DATA WAREHOUSING

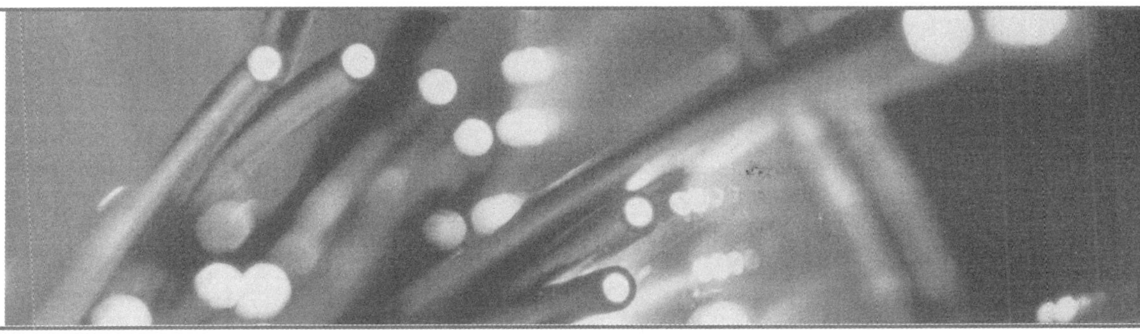

and the AS/400

Scott Steinacher

DUKE PRESS
A Division of
DUKE COMMUNICATIONS INTERNATIONAL
221 E. 29th Street • Loveland, CO 80538
(800) 621-1544 • (970) 663-4700 • www.dukepress.com

Library of Congress Cataloging-in-Publication Data

Steinacher, Scott, 1965 –

Data warehousing and the AS/400 / by Scott Steinacher.
p. cm.
Includes index.
ISBN 1-882419-63-4
1. Data warehousing. 2. IBM AS/400 (Computer) I. Title.
QA76.9.D37S74 1998
005.74—dc21 97-45298
CIP

Published by DUKE PRESS
DUKE COMMUNICATIONS INTERNATIONAL
Loveland, Colorado

It is the reader's responsibility to ensure procedures and techniques used from this book are accurate and appropriate for the user's installation. No warranty is implied or expressed.

This book was printed and bound in Canada.

ISBN 1-882419-63-4

1 2 3 4 5 6 7 WL 0 9 8

To my parents,
Bill and Helen Steinacher,
who taught me that the true measure of one's character
is most apparent when one is anonymous.

Acknowledgments

A number of outstanding people contributed to this book in many ways, both directly and indirectly, and I'd like to express my gratitude to them.

First, a special thanks to Mark Wulf at IBM for reviewing the original manuscript and providing me with invaluable insight based on his many years of data-warehousing and data-mining experience. Thank you, Mark. Others at IBM to thank are René Tragatsch, Rick Landon, and Joe Eisenberg for their input on Intelligent Miner; Jim Flanagan for his input on DataPropagator; and Bob Kaufmann, Van Symons, and John Fulton for providing me with a wealth of valuable information. These people are one reason why IBM's stock has quadrupled in the past few years.

I thank Shaku Atre of Atre, Inc., for reviewing the transcript and providing me with her insight and excellent suggestions about data warehousing.

Next, I am grateful to the vendors and industry players who supported this project. Many thanks to Chuck Bernstein and Rob Peterson at ASC; Eric Figura at BCD; Allen Perry and Christine Brinkley at Coglin Mill; Barbara Wood, Jason Weir, and Nigel Stokes at DataMirror; Jerry Kosmachuk, formerly of DataMirror; Scott Baker, Linda Lammi, Carl Lambert, Marco Peterson, Nicole Duty, and Jim Ward at Datawatch (have you seen OLAP boy?); Duncan Kenzie and Kevin Cronin at ExcelSystems; David Newman at FIS; Katherine Hammer and Rebecca Borden at the Metadata Coalition; Neil Putterman at the Meta Group; Paul Sutton and Adam Winkelmann at Olympic amis; Angie Grimm, Lisa Reickes, and John Friend at ShowCase; and John Hughes and Mike Booth at Silvon.

I am also thankful for the support of Duke Press. First, many thanks to Dave Bernard for his guidance throughout this project. Dave, you lead a truly great team! A special thanks also to Sharon Hamm, the editor of this book. Sharon, if there is one person responsible for the clarity and brevity of this work, it is you. I am forever thankful for your tireless efforts and personal devotion to this project. Another special thank-you to Veronica Patterson, co-editor of the book. Thank you for so many improvements, Ronnie! Thanks also to Martha Nichols for a wonderful job with the book's production and layout. Thanks to John Morris-Riehl for the cover design and CD-ROM. Thanks also to Trish McConnell, Dale Agger, Karen Forster, and Lori Piotrowski for too many things to mention here.

Next, thanks to everybody I've worked with over the years. In particular, I am forever indebted to Bruno D'Agosto, formerly of General Semiconductor, for introducing me to IBM's midrange machines more than 10 years ago. As a manager, Bruno taught me RPG. As a mentor, he introduced me to corporate America. As a philosopher, he helped shape the way I view the world. Enjoy your retirement, Bruno, and leave a few fluke in the bay for me. Others also at General Semiconductor I thank are Bob Lamendola and Jorge Restrepo for their guidance and support, and Linda Perry for serving as an enormously positive role model. Linda, you have taught me more than you realize. And thanks to Mary Capria, Judy Tsai, and Annelie Weidenmuller for keeping things humming. Finally, thanks to the IT department in Taiwan, Germany, Ireland, and the United States.

I also thank everyone from the Business School at the State University of New York at Albany for a first-rate education. I still rely upon the lessons I learned as an MIS undergraduate at SUNYA. My sincerest thanks to Professors Salvatore Belardo, William Bray, Peter Duchessi, Joshua Levy, Harold Pazer, and every other professor who introduced me to technology and the business world. Your influences are evident throughout this book. And a very special thanks to John Levato, Assistant Dean of the Business School. John, you already know that your guidance has had a tremendous impact on countless careers, including mine. What you may not know is that your guidance transcended education and made us better human beings. Thank you, John. And thanks to Professor Berit Brown at Long Island University, Professor Susan McClive at New York University, and Professor Peter Seagle at SUNYA for everything you've taught me.

Next, I thank my friends for their constant support and friendship. First, a special thanks to Anne Mangieri, Catherine Kappenberg, and Dana Shatzkin for smoothing out life's rough spots. A special thanks also to Brenda Brunner for everything (say hello to Itchy). And many thanks to Charles "Sluggo" Feld, Joseph "Yopus" Pajkowski, "Captain" James T. Halka, Joseph "The Hammer" Rosenblum, Ellen Gnam, Susan Weingardner, Eileen Reid (see you on Thursday), Larry Feld, Rob Adcock, Richard Granahan, Dave Winthrop, Robert "Bromo" Pipia, Elaine Hansen, Tom "Dudemaaan" Lamendola (please pass the gator chips), Cathy Quinn, Shelly Prophet, Jackie Davidson, Patricia Fredal (da-da-dee), Christa Bejcek, John Turner, Debbie Kinahan, Chris Nickum, Farida Danninger, Mike and Anne McGregor of Dundee, Andreas Wanke and Monika Plattman, Danielle Visser of Haarlem, Jos and Mary van Loo, Larry and Sharon Lasher, Bob and Kathy Engel, the Dawers, Alex Dennis at Sears, and all my brothers and sisters at the Dix Hills Fire Department (I'll see you at the big one).

Finally, and most importantly, I thank my family for their love and for making life what it is. Thanks to Stewart Steinacher, Stephanie Steinacher, Synthia Steinacher, Steven and Linda Steinacher, James West, Amanda West, Robert Wachsmann, William Jr. and Gloria Bubenheimer, William Sr. and Helen Bubenheimer, Dorothea and Maria Ferdinand, Duke, and most of all, thank you, Mom and Dad. If my future children feel about me the way I feel about you, then I will be the most successful parent in the world!

Table of Contents at a Glance

Table of Contents

Foreword

Data warehousing is the latest incarnation of a grand idea. The idea, which is not new, is to use data to make business decisions. The idea comes around about once every four years. So what makes this time different? I think that answer lies in this book, in which Scott Steinacher discusses the many factors that have come together to make data warehousing an idea whose time has come — the culmination of advances in hardware technology and the decreasing cost of that technology; the availability of sophisticated software to make data warehousing faster, easier, and more effective for users at all levels; the methodology to implement a solution; and the measurable advantages data-warehousing and data-mining solutions can offer in today's competitive business environment.

You will make many choices as you implement a data warehouse, and because technology changes rapidly, your choices must be based on up-to-date, accurate information. You will need to provide vendors with key information about your business. You will need to decide whether to buy a predefined template or build your data-warehouse system. You will need to keep future growth in mind. You will need to be prepared to iterate and upgrade. This book contains the essential information to help you make those choices quickly. It details the components that go into comprehensive data-warehousing solutions, including a focus on data mining as a means to improve your business and capitalize on your data-warehouse investment. In addition, the book includes evaluations of the key features and limitations of 10 representative AS/400 data-warehousing and data-mining vendor solutions.

If you already run your business with AS/400 systems, this book will increase your appreciation for how the technology you have been using has advanced in performance, database scalability and functionality, openness, extensibility, and application support to help make it a strong data-warehouse server. If you have no AS/400 experience, this book will introduce you to both data warehousing and how the AS/400's basic architecture supports this technology. Although no book can tell you everything you need to know to implement a successful data-warehousing solution, *Data Warehousing and the AS/400* gives you the background you need, and the kind of how-to and product information to help you make intelligent decisions.

In the end, your data warehouse will become as important as, if not more important than, the applications that run your business. With this book to guide you, what you might have considered just a basic decision-support tool will become one of your mission-critical applications.

MARK WULF

MANAGER, PARTNERS IN DEVELOPMENT DATA SOLUTIONS CENTER
IBM, ROCHESTER

Preface

In late 1988, I arrived fresh at the doors of General Semiconductor's (GS's)[1] Long Island site with a bachelor's degree in MIS from the State University of New York at Albany (SUNYA). I had written quite a few programs at SUNYA and was anxious to test my skills in the business world. My first interview was conducted by Bruno D'Agosto, an IT project manager who would later become both a mentor and close friend. After talking about everything from my grade point average to Bruno's hometown in Italy, Bruno mentioned that GS had a computer called a System/38 and asked whether I was interested in learning RPG. Bruno looked a lot like Albert Einstein, so I assumed he had much to teach. I was not disappointed. Having programmed on a DEC PDP-11, I was soon awestruck by the capabilities of the S/38 and of RPG. The following year, when I thought that my job could not possibly get any better, a powerful new AS/400 arrived.

Despite the AS/400's formidable capabilities, managers outside of IT were fairly dissatisfied with the folks in IT. Their issue was not an operational one. We had already installed systems that effectively supported accounting, order entry, inventory management, and other critical day-to-day functions of the business. Rather, their dissatisfaction was rooted in our failure to provide them with decision-support tools. For example, when users wanted to analyze data that was not already in a report or on a screen, they had to fill out a Support Request form. If they were lucky, a new program would be ready in a month or two. This is not to say that we in IT had anything against providing immediate answers to questions. On the contrary, we were very accommodating when there was an urgent need for information. Using Query/400, we would join a half dozen or more files and run some powerful queries — of course, the AS/400 disk devices lit up like a Christmas tree and nobody else in the company could sign on for a while!

Obviously, this situation was unacceptable. Bob Lamendola, a gifted analyst who would later become a good friend and vice president of IT at GS, had been toying with the idea of creating denormalized summary files from our OLTP databases. Bob designed some file formats, and I wrote several thousand lines of RPG code to fill the summary files with denormalized, decoded data. We then did some significant reconciliation activity, in which we compared the data in the summary files to data on operational reports.

About this same time, I read an article in *NEWS 3X/400* (now *NEWS/400*) magazine about a DOS-based query tool from IBM — Menu-Based Natural

[1]In July of 1997, General Instrument Corporation was split into three separate public companies. Formerly known as the Power Semiconductor Division of General Instrument, General Semiconductor, Inc., emerged as an independent corporation listed on the New York Stock Exchange (NYSE).

Language Query (MBNLQ). According to the article, we could use MBNLQ to create English-language-like phrases on personal computers. MBNLQ would then translate these phrases into SQL programs that would run on the AS/400 in batch. Afterward, MBNLQ would return query results to the PC; if necessary, it could also download the results into a Lotus spreadsheet for further analysis. I reasoned that if we installed MBNLQ on end users' PCs, they could write their own queries. We ordered a copy of MBNLQ in the fall of 1990.

When MBNLQ arrived, we installed it on a PC and directed it to process the DDS specifications for our AS/400-based summary files. After reading the DDS specs, MBNLQ automatically created PC-based interfaces over the files. It then let us customize these interfaces with descriptive text, color cues, industry-specific jargon, and context-sensitive pop-up windows. And that's where the fun began. We clicked on words and phrases and created sentences such as "For each customer, find the total net sales value with region the same as Northeast and with year equal to 1990."

MBNLQ then used PC Support's Source Transfer Facility (STF) to query the AS/400 summary files and retrieve the desired information. Several weeks later, calling our new application WWMS (WorldWide Marketing System), Bob and I unveiled MBNLQ to a skeptical group of managers. (Like IBM at that time, we were an acronym-happy team.)

WWMS was a smash! With it, managers and their assistants were able to perform ad hoc analyses in minutes instead of weeks. In the process, they threw off the oppressive yoke of IT dependence. For our part, Bob and I received a corporate-wide performance award and some much-needed beer money.

Not until 1992, when I read an article about data warehousing, did I realize what we had started to do at GS. Like WWMS, data warehouses extract raw data from operational databases, transform that data into meaningful information, then let end users analyze that data. Using data warehouses, managers can retrieve the information they need, when they need it, and in the format in which they like to see it.

As I read more articles about data warehousing, I became more excited about its potential. At the same time, I was perplexed that the AS/400 was rarely referred to as a viable data-warehousing platform. Sure, the machine was on its way to becoming the most popular multiuser business computer in history. But almost everyone seemed to feel the machine was suited only for transaction-oriented operational applications, not query-based data warehouses. That perspective changed in 1995 when IBM Rochester introduced a new line of 64-bit AS/400s that employed PowerPC processors.

Launched from a springboard of technological innovation, those AS/400s (known as Advanced Servers) quickly began to deliver the strategic benefits of data warehousing to an information-hungry market. Through significant advances in performance, database technology, storage capacity, and operating-system functionality, these servers are among the most powerful in the world. In fact,

IBM positions the AS/400 as a highly scalable, enterprise-wide data warehousing machine. In recognition of the AS/400's functionality and performance, leading software developers quickly introduced a variety of AS/400-based data warehousing tools and applications.

I wrote this book with two objectives in mind. First, I want to get people excited about data warehousing. This application streamlines the analysis process in companies of all sizes, in all fields. In addition, it lets companies perform analyses that otherwise would be impractical. Data warehousing may well be the most potent application IT has ever delivered to its charges. Without data warehouses, companies risk falling behind in their markets.

Second, I wrote this book to tout the AS/400's data-warehousing capabilities. Despite its enormous success and popularity, the AS/400 is often referred to as IBM's best-kept secret. That perception is starting to change as IBM aggressively markets the AS/400's capabilities in international ad campaigns. In short, through this book, I hope to educate current and future AS/400 customers about the AS/400's data-warehousing capabilities.

To be truly effective, any discussion about the AS/400's suitability as a data-warehousing server must be preceded by an in-depth discussion of data warehousing. To that end, the opening chapters of this book discuss the components of comprehensive data-warehousing solutions. Chapter 1 explains what a data warehouse is and briefly examines its history and its major components. This chapter also touches upon the AS/400's applicability in data warehousing. Chapter 2 picks up with an in-depth discussion of data-warehouse database schema. Chapter 3 details how raw operational data is extracted, transformed, and moved into data warehouses. Chapter 4 examines the types of tools that enable end users to analyze data-warehouse information. Chapter 5 looks at metadata, or "data about data." A detailed discussion about data mining, a data-driven approach to knowledge discovery, comprises Chapter 6. Chapter 7 explores in depth the AS/400's merits as a data-warehousing platform. The remaining chapters, 8 through 17, examine 10 leading data-warehousing applications that are available to AS/400 customers: Advanced Systems Concepts' SEQUEL, Coglin Mill's RODIN, DataMirror Corporation's Transformation Server for AS/400, Datawatch Corporation's Monarch, Ferguson Information Systems' InfoManager, IBM Corporation's Data Propagator, IBM Corporation's Intelligent Miner for AS/400, Olympic amis Ltd.'s amis V8, Showcase Corporation's STRATEGY, and Silvon Software's DataTracker. You can find a more detailed overview of these chapters in the "Introduction to Section II" (page 117).

Chapter 1

Introduction

As one of the most exciting developments in the field of information technology, data warehousing is ushering in a new phase of the Information Age. Before data warehousing, nearly all mainstream computer applications focused on automating manual tasks. Think about the volume of mundane work that computers now perform. Functions such as accounts receivable and accounts payable maintenance are not done on paper anymore. Similarly, because word processing has transformed typewriters into relics, typewritten documents are rarely used in business. And when was the last time you spoke to a telephone receptionist? Computer-based telephony systems have all but eliminated this position in many businesses. Corporations of every size in every industry have saved billions of dollars as technology has eliminated or streamlined manual processes. And computer automation is by no means limited to corporate settings. This year, I made my first purchase over the Internet from home. Internet-based applications have made it possible to automate order fulfillment from the moment an order is placed right up to the point it is shipped — the future does not bode well for order-entry clerks. And the revolution is far from over. In a few short years, the proliferation of home computers and the Internet will transform the retail industry as billions of dollars of goods are sold online. What do all of these applications have in common? They automate manual processes.

Data warehouses also automate manual processes. These specialized systems programmatically extract data from operational databases, transform that data into meaningful information, then provide end users with the means to access and analyze that information. In organizations without data warehouses, end users must manually gather data from reports or other sources and then rekey that data into analytic tools. However, data warehouses are much more than "task automation" systems. Unlike these traditional applications, data warehouses are designed to deliver seeds of knowledge, insight, and understanding to the desktop. And an experienced end user can cultivate those seeds to support better, more timely decisions. The *raison d'être* of a data warehouse is decision support and knowledge enablement, not task automation.

Because data warehouses transform raw data into useful information, they help companies learn about the key aspects of their businesses: buying patterns, pricing strategies, customers, products, margins, revenues, profits, and so on. When coupled with data-mining algorithms that can discover patterns hidden in a morass of data, data warehousing becomes the first mainstream knowledge-enabling application of the Information Age. As such, data warehousing may be the most potent competitive weapon IT has ever designed, with the potential to redefine IT's role in tomorrow's corporate arena.

In this chapter, I examine why traditional computer applications cannot effectively help end users learn about their businesses. I also explore how we as IT professionals attempted to solve this dilemma before the rise of data warehousing. An overview of the major components in a data warehouse follows that discussion. Finally, I round out the chapter with a discussion about the AS/400 and its applicability in the data-warehousing arena.

The Deficiencies of Traditional Applications

IT departments expend most of their resources on the installation and maintenance of online transactional processing (OLTP) systems such as order entry, accounts receivable, accounts payable, general ledger, inventory management, and sales tracking — systems that process an organization's work flow. In a basic sense, these systems meet the daily processing needs of a business.

Typically using relational databases, OLTP systems employ normalization to limit data redundancy and to minimize response time. Normalized data is stored in numerous tables and derives meaning through its interrelationships with the contents of other tables. However, an obvious trade-off for this efficient storage technique is that normalized data is difficult to access precisely because it is stored in multiple tables. What's more, normalized data often consists of codes and abbreviations that further enhance database and application efficiency at the expense of intuitive data access.

Consider a basic invoice, for example, that an order-entry system at a department store could generate. In normalized databases, a single invoice comprises numerous data elements stored in several files. Such databases typically include a customer information file, order header file, order detail file, and parts master file. To illustrate the concept of normalization, I have detailed portions of sample files in Figure 1.1. I have also created an invoice (see Figure 1.2 on page 4) derived from the data elements in the sample files.

To generate an invoice, computer programs must retrieve each data element (noted in shaded areas) from the files in Figure 1.1. This is not a simple task. Normalization complicates the accessibility of something as elementary as an invoice. And as any programmer knows, this example is a simplification. A more realistic invoice would contain data gleaned from a dozen or more files! It is easy to see why the ad hoc analysis of sales data, which may consist of thousands of invoices from many files, is so inordinately difficult in an operational environment. Retrieving normalized data requires intimate knowledge of both a programming language, such as RPG or Cobol, and the production database schema. That is why highly trained programmers often are left to write applications that perform basic tasks such as invoice printing and sales reporting.

FIGURE 1.1

Invoice Data as Stored in a Normalized Relational Database

Customer File

CUSTID	LSTNAM	FSTNAM	SAL	ADDR1	ADDR2	CITY	STATE	ZIP	CNTRY
1000	Johnson	Tom	Mr.	3 Spruce Rd.	Apt 15A	Melville	NY	11747	USA
1001	Acorn	Lisa	Mrs.	4 Bell Pkwy.	Suite 14	Brookline	MA	02167	USA
1002	Smith	Bob	Mr.	12 Main St.	Suite 5	Commack	NY	11725	USA

Order Header File

CUSTID	ORDID	TERMID	ENTMM	ENTDD	ENTYY	ENTCC	CSREP
1000	2566	N30	03	22	96	19	JM
1001	2401	N60	08	31	96	19	LS
1001	2952	N60	11	13	96	19	LS
1002	3565	N30	02	26	96	19	DP

Order Detail File

ORDID	ITEMID	PARTID	QTY	PRICE
2566	01	1-A	1	175.00
2566	02	3-A	2	20.00
2401	01	1-A	1	175.00
2952	01	2-A	1	22.00
2952	02	3-A	1	20.00
3565	01	2-A	1	22.00

Parts File

PARTID	DESCRP	COLOR	MATRL	STDPKG
1-A	OVERCOAT	BLACK	WOOL	1
2-A	SCARF	BLACK	WOOL	1
3-A	GLOVES	BROWN	LEATHER	1

But even these basic tasks require a predefined set of input parameters. For example, end users are usually prompted for a specific customer ID or order ID before a program can gather data from an OLTP database. Most programs are designed to access data in a very specific manner. If an end user requires information in a new format, then a programmer must change the existing program or write a brand new one. For all their usefulness, OLTP applications are deficient in terms of accessibility and decision support.

Such deficiencies were particularly acute in the 1980s, when query tools, report writers, program generators, and EIS products were not yet commonplace. To properly frame the history of data warehousing then, let's go back to the earliest days of the AS/400, before query tools and the like became popular.

Let me illustrate how a request for information was processed back then. Suppose a manager in a sales organization asked an IT manager for a report detailing sales history by customer. If an experienced programmer were available, he would design, code, and test the new report program. Upon its completion, the sales manager would run the new report. Now assume that the sales manager noticed a sharp decline in sales revenue for a particular customer.

FIGURE 1.2
Sample Invoice Derived from Data in Sample Files

ABC Department Store, Inc.
2939 Route 9
Woburn, MA 02169

Order No.: 2952
Customer No.: 1001
Payment Terms: Net 60

Invoice Date: 11/13/96
C/S Rep ID: LS

CUSTOMER BILL-TO:
Mrs. Lisa Acorn
4 Bell Pkwy.
Suite 14
Brookline, MA 02167

CUSTOMER SHIP-TO (If different)

Item	Description	Color	Qty	Unit Price	Total
01	SCARF	BLACK	001	22.00	22.00
02	GLOVES	BROWN	001	20.00	20.00

Subtotal:	42.00
Tax:	3.36
Delivery:	8.00
Total:	$ 53.36

Thanks for your order! Our toll-free customer-service number is
1-800-123-4567

Most likely, her next step was to examine that customer's sales history on a product-by-product basis. If such information were not readily available, the sales manager had to go back to the IT manager and ask for a new sales report, one with product data.

If the dejected programmer was able to work on the new request immediately, the sales manager may have received the new report in a few days. In such an organization, however, a formidable backlog of similar requests probably existed, and the sales manager would have waited several weeks or even months for the second report. And so it went. The programmer felt as though he was walking up an escalator the wrong way, expending energy but never really going anywhere. For her part, the sales manager remained frustrated. She could not get the information she needed, so she could not address and rectify the deteriorating sales situation. In the end, business suffered.

ADDRESSING THE SYMPTOM INSTEAD OF THE CAUSE

In the late 1980s and early 1990s, IT departments embraced report writers, query tools, and program generators in an attempt to address this problem. And for a short time, the situation did improve. When end users required access to OLTP data in a new way, programmers used these tools to create reports and inquiries faster than ever before. (Of course, for complicated tasks, RPG and Cobol programs remained the norm). Thanks to the new tools, programmers were more productive and support backlogs began to diminish. But then something unexpected happened. Having been given more timely access to data, end users became more demanding and support backlogs began to grow again. As soon as one request was filled, two more took its place and IT departments were back on the treadmill, expending lots of energy but never really going anywhere.

It wasn't long before IT managers decided to try giving end users direct access to OLTP data. The reasoning was that programmers didn't have time to create new programs, queries, and reports whenever end users needed to see data in a different format. The goal was to train users to access data themselves. Although this idea was sound, we soon learned that end users couldn't use report writers and query tools if the underlying databases were left unchanged. Most end users did not have the time (or desire) to learn about the vagaries of database normalization. And even if these users were so inclined, many of our OLTP databases contained too many arcane abbreviations, codes, inaccuracies, and quirks to be of much use anyway. And as many of us in IT saw, end-user queries were often poorly constructed (e.g., too many joins) or did not make sense (e.g., summing customer ID numbers), resulting in queries that degrade system performance.

Despite good intentions, this attempt to empower users failed because it focused on a symptom (data starvation) instead of its cause (inaccessible, mazelike databases). This is why query tools, report writers, program generators, and even more programmers cannot effectively address a burgeoning support backlog in the long run. If end users are not given *direct, intuitive access* to data, then attacking a support backlog is about as effective as using a sponge to sop up water from a leaking pipe. Building a data warehouse is like fixing the pipe.

Before I continue, I want to point out that OLTP databases themselves are not a problem. On the contrary, OLTP databases are ideally suited for their intended purpose: the efficient storage and maintenance of formidable volumes of dynamic, transactional data, and they will serve as the foundation of mission-critical applications for many years to come. These databases never were designed to meet the needs of information-hungry end users, and any attempt to use them for this purpose is tantamount to using a hedge trimmer to mow a lawn. As every homeowner knows, different jobs require different tools. And when it comes to providing flexible, intuitive access to reams of information, a data warehouse, and in particular, an AS/400-based data warehouse, is one of the best tools available.

Effective End-User Access to Data

Data warehouses transform complex operational data into meaningful information, which is then stored in databases designed specifically to support flexible, intuitive, ad hoc analyses. In addressing the underlying cause of user frustration, data warehouses empower end users to satisfy their own information needs. And market trends confirm the widespread growth of data warehouses. According to the META Group, a consulting and research firm based in Stamford, Connecticut, the market for data-warehousing hardware, software, and services will grow to $12 billion by the year 2000. This figure represents a six-fold increase over 1996 sales of roughly $2 billion. As we shall see, powerful forces are driving these rosy growth projections.

As a concept, data warehousing has existed since the 1970s; the need for intuitive access to data has existed even longer. Yet data-warehousing articles and books did not become commonplace until the early- to mid-1990s. Why did data warehousing become popular at this particular time? Several factors are directly and indirectly responsible for its en masse acceptance.

First, as we saw earlier in the chapter, many IT departments learned through trial and error that the only way to satisfy users' insatiable appetite for data is to provide them with timely, intuitive access to data. In this light, data warehouses are the result of evolution, not revolution.

Second, data warehouses require significant memory and storage space to accommodate the massive amounts of information they manipulate. The cost of main memory and disk storage at both the client (e.g, personal computer) and server (e.g., AS/400) levels has decreased sharply during this decade. At the same time, the amount of available memory and disk space has increased dramatically. For example, AS/400s are now available with 20 GB of main memory and 1 terabyte (TB) of disk storage (a gigabyte is equal to one million bytes, while a terabyte equals one *trillion* bytes).

Third, data warehouses are resource-intensive applications that require high-performance servers. Ever-more-powerful systems for less money became the norm in the 1990s. As an example, consider the dramatic increases in affordable processing power that have resulted from IBM's introduction of powerful 64-bit, RISC-based AS/400s.

Operational systems themselves are another force behind the growth of data warehousing. During the past decade, both online and archived databases have accumulated an enormous amount of data. Organizations finally have both the data and computing resources to support strategic analyses.

Another reason for the data-warehousing phenomenon is education. Professionals in every functional area of business have learned about the benefits of data warehousing through magazine articles, seminars, print advertisements, and even television commercials. In a global economy characterized by fierce competition, organizations are more apt to evaluate any measure that can provide a competitive edge.

Finally, the availability of specialized software applications is another factor behind the growth of data warehousing. This influence is especially true in the AS/400 arena, where we find a bevy of world-class data-warehousing products designed specifically for the AS/400.

Up to this point, we've examined the circumstances that led to the growth and acceptance of data warehousing. In the next section we actually define data warehousing and look at the fundamental components of a comprehensive data warehouse.

Data Repositories

To stimulate demand and market their products, many software companies use the term *data warehousing* far too liberally in promoting their wares. Not surprisingly, this has led to a good deal of confusion, and many IT professionals find it difficult to define data warehousing. Data warehouses are not off-the-shelf products (although that is slowly changing). Rather, data warehouses are customized solutions that support flexible, intuitive, and timely access to meaningful information. Let's take a look at the fundamental components of a comprehensive data warehouse.

Comprehensive data warehouses consist of two types of databases: the primary repository and the data mart. These specialized databases embrace aggregation (a transformation function that subtotals and summarizes detailed operational data) and eschew the highly normalized schema found in typical OLTP systems. Taken together, primary repositories and data marts may contain many gigabytes, or even several terabytes, of data extracted from a number of disparate OLTP databases. In many implementations, multiple data marts exist alongside a single primary repository.

Primary repositories store homogenized, consolidated data that may be extracted from a number of disparate OLTP databases. In many cases, primary repositories are the only available source of enterprise-wide information. Primary repositories vary in terms of schema. Unsophisticated examples may consist of nothing more than a series of large, two-dimensional, flat tables. Others may be denormalized relational databases that consist of numerous aggregate files. It is important to note that there is no unique primary repository schema per se. Figure 1.3 highlights the major differences between OLTP databases and primary repositories.

FIGURE 1.3
Comparison of OLTP Databases and Data-Warehouse Primary Repositories

OLTP Databases	Data-Warehouse Primary Repositories
Are created by end users	Are created by propagation tools
Generate raw data from manual processes	Convert raw data into meaningful information
Contain relatively new information	Maintain historical perspectives
Are optimized for transactional processing	Are optimized for retrieval and analysis
Are updated constantly	Are updated at specific times or by specific events
Coexist with many other OLTP databases on one machine	Are stored on dedicated servers
Often contain inconsistencies and even errors	Must contain the "one truth"
Are highly normalized	Usually are denormalized
Contain very detailed information	Contain summarized information

Primary data-warehouse database repositories also may serve as the origin of smaller databases that are designed for specific departments or purposes. Known as data marts, these flexible systems employ unique storage schema and software to deliver online analytic processing (OLAP) to the desktop. OLAP technology enables analysts to quickly drill up, drill down, and drill across information. OLAP applications also support "what if" analyses, time-series analyses, budgeting, forecasting, and other advanced analytic modeling. Comprehensive OLAP applications even allow users to update the data mart online with critical variables such as exchange rates and interest rates.

To minimize response times and support speed-of-thought analyses, data marts store and/or present data in a multidimensional format. The most common implementations are based upon either multidimensional OLAP (MD-OLAP) or relational OLAP (ROLAP) databases. In Chapter 2, we explore these database schema in detail. Before we move on, it is important to note that primary repositories, although not designed for the same purpose as data marts, may also employ relational OLAP schema.

TRANSFORMATIONAL REPLICATION TOOLS

Before operational data can be moved to data warehouses, that data must be denormalized and decoded. Transformational replication tools refine and map OLTP data to data warehouses. This process may consist of five related functions: filtering, standardization, aggregation, consolidation, and cleansing. I present examples of each function in Chapter 3. Briefly, *filtering* is a process whereby valuable information is isolated in OLTP databases. *Standardization* is a transformation function that creates data elements that are consistent in terms of syntax, size, description, and meaning. *Aggregation* is an essential transformation function that subtotals and summarizes detailed operational data. *Consolidation* is a process that groups together OLTP data from separate databases, applications, and/or platforms. *Cleansing* is a transformation process that modifies data elements via value-translation algorithms.

Metadata

Metadata, or data about data, describes data-warehouse repositories and the processes used to populate them. Metadata falls into one of two categories, depending upon its nature and intended audience.

IT staff, software, and the AS/400 itself all maintain *technical metadata* that describes warehouse schema, data-transformation processes, security controls, and so on. This information may be stored online or offline, and end users usually do not access it. From a programmer's point of view, technical metadata provides a comprehensive overview of every field, file, and program in a data-warehousing application.

Unlike technical metadata, *business metadata* is designed for end users. Although end users do not need to know field attributes or file names, they do require information about the data in data warehouses. End users typically want to know how up-to-date the information is (e.g., How recent are these figures?), where it came from (e.g., What system generated these figures?), and how it was derived (e.g., What exchange rates were used to compute these figures?). Business metadata describes data warehouses in familiar, nontechnical terms.

Analysis & Presentation Tools

To leverage the resources invested in the implementation of a data warehouse, IT professionals must provide end users with intuitive access to information. *Analysis and presentation tools* are specialized programs, typically PC-based, that can be used to navigate and analyze the contents of data warehouses. These tools provide the means to graph, chart, subtotal, combine, summarize, and manipulate warehouse data in a graphical environment.

Examples of analysis and presentation tools include report writers, spreadsheets, Internet browsers, decision-support systems, executive information systems (EISs), and graphics software. I examine these tools in detail in Chapter 4.

Data Mining

A natural outgrowth of data warehousing, *data mining* refers to the use of specialized software to discover hidden patterns, trends, and correlations in databases. To make use of data-mining tools, IT personnel must extract, transform, and propagate OLTP data to relational databases or flat ASCII files. In this light, data-mining solutions mimic the basic architecture of data warehouses. Unlike data-warehouse applications, however, data-mining programs require transaction-level detail. As we will see in Chapter 6, data mining represents the next stage in the evolution of corporate information systems.

Support Staff

Often overlooked in articles, books, and discussions about data warehousing, IT support staff are an essential component of any data-warehousing solution. Data warehouses grow and evolve rapidly, more so than OLTP applications do. Take a moment to consider the stability of accounting software, which changes very little over time because accounting itself is relatively static. If implemented properly, an accounting application does not require significant IT support. By contrast, data warehouses reflect dynamic business environments and subjective analytic models. In this fundamental sense, data warehouses solutions differ from traditional computer applications and necessarily require higher levels of support. If you don't commit appropriate human resources to the long-term viability of data warehouses, the utility of these systems will diminish over time.

The AS/400 and Data Warehousing

Computers designed to support OLTP applications are tuned specifically for workloads associated with interactive jobs. Data-warehouse servers, on the other hand, must efficiently support batch-oriented workloads commonly associated with query and reporting jobs. For this reason, OLTP and data-warehousing applications should not reside on the same machine. If they do, performance for both applications can degrade significantly. In recognition of this, IBM introduced server models of the AS/400 beginning in May of 1994. These AS/400s are designed specifically for resource-intensive batch processing, database serving, and communications serving. IBM, in equipping AS/400 servers with cutting-edge technology, offers a scalable and extensible data-warehousing platform. Let's take a closer look at these servers to understand why they are so well-suited for data warehousing.

Performance is of paramount concern when you are choosing a data-warehouse server. Data warehouses applications may process several million records every day. To support processing of this magnitude, the AS/400 can utilize four types of parallel processing: *parallel I/O processing, superscalar processing, symmetric multiprocessing (SMP)*, and *multisystem parallel processing*. I examine the AS/400's parallel-processing capabilities in detail in Chapter 7.

In addition to comprehensive support for parallel processing, the AS/400 features a 64-bit operating system (OS/400), a 64-bit relational database (DB2/400), and up to twelve 64-bit RISC processors. In terms of performance,

64-bit technology is vastly superior to 16-bit and 32-bit technology. Because of their 64-bit design, AS/400 PowerPC AS processors can directly address more than 18,000,000,000,000,000,000 (2^{64}) bytes (or 18.44 million terabytes) of memory, which is roughly a million times larger than the theoretic limit of 4 GB imposed upon 32-bit processors. The capability to directly address such a vast amount of data extends to disk storage as well. That is, a 32-bit machine can directly access only 4 GB of disk storage. Designers of 32-bit machines may sidestep this restriction by employing two-phase addressing schemes, but that approach can hinder system performance. The AS/400, in supporting a 64-bit virtual addressing scheme, can directly manage vast amounts of main memory and disk storage. As a result, performance is enhanced. A resource-intensive application such as data warehousing requires the benefits of an integrated 64-bit solution. We explore the AS/400's 64-bit architecture in more detail in Chapter 7.

To further enhance performance, the AS/400 uses specialized, dedicated I/O processors to off-load tasks that CPUs traditionally perform. I/O operations are one of the most common functions the AS/400 performs; they occur each time the machine communicates with a hardware component such as a disk device or workstation. Attached via high-speed, laser-driven fiber-optic buses, AS/400 I/O processors also are responsible for managing printers, communications devices, optical libraries, and so on. By off-loading such tasks from the CPU, the AS/400's I/O system has a dramatic impact on system performance.

You also must consider database functionality and scalability when you are choosing a data-warehouse server. Every AS/400 ships with a highly scalable relational database known as DB2 for OS/400, or simply DB2/400. This database is tightly integrated with OS/400, the AS/400's 64-bit, multithreading, multitasking operating system. In addition to advanced functionality that supports parallel processing, multiple-terabyte scalability, query optimization, stored procedures, database triggers, referential integrity, and a predictive query governor, DB2/400 is managed by the AS/400 system itself. There is no need to hire a database administrator to manage DB2/400 databases. Furthermore, a single AS/400 can accommodate DB2/400 databases of up to 1 TB in size. If that's not sufficient, up to 32 separate AS/400s can be linked together in a *loosely coupled, shared-nothing cluster*. In this scenario, databases on separate machines appear as one logical repository to users and applications. Because each machine, or node, in an AS/400 cluster can support 1 TB of storage, the AS/400 platform can support 32 TB of data. To put this into perspective, consider that one of the largest data warehouses in the world is approximately 7.5 TB in size. DB2/400 also is the most widely used multiuser relational database in the world. Because so much DB2/400 data exists in operational systems, it makes sense to also use DB2/400 in data warehousing, because there is less need to convert data in a homogenous DB2/400 environment.

Extensibility is another highly desirable feature in data-warehouse servers. We can define extensibility as a server's ability to accommodate technological advances without disrupting system functionality or necessitating costly upgrades. This is an important consideration in the data-warehousing arena because data warehouses require significant resources to build. For this reason, data-warehouse servers must protect today's investment when they use tomorrow's technology. As evidenced by a relatively painless migration from CISC to RISC processing, the AS/400 is a highly extensible machine. In Chapter 7, we examine the AS/400's technology-independent machine interface (MI) to learn how it supports new technology without disruption.

Because data-warehousing solutions may have to extract data from a variety of different computers, openness is another critical consideration when you are selecting a data-warehouse server. The AS/400 supports a wide variety of industry-endorsed standards, including ODBC (Open Database Connectivity), TCP/IP, APPC (Advanced Program-to-Program Communications), APPN (Advanced Peer-to-Peer Networking), DRDA-2 (Distributed Relational Database Architecture), Apple's DAL (Data Access Language), the X/Open SQL CLI (Call Level Interface), and several SQL (Structured Query Language) specifications, including ANSI, ISO, and FIPS. The AS/400 also provides POSIX-compliant (Portable Operating Systems Interface) operating-system services for Unix application vendors. Furthermore, the AS/400 supports transmission protocols such as ANSI X3.135.1992, ISO 9075-1992, and FIPS 127-2 SQL. In a corporate landscape dotted by companies that have grown through mergers and acquisitions, the capability to create a homogenous data warehouse in a heterogenous, often distributed computing environment is critical. As an open system, the AS/400 supports this need. And there is little doubt that IBM will continue to enhance the AS/400's open-system capabilities.

Application support is another important consideration when you are selecting a data-warehouse server. A number of independent software vendors (ISVs) have already released software tools and applications that simplify the implementation and maintenance of AS/400-based data warehouses. These firms include software developers such as Angoss Software, Brio Technologies, Business Objects, Carleton (which has been purchased by Apertus Technologies), Coglin Mill, Cognos, DataMirror, Datawatch, Evolutionary Technologies International, Ferguson Information Systems, Lakeview Technologies, Logic Works, MicroStrategy, NewGeneration Software, Olympic amis, SAMAC, ShowCase, Silvon, and Vision Solutions. In Chapters 8 through 16, I examine several of these solutions in detail.

Conclusion

As we've just seen, data warehouses are complex systems comprising numerous components. To tie together what we have covered thus far,

Figure 1.4 provides a schematic overview of a generic AS/400-based data warehouse.

FIGURE 1.4
Data Warehousing Overview

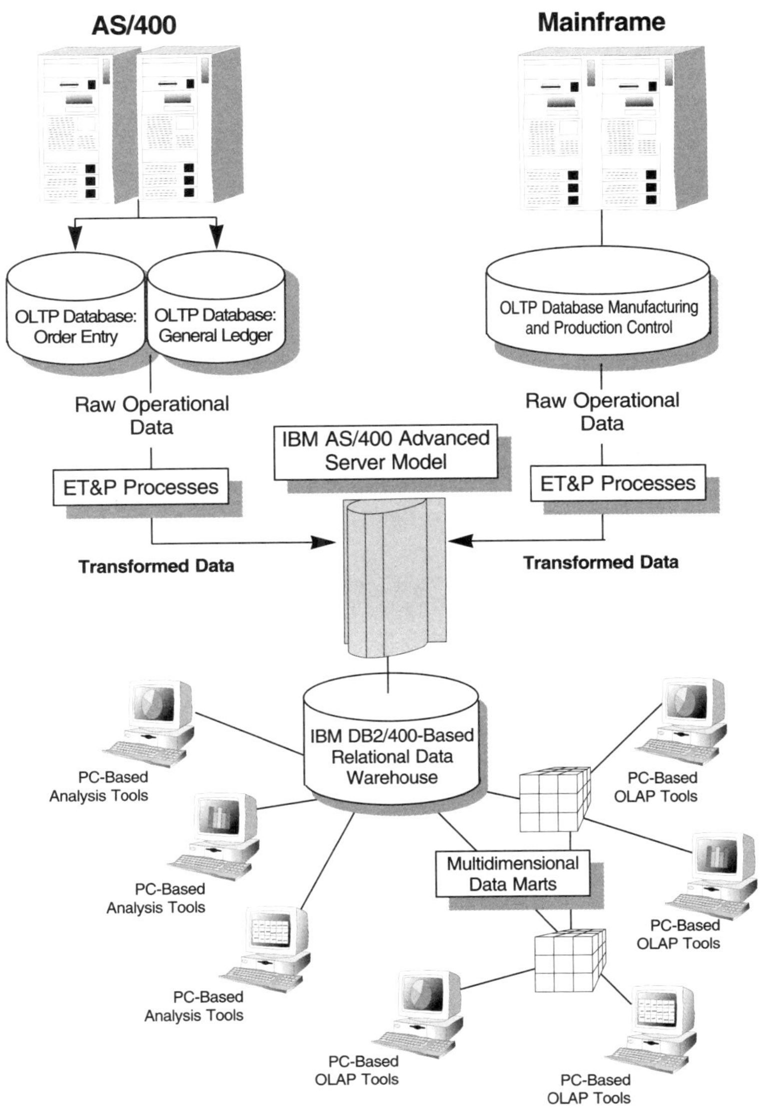

Before moving on to Chapter 2, where I explore data-warehouse repositories in detail, let's determine whether your organization is a candidate for a data warehouse. Figure 1.5 is a simple questionnaire that can help identify organizations likely to benefit from a data warehouse. If you answer the majority of these questions affirmatively, then data is not flowing freely through your company and a data warehouse may be what you're looking for.

FIGURE 1.5
Data Warehousing Needs Assessment

1. Do your end users frequently print lengthy reports and then search through many pages for subtotals or other select figures?
2. Do your end users frequently re-key data from reports and inquiries into spreadsheets to perform additional analyses?
3. Do your end users frequently save reports for long periods of time?
4. Does your IT department maintain a backlog of requests for new reports and inquiries, often of an analytic nature?
5. Does your support backlog continue to grow no matter how much time and effort your IT staff devotes to it?
6. Is your support backlog computerized so it can be tracked by user, request date, department, and so on?
7. Are programmers assigned to work full-time on the support backlog?
8. Are departmental managers generally dissatisfied with your IT group?
9. Do your accounting personnel spend considerable time reconciling figures from various systems, applications, and databases?
10. Do your end users spend more time gathering data then they do analyzing it?
11. Do your end users feel the need to prove that data is accurate by comparing data on several reports and screens?
12. Can your end users quickly access essential figures without running a report?
13. Is your organization made up of autonomous divisions that maintain their own IT departments and computer systems?
14. Is there a variety of major computing platforms in use at one location in your organization? (e.g., IBM AS/400s, HP 9000s, Digital Vax units)
15. Do these systems experience bottlenecks caused by queries and reports?

Chapter 2

Data Repositories

Let's begin our discussion of data repositories with a brief review of the concepts and terms related to this topic that I presented in Chapter 1. You may recall that a data warehouse is designed to store massive volumes of summarized information. To effectively accomplish this task, data warehouses rely on two different types of data stores: the primary repository and the data mart. The main function of a primary repository is to maintain a homogenized version of data pulled from multiple OLTP applications. (A data warehouse typically has just one primary repository.) In contrast, data marts contain information from a single application. For example, a data mart may contain sales data, marketing data, or financial data. Multiple data marts often coexist with one primary repository. As we shall see, primary repositories and data marts serve different purposes.

PRIMARY REPOSITORIES

Primary repositories contain the results of transformation processes that extract data from multiple application databases. These application databases could include information from accounting systems, order entry systems, inventory management systems, financial management systems, and so on. In addition to these application databases, primary repositories may contain data extracted from numerous other data sources, including spooled files, spreadsheets, PC databases, and the like.

Typically, decision-makers access primary repositories when they must simultaneously examine detailed information from separate applications or functional areas. For example, a manager seeking comparisons by month between last year's sales revenue and this year's order backlog would most likely query a primary warehouse repository. Primary repositories are also an excellent source of information in enterprises that have grown through mergers and acquisitions. These organizations often let acquired companies function as autonomous business units. As such, these units maintain their respective IT staffs and infrastructures, so it is not uncommon to encounter Fortune 500 companies with a hodgepodge of hardware and software: mainframes, midrange systems, local area networks, various database products, homegrown programs, and canned applications. In such heterogenous environments, a primary warehouse repository is often the only means to create one source for enterprise-wide data. We can think of primary repositories as decision-support databases that serve an entire enterprise. Figure 2.1 presents a high-level schematic of a primary warehouse repository.

FIGURE 2.1
Primary Warehouse Repository

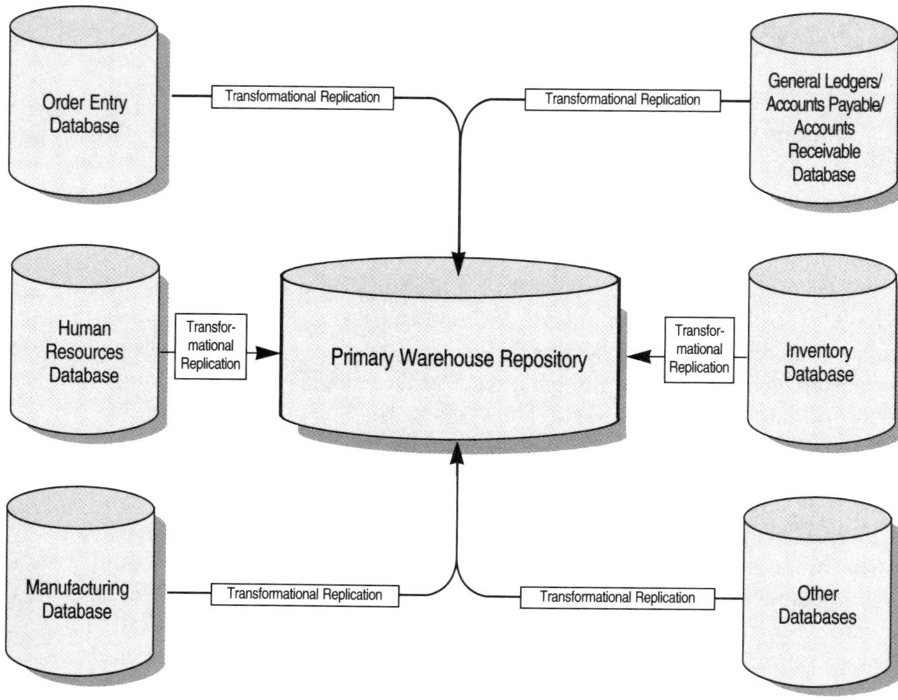

As we noted in Chapter 1, primary repositories vary in terms of schema. Unsophisticated examples may consist of enormous, unrelated tables, while complex varieties may employ specialized relational architectures. In fact, we often find one such complex architecture in both primary repositories and data marts. Known as relational OLAP, or ROLAP, this architecture makes use of standard relational-database technology to organize large volumes of data in a way that enhances query performance. Bear in mind that both primary repositories and data marts employ this architecture. In a few moments, we will explore ROLAP schema in detail.

DATA MARTS

Data marts, the contents of which are often extracted from primary warehouse repositories, are designed for specific purposes and audiences. Accountants can examine budget variances using a financial data mart, for example, while analysts can measure profitability by product line using a marketing data mart. To enable such analyses, data marts contain information that has been highly refined by preprocessing functions. Batch processes, for instance, can precompute budget variances each time data is moved from a primary repository into a financial data mart. Similarly, a marketing data mart can store profitability figures in multiple currencies.

Data marts hold considerable appeal for a number of reasons. First, because the information in a data mart exists to meet the specific needs of a particular audience, that information can be consolidated and customized to a greater extent than information in a primary warehouse repository. Primary repositories must be of a general nature because they exist for the benefit of an organization's general population. In practice, many companies choose to implement data warehouses that contain only data marts without a primary repository.

Data marts also enhance query performance more than primary repositories can, for two main reasons: 1) Data marts contain less data than primary warehouses, so queries require fewer resources and less time to execute. 2) Data marts summarize data more than primary repositories do, which also helps to limit response times.

A third benefit of data marts is that they improve system utility through the use of customized interfaces. Designed specifically for particular audiences, these interfaces let end users construct queries and manipulate results with minimal time and effort. By contrast, access to primary repositories is via interfaces that sacrifice power and elegance for general-purpose functionality.

A fourth reason for the popularity of data marts is that they afford a greater degree of user-initiated control over their contents. Many systems provide facilities by which users can enter and maintain a variety of external data. For example, financial analysts may add currency exchange rates to a data mart on a regular basis. Marketing analysts may enter competitive pricing information whenever it is available. (As we shall see in Chapter 5, metadata that includes date, time, and user-profile stamps describes these processes.)

Data marts consist of four major components, including presentation and analysis tools, a database management system (DBMS), propagation and maintenance programs, and metadata. The presentation and analysis software typically includes a PC-based graphical user interface (GUI), spreadsheet and OLAP functionality, charting capabilities, and a variety of customized analytic models. The database management system may include a combination of DB2/400 physical and logical files, along with various arrays and other data structures. As is the case with operational systems, the AS/400 itself performs most database management functions. Customized programs or specialized replication software typically maintain data marts. These tools extract data from the primary repository or OLTP databases, transform that data in batch-oriented processes, then finally move that data to the data mart. We can use products such as IBM's DataPropagator and DataMirror's Tranformation Server to simplify and synchronize these processes. Finally, metadata contains information regarding both the content of data marts (file layouts, data structures, field and cell descriptions, etc.) and the processes that maintain data marts.

Data marts are a natural outgrowth of primary warehouse repositories. As we have already discussed, data marts may be constructed before or in lieu of a primary warehouse repository. In such scenarios, information is extracted from operational databases and moved directly to the data mart after consolidation and preprocessing. Reasons for this implementation strategy vary. Some organizations simply do not have the financial or technical resources to implement a comprehensive warehousing solution. In other cases, the need for particular information may be so acute that time constraints dictate a more focused approach. And because of the many significant benefits data marts provide to end users, businesses often develop data marts first and use them to justify comprehensive data warehouses that include primary repositories.

If an organization chooses to build data marts before it builds a primary repository, it must take great care to coordinate the effort. Otherwise, a plethora of databases and propagation processes results in the same problems (e.g., inconsistent field attributes, variable database schema, data redundancy) that so often plague legacy systems. And should that situation occur, data marts will prove to be more expensive in the long run than a comprehensive data warehouse.

Although primary repositories and data marts have many similar features, they also have many notable differences. Figure 2.2 highlights the major distinctions between primary repositories and data marts.

FIGURE 2.2
Comparison of Primary Repositories and Data Marts

Primary Repositories	Data Marts
Are designed for simple, list-oriented queries	Are designed for advanced analyses
Address an entire enterprise	Address a specific department or function
Have variable response times	Have consistently fast response times
Contain summarized OLTP data	Contain derived data (e.g., ratios and variances)
Employ denormalized, relational schema	Often employ multidimensional schema
Contain data that is read-only	Contain data that can be updated
Are focused on the past	Are focused on the future

Online Analytical Processing (OLAP)

Data marts employ specialized storage schema to deliver online analytical processing (OLAP) to the desktop. The term OLAP describes a relatively new class of applications that lets end users interactively examine large sets of data from numerous perspectives. They typically use these applications to forecast sales, analyze manufacturing mixes, consolidate financial information, examine customer segments, perform time-series analyses, and test what-if hypotheses. What's more, OLAP functionality lets these advanced analyses be performed in a timely, ad hoc manner.

By storing information in schema that help set predictable limits on response time, data marts serve as the foundation of many OLAP solutions. Two distinct classes of OLAP database technology are in use today. MD-OLAP solutions rely on data marts that use proprietary multidimensional database (MD or MDD) technology. Also called MOLAP applications, these systems have grown in popularity since their introduction in the early 1990s. ROLAP solutions, the second class of OLAP technology, employ relational-database technology to store information.

As a versatile computing platform, the AS/400 supports both MD-OLAP and ROLAP data-warehousing solutions. In addition to its industrial-strength relational database (DB2/400), the AS/400 provides software developers with three different types of arrays, numerous data structures, and a variety of low- and high-level programming languages. We examine the AS/400's database and development tools in detail in Chapter 7.

Although both ROLAP and MD-OLAP applications provide similar benefits, each does so in a unique manner. Before we examine these database architectures in detail, let's summarize the major characteristics of OLAP. First coined by E. F. Codd and colleagues at Codd and Date Incorporated, the term OLAP describes a relatively new class of decision-support applications. (For those interested in database history, E. F. Codd introduced the concept of varying degrees of normalization in relational databases.) OLAP solutions complement traditional OLTP applications by addressing end users' needs for analytic capability. Codd et al. identified 12 characteristics that, in their view, appear in a true OLAP solution.

Codd's first requirement for an OLAP model is that it support *multidimensional conceptual views*, or that users of OLAP tools be able to analyze information from a number of perspectives. For example, they can examine revenue figures not only by product, customer, or region, but also by any combination of these dimensions.

The second OLAP requirement Codd specified concerns the *transparency* of these solutions. OLAP tools should fit seamlessly into an open-systems architecture, which means that OLAP users should not be required to know that they are utilizing OLAP functionality. Also, OLAP tools should be capable of accessing and converting source data to present a consistent multidimensional view of that data to users.

The third OLAP rule Codd devised, *accessibility*, holds that OLAP solutions must support the creation of an interface between their own logical structures and those of heterogenous data sources.

Codd's fourth rule concerns *reporting performance.* As the number of dimensions in an OLAP database increases, system performance should not degrade appreciably in response to user queries.

And because many organizations already use personal computers to analyze data stored on mainframes and midrange systems, OLAP solutions also must work effectively in a *client/server environment.* This capability comprises Codd's fifth rule.

Generic dimensionality, the sixth rule, holds that every dimension in an OLAP model must be equivalent in its structure and its functional characteristics. This means that every mathematical operation that can be performed on revenue by product, for example, should also function with revenue by customer and revenue by region.

Codd's next rule, that OLAP models support *dynamic sparse matrix maintenance,* applies only to MD-OLAP models. I examine sparsity in the next section of this chapter.

Codd's eighth rule for OLAP solutions concerns *multiuser support.* OLAP products should facilitate the concurrent access and manipulation of data, as well as user-based security measures.

According to Codd, ideal OLAP products also should support *unrestricted cross-dimensional operations.* We already know that OLAP users should be able to perform the same functions in any dimension. This additional rule holds that the OLAP solution itself should manage related calculations across dimensions.

Of course, one reason for the popularity of OLAP applications is their capability to support the *intuitive manipulation of information.* Codd's tenth rule holds that such functionality, which typically supports ad hoc consolidations and hierarchal data manipulation, should not require the use of menus or multiple passes across the user interface.

Another reason for the widespread acceptance of OLAP tools is their provision for *flexible reporting,* expressed as Codd's eleventh rule. Users should be able to access and present/organize any view of the information in the OLAP database — such as the reorientation of columns and rows and the logical grouping of cells (in an MD-OLAP model) close to one another.

Codd's final OLAP rule holds that these tools accommodate at least 15 data dimensions within a common analytical framework. The dimensions also should facilitate a virtually unlimited number of user-defined aggregation levels within any particular consolidation path.

In practice, OLAP solutions do not have to adhere to every one of Codd's rules to be effective. While the rules provide a useful guideline for evaluating OLAP solutions, they should not be used as the only basis upon which solutions are judged. If they were, many useful ROLAP applications would not occupy their well-deserved place in the OLAP market today.

Multidimensional OLAP (MD-OLAP)

The defining characteristic of MD-OLAP applications is their use of multidimensional data structures. To illustrate multidimensionality, let's compare a simple list to true multidimensional structures. The list in Figure 2.3 contains sales information from a fictitious department store.

FIGURE 2.3
Sales List

Product	Color	Sales Volume
Overcoat	White	4
Overcoat	Gray	10
Gloves	Gray	8
Gloves	Black	7
Overcoat	Black	7
Overcoat	White	3
Scarf	Gray	4
Overcoat	Black	8
Scarf	White	6
Scarf	White	6
Scarf	Black	1
Gloves	Gray	5
Gloves	Black	3
Gloves	White	5
Scarf	Black	3

From careful inspection of this list, we can determine that three different products were sold at our store, each in three colors. This conclusion is not readily apparent, however. We have to examine each value in each row and then manually synthesize the data. Figure 2.4 presents the same information in an alternative format. As you can see, we can instantly determine that exactly three products were sold in exactly three colors simply by looking at this matrix, or two-dimensional array. What's more, we can discern relationships that exist between the various data elements; for example, more gray gloves were sold than gray overcoats.

In an array, each axis is referred to as a *dimension*. The array in Figure 2.4 has two dimensions: product and color. Each of these dimensions has, in turn, three members. That is, the product dimension includes overcoats, scarves, and gloves. The color dimension includes black, white, and gray. Multiplying the number of members in each dimension in an array yields the total number of cells in that array. In this case, there are 3 × 3 = 9 cells. Cells contain specific values known as *variables*.

FIGURE 2.4
Two-Dimensional Array

PRODUCT \ COLOR	Black	White	Gray
Overcoat	15	7	10
Scarf	4	12	4
Gloves	10	5	13

In storing information in a way that confers meaning upon their contents, arrays group similar data elements together. As we look at Figure 2.4, we can quite easily determine the total number of overcoats or gloves that were sold. We simply need to add together the variables in a particular column or row. Unlike the list or file in Figure 2.3, the structure of the array itself actually lends context to its contents.

The array in Figure 2.5 includes precomputed totals, or consolidations. In a multidimensional data model, these computed variables are stored in cells that are sometimes referred to as *output cells*. Each consolidated column or row may, likewise, be referred to as an *output member*.

FIGURE 2.5
Two-Dimensional Aggregate Array

PRODUCT \ COLOR	Black	White	Gray	Total
Overcoat	15	7	10	32
Scarf	4	12	4	20
Gloves	10	5	13	28
Total	29	24	27	80

To improve performance, multidimensional database designers attempt to precompute and store all output members (which is not to say that MD-OLAP models are incapable of performing ad hoc consolidations). But while multidimensional systems can consolidate considerable volumes of data, these processes consume significant resources. MD-OLAP applications that derive variables in an ad hoc manner necessarily trade increases in response time for reductions in storage capacity and load times. In such models, the specific values in derived output members are referred to as *derived variables*. End users should not need to know the difference between permanently stored variables and variables derived on an ad hoc basis.

Getting back to our department store, let's suppose that overcoats and scarves are not available in white. To reflect this fact, the array contains two empty cells, as depicted in Figure 2.6. *Sparsity* describes the number of empty cells in an array or data structure relative to the total number of cells. A sparse array contains a relatively high percentage of empty cells, while a dense array contains relatively few empty cells. A second measure of sparsity concerns cells that have the same variable, or value. Rather than filling numerous cells with the same value, advanced multidimensional products use codes to represent repeated values.

FIGURE 2.6
Moderately Sparse Two-Dimensional Array

PRODUCT	Black	White	Gray	Total
Overcoat	15		10	25
Scarf	4		4	8
Gloves	10	5	13	28
Total	29	5	27	61

COLOR

Thus far, we have examined a very simple two-dimensional array. Now suppose that each product were available in three sizes: small, medium, and large. How could we incorporate this new information, or dimension, into our model? Figure 2.7 presents a three-dimensional array, or cube, that includes product, color, and size. Contrast this cube with the list in Figure 2.8.

As you can see by looking at Figure 2.8, discerning patterns in a list becomes increasingly difficult as more data is added to it. The cube, however, retains its ability to store data in an inherently meaningful manner. Multidimensional databases support complex analyses because analysis itself is multidimensional

FIGURE 2.7
Three-Dimensional Array

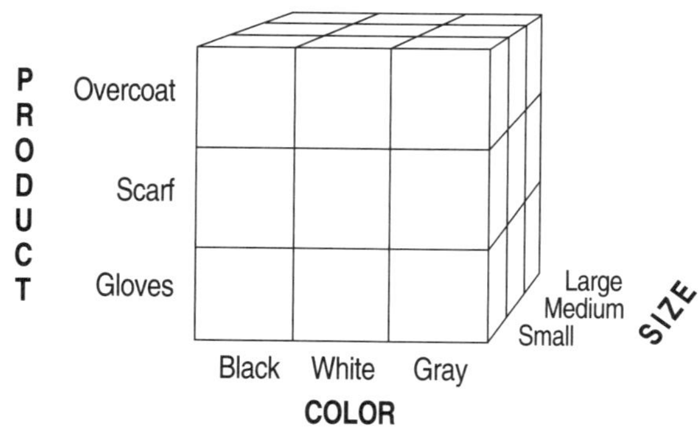

FIGURE 2.8
Sales List with Additional Dimension of Size

Product	Color	Sales Volume	Size
Overcoat	White	4	Small
Overcoat	Gray	10	Large
Gloves	Gray	8	Small
Gloves	Black	7	Medium
Overcoat	Black	7	Medium
Overcoat	White	3	Small
Scarf	Gray	4	Large
Overcoat	Black	8	Large
Scarf	White	6	Medium
Scarf	White	6	Small
Scarf	Black	1	Large
Gloves	Gray	5	Medium
Gloves	Black	3	Small
Gloves	White	5	Large
Scarf	Black	3	Small

in nature. That is, end users want to examine figures based on various combinations of key business dimensions. In the retail industry, these dimensions typically include customer, product ID (or SKU), product name, product color, product size, sales department, store locale, state, region, country, vendor, sales day, sales month, and sales year. End users in banking tend to focus on customer, household ZIP code, household income, account type, branch locale, fiscal month, fiscal quarter, and fiscal year. An end user who examines two or more dimensions simultaneously, even on a report that lists product revenue by customer and store ID, is performing multidimensional analysis.

Although we cannot show it, several cells in Figure 2.7 are empty. For example, there are no small, gray scarves. Well-designed multidimensional database products are designed to automatically detect and remove empty cells from a cube. The entire structure is then compressed, reducing storage requirements and improving response times.

To further highlight the capabilities of a multidimensional database, let's explore how its structure supports the examination of data via different views, or *slices*. After all, different analysts examine different subsets of data. Our three-dimensional cube can support 6 distinct views, as Figures 2.9 through 2.14 demonstrate. Note that the data is not manipulated to present another view. Rather, the entire cube itself is rotated 90 degrees in each figure to let its contents be examined from a different perspective. Each rotation reveals a new two-dimensional slice of information. Through this exercise, we see that a three-dimensional structure supports 6 (3 × 2 × 1) different views. A four-dimensional model supports 24 views, and a five-dimensional structure supports 120 different views.

Note also that as the number of dimensions in an MD-OLAP model increases, the number of cells increases exponentially. A 3-dimensional model with five members in each dimension has 125 cells (5 × 5 × 5), while a 16-dimensional model with the same number of members in each dimension has more than 150 *billion* cells.[1]

Of course, users may not be interested in examining the entire data set in a multidimensional database. For example, suppose that a product manager wants to examine only overcoats and gloves. An effective multidimensional database system would let the product manager create a smaller cube from the larger cube, a process known as *dicing*. Afterward, the manager would be free to manipulate the derived cube in the same way he could manipulate the parent cube. Figure 2.15 on page 28 demonstrates the creation of a derived cube.

[1] *An Introduction to OLAP, An Explanation of Multidimensional Terminology and Technology*, white paper, Pilot Software, Inc., 1996.

FIGURE 2.9
Product by Color by Size

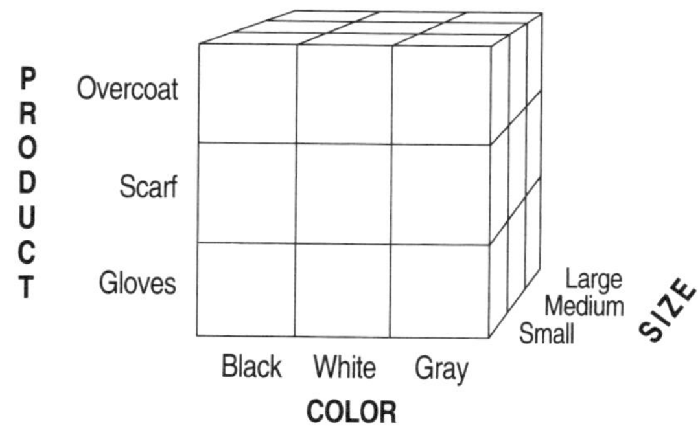

FIGURE 2.10
Color by Product by Size

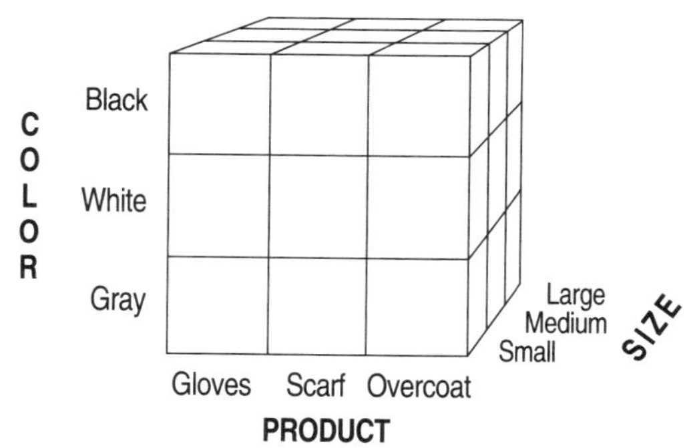

FIGURE 2.11
Color by Size by Product

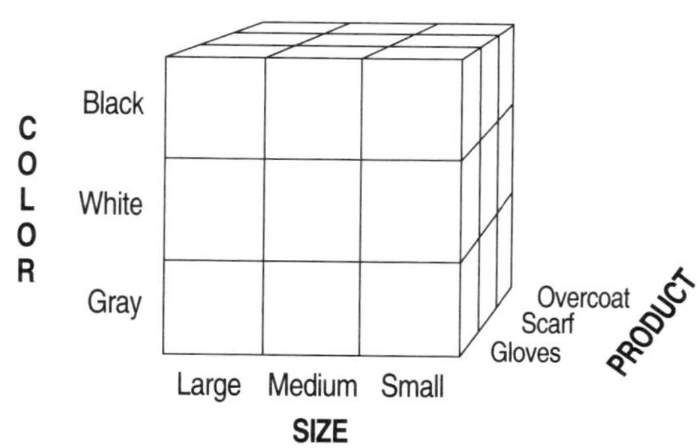

FIGURE 2.12
Size by Color by Product

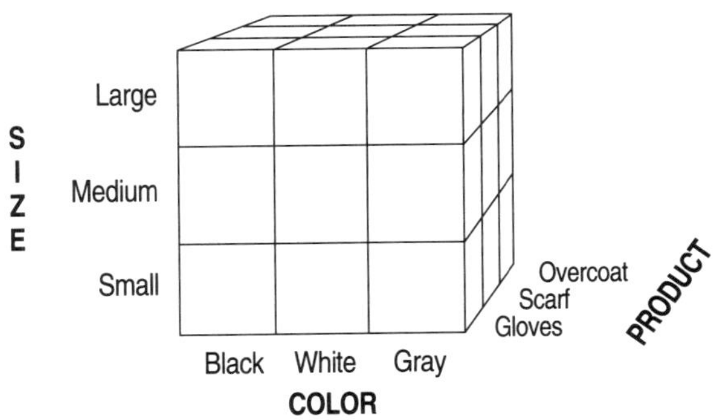

FIGURE 2.13
Size by Product by Color

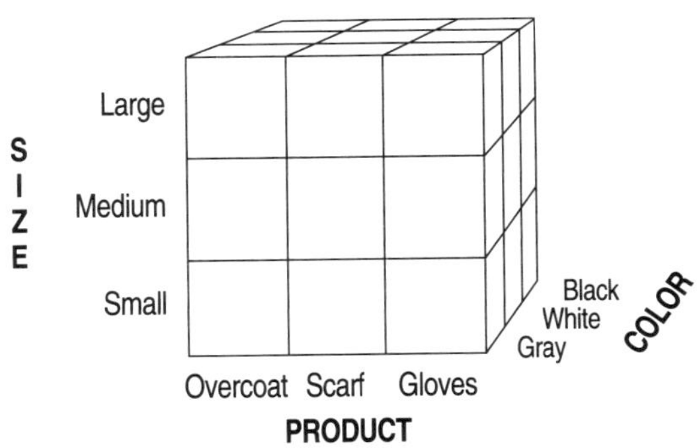

FIGURE 2.14
Product by Size by Color

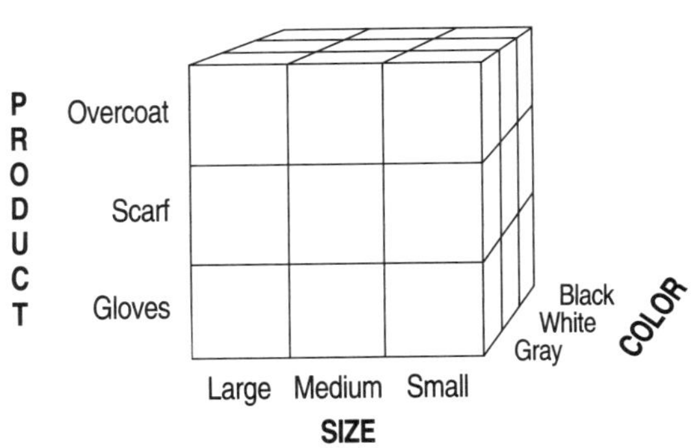

FIGURE 2.15
Multidimensional Dicing

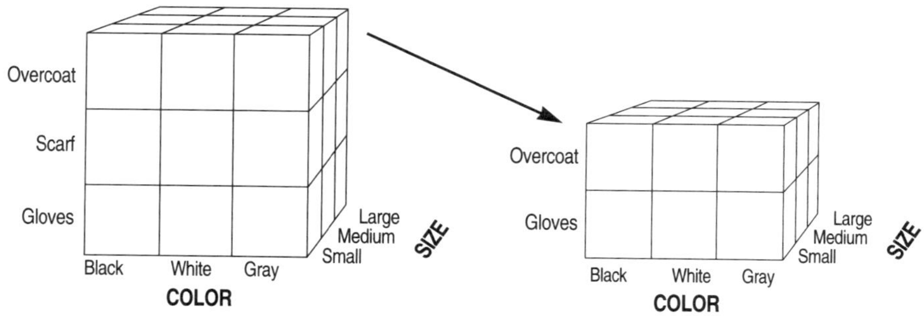

Now suppose that our department store is part of a nationwide retail chain organized by store ID, state, and region. The national sales manager certainly would need the capability to analyze sales volume at a regional level (Northeast, Southeast, Midwest, and West), a state level (e.g., NY, CT, MA, NH), and an individual store level (e.g., store 001, 002, 003). What action would the manager take if he notices that sales in the Northeast region have slumped during a particular month? His first step probably would be to examine sales volumes by state in that region. If he notices low figures in a particular state, such as NY, he might then choose to examine monthly volumes at each NY store. This style of iterative analysis is known as *drilling down*. Conversely, examining sales at a store level followed by the associated state and regional levels would be an example of *drilling up*. These terms are synonymous with *rolling down* and *rolling up*.

You might think that adding a new dimension such as state or region to a multidimensional database is an ideal way to support drill-ups and drill-downs that require this additional data. Although additional independent dimensions would enable this functionality in such a schema, there is a more efficient method. Advanced multidimensional products have facilities that support the creation of *multiple hierarchies* within dimensions. For example, a multidimensional database could contain a dimension called *company* that consists of individual stores, states, and regions. Figure 2.16 presents such a structure.

As I mentioned earlier, determining the total sales volume for a particular dimension in a cube is a relatively trivial exercise. In grouping similar data elements in rows and columns, MD-OLAP databases facilitate such mathematical consolidations. Sophisticated analytic models, however, often require values that can be computed only through the manipulation of other variables. A variance, for example, is calculated by deducting actual results from budgeted figures. Similarly, our department store manager may want to compare actual sales of overcoats to projected sales of overcoats. Through *vector arithmetic*,

FIGURE 2.16
Hierarchical Dimensions

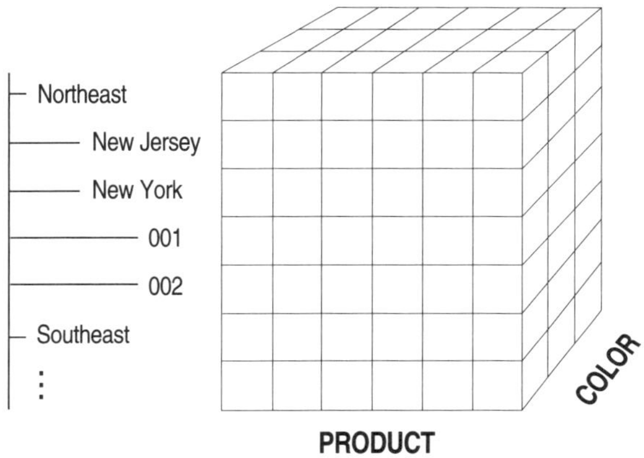

MD-OLAP applications can calculate derived figures in an array with a single operation. Vector arithmetic lets entire slices, or planes, be manipulated along with other slices. Figure 2.17 depicts an array using vector arithmetic. MD-OLAP databases, in supporting such operations, let applications maintain consistently low response times. Because analysts who continually swap dimensions and derive new variables require speed-of-thought response, this feature of OLAP is a necessity.

FIGURE 2.17
Vector Arithmetic

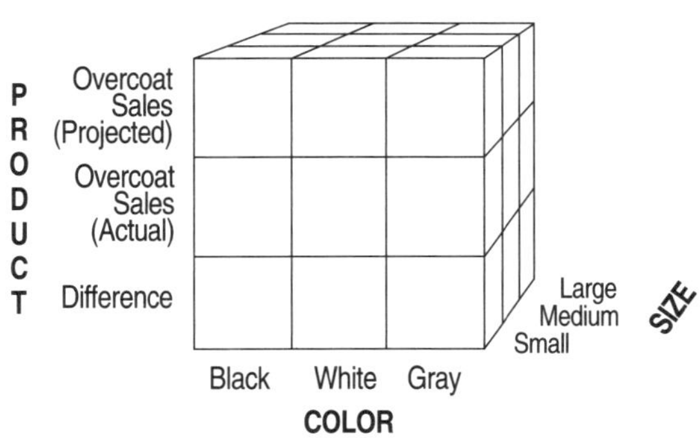

Now suppose that our three-dimensional array were to include 100 members in each dimension. Such a structure would contain 1 million cells — a total computed by multiplying the number of members in one dimension by the number in each of the others (100 × 100 × 100). To locate data in any particular cell, a search engine would have to evaluate a maximum of only 300 members (i.e., 100 members per dimension) in the cube. On average, only half as many members would actually be evaluated. Many MD-OLAP solutions employ specialized indices and hashing algorithms to further improve seek performance. These index structures, which may comprise less than 5 percent of the cube's total size, often can reside entirely in main memory. By eliminating the need to physically access indexes on disk, these models support enhanced query performance. Fortunately, the AS/400 can support up to 20 GB of main storage.

I have limited our discussion to multidimensional database models that contain three dimensions. Real-world analyses, of course, require many more. According to E. F. Codd, an industrial-strength OLAP tool should be capable of supporting 15, and preferably 20, different dimensions. These models are difficult to visualize, but intuitive interfaces shield users from such complexities. For example, suppose that a fourth dimension, time, is added to our three-dimensional cube. Suppose further that analysis is performed on annual sales volumes for each of the past five years. In theory, an MD-OLAP product could maintain five individual three-dimensional cubes, each of which contains data corresponding to a particular year. From an end-user perspective, these cubes then can be manipulated as if the data were in a single structure.[2]

Relational OLAP (ROLAP)

Another popular class of OLAP tools relies upon relational-database technology. Known as ROLAP solutions, these applications do not store data in a multidimensional format. Instead, through the use of indices and denormalized aggregate tables, these systems employ relational-database technology to support multidimensional analyses. Because relational OLAP databases are capable of storing vast amounts of data, primary repositories often use them as well.

The most basic of ROLAP implementations relies on a database architecture known as the *star* schema. Built for simplicity and speed, this relational model includes a central fact table that consists of keys and numeric variables, or facts, such as sales quantities and sales dollars. A generic star schema appears in Figure 2.18. Radiating outward from the central fact table in this example are four denormalized files, or dimension tables. Dimension tables contain descriptive, textual data such as product names. The star model is aptly titled; in large examples, numerous dimension tables appear to be connected through rays to a central point, thus resembling a star.

[2]Portions of the preceding section were derived from the following white papers: *Introduction to Multidimensional Database Technology*, Kenan Systems Corporation, 1993–1995, and *An Introduction to OLAP, An Explanation of Multidimensional Terminology and Technology*, Pilot Software, Inc., 1996.

FIGURE 2.18
Generic Star Schema

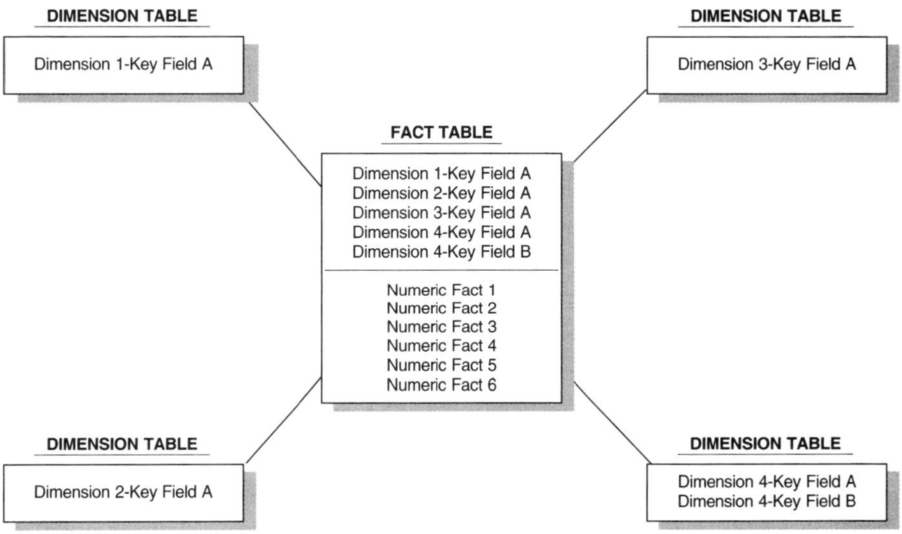

To retrieve information from a star schema, queries first compare selection criteria to the data contained in various dimension tables. After isolating records in appropriate dimension tables, the query quickly accesses values in the fact table via joins. In the case of the AS/400, joins refer to joined-logical files. These specialized objects contain indexes that enable access to data contained in multiple physical files. Through joins, dimension tables are related to fact tables. A 4-dimensional ROLAP data mart would require 4 dimension tables; similarly, a 15-dimensional model would maintain at least 15 dimension tables. ROLAP databases with more than three dimensions are much easier to visualize than similar MD-OLAP models.

By adjusting our department store information for this model, we can construct a very simple star schema, effectively depicted in Figure 2.19. Notice that a level indicator field appears in each dimension table. Referring to the store file, this level indicator is required to differentiate aggregate data (e.g., revenue per region) from more detailed figures (e.g., revenue per store). In this file, we assign different codes to each unique aggregation level. For example, "01" can refer to the store level, while "02" and "03" can refer to the state and region levels, respectively. In this way, ROLAP databases can define a hierarchy within a single dimension, just as our MD-OLAP model did in Figure 2.16.

In environments that consistently require the addition of new dimensions or the removal of obsolete ones, however, level indicators may have negative consequences. Because level structures are physically defined in each record of

FIGURE 2.19
Simple Star Schema with Central Fact Table

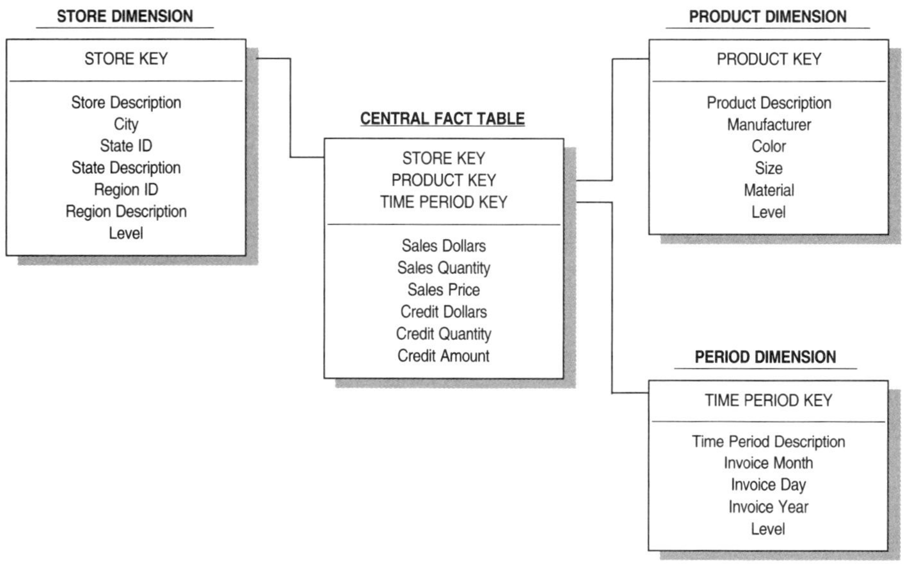

a dimension file, the addition or removal of a level necessitates updates to both the dimension key and the fact table key. In files with several million records, these processes require significant resources as access paths are updated. Also, the level concept may lead to confusion if end users are not aware of its significance. If a query is constructed without a level ID parameter, for example, incorrect query results are returned to the end user. This occurs because the query performs operations on detailed as well as aggregate data. Simple star schema that employ the use of level indicators also must account for all combinations of aggregate information, or at least views of every combination. For example, if our model did not include aggregate data by region, then a query seeking regional revenue totals would return a value of zero because no records meeting that criterion would be processed.

To obviate the need for level indicators in a ROLAP model, we can fortify the simple star schema with additional aggregate fact tables. In this way, the database consists of numerous consolidated files that will be accessed when queries seek summarized information. A typical use for this more robust architecture is in drill-up and drill-down operations.

Figure 2.20 demonstrates how the addition of state and region fact tables to our simple star schema can provide summary results in a more timely way. Returning to our national sales manager, suppose that he is in the process of examining the results of a particular store. For comparative purposes, he may

FIGURE 2.20
Multiple Fact Tables

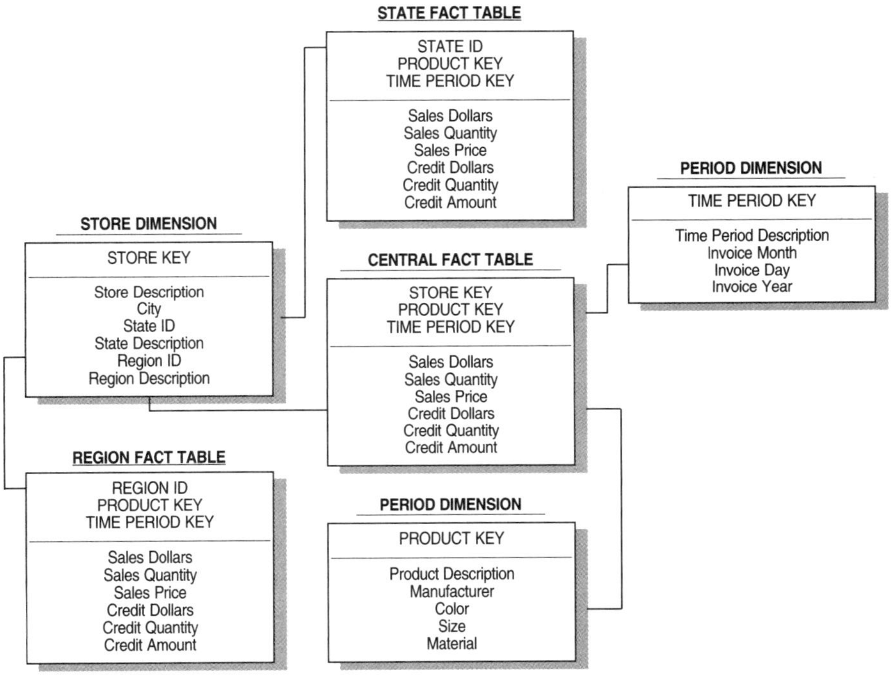

wish to view the results of the state in which the store is located. In constructing an appropriate query, the manager would, in effect, execute a chain operation to the state fact table; the state ID would serve as the key. This single operation would provide the answer to the manager's query because the state fact table would contain pre-computed sales figures for each state in which products were sold. I should note that ROLAP products do not require knowledge of a programming language such as SQL, RPG, or Cobol, as is sometimes thought. As is the case with MD-OLAP solutions, ROLAP applications provide intuitive user interfaces that effectively shield end users from complex schema.

As you can imagine, star schema that employ multiple fact tables can grow quickly in size and complexity. An alternative ROLAP design approach is to normalize each dimension table by attribute level, thereby creating progressively smaller dimension tables that are linked to appropriate aggregate fact tables. This particular ROLAP model is known as the *snowflake* schema. Figure 2.21 presents such a schema. Keep in mind that in this case, the store dimension maintains the most detailed level of information. Stated another

FIGURE 2.21
Snowflake Schema

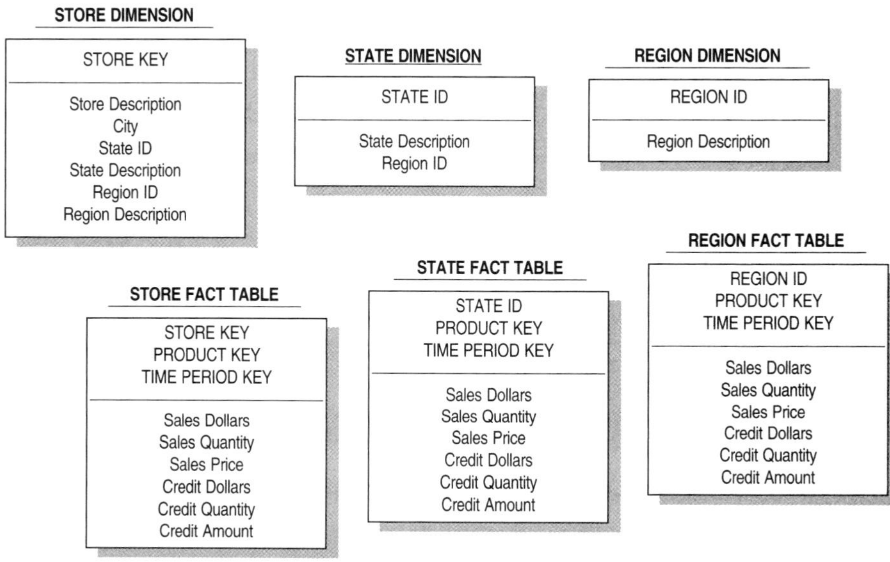

way, the store dimension possesses the finest *granularity*. Every record in the store dimension that is associated with the next hierarchy (e.g., state) would be extracted, consolidated, and included in the aggregated state fact table. Fields that do not pertain specifically to the state dimension or to the next level in the hierarchy (e.g., region) would not be included in the state dimension. This process of aggregate decomposition occurs until the coarsest dimension of data is created. In this simple example, that dimension would be region. As in any normalized database, it is imperative that column names remain consistent throughout ROLAP schema.

ROLAP databases effectively support ad hoc, multidimensional analyses. These models can maintain derived data as well. For example, separate dimension tables may be designed to hold variances by product, state, and region. Similarly, ROLAP data marts also can store ratios. And users of these systems are free to drill up and down through various levels of consolidated information. System designers, who must foresee end-user requirements and create appropriate fact and dimension tables with appropriate levels of aggregation, hold the keys to a successful ROLAP implementation. As with MD-OLAP solutions, there is a fine line between too much pre-aggregation and not enough — the former may result in intolerable load times, the latter in unacceptable query performance.

OLTP Applications and OLAP Technology: A Potent Combination

We have seen that both MD-OLAP and ROLAP databases can effectively support the analytic needs of knowledge workers. You may now be wondering whether you simply should store all your operational data in an MD-OLAP or ROLAP database. The answer, of course, is a resounding "No!" You should view OLAP technology as a complement to, and not a replacement for, operational systems. Let's examine why.

Suppose that the national sales manager in our earlier example would like to store the ages of his sales representatives in a multidimensional database such as an array. He could list Social Security numbers on the vertical dimension and last names on the horizontal dimension. In each cell, he would place the age of the corresponding employee. As you can see in Figure 2.22, the result is a very sparsely populated array. What value is provided by such a structure? Very little. It is doubtful that the sales manager would benefit from discerning a relationship between Social Security number and age. Similarly, the aggregation of ages in this case just doesn't make sense. The same holds true for storing names and Social Security numbers in separate dimension tables in a star or snowflake schema. Although this example is a bit simplistic, it highlights a fundamental characteristic of OLAP data models; that is, the greater the number of interrelationships between the elements in an OLAP database, the more likely that database is to yield value in the form of business intelligence. Data sets that do not contain multiple interrelationships are not good candidates for inclusion in an OLAP application.

FIGURE 2.22
Sparsely Populated Array

SOCIAL SECURITY NUMBER	Smith	Jones	Wilson	Katzen	Field	Halka	Pajkowski	Brown	Dawer	Lasher
111-11-1111		32								
222-22-2222	45									
333-33-3333			27							
444-44-4444				33						
.							28			
.								39		
.									53	
.					19					
.										47
.						47				

LAST NAME

Also, keep in mind that OLTP databases are updated continually throughout the day. They are designed to maintain highly granular data sets that are in a constant state of flux. OLAP databases, on the other hand, are maintained by customized, batch-oriented, resource-intensive propagation routines. In practice, many OLAP databases are updated only on a daily, weekly, or even monthly basis. They are simply not designed to store large volumes of transaction-level data. In providing for advanced decision-support capabilities, however, OLAP applications are a wonderful complement to traditional OLTP applications.

MD-OLAP and ROLAP: A Comparison

Because there is a strong need for analyses in business, there is clearly a need for OLAP functionality as well. What is not clear is whether to choose multidimensional OLAP or relational OLAP technology. Although these competing architectures provide similar benefits to decision makers, each does so in a unique manner. Vendors who offer one or the other are quick to recite performance benchmarks and scaling statistics that seem to prove their particular methodology superior. But I have always looked at benchmarks with a healthy dose of skepticism — it has been said that benchmarks support what the sponsoring company wants to prove.

How then can you make a choice between a relational OLAP application and a multidimensional OLAP solution? Unfortunately, there is no easy answer to this question. Rather than attempting to resolve what has become a heated debate, I offer you some noteworthy points of comparison regarding these respective solutions that may prove useful in your search for an OLAP tool.

On the positive side, MD-OLAP databases are inherently multidimensional. In addition, MD-OLAP solutions create relatively small indexes that often can reside entirely in main memory. This means that fewer physical I/O operations are required to access data, which enhances performance. However, MD-OLAP is based on proprietary designs that may differ dramatically from one vendor to the next, so programmers who are familiar with one solution cannot readily apply that knowledge to another. Another potential disadvantage is that MD-OLAP databases may be somewhat difficult to visualize in the design stage (what does a 10-dimensional cube look like anyway?). Another downside of MD-OLAP is that the multidimensional database industry has yet to devise a standard data-access and data-manipulation language for this type of solution; major MD-OLAP vendors, however, do provide APIs with their products.

ROLAP solutions provide OLAP functionality even though the data itself is not stored in an inherently multidimensional manner. Even a simple table with columns and rows can yield information in a multidimensional format. Also, recognize that ROLAP solutions are based on a proven database-design approach. The relational-database industry exceeded $10 billion in revenue in 1995. A market this size is obviously supported by a considerable number of IT professionals conversant in its technology. Another advantage is that multidimensional ROLAP databases are easier to visualize in the design stage than are corresponding MD-OLAP models. Finally, an advantage of ROLAP is that relational databases conform to a standard access language, ANSI-standard SQL.

By no means am I implying that ROLAP technology is the preferred choice for OLAP-based systems. Because ROLAP schema consist of multiple-join files, the operations that create and maintain these files can consume an enormous amount of system resources. Also, unlike MD-OLAP models, ROLAP solutions are typically inefficient at providing answers to queries that seek single-figure results. Furthermore, ROLAP solutions often employ extremely large fact and dimension tables, with very large indexes.

If I were forced to make a choice, I would recommend ROLAP schema in instances where a considerable volume of data (i.e., more than 10 GB) is maintained and standard analyses (e.g., drill-ups, summaries) can suffice. In environments characterized by smaller data sets and the need for more sophisticated analyses, an MD-OLAP tool is probably the better choice. Bear in mind that you also can implement both methodologies simultaneously.

One important note of caution: When you evaluate OLAP solutions, do not equate the number of dimensions that a given product supports with database capacity. One vendor's idea of a six-dimensional model may be the functional equivalent of another vendor's four-dimensional model. As evidenced by multiple hierarchies within a single dimension, both ROLAP and MD-OLAP solutions give developers a great deal of flexibility in the definition of dimensions.

We have seen that data-warehouse database schema are inherently different from operational database schema. In terms of content, structure, and purpose, both primary repositories and data marts are designed to support the decision-making process. In contrast, operational databases are designed to store massive volumes of continually changing, transaction-level data. Without primary repositories and data marts, data warehouses could not provide business intelligence to end users. As you will see in Chapter 3, the processes that maintain data-warehouse repositories are as important as data-warehouse database schema.

Chapter 3

Loading the Data Warehouse

In Chapter 2, we examined the foundation of data warehouses: primary repositories and data marts. In this chapter, we focus on three related procedures that we can use to move data into these specialized databases: data extraction, data transformation, and data propagation. As I stated in Chapter 1, data-extraction procedures programmatically access information stored in OLTP databases. For example, we can use customized programs (i.e., RPG or Cobol) or third-party replication tools to collect information from a highly normalized sales database. After we collect the raw data, we use data-transformation procedures to translate the data into more implicitly meaningful information. The denormalization and aggregation of OLTP data are common examples of data transformation. Finally, we use data-propagation routines to physically map the transformed data into a data warehouse. A procedure that manages the movement of transformed mainframe data into an AS/400-based data mart is an example of a propagation process.

At a major data-warehousing conference in 1996, surveys indicated that getting data into data warehouses is one of the most difficult challenges we face during the lifetime of these projects. Several factors account for this difficulty.

First, normalized legacy data isn't stored in intuitively accessible structures. Because normalized databases use multiple files and are designed for operational efficiency, they're inherently difficult to access. What's more, these databases make extensive use of flags, codes, and abbreviations. Although these features enhance operational efficiency, they do so at the expense of intuitive access to data.

Second, OLTP database schema are often inconsistent, especially in organizations that manage both home-grown and canned applications. Just as no two snowflakes are ever the same, different application databases rarely embody the same design characteristics. In particular, I recall one organization that maintained a denormalized accounts-payable database consisting of numerous multimember files. Surprisingly, a highly normalized, efficient order-entry database operated alongside this accounts-payable application.

Inadequate legacy-system documentation also contributes to the difficulties we encounter as we maintain data warehouses. Although documentation is very useful because it details system processes and database schema, system designers and programmers unfortunately often treat it as an afterthought. So if your operational systems have inadequate documentation, be prepared to spend considerable time examining applications and databases.

Finally, inaccurate legacy data can further complicate the migration of data into data warehouses. Many OLTP systems contain minor errors that, when taken alone, do not pose a major problem. However, as operational data is summarized, the effects of even minor errors are compounded time and again. A small difference in currency exchange rates, for instance, might cause serious problems when that difference is summarized over the course of several years. So be aware that you may find it necessary to correct OLTP applications and update their databases before you can extract data for your warehouse. Of course, data quality in any computer application is of paramount importance. In a data-warehousing environment, however, data integrity takes on heightened significance. Analysts who examine warehouse data rely on its accuracy to make decisions. In some cases, these decisions can have a dramatic impact on an organization's future.

Consider a data warehouse of information gleaned from a hypothetical department store chain. Management may subject this information to numerous complex analyses to determine whether a particular region needs a new store. What if the data warehouse was inaccurate, and management opened an outlet in a saturated market? Such a decision could have dire financial consequences for the company.

Now that we've seen why moving data into data warehouses can be very difficult, let's examine the processes we can use to accomplish this task.

Data Extraction

The first step in data extraction is to identify the specific elements that warrant inclusion in the data warehouse. End users know what data is valuable, so this identification process involves interviews with them. But although they know what's important, many end users do not know how to explain completely and exactly what they require. For example, a sales manager may simply state, "I need to examine sales volume by region." You must make sure she knows precisely what sales volume means in this case. Is it sales quantity? Is it sales revenue? Is it both? Should these figures include damaged goods, returned goods, and other credits? What precisely does region mean? You should ascertain that the manager's definition of a region does not differ from the operational system's definition. When possible, it is advisable to ask end users to point out specific examples of the data they require, such as figures listed on a report. This will help you more easily locate the source of the data.

Once you have identified critical data elements for the data warehouse, you must locate that data before you can extract it. To locate specific data elements, you may have to examine multiple application databases on a variety of machines. And in the case of third-party software applications, this can be a daunting task, because many canned applications use inherently complex database architectures.

Once you have located and isolated the requisite data elements, you can begin creating extraction procedures. As I noted in Chapter 1, normalized data is stored in many files — not a design conducive to efficient extraction processes.

In essence, the data-extraction phase of warehouse propagation requires you to reconstruct operational data field by field, record by record, and file by file. And multiple database structures (variable-length records, internally described records, data structures, data queues, multimember files, logical files, physical files, join-logical files, open query files); inconsistent field names; inconsistent file names; and inadequate or non-existent documentation often conspire to complicate this arduous task.

Because many fields in normalized databases contain data that has been encoded to further reduce redundancy and disk space, you must determine precisely what these codes mean — a time-consuming task that often results in the discovery of obsolete codes.

When you are ready to actually extract data from your OLTP databases, you should consider using a transformational replication tool. These products are specially designed to access legacy OLTP applications, and they can substantially reduce, and sometimes even eliminate, the need to write customized extraction programs. In later chapters, I examine several such products in detail, including ASC's SEQUEL, Coglin Mill's RODIN, DataMirror's Transformation Server, Datawatch's Monarch, and IBM's DataPropagator.

REPORT MINING

You've seen why extracting data from databases can be difficult. Happily, another source of OLTP data may significantly reduce the need to directly access operational databases. Spooled files (reports that have not yet printed) contain data that has *already* been extracted from operational databases, and you can use report mining to access this data. For several reasons, report mining holds considerable appeal for those tasked with loading data into a data warehouse.

Almost every OLTP application, whether canned or home-grown, generates a comprehensive suite of reports. Because they provide valuable information to end users in a relatively intuitive way, reports mask the complexity of underlying OLTP databases. Furthermore, report programs have already located, accessed, extracted, and consolidated valuable operational information. For example, consider an RPG program that creates a monthly sales report. This report program *is* an extraction procedure because it pulls data out of an operational database. By leveraging the effort already invested in this program, you may not need to determine how invoices are stored in the underlying OLTP database.

Reports also can serve as effective sources for data warehouses because reports are often archived longer than operational data. Most organizations purge or offload OLTP data regularly to maintain system performance. Restoring this information to disk for warehouse propagation is a time-consuming, resource-intensive task, so many organizations use specialized applications to store and access reports. Known as computer output to laser disk (COLD) systems, these products use optical media and advanced indexing to store thousands of compressed spooled files. Users can then access the spooled files using intuitive, PC-based interfaces. While comprehensive COLD products support report mining directly, many others provide the means to integrate spooled data with third-party report-mining tools.

Finally, reports can be handy sources for data warehouses because they maintain metadata in the form of column headings, date ranges, titles, and other descriptive text. In a world where truly effective documentation is rare, reports are valuable allies.

Of course, reports aren't a panacea for the problems you encounter during data extraction — reports can contain the same inaccuracies and errors that exist in operational data. Furthermore, reports may apply subtle biases to data. For example, a particular set of reports may use currency exchange rates that haven't been effectively rounded. If the underlying code and database aren't examined in detail, this bias will be passed on to the data warehouse.

Also, keep in mind that data extraction from reports is a multistep process. You must first execute the report program, download the spooled file (to convert it into ASCII), run the extraction procedure, then load the extracted data into AS/400 files. However, in many cases, the benefits of report mining clearly outweigh the drawbacks. (In Chapter 11, we examine Monarch, a popular report-mining tool from Datawatch Corporation, in detail.)

Thus far, our discussion has assumed that required warehouse data exists in your operational databases and/or reports. In some instances, this is not the case; you may have to design procedures to capture data that's not stored in any of your systems. The classic example is a sales organization that purchases demographic data for analysis. Many companies, especially those without data warehouses, conduct much of this analysis offline. However, once your data warehouse has proven itself and users are familiar with its analytic functionality, be prepared to field requests for the inclusion of "new" information.

Whether you implement extraction procedures through custom coding, vendor tools, report mining, or a combination of the three, the process is time-consuming and often requires significant resources. You should allocate these resources to the project from its inception. Also, plan to acquire in-depth knowledge of your OLTP applications. Without these steps, your data warehouse is doomed.

Data Transformation

Once raw data has been extracted from OLTP databases, it must be reformatted and refined for the data warehouse. As we have already seen, the nature and content of operational data — it is transaction-oriented and consists of many codes — differs from that of warehouse repositories. The transformation of this granular, cryptic data into intelligible information comprises five related activities:

data aggregation, data filtering, data combining, data standardization, and data cleansing. I describe each of these activities in the following sections.

Data Aggregation

Aggregation is an essential transformation function that summarizes operational data. For example, suppose each invoice in a simplified accounts-receivable application is stored in two files, a header file and a detail file. Although this design makes perfectly good sense in a normalized environment, it makes no sense at all in a data warehouse. We cannot expect end users to explicitly join these two files, nor can we expect users to understand the concept of normalization as it relates to the relationship between header and detail records. The goal of aggregation in this case is twofold. First, the aggregation process should combine the header and detail records into one record or block (*interfile aggregation*); second, multiple invoices should be summarized according to a unique key that coincides with the desired degree of granularity (*intrafile aggregation*). A typical sales aggregation program would use a key to create one data-warehouse record or cell from multiple invoices. Keep in mind that the goal of aggregation processes is the creation of summarized information for analysis. You always can use reports and inquiries to obtain detailed information directly from OLTP applications.

The degree to which warehouse data is aggregated directly affects query performance. For example, queries that dynamically calculate results consume far more computing resources than queries that retrieve highly aggregated data. However, there is also a direct relationship between the chosen degree of aggregation and the time required to load data warehouses: the higher the degree of aggregation, the longer the load time. Furthermore, as the degree of aggregation increases, there is also a diminishing marginal return on incremental gains in query performance. This means that a low degree of aggregation requires shorter load times, yet generates the highest degree of relative query performance improvement. As the degree to which data is aggregated increases, corresponding load times increase and relative query performance improves marginally. You'll need to conduct trials to determine the optimal level of data aggregation for your environment.

Several variables are responsible for the relationships between data aggregation, load times, and query performance. Of course, the volume of OLTP data processed has a major impact on these measurements. As the amount of data increases, aggregation routines consume more computing resources and are likely to take longer to run.

In addition, as data warehouses expand to include more levels of aggregation, the data warehouses require ever-increasing amounts of disk space. For example, the storage-expansion factor for a highly aggregated five-dimensional database is approximately 32. This means that 100 MB of granular OLTP data will require about 3.2 GB of disk storage in the associated data warehouse.

Dimensionality is another factor that has a dramatic impact upon aggregation routines and load times. As more dimensions are added to a warehouse model, the associated processing requirements increase exponentially as the degree of aggregation rises.

Finally, the volatility of operational data also affects aggregation and load times. If OLTP data elements change frequently, or if the rules for aggregation are modified, then warehouse load times increase as these changes are reflected retroactively in the data warehouse. Date elements are an example of data with a low degree of volatility. Dimensions consisting of day, month, and year rarely change because the element of time is stable. Product structures, however, are apt to change on a continual basis as product lines are frequently modified. Of course, increases in computing power (e.g., more memory, additional processors) tend to mitigate the impact of dimensionality and volatility on warehouse aggregation procedures, load times, and query performance. However, there will always be a trade-off between chosen levels of aggregation, load times, and query performance.

Data Filtering

Transformational processes also may *filter* relevant information from OLTP databases. For example, a marketing analyst who must examine sales trends would probably have no interest in invoice numbers or order numbers. These and other extraneous data elements would not be transferred to a data warehouse. Furthermore, suppose that a marketing data mart is to include expense information for marketing personnel. During the construction of such a data mart, pertinent information that pertains only to the marketing department may be filtered from databases that contain enterprise-wide information. For example, filter routines may examine only general-ledger account records associated with marketing employees. Effective replication software lets users specify selection criteria at both the column and row level for propagation to warehouse repositories.

Data Combination or Combining Data

A third transformation function may *combine* OLTP data from separate applications and platforms. The growth of distributed-processing environments has resulted in operational databases that are scattered around the world. Data warehouses often must combine data elements from these disparate systems. To make matters worse, information systems professionals have traditionally viewed business functions as distinct entities. As a result, different programs writing to separate databases often maintain functional data. And this practice occurs even in centralized data-processing environments. One set of files, for example, may contain sales data while another group contains booking information. If these applications are somewhat mature, many bookings and sales reports have probably been created for the user community. But what happens when management wants to compare current booking figures to previous revenue levels? Without a data warehouse, most IT shops would have to allocate significant programming resources to this task. Data-warehouse maintenance procedures alleviate the need for this use of resources.

Data Standardization

Data-transformation processes *standardize* data elements and the metadata that describes those elements. The difficulties caused by poor or even nonexistent documentation underscore the need for consistency. Basic field attributes such as content, size, type, and description often differ across multiple applications, or even within a single application. The inconsistent use of codes is a frequent problem, as well. The first step in data standardization is to determine the possible values for every field being moved to the warehouse. For example, suppose that a poorly designed legacy database has several thousand records containing a customer field, CUSNAM. After examining these records, you may discover that the information relating to the same customer is represented in several different ways, as the following shows:

CUSNAM Field Contents	Frequency
AT&T	45
ATT	32
AT & T	16

After you have made a decision about a standard spelling representation of AT&T, you can write a program to standardize this field for the data warehouse. Figure 3.1 depicts conditional RPG logic you could use in this simple example. Alternatively, you could use higher-level replication software for this function.

FIGURE 3.1
Conditional RPG Logic Sample

```
NØ1Factor1+++++OpCode(E)+Factor2+++++++Result++++++Len+++HiLoEq....
C   CUSNAM      IFEQ      'ATT'                                      Case 1
C   CUSNAM      OREQ      'AT & T'                                   Case 2
C               MOVE      *BLANKS       CUSNAM                       Clr Field
C               MOVEL     'AT&T'        CUSNAM                       Inz Field
C               ENDIF                                                Endif
```

Flag fields can present a similar problem in OLTP databases. In many systems, a confusing mix of Y, N, 1, 0, X, and blanks is used to denote off and on conditions in these fields.

Another common problem in legacy-system data arises from the various ways numeric data may have been stored. Numeric fields may include leading or trailing negative signs, plus signs, implied decimal points, brackets, scientific notation, and even alphabetic symbols that represent a combination of a number and a negative sign. A generally accepted data-warehousing standard is to store numbers with explicit decimal points.

Date fields present another transformation dilemma because legacy systems include a wide variety of date representations. Single-field formats include MMDDYY, YYMMDD, YYYYDDD, and CCYYMMDD. Dates also may be represented by multiple fields (MM DD YY), textual abbreviations (JAN, FEB, etc.), and codes (01, 02, etc.) A generally accepted standard is to represent dates as single fields in CCYYMMDD format; given the issues related to representing the coming century, this is a timely solution. Text fields, and in particular comment fields, often require standardization as well. Many legacy systems, for example, do not validate the case of text fields.

The role of standardization is especially critical in warehouse applications designed for international companies. What does 4/3/95 mean to you? If you are an American, it represents the third of April. To a European, it means the fourth of March. Similar confusion occurs with units of measure (liters vs. gallons), currencies (US vs. Canadian dollars), and even language (American words vs. English words).

In many legacy systems, values are also stored without appropriate units of measure. Often, the designers of these systems assumed end users would know which units apply. These issues must be resolved before operational data can be moved to a data warehouse. Standardization routines are essential components of every data warehouse; without them, end users would not know which values they could use in queries.

Data Cleansing

Another function data-transformation programs perform is that of *data cleansing*. Most IT shops boast an impressive set of procedure manuals designed to ensure data integrity, but, as I mentioned earlier, many OLTP databases do contain errors. An effective transformation product supports the cleansing of data via value-translation algorithms that change field contents and attributes. We use data-transformation procedures to ensure the accuracy of warehouse repositories.

Data Propagation

Data-propagation procedures physically move transformed OLTP data to data warehouses. The data itself may be moved from an OLTP computer to a separate warehouse server, or it may simply be copied from one database to another on the same machine. As we saw in Chapter 1, moving the data to a separate server is the recommended approach for optimum performance.

We can perform data-propagation procedures periodically or continuously. Periodic replenishment occurs at regular intervals — i.e., daily, weekly, or monthly — and is sometimes referred to as *snapshot propagation*. In essence, this approach replicates the state of operational systems at a specific moment in time. Because changes in operational data are not immediately reflected in the data warehouse, end users will not have access to the most current information. However, end users often use data warehouses only to examine trends, so they may have no overwhelming need for up-to-the-moment information. Furthermore, OLTP systems do provide reports and inquiry screens that provide current — albeit rudimentary and static — information.

When end users require current information, we employ continuous-propagation procedures. In this scenario, propagation occurs throughout the day on a real-time basis. As changes are made to OLTP data, the warehouse repositories are updated. Continuous replication requires dedicated communications channels (e.g., leased lines or high-speed LAN connections) so that data warehouses remain synchronized with OLTP applications. Real-time data-warehouse applications are becoming more popular as competition in the communications arena drives the associated costs down.

Both periodic and real-time propagation processes maintain snapshots of warehouse data over time. For example, consider a data mart that stores information about bookings, or orders that have not yet been filled. Bookings transactions consist of new orders, deleted orders, and changes to existing orders. Obviously, bookings figures fluctuate throughout the day as orders are updated. End users may have to forecast bookings levels so they can allocate resources for activities such as manufacturing. A data warehouse that contains only current bookings information is of limited use to end users if does not also contain historical trends. So nearly all data warehouses retain weekly or monthly snapshots of their own data repositories, which lets end users perform trend analyses.

Effective propagation tools support both periodic and real-time data replication. Comprehensive products also support propagation on a net-change basis. In this way, only the data that has been modified is transmitted to the data warehouse. Unlike full-refresh methodologies, this approach requires minimal communications resources because it transmits only modified data. DataMirror Corporation's Transformation Server is one example of a product that supports all of the preceding propagation strategies.

Once defined, propagation processes should execute automatically in one of two ways. *Log-based replication* gathers transactions from AS/400 journal receivers. These specialized objects store audit trails, or change histories, for specified data files. AS/400 journals capture such transactions. Because it operates asynchronously, log-based warehouse propagation has the least effect on response time and system performance. Of course, data in files that are not journaled cannot be processed with this approach. In contrast, *trigger-based replication* relies upon actual database transactions to invoke the propagation procedure. Database triggers ensure application integrity by making the database itself responsible for events that depend upon its contents (e.g., warehouse write transactions). If many updates occur at once, however, this process tends to degrade system performance more than log-based replication does.

Transformed OLTP data is either pushed into a data warehouse by the source machine or pulled into the data warehouse by the warehouse server. With the first approach, event triggers or scheduled batch jobs that reside on the OLTP machine initiate propagation processes. With the second approach, end-user queries pull OLTP data through a communications gateway on an as-needed basis. In addition, scheduled propagation jobs that reside on the data-warehouse server can pull data. Of course, pull procedures do not support data concurrency, because OLTP data is transmitted only periodically.

Propagation procedures also can be designed to use both push and pull processes. In this scenario, the source application typically pushes data to an intermediate, or staging, database. The staging database can reside on either the OLTP machine or the warehouse server. Normally, transformation processes update the staged information, which queries or scheduled jobs then pull into the warehouse. This mixed-mode replication approach requires increased disk space, but it can improve performance in some instances.

Some data warehouses reside on a single server fed by one or more OLTP machines. This architecture uses a one-way replication approach because the warehouse server can only receive data. In this case, each OLTP machine has a "master–slave" relationship with the warehouse server. In other cases, data warehouses may reside on multiple servers. For example, a mainframe-based manufacturing system may function as a data source for several distributed AS/400-based data marts. Instead of multiple master–slave relationships being enforced between the operational machine and the warehouse servers, cascading replication can propagate the data. In this approach, transformed OLTP data is transmitted to warehouse servers that in turn pass additional copies of the data directly to other warehouse servers. Each intermediate server functions as both a warehouse platform and a replication server. In effect, cascading replication distributes the processing workload from an OLTP computer to multiple warehouse servers. Figure 3.2 details a master–slave replication architecture, while Figure 3.3 on page 50 presents a cascading replication architecture.

Data Verification

Data-warehouse maintenance procedures, like any other applications, are vulnerable to errors. In many cases, IT personnel verify the integrity of a data warehouse only once, after it has been initialized with the very first bulk transfer of transformed OLTP data. Typically, they verify data by manually comparing warehouse query results to known OLTP figures. For instance, they might compare monthly revenue figures generated by a data-mart query to

FIGURE 3.2
Example of Master–Slave Replication

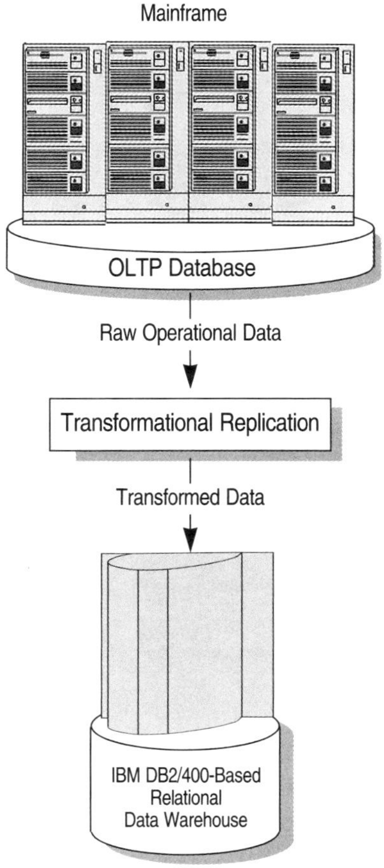

monthly revenue figures as they appear in a general ledger. But this piecemeal approach to data verification is insufficient.

To maintain warehouse integrity, IT staff must design systematic procedures to periodically compare warehouse information to operational data. In some cases, a series of integrity reports may be generated each time a propagation process has executed. These reports can compare key figures gleaned from both warehouse and OLTP databases. A computer operator might examine this report for discrepancies each time it is generated. Comprehensive integrity reports may also include information about the propagation procedure used, such as program names and run-time statistics taken from associated job

FIGURE 3.3
Example of Cascading Replication

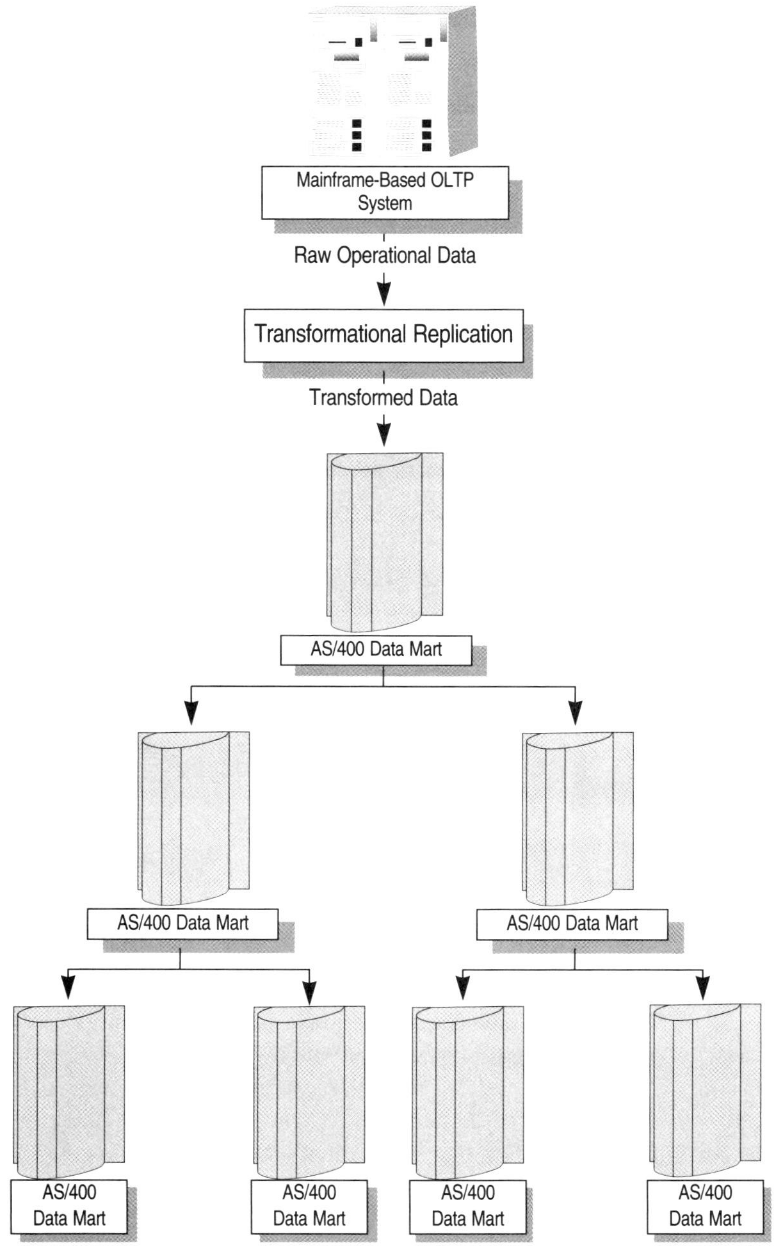

logs. Alternatively, integrity procedures can send detailed break messages to the system message queue if designated significant differences between warehouse and operational data are found.

Such steps are necessary because operational systems, much like the business functions they automate, are subject to change, which is why data-warehouse integrity may deteriorate over time. Maintenance programmers constantly modify production applications to reflect operational shifts in business. If these programmers don't know what impact these changes have on associated data warehouses, they will fail to update the procedures that maintain the data warehouses. A well-defined set of verification procedures should be an integral component of any data-warehouse application.

Conclusion

As we have seen in this chapter, extraction, transformation, and propagation, the three processes that move data into warehouses — as well as verification procedures — are all important elements in creating and maintaining effective data warehouses. Figure 3.4 on the following page presents an overview of these interrelated processes.

In many cases, a replication product can perform much of the work necessary to implement these procedures. Of course, you can opt to develop customized CL, SQL, and RPG programs to load your data warehouse, but it is usually difficult to justify the requisite programming costs when you compare them to the price of transformation tools. The growing need for replication tools is fueling an active market. In fact, the Gartner Group estimates that the market for transformational replication tools used for data warehousing will grow to $210 million by 1999. Given 1994 levels of $65 million, this figure represents a healthy compound annual growth rate of approximately 26 percent.

Now that you understand the various ways in which we can move data into the data warehouse, let's go to Chapter 4, where I examine how end users access and analyze the data that has been moved.

FIGURE 3.4
Data-Warehouse Maintenance Procedures

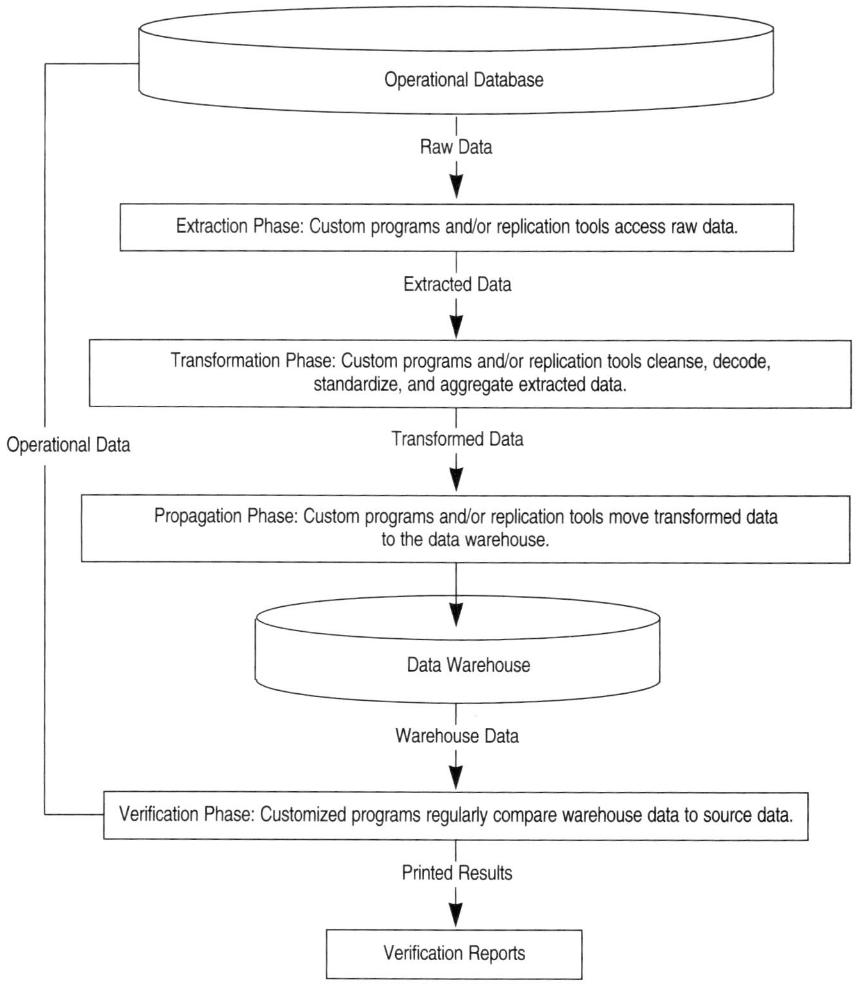

Chapter 4

Analysis and Presentation Tools

In addition to data repositories and tools to maintain those repositories, data warehouses require software that lets end users analyze and view warehouse information. Typically PC-based and featuring graphical user interfaces (GUIs), analysis and presentation tools enable this functionality. As an IT professional, you have probably worked with a variety of analysis and presentation tools. Categorized by functionality, these products comprise several major classes of software, including query tools, spreadsheets, graphics software, OLAP tools, report writers, Web browsers, and executive information systems (EISs). You can acquire these components as part of a comprehensive data warehouse, or you can purchase them separately as you build your data warehouse. In this chapter, I examine each major class of analysis and presentation software.

Query Tools

Query tools provide end users with the means to extract information from data warehouses. Queries, which are simply statements or specifications designed to access and manipulate data, enable this functionality. Effective query tools let end users who have little or no programming experience access data in an intuitive manner. To support this goal, many query tools feature natural language processing, or NLP. Broadly defined, natural language processing lets end users access data via common words and phrases. For example, an end user who is seeking revenue information in a data warehouse can create a statement such as, "Show me 1997 sales revenue by product line." Once constructed, the host AS/400 translates this statement into standard SQL statements and executes it. The translation process should be transparent to the end user.

Of course, English is just one "natural language." Comprehensive products that feature NLP should provide support for other languages as well. Because few users have experience with programming languages such as SQL, yet all are intimately familiar with natural languages, NLP is an ideal complement to a data warehouse.

In a data-warehousing environment, end users often execute queries in an iterative way. For example, in the early stages of an analysis project, end users might construct queries that access thousands of records in a data warehouse. Such queries tend to focus on primary repositories. After examining the results of these queries, users often refine their queries until they have isolated the most pertinent data. Often, these queries focus on data marts. Response times for queries against primary repositories tend to vary; some will execute in seconds, while others may require several minutes. In cases where the same or similar queries are executed periodically, you should pre-aggregate the requisite data.

Once you have equipped end users with query tools, you should be prepared for the potential hazards of poorly constructed queries. For example, end users may design queries that access too much data and as a result overwhelm system resources. The classic runaway query is one in which the user has neglected to include a date range. To prevent such scenarios, the AS/400 features a predictive query governor. Unlike most query governors, the AS/400 query governor estimates the runtime of queries before they begin executing. As we shall see in Chapter 7, queries that would execute longer than a specified period of time can be cancelled before valuable system resources have been consumed.

Query tool users are typically more interested in raw results than in the advanced presentation of those results. In many cases, simple two-dimensional lists suffice. However, many query products do provide graphing facilities by which analysts can visually depict query results. In addition, many query tools provide spreadsheet functionality or can export data directly to leading spreadsheet packages.

SPREADSHEETS

Unlike query tools, whose primary function is to extract information from a data warehouse, the purpose of spreadsheets is to analyze data. End users often run queries to extract information from a data warehouse, then export that information to a spreadsheet for analysis.

As one of the first mainstream, PC-based applications, spreadsheets have become permanent fixtures on the corporate desktop. Because of their widespread availability, high utility, and relatively low cost, leading products such as Lotus 1-2-3 and Microsoft Excel are the most popular analysis tools in the data-warehousing arena. With spreadsheets, of course, analysts can organize data in a series of rows and columns. They can then freely manipulate this data by applying mathematical formulae, statistical functions, conditional logic, and a host of other analytic constructs. For example, suppose that an analyst has executed a query against a data mart containing our department stores' revenue figures. The query results might appear as follows:

Northeast	$ 342,103.44
Southeast	$ 203,453.31
Midwest	$ 239,293.22
Northwest	$ 301,225.34
Southwest	$ 293,811.34

Suppose further that the analyst is interested in the ratio of each region's revenue to the total revenue. If the data warehouse is integrated with a product such as Lotus 1-2-3 or Excel, the analyst can export the query results to a spreadsheet, where she can calculate the desired results. Figure 4.1 depicts a spreadsheet that we have used to analyze our regional sales figures.

FIGURE 4.1
Spreadsheet Depicting Regional Sales Figures

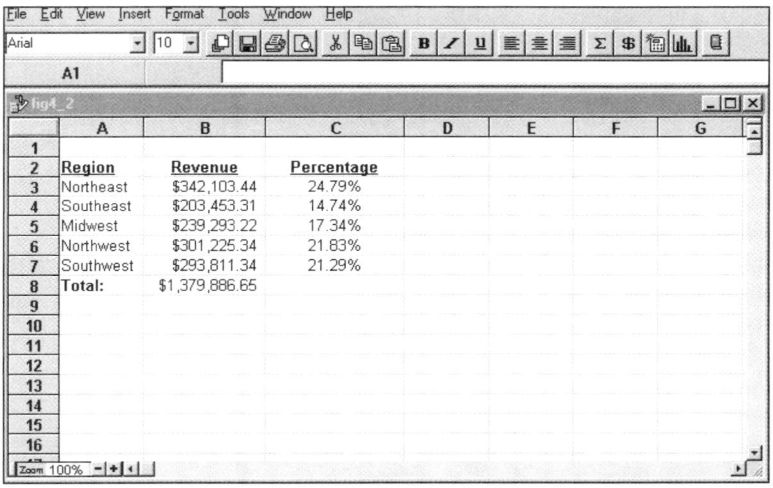

Although offline analyses may result in better performance at the warehouse server level, they may also lead to erroneous results as users introduce errors into the analytic model. Note, too, that the data mart in this example could have been designed to store pre-aggregated regional sales ratios. IT personnel must make such design choices after careful consultation with end users. In any event, spreadsheet products will continue to dominate the personal productivity landscape for many years to come. In recognition thereof, many data-warehousing products provide links to Lotus 1-2-3 and Microsoft Excel.

GRAPHICS SOFTWARE

We have learned that query tools help us extract data from data warehouses, while spreadsheets help us analyze extracted data. Unlike these tools, graphics software focuses on the presentation of data in an intuitive, highly visual manner.

In a basic sense, numbers are merely symbols that represent the magnitude of underlying units of measure. The human mind can evaluate individual numbers quite easily. For example, most of us implicitly understand that $3.27 represents three units of one dollar each and 27 percent of a fourth unit of one dollar. The human mind is less facile, however, when relative comparisons are to be made between two or more numbers. For instance, we easily comprehend the magnitude of individual region's sales figures in the preceding spreadsheet example. However, if asked for the relative difference between the regions' sales, most of us would require some time to answer. Typical business analyses (e.g., ratios, variances, and trend analyses) are similar to this example because they require numeric comparisons. Graphics software provides the means through which we can present these comparisons visually.

Graphics software, as its name implies, is used to create graphs. Most of us are familiar with graphs and have used them on many occasions. Let's look briefly at the most common graphs used in data-warehousing. Vertical or horizontal bar graphs, as well as histograms, employ area-based columns to visually depict underlying values. Pie charts, on the other hand, use proportional slices of a circle to represent numbers, while scatter diagrams express figures with plotted dots or other symbols. Another popular figure, the line graph, uses connected coordinates to represent related values. Figure 4.2 expresses the regional dollar figures from our spreadsheet example in a vertical bar chart; Figure 4.3 uses a pie chart to express the same information. As you can see, data visualization emphasizes the significance of numbers and is an intuitive way to examine data.

FIGURE 4.2
Bar Chart Depicting Regional Dollar Figures

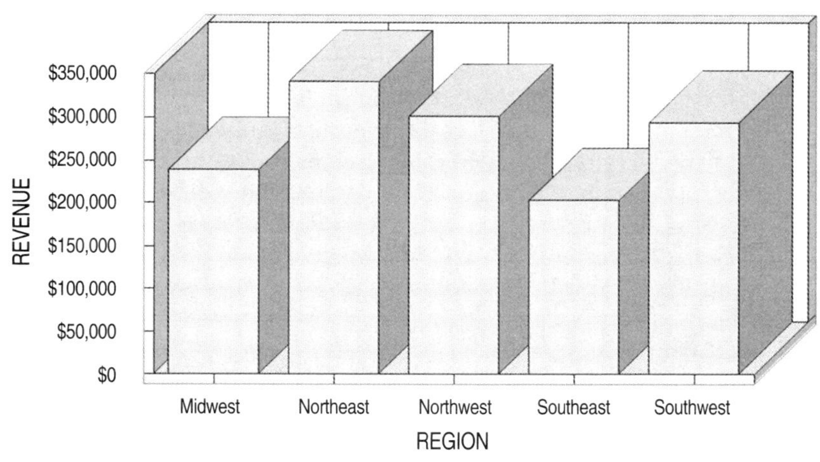

Of course, these examples are relatively simple. Let's invent a more complicated data set for our fictitious department store chain. Suppose that the list depicted in Figure 4.4 represents sales quantities and sales values by region and by product for our stores. The accompanying three-dimensional bar graph in Figure 4.5 shows both quantities and revenue by region, while Figure 4.6 depicts the same variables on a product-by-product basis. Finally, the graph in

FIGURE 4.3
Pie Chart Depicting Regional Dollar Figures

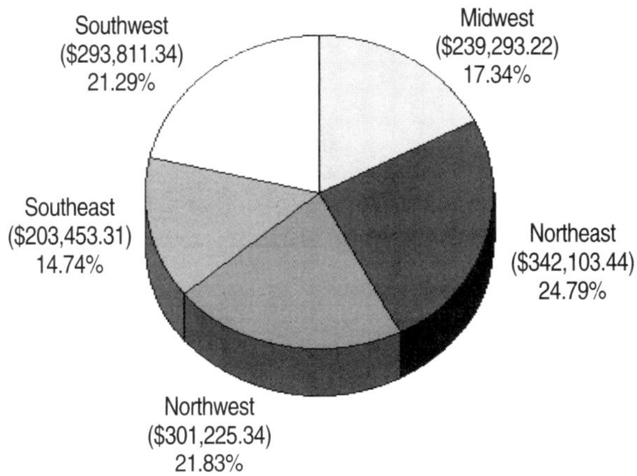

FIGURE 4.4
Sales by Region and Product

Region	Product	Units Sold	Total Revenue
Northeast	Gloves	2,000	$ 10,320.45
Northeast	Scarf	2,400	$ 11,294.33
Northeast	Overcoat	2,500	$ 26,940.62
Southeast	Gloves	4,000	$ 15,150.45
Southeast	Scarf	3,000	$ 12,234.43
Southeast	Overcoat	2,400	$ 25,931.42
Midwest	Gloves	1,900	$ 10,020.90
Midwest	Scarf	7,500	$ 21,894.13
Midwest	Overcoat	2,400	$ 25,749.37
Northwest	Gloves	2,200	$ 10,827.49
Northwest	Scarf	6,300	$ 30,394.13
Northwest	Overcoat	2,600	$ 27,440.22
Southwest	Gloves	2,200	$ 11,620.76
Southwest	Scarf	2,000	$ 9,347.58
Southwest	Overcoat	9,600	$ 57,422.68

Figure 4.7 depicts quantity and revenue per product for the Northeast region alone. Note that these graphs employ a third axis, known as the z-axis, to support a third dimension.

FIGURE 4.5
Bar Graph Showing Quantity and Revenue by Region

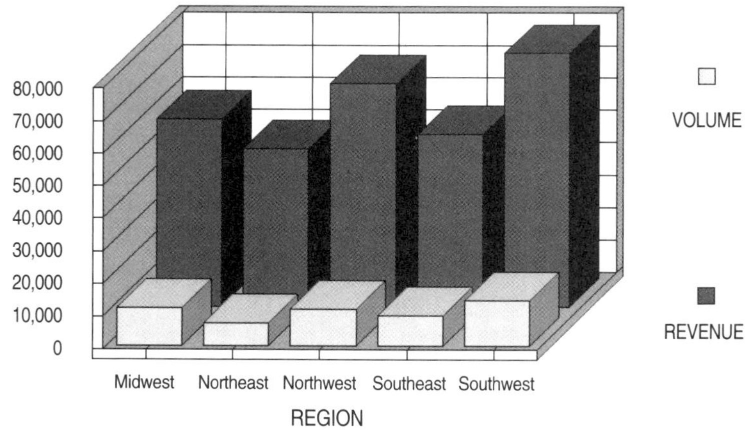

FIGURE 4.6
Bar Graph Showing Quantity and Revenue by Product

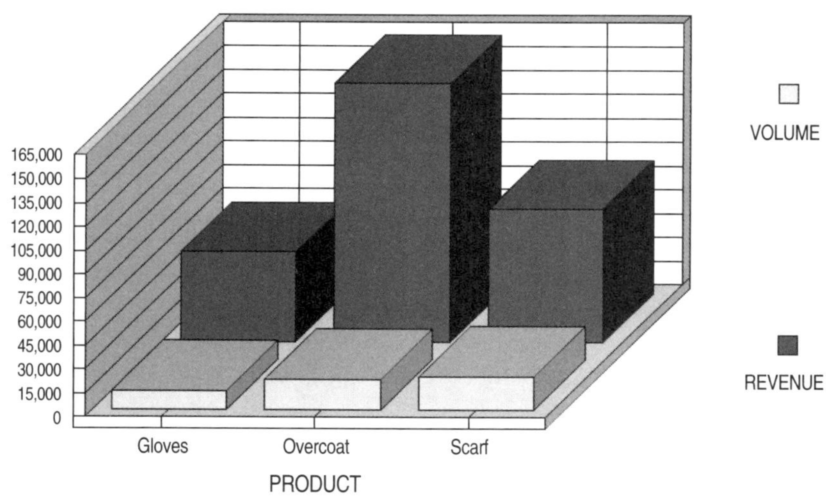

Comprehensive data warehouses include software that lets end users view data graphically. As users of these tools drill up and drill down through various levels of information, related graphs can often be refreshed dynamically.

Figure 4.7
Bar Graph Showing Quantity and Revenue by Product Northeast Region Only

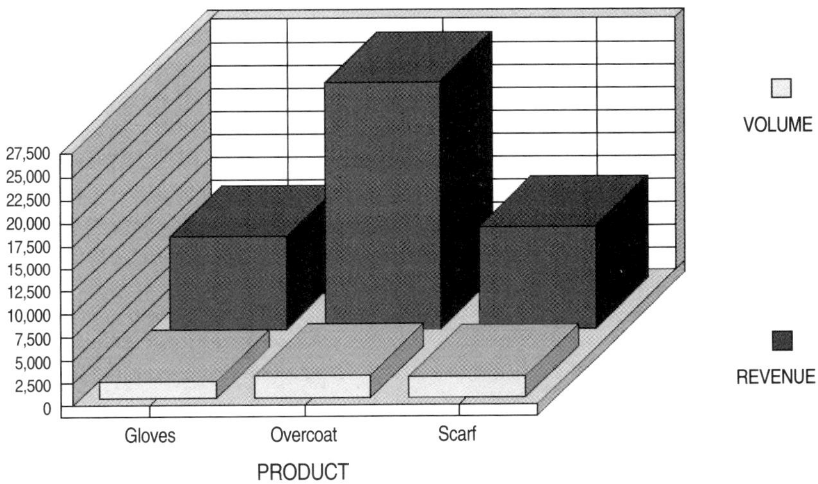

Most data-visualization tools let end users freely switch from one graph type to another.

In the early 1990s, general-purpose business graphics packages such as Harvard Graphics comprised one of the best-selling categories of PC-based software. Today, general-purpose business graphics software is not sold as a standalone product. On the contrary, as applications such as spreadsheets and query products evolved, software developers enhanced these products to support graphs and charts. In the AS/400 arena, many data-warehousing vendors license best-of-breed graphics technology rather than design it themselves. This explains why many data-warehousing solutions feature similar graphical components.

OLAP Tools

Primarily an analysis tool, OLAP products let analysts interactively examine and manipulate large sets of data from numerous perspectives. Featuring functionality similar to that found in spreadsheet programs, OLAP tools are designed to support advanced ad hoc analyses that require numerous dimensions of data. In fact, the primary difference between OLAP software and spreadsheet products lies in OLAP software's capability to depict and manipulate data in a multidimensional manner. End users who are equipped with OLAP tools can quickly exchange the key business dimensions in a business model. For example, an OLAP product for a sales data mart might let analysts freely examine revenues by varying combinations of product, customer, state, region, purchase date, and store ID. By contrast, spreadsheets are best suited for two-dimensional, list-oriented analyses. However, leading spreadsheet vendors are starting to add OLAP functionality to their products. Conversely, many OLAP vendors offer tools that feature spreadsheet-like interfaces and links to spreadsheet packages. And as I mentioned in Chapter 1, analysts often use OLAP software to forecast sales, analyze manufacturing mixes, consolidate financial information, examine customer segments, perform time-series analyses, and test what-if hypotheses.

Report Writers

Thus far, our discussion of data analysis and data presentation has been limited to on-screen, or "soft copy," usage. In addition to interactively viewing data in soft-copy form, end users often require information from data warehouses in hard-copy form. Comprehensive data warehouses let end users create and print presentation-quality reports and documents at the desktop. Through advanced solutions such as ShowCase STRATEGY, users can create colorful reports that include both text and graphics.

To create hard-copy documents that present information from data warehouses, users typically design templates that specify font characteristics, color specifications, page orientation, data-selection parameters, summary-level definitions, sort orders, derived field attributes, title and heading descriptions, and other basic reporting characteristics. They then execute these templates periodically or as needed.

Web Browsers

A relatively new category of software, Web browsers provide access to data via the Internet or corporate intranets. In a basic sense, Web browsers are interfaces. As such, they facilitate access to data warehouses and thereby enable both the presentation and analysis of data warehouse information. In leveraging the rapid growth of the Internet and corporate intranets, Web browsers such as Netscape's Navigator and Microsoft's Explorer are economically delivering the benefits of data warehousing to remote users throughout the world. For example, Figure 4.8 illustrates how ShowCase Corporation uses Microsoft's browser to deliver business intelligence to STRATEGY users via the Internet.

For many reasons, Web browsers and the Internet have considerable appeal in the data-warehousing arena. First, Web browsers are inexpensive and relatively easy to deploy. In many cases, they can be installed from a server in minutes. Second, because Web browsers are already a significant presence on the desktop, Web-enabled data warehouses can leverage an installed base of browsers. Third, the Internet and corporate intranets provide a cost-effective means of accessing warehouse data from remote locations. For the price of a local phone call, users can dial into data warehouses across the

FIGURE 4.8

Accessing a Data Warehouse via a Web Browser

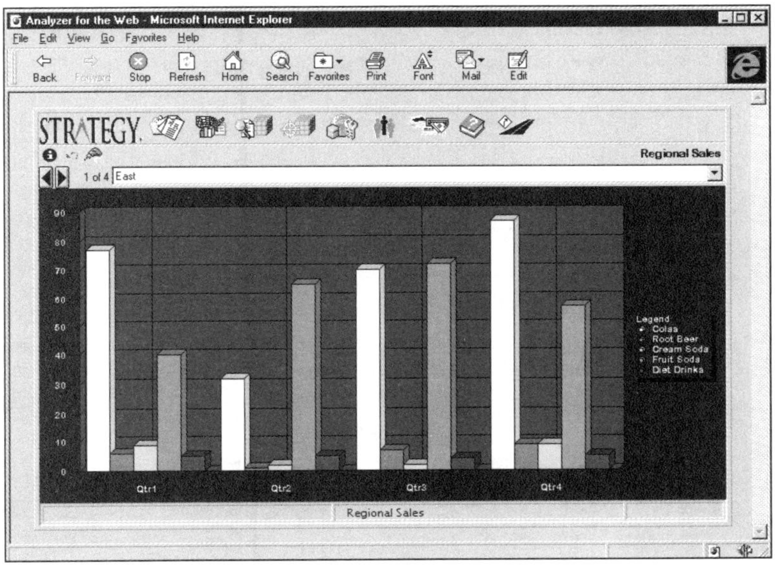

globe. Fourth, browsers are extremely easy to use. Millions of computer users already know how to access information with Web browsers. Finally, browsers are platform-independent. In addition to OS/2 and Windows computers, these software programs run on Unix-based workstations as well as Apple machines.

Web-enabled data warehouses provide software to convert user-defined queries from static HTML screens into either SQL or proprietary MD-OLAP data-access commands. Once the user has extracted query results from the data warehouse, these results are converted into HTML format. As is the case with any remote application, Internet users will experience some delay in response times. Individuals with direct intranet connections can expect communications delays of only a second or so. Dial-up users, however, may experience delays of 2 to 5 seconds. For standard Internet users, response times will increase by 3 to 10 seconds, assuming that the service carrier has available line capacity. Despite these delays, Web-enabled warehouse applications hold considerable appeal and will continue to gain support in the warehouse arena. (In Chapters 16 and 17, I examine two Web-enabled data-warehousing products: STRATEGY, from Showcase Corporation, and DataTracker, from Silvon Software.)

EXECUTIVE INFORMATION SYSTEMS

In many organizations, upper-level managers do not have time to engage in serious number crunching. Most often, these individuals simply want to monitor key operating benchmarks and are not inclined to perform in-depth analyses. Specialized applications known as executive information systems (EISs) let these managers examine warehouse information using highly intuitive screens. These systems feature interfaces that have been custom designed for strategic decision makers. Because EIS users often have limited computer experience, they require interfaces that are extremely easy to use. For example, an EIS interface for a sales data mart may present revenue figures to a marketing vice-president via color-coded maps of the world. The map image itself would include hot spots that support push-and-click, drill-down analyses, with relevant information typically accessible via a single mouse-click. EISs that provide extensive mapping support are referred to as geographic information systems (GISs). These models are very popular in warehousing applications that maintain data by country, state, region, and other locale-oriented dimensions. An example of one such interface, as created with InfoManager OY's InfoManager, appears in Figure 4.9. We look more closely at InfoManager in Chapter 12.

FIGURE 4.9

Accessing a Data Warehouse via an EIS Interface

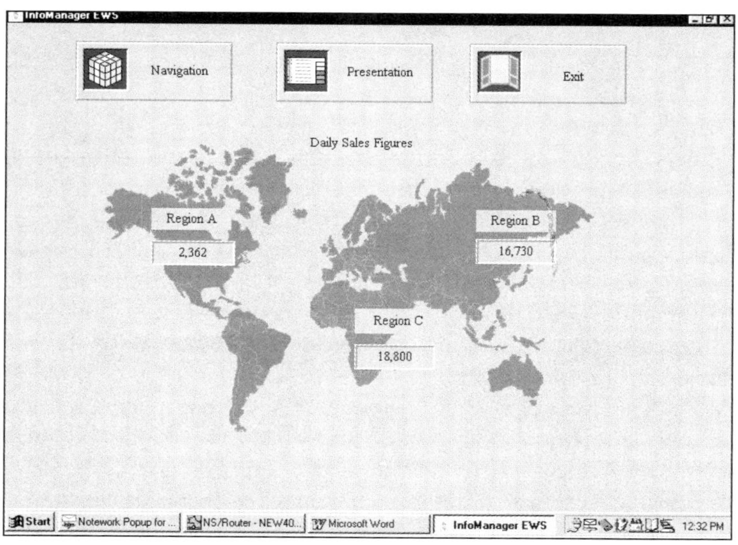

Most EIS applications are characterized by limited breadth but considerable depth. The scope of a sales EIS, for instance, typically is confined to preaggregated sales figures. However, within the space of those figures, EIS users can drill down to very detailed levels of sales information.

At the inception of an EIS program, relatively few performance measures may be made available to end users. However, as managers gain familiarity with the EIS, they inevitably ask for access to additional warehouse data. Such requests indicate that the system is gaining acceptance. Because EIS users tend to have limited computer experience, programmers typically write SQL queries to retrieve information, then link the queries to the EIS interface via hot spots and other structures. Designing queries for an EIS is an ongoing process that may require significant IT support.

Because executives generally do not expect to wait more than a few seconds for results, EISs must enforce predictable limits on response time. To sustain such performance, EISs process highly aggregated sets of data stored in data marts. These applications rarely access primary warehouse repositories.

It may be helpful to think of an EIS as diagnostic equipment for your business. Managers use EIS applications to evaluate the overall health of organizations just as doctors use medical devices to evaluate the overall health of patients. Many EISs provide alarms that proactively notify managers when business conditions warrant attention. Similarly, hospital monitors automatically sound when medical attention is required. As is the case with queries, the meaning of EIS data is always open to interpretation. Just as it takes a seasoned doctor to effectively evaluate a patient's vital signs, an EIS will not produce significant benefit in the hands of an inexperienced manager.

EISs promote managerial effectiveness on many levels. In addition to simply monitoring the performance of an organization or department, these applications provide managers with a means to examine critical performance criteria in a historical context. They also reduce the need for managerial support staff to manually collect and synthesize relevant information. As the penetration of data warehousing in the corporate arena deepens, executives will use EISs more frequently to support decision making. These systems are inherently different from query tools. Figure 4.10 summarizes the major distinctions between query products and EISs.

FIGURE 4.10
Comparison of Query Tools and Executive Information Systems

Query Tools ...	Executive Information Systems ...
Are designed for data access and manipulation	Are designed for data presentation
Let end users design their own queries	Require programmers to build queries for end users
Are employed by midlevel analysts	Are used by upper-level management
Have variable response times	Have consistently fast response times
Access primary repositories and data marts	Access data marts
Require significant training to use	Require little training to use
Require relatively limited ongoing IT support	Require extensive IT support
Are designed for entire departments	Are customized for a few key users

CONCLUSION

Effective end-user tools for analysis are essential to both the acceptance and effective use of data warehouses. Data is of little value if end users cannot readily access and manipulate it. Most end users cannot appreciate the challenges IT personnel who design data-warehouse schema face. For example, many end users cannot understand the difficulties associated with transforming normalized operational data into meaningful information. However, nearly all end users appreciate effective, intuitive analysis tools.

Well-designed analysis tools will have a dramatic impact on how well a data warehouse supports a company's business goals. Conversely, ineffective tools will quickly undermine users' acceptance of a data warehouse, even if the underlying database technology and associated replication routines are first-rate. To that end, expect your AS/400-based data warehouse to provide end users with GUIs. These interfaces employ option (aka radio) buttons, bubble Help, pop-up windows, drop-down lists, hot spots, button bars, icons, dialog boxes, and other features that can accelerate learning and spark interest in a data warehouse. As we shall see in Chapters 8 through 17, a wide variety of GUI-based end-user tools is available for AS/400-based data warehousing.

Chapter 5

Metadata

Can you imagine how difficult it would be to find a book in a library without using a card catalog? Even though libraries store books in a logical way (e.g., by subject), it would be inordinately difficult to find a specific publication without first referencing a card catalog. Just as card catalogs let readers quickly locate books in libraries, metadata lets end users effectively access data in data warehouses. As we have seen in the preceding chapters, data warehouses are complex applications that consist of numerous components. Without metadata, end users cannot effectively locate information in these systems, nor can IT personnel effectively maintain such systems.

The term *metadata* is commonly defined as "data about data." Although metadata primarily does describe database schema and data elements, it has other important uses as well. In addition to data, metadata also describes business rules, operational processes, data-transformation procedures, and virtually every function through which data is created and maintained. These two kinds of metadata — which I refer to as *technical metadata* and *business metadata* — are critical components of data warehouses.

Although metadata is commonly associated with computer systems, its use is not limited to the IT field. As I just discussed, metadata is at the heart of every library. In fact, most of us access and manipulate metadata every day. In addition to card catalogs, common metadata repositories include telephone books, magazine indexes, tables of contents, and street listings on road maps. In a basic sense, these structures contain information about data. Again, consider the card catalog, either in physical or electronic form. This specialized filing system contains information about books, periodicals, magazines, and journals. Data elements we find in card catalogs include titles, descriptions, publication dates, authors, ISBNs, and shelf locations. Without a card catalog, readers could not determine what data (e.g., books) exists in a library, nor could they determine where that data is located. Card catalogs are particularly effective metadata repositories because they adhere to a widely recognized indexing standard, such as the Dewey Decimal or the Library of Congress classification system, by which readers can locate data in libraries throughout the United States.

As one would expect, metadata structures abound in the IT field. Data dictionaries, data-flow diagrams, data-description specifications (DDS), library lists, object descriptions, online Help, job logs, program comments, reference manuals, query definitions, field names, file names, and field reference files are all examples of effective metadata structures. In data warehousing, metadata is classified according to its purpose and intended audience.

Technical Metadata

Designed to support IT professionals, technical metadata uses specialized terminology to describe data-warehousing applications, databases, and data. The user community rarely accesses technical metadata, which is often stored in a relatively raw form. A DDS source member for an AS/400 physical file is a good example of technical metadata. Of limited use to end users, source members provide programmers with a wealth of information about AS/400 files. Figure 5.1 presents a sample DDS specification for a physical file.

FIGURE 5.1
Technical Metadata in the Form of an AS/400 File Specification

```
...1....+....2....+....3....+....4....+....5....+....6....+....7....
                                         UNIQUE
     R CUSTØ1P                           TEXT('CUSTOMER FILE')

       CUSID          9P Ø               TEXT('CUSTOMER ID NUMBER')
       CUSNAM        25A                 TEXT('CUSTOMER NAME')
       BILAD1        25A                 TEXT('BILLING ADDRESS 1')
       BILAD2        25A                 TEXT('BILLING ADDRESS 2')
       BILAD3        25A                 TEXT('BILLING ADDRESS 3')
       BILCTY        25A                 TEXT('BILLING CITY')
       BILSTT        25A                 TEXT('BILLING STATE')
       BILZIP         9P Ø               TEXT('BILLING ZIP CODE')

     K CUSID
```

By examining the source member in Figure 5.1, experienced AS/400 programmers can learn a great deal about its associated file. For example, they can tell that the file is a physical file consisting of eight fields and one key. Each address field, of which there are three, can contain up to 25 alphanumeric characters. Also, the customer ID and ZIP-code fields are numeric and can contain up to 9 digits each. Furthermore, the key field (customer number) in this file is unique. In a basic sense, all this information is "data about data."

Figure 5.2 presents another example of technical metadata. In this case, program comments and RPG code detail information about a data element and an associated transformation process (you may recall that Figure 3.1 presented pseudocode for this transformation process). Through this coding, AS/400 programmers can determine that a customer name field was improperly validated in an operational system. Furthermore, they can ascertain the way in which a particular customer's name is standardized for use in a data warehouse.

The AS/400 automatically maintains a vast array of technical metadata, as well as the means to access it. For example, a special object known as a *data dictionary* contains the descriptions of every component in every physical and logical file on an AS/400. This metadata repository provides IT personnel with

FIGURE 5.2

Technical Metadata in the Form of RPG Code and Program Comments

```
NØ1Factor1+++++OpCode(E)+Factor2+++++++Result++++++Len+++HiLoEq....
  *
  * IN THE ORDER ENTRY SYSTEM, THE CUSTOMER NAME FIELD WAS NOT
  * VALIDATED PROPERLY. THE FOLLOWING ROUTINE STANDARDIZES
  * THE CUSTOMER NAME BEFORE WRITING IT TO THE SALES DATA MART.
  *
C  CUSNAM      IFEQ      'ATT'                            Case 1
C  CUSNAM      OREQ      'AT & T'                         Case 2
C              MOVE      *BLANKS       CUSNAM             Clr Field
C              MOVEL     'AT&T'        CUSNAM             Inz Field
C              EXSR      WRTRCD                           See Subrtn
C              ENDIF                                      Endif
```

a comprehensive overview of application databases. The data dictionary is updated automatically each time a file is created or deleted. As a result of enhancements to Version 3 of OS/400, the data dictionary now contains information about DB2/400 files, fields, referential integrity constraints, and object cross-reference details. Although most people don't think of DB2/400 in terms of interfaces, it actually has two: DDS and SQL. Under SQL, the data dictionary is known as the *systemwide catalog* in much the same way that table means file, column refers to field, and row refers to record.

The AS/400 provides many ways to access technical metadata. For example, to determine the size, type, and structure of any file, programmers need only execute the DSPFD (Display File Description) command. While such facilities are very useful, the AS/400's metadata facilities alone cannot maintain enough information to effectively document data warehouses. For example, the AS/400 cannot automatically record the meanings of codes in a table file or describe the processes used to create those codes. To address such needs, many data warehouses include their own centralized data dictionaries. In addition to the attributes of fields and files, these structures store descriptions of the processes used to create data. In addition to metadata repositories such as the DB2/400 system catalog and third-party data dictionaries, IT personnel often maintain metadata in the form of data-flow and entity-relationship diagrams. Such structures go a long way toward supporting application maintenance.

BUSINESS METADATA

Unlike technical metadata, business metadata uses common terminology and intuitive interfaces to describe the contents of data warehouses to end users. Users typically want to know how up-to-date information is (How recent are these figures?), where it came from (What system generated these figures?), and how it was derived (What exchange rates were used to compute these figures?).

When users need this information, they should be able to access it online. For example, online Help systems that consist of field definitions are frequently used to present business metadata to end users. Such definitions may also include a list of sample field values and any applicable field aliases. Field aliases are different words or phrases used to describe a data element. As I discussed in Chapter 3, many companies, for example, alternatively refer to order number as PO number, pull number, or tracking ID — a very common situation when companies have grown through mergers and acquisitions. In many cases, the employees of an acquired company fail to adopt the vernacular of the parent company, and vice versa. Online Help systems also can reduce ambiguity in instances when a single word or phrase has several different meanings. For example, engineers may consider a product line to be a group of discrete products with similar bills of material. In contrast, sales professionals may view a product line as a collection of products with similar functions. In Chapter 3, I discussed the significance of transformational replication and its primary purpose: the creation of "one truth." In a data warehouse, the term *product line* would have only one meaning.

Online Help provides users with the means to reconcile the "one truth" with ambiguity that exists outside the data warehouse. Indexed and often accessible via context-sensitive pop-up windows, online Help facilities also can provide users with query examples, business rules, and additional forms of business metadata. An example of an online Help application screen for business metadata appears in Figure 5.3.

FIGURE 5.3
Screen Showing Online Help for Business Metadata

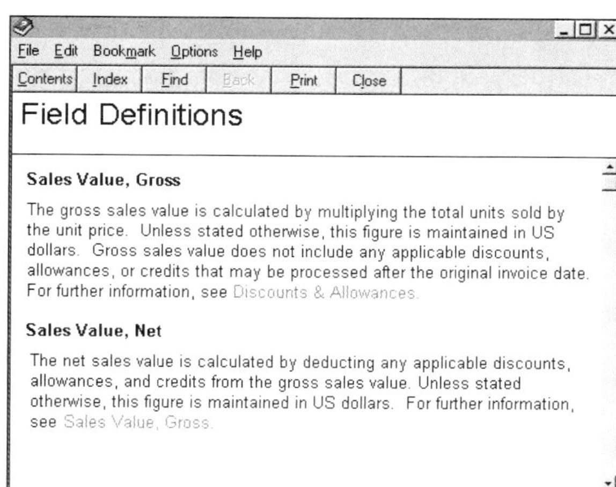

In addition to online Help, data warehouses should let you associate descriptive text with cryptic file and field names. Also known as aliases, this form of metadata supports intuitive end-user access to data warehouses. For example, assume that a dimension table used to store time periods in a DB2/400-based ROLAP repository is called PERDIMTA. Assume further that this file uses three fields to describe an invoice date: INVYR, INVMON, and INVDAY. These relatively cryptic file and field names would be of limited value to end users. Using metadata, programmers can associate more descriptive phrases such as Time Periods, Invoice Year, Invoice Month, and Invoice Day with the file and field names. End users access warehouse information through this layer of metadata and see the less cryptic terms on their screens. In this way, business metadata masks system complexity and facilitates intuitive access to information. In so doing, it also smoothes learning curves and accelerates end-user acceptance of data warehouses.

The Need for Standards

During the 1990s, a dizzying array of database products (e.g., DB2, Oracle, Sybase, Informix, Windows NT SQL Server) and hardware platforms (e.g., mainframes, midrange machines, workstations, LANs, personal computers, network computers) conspired with shifting architectural paradigms (e.g., distributed processing, client/server computing, the Internet, and intranets) to complicate the management of corporate information. Ten years ago, it was not unusual for organizations to purchase all software and hardware from one company. But such homogeneity rarely exists in today's dynamic corporate arena. For example, many organizations that have grown through mergers and acquisitions maintain numerous applications running on multiple platforms.

Data warehousing, as an application that demands access to data across an enterprise, has made software vendors and IT personnel painfully aware of the difficulties heterogeneity causes. To extract enterprise data amid such diversity, IT professionals must understand several operating systems, databases, and software packages. Largely as a result of data warehousing, a universal standard for technical metadata clearly became necessary. Such a standard would allow vendors to design software tools that use uniform methods for accessing enterprise data without special consideration for source databases, host platforms, or originating applications.

The Metadata Coalition and its Metadata Interchange Specification (MDIS)

To address the need for such a standard, a group of six application vendors founded The Metadata Coalition[1] in October of 1995 to define standard specifications for the interchange of metadata between software tools. Now comprising

[1]You can learn more about The Metadata Coalition by contacting its Web site at http://207.33.3.206.

representatives from 24 data-warehouse application vendors including IBM, ETI, and Arbor Software, the coalition meets several times each year and is open to both vendors and end users. A platform-independent organization that does not focus on particular databases or machines, the coalition is working toward several goals. These goals include defining metadata interchange standards; creating a vendor-independent application programming interface (API) for metadata interchange; defining an infrastructure to facilitate product compliance with metadata interchange standards; and finally, designating procedures to maintain and incorporate changes to metadata interchange standards. In 1998, the first generation of MDIS-compliant software will come to market. Although these initial products will probably focus on the mainframe arena, we can assume that AS/400 vendors ultimately will comply with the standard.

Despite its brief history, The Metadata Coalition already has proposed an open specification for the interchange of metadata between software packages. Referred to as the Metadata Interchange Specification (MDIS), this specification has four major components: an Interchange Standard Metadata Model, an Interchange Standard Access Framework, a Tool Profile, and a User Configuration.

The *Interchange Standard Metadata Model* refers to ASCII file formats that represent technical metadata for exchange among data-warehousing tools. By avoiding proprietary file formats, tools running on any major hardware platform can access the Standard Metadata Model. According to the coalition, metadata interchange files must describe metadata as well as the application that generated the metadata. Such information includes the name and version number of the tool that created the metadata, date and time stamps denoting when the metadata was exported, a version ID for the MDIS standard in use, the name of the originating host computer, text descriptions of the metadata, and metadata field attributes. These interchange files are the foundation of the MDIS model.

The *Interchange Standard Access Framework* component of MDIS describes the number and types of API functions that a tool must support to be deemed MDIS compliant. Through calls to APIs, customers will be able to create programs that invoke the exchange of metadata. In addition to obligatory APIs, the framework details optional API functions that tools can support at the discretion of tool developers.

The remaining components of the interchange standard refer to the contents of specialized files. The *Tool Profile* is a required file describing each aspect of the Interchange Standard Metadata Model that a particular tool supports. The *User Configuration* is a second file required in each MDIS-compliant tool. This file describes valid interchange paths in an end user's own processing environment. Also included in the User Configuration file is a list of tools from which metadata can be imported. Figure 5.4 details a logical representation of the Metadata Interchange Standard and its components. As a standard in its infancy, MDIS will have limited practical applicability for several

FIGURE 5.4
Logical Representation of the Metadata Interchange Standard

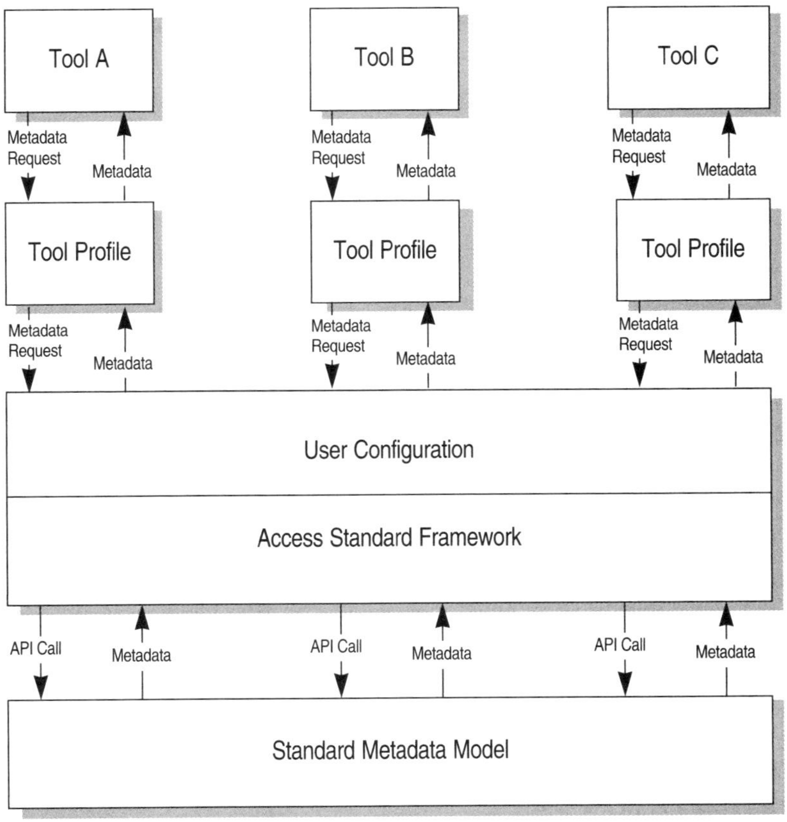

years. In the meantime, proprietary software and the manual efforts of IT professionals will continue to manage metadata.

CONCLUSION

Because data warehouses are complex applications, the need for both technical and business metadata is particularly acute in the data-warehousing arena. Without metadata, end users would have little hope of locating and analyzing information in data warehouses. Likewise, IT personnel could not effectively maintain these applications over time. Effective metadata dramatically enhances the utility of data-warehousing solutions and reduces the need for IT support. As such, it is an important component of every data warehouse.

Chapter 6

Data Mining

In Chapter 2, I examined how primary repositories and data marts can store massive amounts of data in a way that supports sophisticated, ad hoc analyses. In Chapter 3, we explored the procedures needed to load and maintain data warehouses. In Chapter 4, I discussed various tools (e.g., query tools, spreadsheets, graphics software) we can use to access and analyze the contents of data warehouses. In Chapter 5, we saw how metadata provides a road map for the data warehouse.

If you were to put this book down now and design a data warehouse, you would build a system whose utility is completely dependent upon its users. For despite the flexibility and power of primary repositories, data marts, OLAP tools, query products, and the like, the capability to derive business intelligence from a data warehouse remains rooted in the collective experience and knowledge of its users. And in today's fiercely competitive business environment, that may not be enough. Imagine what could happen if data-warehouse users at our fictitious department store did not notice a subtle, yet critical, correlation between sales volume and the location of merchandise on the floor. Such an oversight could easily result in lost revenue and lower profits.

In this chapter, we explore how data mining can augment end users' abilities with tools that can uncover valuable information in a morass of data. More specifically, data mining refers to the use of specialized software to discover hidden patterns and subtle correlations in databases. For example, a data-mining program can examine a credit-card-statement database and determine that customers in a specific age group are more likely to buy certain products on weekends. Marketing personnel can then use this information in special promotions and tailored advertisements.

Once the sole province of large corporations and governmental entities, data mining is poised for significant growth in additional market segments. In fact, the Meta Group estimates that the data-mining business will grow from less than $100 million in 1996 to more than $800 million by the year 2000. Several factors are responsible for data mining's increasing popularity.

First, despite the fact that the two are very different, the advent of data warehousing supports the growth of data mining in several ways. Often, for example, we can use (with little modification) the transformational replication procedures that populate data warehouses to gather and reformat data for data mining. Data-mining tools, unlike data warehouses, require very detailed information. In fact, the currency of data mining is the transaction itself. Before the advent of data warehousing, however, transactional data was often inordinately difficult to access. By collecting and standardizing OLTP data, data-warehouse maintenance procedures perform many of the data-preparation tasks required for data mining.

Data warehousing supports data mining in other ways as well. For instance, many organizations that perform data warehousing elect to do so on dedicated servers. In many cases, data mining would not be feasible without the processing power obtained for data warehousing. The financial investment in data warehousing also provides support for data mining. In an effort to improve the return on investment of data warehouses, many organizations look to data mining.

Another reason for the growing popularity of data mining is the ever-improving price/performance ratio of computing hardware. This is especially true in the AS/400 arena, where IBM remains committed to delivering 70 percent performance gains each year in high-end models. Because data-mining tools process enormous volumes of transactional data, they consume significant computing resources. Dramatic increases in processing power, along with equally dramatic decreases in the cost of memory and storage, have made requisite computing resources more available and more affordable for data mining. The new RISC-based AS/400e servers, which can support up to 1 TB of disk storage and 20 GB of main memory, are well-suited for data mining.

Enhanced software also is responsible for the expanding market in data-mining products and services. Historically, data-mining tools were designed to manipulate flat files in a command-driven environment. Originally used by statisticians and computer scientists, data-mining software has only recently been enhanced for business users with general computer skills. Such enhancements include the incorporation of bit-mapped GUI interfaces and support for user-friendly input devices such as the mouse. One AS/400-based data-mining product, IBM's Intelligent Miner for OS/400, supports DB2/400 and a Windows-based GUI interface. (I examine Intelligent Miner in detail in Chapter 14.)

A growing realization that databases are competitive weapons is another reason for the burgeoning market in data-mining products. The popular press has proven to be an invaluable ally in this regard, as data-mining articles appear regularly in mainstream business magazines, technology publications, and even television commercials.

At this point, let's explore some of the details of data mining.

Pattern Recognition: The Force Behind Data Mining

The power of data-mining software lies in its ability to recognize patterns in data. Patterns, of course, are measurable sets of characteristics that we can associate with events or other sets of characteristics. In many ways, patterns are the lifeblood of business analyses. For example, when taken alone, a single sales figure for cologne at our fictitious department store is not likely to cause management to take action. But suppose cologne sales were related to shoppers in the following way: When men aged 20 to 24 shop on a Saturday morning and buy clothes, they are also likely to purchase cologne. This relationship, or pattern, is called an *association*. We identify such patterns when we can link events to one another during a discrete period of activity, such as a shopping trip.

In and of itself, this association is relatively useless without a related degree of likelihood, or *confidence*, to indicate the strength of the connection. In the case of our department store, analysts would need to know how likely a male shopper in that age group is to buy cologne after making a clothing purchase. If 90 percent of such shoppers buy cologne, the store manager may decide to move cologne as far away as possible from the clothing department. The reason, of course, is that these shoppers may see something of interest as they walk to the cologne counter. In contrast, a figure in the 10 percent range may cause the manager to move cologne closer to the clothing department in an attempt to stimulate sales. Confidence measures are a critical component of associations.

Support levels, another important factor used in conjunction with associations, are figures that express the relative percentage of members in a sample or population who possess the attributes or behavior in question. For example, if 7 percent of all male shoppers in that age group buy cologne after purchasing clothing, then a support level of 7 percent is said to apply to the association.

Although measures of confidence and support are critical, they have little use if a pattern is not *actionable*. Our cologne example is an actionable situation because management can reasonably expect to influence the sale of cologne. Actions in this case could include modifications to the store's arrangement or special weekend promotions.

Finally, we also must assign some measure of *significance* to data-mining output, because actionable hypotheses with a high degree of support and confidence may not necessarily improve the bottom line. For example, if our target group of male shoppers buys inexpensive cologne with razor-thin margins, then special measures may not be worthwhile. As with any analysis, it is important to relate the findings of data-mining software to normal measures of operating performance.

Now that I have highlighted the significance of patterns, let's explore the ways in which data-mining software uncovers them.

Data Discovery

Data mining represents a fundamental shift in how we derive business intelligence from data. In data-warehousing environments without data mining, all the analyses that could lead to pattern recognition originate with a person. To illustrate this point, let's refer to our earlier example in which male customers purchased cologne along with clothes. Without data-mining software, only a person could uncover this association. For example, a sales manager might recognize the correlation while examining the results of a product-customer sales query. There is a good chance, however, that the correlation would go unnoticed. Without data mining, the success of data warehouses is dependent upon the end users' ability to notice patterns in data. In addition, end users interpret information in a way that is consistent with their own experiences. Given a common set of query results, different end users will notice different things.

Traditional data warehouses adhere to this user-driven approach to data analysis and are often referred to as *verification-driven* applications. By contrast, data mining is a *discovery-driven* application because it programmatically uncovers patterns in data — in other words, the system itself discovers relationships and correlations. What's more, data mining does so without user-initiated queries.

Unlike the preceding example in which the sales manager discovered a correlation by chance, data-mining tools can be programmed to detect associations algorithmically. After data-mining software has isolated patterns such as associations, end users can run traditional queries to evaluate the significance of the newly discovered patterns. As a discovery-driven application, data mining is valuable because it can uncover subtle patterns in data that otherwise would go undetected. Data mining can do this because computers can analyze far more data than humans can. It is also important to note that data mining discovers patterns based solely "on the numbers." It does not apply subjective biases to data. To derive the most value from your data, you should augment your data warehouse with data mining.

The Value of Modeling

To effectively evaluate data mining, users must understand the concept of modeling. A model, of course, is a structure or system designed to embody the salient features of objects, events, and people. The fundamental architecture of a model consists of input, processes, and output. In data mining, the input consists of one or more data elements known as *independent variables.* The processes are *mathematical and statistical functions.* Finally, the output comprises data elements called *dependent variables.*

Data-mining applications use two basic types of models. *Deterministic models* reflect situations when a known equation can process specific input to yield predictable output. For example, a deterministic model can compute the simple interest earned on a certificate of deposit. In this case, the model's input includes principal value, interest rate, and deposit period, or term. Its process consists of an equation that multiplies the principal amount by the rate and term. Finally, the model's output is a single result called interest earned. There are an infinite number of possible combinations of input variables for this model. In one instance, the principal value may be $500, the interest rate 5.25 percent, and the term one year. The interest earned is calculated as follows: (500) (.0525) (1) = $26.25. In another case, the principal value may be $700, the interest rate 5.50 percent, and the term 2 years. The interest earned in this case is $77. Because there is no limit to the possible values and combinations of principal, interest rate, and term, there is an infinite number of input data sets. However, once we have identified a particular set of input data, our interest rate model computes a single, unambiguous result, which is the essence of a deterministic model. Deterministic models function well in situations that have a limited number of inputs with well-defined relationships.

In contrast to deterministic models, *probabilistic models* generate output in cases where there are too many input variables to consider and/or when the relationships between variables are not well defined. For instance, consider a golfer who attempts to predict the distance a particular drive will travel. In this case, many variables — wind speed, the angle and striking force of the club head, the condition of the ball, the condition of the fairway, the topological features of the course, and so on — will have an impact on the ball's flight. Even if we could identify all factors that affect the golfer's drive, we could not identify their interrelationships.

In many cases, we cannot design probabilistic models to account for every possible input variable. Instead, we design these models to focus on known outcomes that are based upon a limited set of critical, identifiable inputs. For example, many golfers can closely predict the distance of a drive based on their own experiences with varying combinations of wind velocity, striking force, flight angle, and grass height. These golfers have, in effect, built probabilistic models based on known outcomes and associated critical input variables. What's more, these models are flexible enough to support accurate predictions in circumstances that have not yet been encountered. For example, golfers may have no experience playing in gale force winds, but they still can estimate how far a drive will travel the first time they encounter such conditions. The human brain is particularly adept at probabilistic reasoning.

To support both deterministic and probabilistic models, data-mining applications use two basic architectures — artificial neural networks (ANNs) and decision trees. Let's define and examine these architectures in detail.

Artificial Neural Networks (ANNs)

ANNs are computer systems that strive to mimic the functionality of their biological counterpart, the human brain. Well-suited for probabilistic modeling, ANNs attempt to recognize patterns and generate useful predictions in situations characterized by vast amounts of input. These networks consist of interconnected elements, or neurodes, that process numerous inputs. In practice, neurodes are schematic representations of algorithms that evaluate inputs then generate outputs. Because each neurode in an ANN can process data asynchronously, these systems are a good fit in parallel-processing environments. Another characteristic of neural networks is their ability to adapt to changing sets of inputs. An example of a single-unit ANN appears in Figure 6.1.

FIGURE 6.1
Single-Unit Artificial Neural Network (ANN)

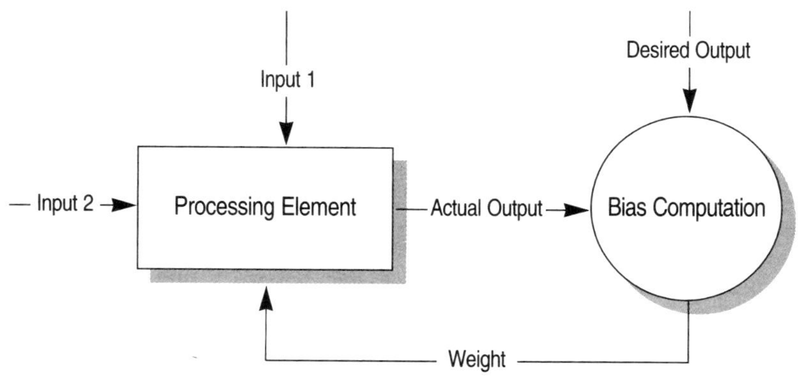

In this simple case, one neurode that generates output processes two independent variables, Input 1 and Input 2. An additional variable known as *bias* is responsible for weighting input so that the network can adapt, or learn. Depending on the particular ANN scheme in use, an equation that compares output to input typically calculates the bias factor. For example, the processing algorithm might use a bias to change (or weight) the inputs by an amount proportional to the difference between actual and expected output. After evaluating a large number of cases, the unit will have adjusted its processing element to meet the desired output. Actual ANNs consist of many such units, as well as hidden processing layers that actually can recode inputs. Hidden layers are designated according to rules derived from patterns found in various sets of inputs. A generic neural network appears in Figure 6.2. We refer to networks that require expected (or desired) outputs as *supervised networks*.

FIGURE 6.2
Generic Neural Network

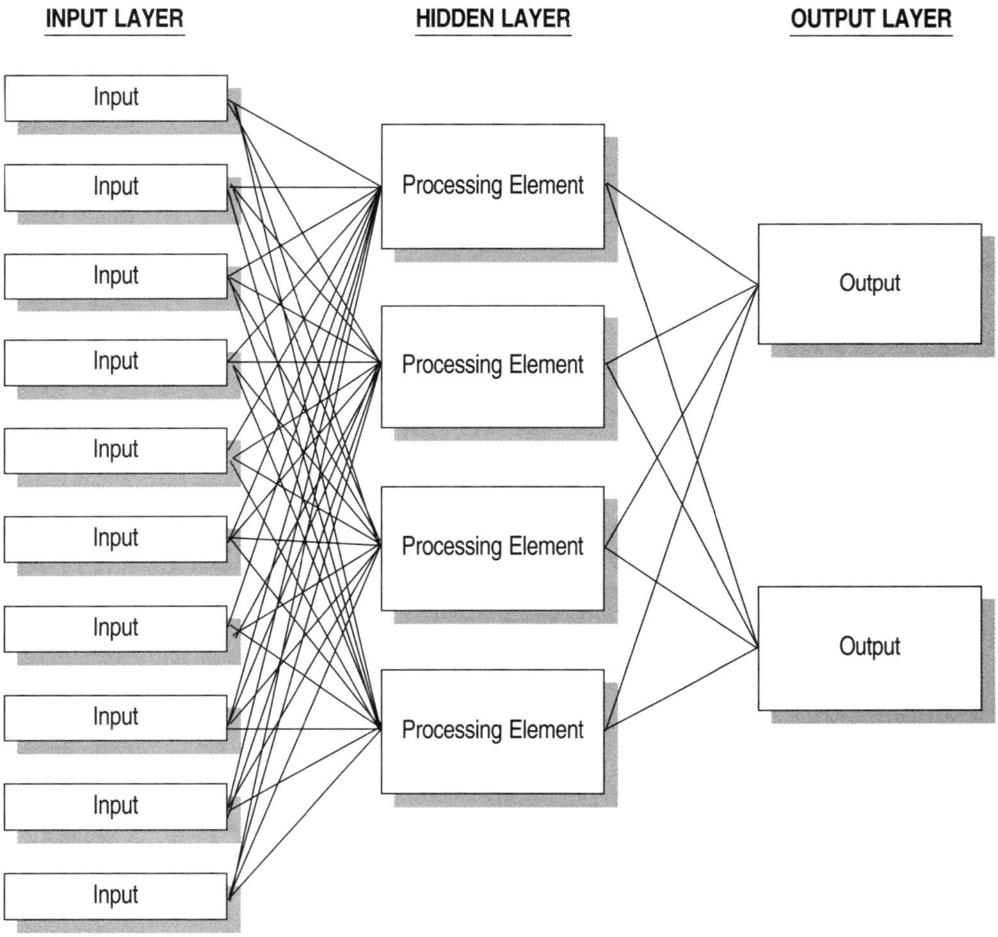

We frequently use neural networks to model situations that we cannot readily describe by hard-and-fast rules or rigid algorithms. In many cases, there are simply too many variables to consider. In others, we may not know the precise algorithms. Many data-mining applications are based upon neural-network technology. In the investment arena, for instance, forecasters use these models to help predict the movement of stock prices relative to changes in market indexes, interest rates, and the prices of related stocks. Other interesting applications for ANNs include the detection of credit-card fraud, and computer-based voice and fingerprint recognition.

Decision Trees

A popular data-mining architecture that is especially well-suited for deterministic modeling is the decision tree. Unlike ANN-based tools, tree-based products isolate patterns in databases then construct if-then hierarchies to describe those patterns. The hierarchies lend structure to numerous rules, or equations, that are later used to classify individual data elements. During this classification process, an analysis engine isolates the key attributes of each individual data element. The system then plugs these attributes into equations represented by nodes in the tree structure. The output of each equation determines which node is processed next. This procedure continues until a result is obtained at the end of a branch. Figure 6.3 presents a simple decision tree that we could use to gauge the credit risk of charge-card applicants at our fictitious department store.

One common technique used in the design of decision trees is known as *chi-square automatic interaction detection,* or *CHAID*. This method employs chi-square tests to create multiway branches that are used to segment databases. To demonstrate how chi-square tests function, let's look at a simple case.

Suppose that an insurance company wants to identify policy holders who are likely to select a particular homeowner's policy. A data-mining tool might use a chi-square test to determine whether the choice of policy is related to age. For example, suppose that the frequency of three policy options (A, B, and C) is examined relative to two age groups, under 50 and over 50. The table below shows fictitious data for 1,250 current policy holders.

	Policy A	**Policy B**	**Policy C**	**Totals**
	(Number of Policy Holders)			
Under 50	300	290	160	750
Over 50	120	330	50	500
Totals	420	620	210	1,250

In this example, we can use a chi-square test to determine whether the variables "age" and "policy choice" are independent or related. The first step in this process is to calculate the expected count for each cell based upon the row and column totals. For example, the expected count for the last cell (i.e., in the lower right corner) would be

$$\frac{\text{(row total) (column total)}}{\text{population total}} \quad \text{or} \quad \frac{(500)\ (210)}{1250}$$

FIGURE 6.3
Decision Tree

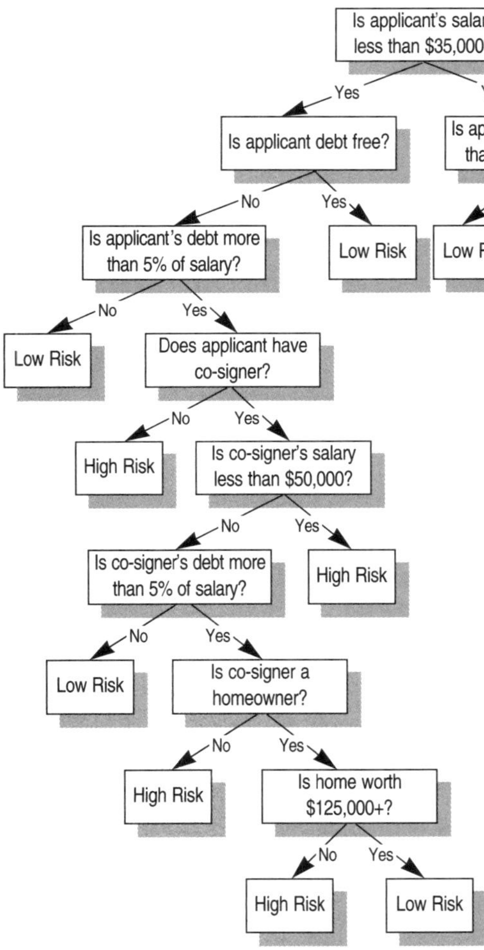

which equals 84. Computing the expected counts for each cell and placing those results in parentheses yields the results in the following table:

	Policy A	Policy B	Policy C	Totals
	(Number of Policy Holders)			
Under 50	300 (252)	290 (372)	160 (126)	750
Over 50	120 (168)	330 (248)	50 (84)	500
Totals	420	620	210	1,250

The next step in a chi-square test would be to compute the value of the following formula:

$$\chi^2 = \Sigma \frac{(\text{observed} - \text{expected})^2}{\text{expected}}$$

Plugging numbers from our example into this formula yields the following results:

$$\frac{(300 - 252)^2}{252} + \frac{(290 - 372)^2}{372} + \frac{(160 - 126)^2}{126} + \frac{(120 - 168)^2}{168} + \frac{(330 - 248)^2}{248} + \frac{(50 - 84)^2}{84}$$

which equals

$$.914 + 1.808 + .917 + 1.371 + 2.711 + 1.376 = 9.097$$

As the value of χ^2 increases, so does the likelihood that the variables are related. It is not obvious, but the cells that have the most impact upon this calculation are those that have an expected count that is very different from the actual count. Finally, the result of the chi-square test, coupled with a statistical measure known as *degrees of freedom*,[1] is located in a probability distribution table to determine the statistical significance of our finding. In this example, a value of 9.097 leads us to conclude that the two variables (age and policy selection) are not independent.[2] Chi-square tests effectively determine whether or not two variables are independent. In data mining, we can use this information to identify attributes (i.e., age) that help us to segment populations.

Decision trees are very popular in data mining. IT personnel readily understand their architecture, and the requisite conditional logic is generally not too difficult to code. Furthermore, decision trees often provide better performance than other data-mining structures. Decision trees may, however, experience difficulties with continuous variables such as age. Often, such variables must be represented by ranges, such as 18 to 24 years. Unfortunately, when designed improperly, decision trees may overlook patterns that are hidden in ranges. And although their underlying structure is relatively simple, very large decision trees can be extremely complex and difficult to maintain.

[1]The formula for degrees of freedom is (# of rows − 1) × (# columns − 1).

[2]This conclusion is valid with a statistical significance, or alpha (α), of .05.

Rule Induction

Neural networks and decision trees frequently employ inductive reasoning to formulate rules. This process, known as *rule induction*, relies upon measures of statistical significance to connect rules to patterns.

Before we move on, let's talk about inductive reasoning. In the field of reasoning and analysis, there are two types of arguments: *inductive* and *deductive*. With deductive reasoning, definitive proof of an argument's conclusion exists. This means that for a given deductive argument, if the premises are true, then the conclusion must also be true. Deductive arguments, therefore, begin with a premise and are either valid or invalid. In contrast, the conclusions of inductive arguments have no definitive proofs. In the case of induction, premises merely provide some support for the truth of a conclusion. As a result, we characterize inductive arguments as either better or worse than other arguments.

Model designers who use rule induction begin by stating the conjecture that is under consideration. Next, they group similar conjectures and associated proofs into what is known as a *proof plan*. The model builders then refer to this plan as they attempt to formulate hypotheses for the case at hand. Data-mining algorithms often use rule induction to analyze data because business models are rarely deterministic.

Architectural differences notwithstanding, nearly all data-mining products perform one or more of the following functions as they examine the contents of databases.

Classification

Classification algorithms examine the traits of individual items and then determine whether a class exists that embodies the same or similar traits. If the algorithms find such a class, classification routines can then assign the item to it. Classification routines are valuable because members in a given class often exhibit similar behavioral patterns and share common tastes. This information can then be used in target marketing.

For example, consider an established class of middle-aged female shoppers from the same community who shop on weekends and spend at least $200 on clothing each month. Effective classification programs can examine the characteristics of other shoppers in the store's data warehouse and then determine whether these shoppers belong to the class. If they do, store managers may be able to assume that goods purchased by existing members of the class would also appeal to the newly classified shoppers. The store can then mail special promotional materials to these individuals to stimulate demand for products they have not bought in the past.

In practice, classification programs can examine thousands of traits associated with millions of items. Classification routines represent the most common form of data mining in use today.

Clustering

Before data-mining software can classify individual items, discrete classes that describe segments of a database population must exist. The goal of *clustering* software is to create these classes. Clustering algorithms first examine the significance and frequency of traits that belong to individual members of a population. Afterward, clustering routines establish mutually exclusive, trait-based profiles that classification algorithms later use.

Clustering has many uses. The banking and insurance industries, for example, use clustering to define classes based on income, marital status, age, education, gender, credit history, and a host of other traits. They then use these classes as a basis to assign risk, which in turn determines loan fees and policy premiums. In the advertising world, clustering techniques are the mainstay of market-segmentation algorithms. Target marketing, of course, is not possible without the proper identification of market segments. Market segments, or classes, group together individuals who share common purchasing profiles. One example of effective target marketing is the inclusion of customer-specific ads in credit-card statements.

Multiple-choice consumer surveys frequently serve as a basis for market segmentation. A form of clustering known as *relational analysis* is particularly well-suited for survey processing. Conceived by researchers at IBM's European Center for Applied Mathematics, relational-analysis models examine individual answers to questions as well as the patterns of answers on each survey. For example, a model may calculate that 20 percent of the respondents chose A for question one, 30 percent chose B, 45 percent chose C, and 5 percent selected choice D. Similar statistics are then compiled for every question on the survey. Afterward, each consumer's individual answer pattern is analyzed to determine whether a statistically significant number of respondents share the same pattern. The results can be used to identify unique market segments.

Associations

As you recall from the beginning of the chapter, we identify as *associations* events that are linked to one another during a discrete period of activity, or that occur during a transaction. For example, suppose that 1,000 shoppers purchase winter coats (event A). If 200 of those shoppers also buy gloves (event B) during the *same* shopping trip, then an association is said to exist between the purchase of coats and the purchase of gloves. In this instance, the association has a 20 percent observed confidence, which means simply that gloves will be bought with coats, on average, 2 out of 10 times. We refer to statements or hypotheses that include both an association and a confidence factor as *affinities.* In addition to affinities, we also can measure associations by support levels. Typically expressed as a percentage, support levels describe the number of members in a given population to which an association applies. In many associative analyses, more than two different events are analyzed and associated with one another. For example, a multiple-association affinity might state that event D will occur with 80 percent confidence and 7 percent support when events A, B, and C occur together. Market-basket analyses, or examinations of goods purchased during shopping trips, commonly use associative algorithms.

Sequencing

Sequencing algorithms are similar to association routines. The primary difference between these data-mining techniques is that in sequencing, events are linked across multiple transactions, while associations occur during a single, discrete transaction. Sequencing algorithms typically predict how likely event B is to occur during a given length of time (not during an activity) subsequent to event A. For example, when a new car is purchased, a 40 percent chance exists that the buyer will purchase accessories within three months.

Forecasting

Forecasting estimates the likelihood of future events based on the historical trends of those events. Unlike sequencing, forecasting does not consider two or more events. Rather, it predicts the future of a single continuous event based on the history of that event. We can use forecasting models, for example, to predict movements in the Dow Jones Industrial Average based on its historical highs and lows.

Predictive Modeling

Predictive modeling describes processes whereby data-mining algorithms consider a known output value and multiple input values, and then attempt to generate a model that can be used to predict future output values using varying combinations of input values. For example, suppose that a particular house with four bedrooms, two baths, one fireplace, and three acres of property sold for $300,000. Suppose further that a neighboring house with three bedrooms, one bath, two fireplaces, and four acres of land sold for $325,000. In predictive modeling, a data-mining program might examine many such sale transactions and attempt to generate a model that describes the relationship between key inputs (e.g., number of rooms, number of baths, number of fireplaces, number of acres of property) and a single output (e.g., the selling price of a home). We can then use the model to predict selling prices for homes that are still on the market.

Combining Techniques

To derive business intelligence from transaction-level databases, data-mining systems often employ a complement of two or more analytic techniques. For example, a market-basket analysis may use both classification and association routines to formulate a hypothesis. Data-mining vendors typically categorize their products according to supported methodologies or the underlying models that enable those methodologies.

Data Visualization

It is often said that a picture is worth a thousand words. This is especially true in data mining, where programs using the aforementioned techniques regularly manipulate more information than we can assimilate. To help us understand and evaluate this information, data-mining tools rely heavily upon graphics. As its name implies, *data visualization* is a process whereby numeric information is presented to users graphically. As we discussed in Chapter 5, graphs are a very effective way to present and examine numerical data. And as we shall see in Chapter 14, the graphs used for data visualization are more complex than those created by general-purpose business software. For example, data-visualization techniques may use fractal mathematics to simultaneously present the standard deviation, correlation, and skew for many variables in a data set. In other instances, data-visualization tools support the animation of graphics. Some products also let users display and rotate matrices of scatter plots. Because of the meaning it confers upon data-mining output, data visualization is an integral component of data-mining tools.

Text Mining: Making Sense of Words

In addition to the classic data-mining techniques I have discussed so far, a nascent field has significant potential in data mining.

Text mining refers to the use of programs to derive business intelligence from text-based data. Just as data-mining tools unlock usable information buried in databases, text-mining programs uncover interesting facts in text-based archives, or textbases. A textbase is simply a database management system that is optimized for textual data storage. Traditional databases are ill-suited for this task because they maintain very rigid data structures. Textbases, on the other hand, make extensive use of variable-length records, free-form memo fields, and specialized indexes to manage unstructured textual information. Customized software then discovers trends and patterns in the underlying textbase.

To obtain enough information to function effectively, textbase applications often rely upon scanners and optical-character-recognition (OCR) software to convert paper documents into electronic data. In the case of e-mail and other computer-based documents, such conversion processes are unnecessary because the data is already in digital form.

Textbase products share some similarities with both imaging applications and computer-output-to-laser-disk (COLD) solutions. Like imaging applications, textbases store documents and reports as objects. Like COLD, these systems can also decompose document- and report-based data into relational files.

However, there is an important difference between imaging/COLD systems and textbases. COLD systems are designed to provide end users with access to raw, detailed data. By contrast, textbases are designed to present users with meaningful information that has been gleaned from detailed data. For example, a textbase application may examine thousands of e-mail messages to isolate patterns (i.e., customer complaints) in their content, which is more efficient than the manual examination and synthesis of these documents.

At present, the field of text mining is in its infancy but a few commercial applications have already appeared. For example, text mining tools developed at IBM's European Center for Applied Mathematics (ECAM) were recently used to discern a positive shift in opinion about how electric cars were viewed by the press. This work was done for Electricité de France (EDF), an organization that did not have enough manpower to conduct its own research. To accomplish the task, IBM's software examined thousands of press clippings about electric cars on the Internet, then synthesized the results and discerned a pattern.

Because more than 80 percent of the world's information is stored as text in a wide variety of documents (books, letters, legal briefs, blueprints, proposals, contracts, e-mail messages, newspaper articles, magazine articles, insurance policies, resumes, research reports, policy manuals, etc.), we can assume that this practice will advance and eventually lead to more applications.

Lingering Misconceptions

Despite rapid growth and heightened visibility, the data-mining arena is still hampered by a good deal of misconception and confusion. For example, many managers believe, or at least hope, that data-mining tools will quickly transform their organizations into highly profitable enterprises. Although data-mining applications occasionally uncover extremely valuable information, they more typically deliver consistent, incremental improvements to existing operations.

Another misconception holds that data-mining software reduces the need for experienced management, but nothing could be further from the truth. Experienced managers must evaluate data-mining output to determine whether it is an accurate, actionable reflection of the underlying business model.

Some managers also are reluctant to support data mining because they believe it relies upon new analytic techniques. In fact, most of the analytic methodologies found in data-mining software have been known for decades. Neural networks, for example, were developed nearly 50 years ago, and CHAID analyses have been used successfully for decades.

Because data mining borrows heavily from the field of statistics, many managers consider intimate knowledge of mathematics a prerequisite for perspective data miners. Although that may have been true 10 years ago, the current breed of data-mining software does not require a graduate degree in mathematics. Understanding and applying even a few rudimentary statistical techniques to your data can be very revealing.

Another misconception holds that data warehouses contain all the information necessary for data mining. Unfortunately, the contents of most data warehouses is too summarized to effectively support data mining. Data mining requires transaction-level detail such as itemized consumer purchases and detailed credit-card-payment histories. However, companies with data warehouses can usually leverage the existing data-warehouse infrastructure (e.g., extraction and transformation processes) to create data suitable for data-mining software.

Finally, many prospective data miners believe that data-mining techniques are effective only when used to examine an enormous database. Although results are best when large databases are used, data mining can yield impressive results by analyzing representative samples of data. In fact, nearly every data-mining application is first prototyped with samples of data before it's turned loose on entire databases.

Implementation Guidelines

Like any sophisticated application, data mining requires planning to ensure success. The first step in any data-mining program is to define a project domain. For example, you may choose to limit your analysis to sales data. You should also clearly understand what business goals the project is addressing. In this light, do not expect data-mining runs on a sales database to yield suggestions for improved manufacturing processes.

Your next challenge is to isolate data as dictated by your project domain. As we discussed earlier, data-mining tools require transaction-level data. As we saw in Chapter 2, data warehouses typically do not contain highly detailed information. And although OLTP systems do contain transaction-level data, they may not contain all the information you need for data mining. For this reason, data-mining applications may require you to modify existing business processes so you can collect requisite data.

For example. many supermarkets have changed their checkout process to include the use of discount cards and scanners that collect highly detailed purchasing data about customers. Retail stores that do not use shopper discount cards also often collect basic demographic data from customers who purchase goods. Has a cashier asked you for your ZIP code lately? Many stores use data-mining tools to analyze customer purchasing patterns nationwide by residential locale.

Grocers and retailers are not alone in modifying business processes to exploit the power of data mining. To effectively perform data mining in a manufacturing environment, for example, manufacturers may install sensors on the shop floor to measure temperature and humidity. Data-mining software can then examine the measurements to determine whether relationships exist between these conditions and manufacturing benchmarks such as yields and defect ratios.

After you have collected the requisite information, you probably will have to transform and format it for use in your data-mining product (unfortunately, different products require different input file formats).

Once you have collected and prepared the data, you will need to select one or more data-mining models and/or algorithms. You should make this critical decision in consultation with your operational managers and your data-mining vendor. Ideally, your vendor will have knowledge of your industry and your position in that industry. (For its part, IBM employs more than 18,000 experts in its Industry Solutions organization and 80,000 employees in its Consulting and Services organization.)

Finally, bear in mind that data mining is an iterative process. After running one or more algorithms, you will most likely have to adjust your data and re-run the model. After your system has generated satisfactory output, operational managers and IT personnel should work together to interpret results and formulate action plans.

Conclusion

Data-mining is not magic — it won't automatically examine your database and tell you how to improve your business. However, when used properly, data mining can uncover valuable information about customers, products, processes, and virtually any aspect of business that generates detailed operational data. Experienced managers can then use this information to bolster their organizations' competitive positions. Data-mining warrants serious consideration as a means to improve both your business and the return on investment of your data warehouse.

Data mining has already enjoyed considerable success in a number of applications. Among other things, it has been used to detect credit-card fraud, isolate high-risk bank loans, segment customer groups, analyze retail buying patterns, predict product demand, manage inventory, identify telephone usage patterns, correlate financial indicators, and interpret stock fluctuations. Because it augments the analytic abilities of both novice and experienced managers, data mining has a secure future in many organizations.

Chapter 7

The AS/400

Introduction

Now that we have reviewed the major components of a data warehouse, we are in a much better position to evaluate the AS/400 as a data-warehouse server. As you read this chapter, you will learn that many of the features that make the AS/400 a formidable OLTP platform also account for its strengths as a data-warehouse server. For example, performance is one reason behind the AS/400's success in both the OLTP and data-warehousing arenas.

In the first section of this chapter, I examine the technology responsible for AS/400 *performance*, and I also examine the applicability of AS/400 performance in data warehousing.

Then I move on to an in-depth examination of the AS/400's native database, DB2/400. In particular, I examine DB2/400's capabilities in two critical areas: *scalability* and *functionality*. Because data warehouses manipulate and store vast amounts of data, you must carefully consider support for both these factors during your evaluation of any data-warehouse server.

After I review DB2/400, I examine the AS/400's support for open computing standards. Because data warehouses often function in heterogeneous computing environments, you also must consider *openness* when you are evaluating data-warehouse servers.

Next, I discuss AS/400 *extensibility*, or the AS/400's ability to support technological advances without costly disruptions to application functionality. In other words, I'll help you determine how well the AS/400 protects your investment in a data warehouse.

To round out the chapter, I examine one of the AS/400's traditional strengths: *application support*. A data-warehouse server is only as good as its application software. As you will see, the AS/400 supports a wide variety of data-warehousing products.

Now that I've introduced the critical criteria by which any data warehouse server is evaluated, let's move on to an in-depth discussion of these criteria.

Performance

To satisfy the batch-intensive processing demands of data warehouses, servers must be able to manipulate large volumes of data quickly and efficiently. Through comprehensive support for parallel-processing, its 64-bit architecture, and a unique I/O system, the AS/400 can effectively meet the demands of large-scale (i.e., even multiple-terabyte) data warehouses.

And in the fall of 1997, IBM introduced a new line of AS/400s collectively referred to as the AS/400e series. These new machines provide AS/400 customers with a dramatic boost in performance over previous AS/400s (performance may vary depending on the model and application you are running), as evidenced by the graphs in Figures 7.1 through 7.4:

FIGURE 7.1

V3R7 CPW Values on Current Hardware

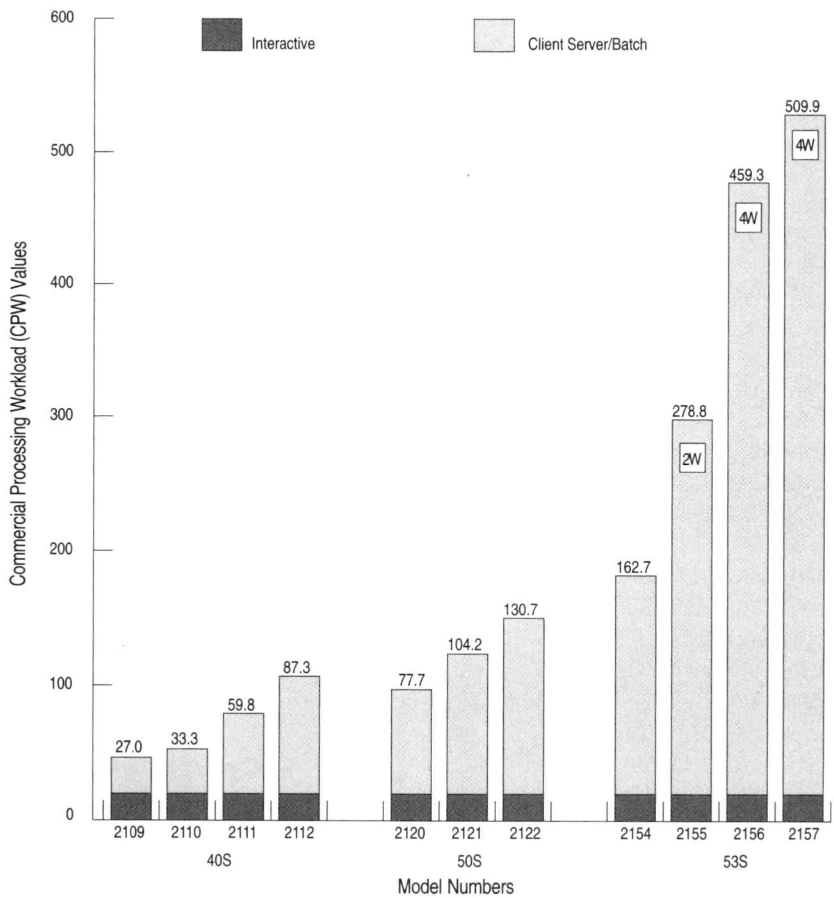

Substantial growth from current processor models to new V4R1 processor models.

- S20 2-way offers up to 3.5× growth compared to high-end 50S model
- S20 4-way offers up to 5.7× growth compared to high-end 50S model
- 1.9×, 3.4×, and 4.3× growth over current high-end 4-way

Source: *AS/400 Magazine*, September 1997, "More Power to You"

FIGURE 7.2

V4R1 CPW Values on V4R1 Hardware

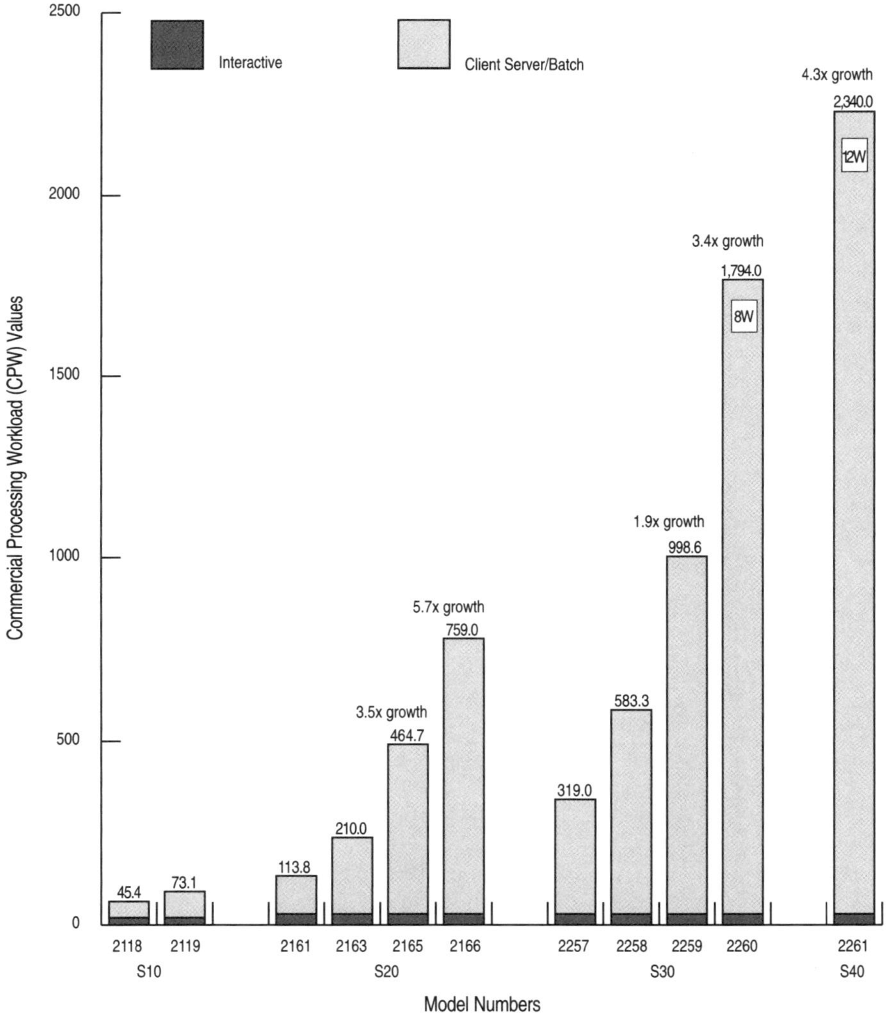

Substantial growth from current processor models to new V4R1 processor models.

- S20 2-way offers up to 3.5× growth compared to high-end 50S model
- S20 4-way offers up to 5.7× growth compared to high-end 50S model
- 1.9×, 3.4×, and 4.3× growth over current high-end 4-way

Source: *AS/400 Magazine*, September 1997, "More Power to You"

FIGURE 7.3
V3R7 CPW Values on Current Hardware

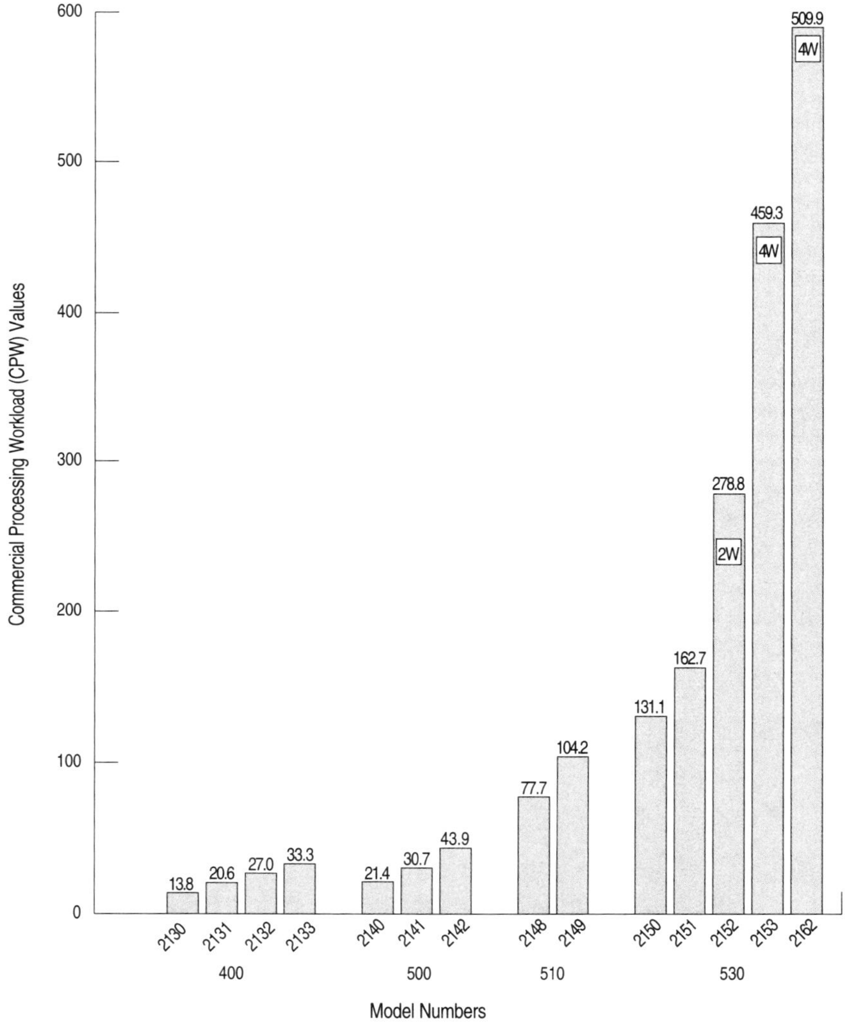

Substantial growth from current processor models to new V4R1 processor models.
- New 600 models up to 2.1× growth over current 400 models
- 620 2-way offers up to 4.4× growth compared to high-end 510 model

Source: *AS/400 Magazine*, September 1997, "More Power to You"

FIGURE 7.4
V4R1 CPW Values on V4R1 Hardware

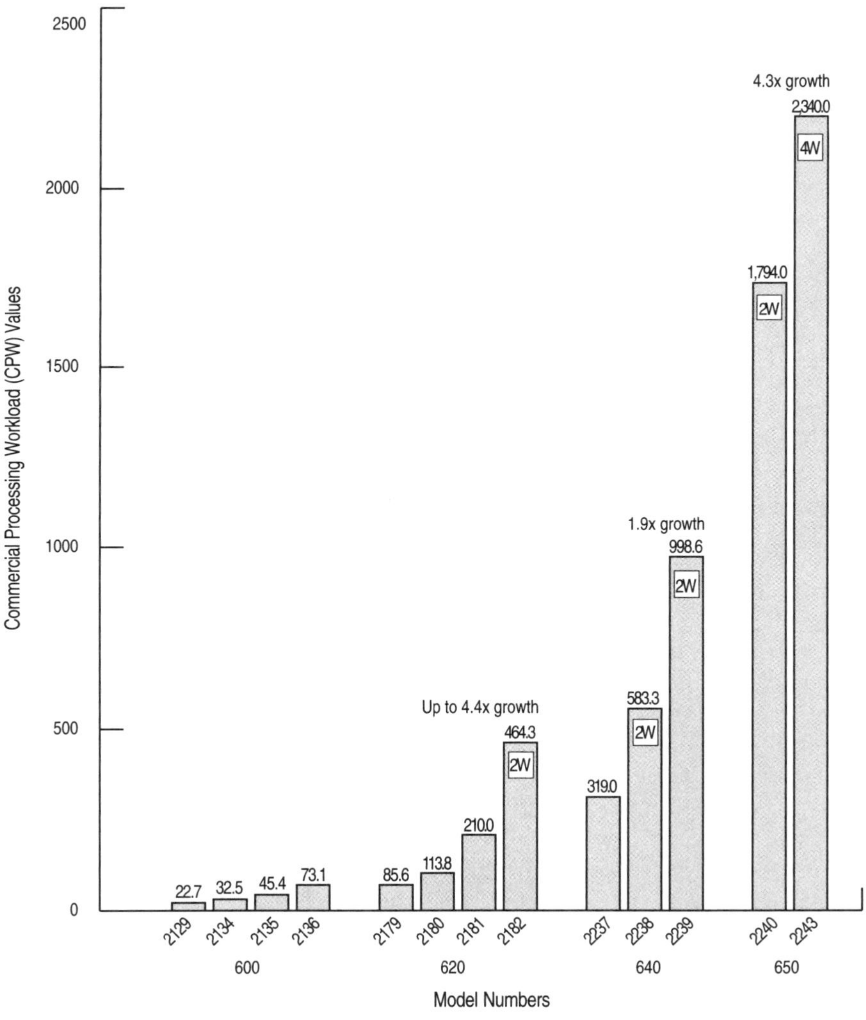

Substantial growth from current processor models to new V4R1 processor models.

- New 600 models up to 2.1× growth over current 400 models
- 620 2-way offers up to 4.4× growth compared to high-end 510 model

Source: *AS/400 Magazine*, September 1997, "More Power to You"

Let's take a closer look at the AS/400's parallel-processing functionality, 64-bit architecture, and I/O system as they relate to performance.

Parallel Processing

One reason for the AS/400's formidable performance is its support for parallel processing. Parallel processing decomposes work into smaller tasks, which lets servers process more work in less time. Parallel processing is commonly defined as the use of multiple CPUs to execute programs in a non-sequential, or simultaneous, manner. In the case of the AS/400, this definition is too narrow because the AS/400 actually supports four distinct types of parallel processing: parallel I/O processing, superscalar processing, symmetric multiprocessing (SMP), and multisystem parallel processing.

Parallel I/O processing occurs on the AS/400 between the CPU and the disk-storage subsystem. The AS/400 always has performed data striping, a technique that distributes data across multiple disks. To perform disk striping, the CPU delegates I/O jobs to specialized I/O processors, each of which can independently read and write data. These processes occur simultaneously, or in *parallel*, across multiple I/O processors and multiple disks. IBM has shown that parallel I/O processing can increase the performance of I/O-intensive queries by up to 700 percent. Every AS/400 performs parallel I/O processing — even those systems that feature a single CPU. Figure 7.5 is a schematic representation of parallel I/O processing as it would function to fulfill a sales query. The sales data in this example is striped across each of the four disk devices.

Superscalar processing, also referred to as CPU parallelism or out-of-order execution, occurs when a single CPU executes multiple instructions simultaneously. Even before their support for RISC processing, AS/400 CPUs could execute instructions in parallel. However, this functionality was restricted to a relatively small subset of the total number of available CPU instructions. The RISC processors' compiler/translators and architecture have been specifically designed to execute a wider variety of instructions in parallel, making these processors truly superscalar. This functionality results in improved performance because CPU tasks are completed in less time.

Symmetric multiprocessing (SMP), alternatively known as tightly coupled processing or uniform memory access (UMA), describes an architecture in which multiple CPUs share the main memory and disk resources of a single machine. Using DB2 Symmetric Multiprocessing for OS/400, the AS/400 can simultaneously use 2, 4, 8, or 12 CPUs to process a single job. Figure 7.6 is a logical depiction of an 8-way, SMP-capable AS/400. As a measure of performance, 12-way AS/400 servers can process tens of millions of records per hour.

FIGURE 7.5
Parallel I/O Processing

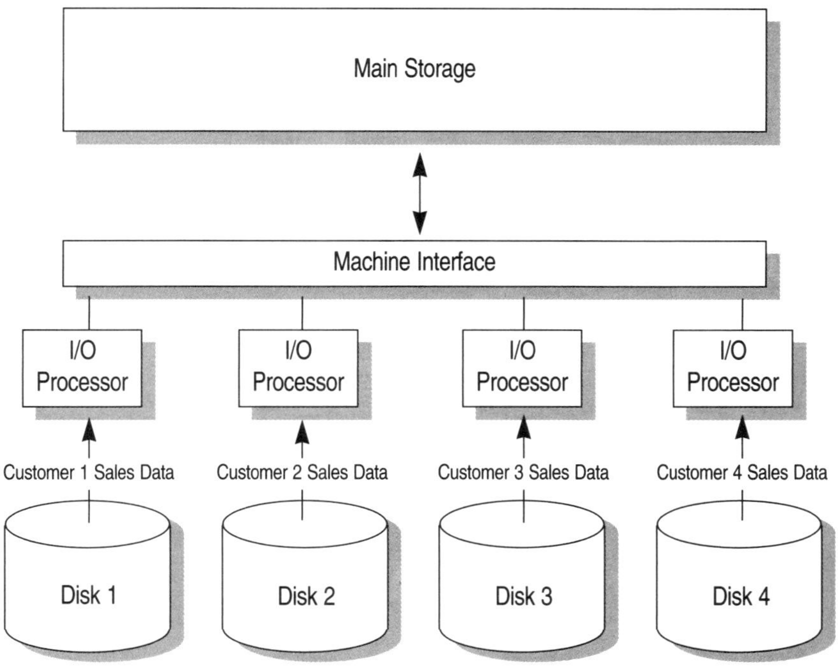

FIGURE 7.6
Eight-Way Symmetric Multiprocessing

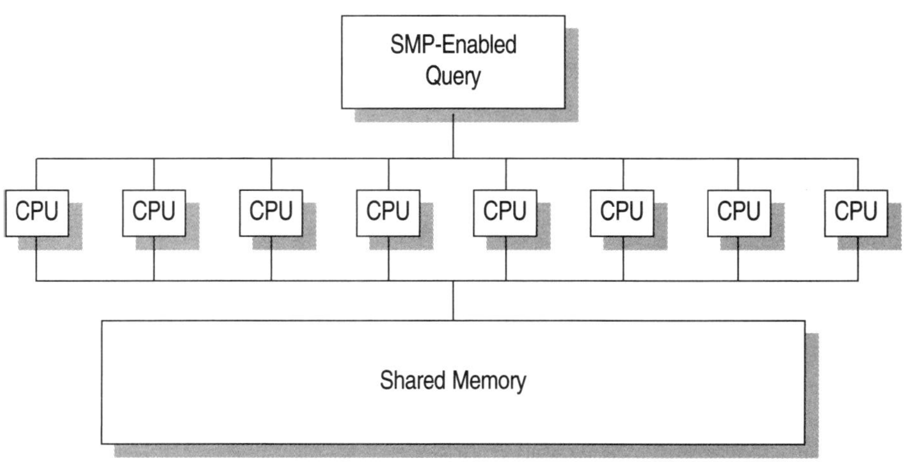

To further enhance parallel-processing performance, DB2 Symmetric Multiprocessing supports both interquery and intraquery parallelism. Interquery parallelism lets only whole SQL statements run on different processors at the same time, while intraquery parallelism can decompose a single SQL statement into tasks that run in parallel on different processors (tasks occur below the machine interface). When queries access large amounts of data, as is often the case in data warehousing, intraquery parallelism can enhance performance significantly.

Nevertheless, in any environment, parallel queries tend to consume considerable memory, disk, and CPU resources. To ensure balanced workloads and acceptable interactive response times, we must carefully manage the number of queries that use parallel processing. In addition, we also should strictly control the degree to which individual queries use parallelism. The AS/400 provides two ways to ensure such management.

First, we can control query processing at the system level through the system value QQRYDEGREE. This system parameter accepts four values: *NONE, *IO, *OPTIMIZE, and *MAX. If we select *NONE, then queries cannot use parallel processing. If we choose *IO, then queries can use only I/O parallel processing. If we specify *OPTIMIZE, then the DB2/400 Query Optimizer can let the query use either parallel I/O processing or SMP parallel processing. (For the optimizer to activate SMP parallel processing, DB2 Symmetric Multiprocessing must be installed.) As you will see in the next section, Query Optimizer automatically determines the most efficient processing technique. When *OPTIMIZE is in effect, the optimizer bases its selection for each query on the relative amount of memory that query is using in a pool. The optimizer also can specify the number of subtasks the system can use to process queries in parallel. Be aware that as the number of subtasks increases, fewer system resources are available to other jobs. If we specify *MAX in the QQRYDEGREE system value, then the same choices are available to Query Optimizer as when *OPTIMIZE is in effect. Under *MAX, however, the optimizer assumes that a particular query can use all the active memory in its pool.

We also can control AS/400 parallel processing at the job level via the DEGREE parameter of the CHGQRYA (Change Query Attributes) command. The DEGREE parameter accepts a total of eight values. In addition to the four I discussed above (which have the same effects here, albeit at a job level), the DEGREE parameter accepts the *SAME, *NBRTASKS, *SYSVAL, and *ANY values. When we specify *SAME, the parallel degree query attribute does not change. When we specify *NBRTASKS, followed by an integer, then the optimizer limits the number of tasks to the specified integer value. This action applies only to situations in which the optimizer chooses to process a query via SMP parallel processing. When we specify *SYSVAL, the QQRYDEGREE system value is the processing option. The last valid value, *ANY, has the same effect as the *IO value — its purpose is to maintain compatibility with prior releases.

As with *OPTIMIZE and *MAX, the optimizer can choose to use parallel I/O processing. To restrict the number of processors that can run a query in parallel, we should limit the number of tasks specified to fewer than the total number of CPUs on the system. For example, if we set this parameter to two on an eight-way AS/400, then only two of the machine's eight processors process the query. The purpose of this parameter value is to balance overall system workloads. If we specify an integer value greater than the number of processors, then all processors on that machine are eligible for use in the query process. Bear in mind that as the number of tasks increases, fewer resources are available for other jobs. Also, adjusting the DEGREE parameter of an active query has no impact on that query, so take care to specify the number of tasks into which a query can be decomposed before you execute the query. Otherwise, the overcommitment of active memory and associated overhead costs can inhibit system performance.

Even when the QQRYDEGREE value or the DEGREE value permits parallel processing, the DB2/400 Query Optimizer may elect to execute a query through non-parallel means. It will choose that option either when the optimizer identifies an available non-parallel-processing method that is more efficient, or as a result of functional restrictions (i.e., when parallel processing resources are not available for the query).

A fourth form of parallel processing supported by the AS/400 is *multi-system parallel processing*, which occurs across several machines, each of which uses its respective processor(s), memory, and disk. In this scenario, a group of interconnected machines, or nodes, is referred to as a loosely coupled, shared-nothing cluster. You need IBM's DB2 Multisystem for OS/400 to implement this method of parallel processing in an AS/400 environment. With DB2 Multisystem, you can link up to 32 separate AS/400s to form a single cluster. Let's take a moment to consider the potential processing power of this arrangement. If each of these machines has eight processors, then a single query theoretically can use the combined power of 256 PowerPC RISC processors!

And in instances where a database grows beyond the capacity of a single server, DB2 Multisystem can partition databases and individual tables across multiple machines. DB2 Multisystem can support databases up to the amount of DASD available (currently, 32 TB is the limit), and individual tables up to 4 TB in size. From an application perspective, these partitioned databases and tables appear as local objects, so we need no additional application coding to access and manage data that may be physically stored on several different servers. An added performance benefit is that partitioning lets queries execute in parallel on separate servers. For example, suppose a single, enormous data-warehouse table contains sales records for four regions: East, West, North, and South. Suppose further that IT personnel have directed DB2 Multisystem to partition this file by region so that separate servers store records for each region. One server contains all West records, another contains all East records, and so on. If a query is designed to group sales by region, we actually can run that query on all four servers at the same time. DB2 Multisystem accomplishes this by decomposing the query into four tasks, each of which is then sent to a different server. After each task has executed, results are automatically combined and returned to the user or initiating process. To implement this functionality, DB2 Multisystem uses a message-passing technique to communicate with each node in the cluster. With this technique, the software sends work (i.e., a query task) to the data instead of sending data to the query; because network traffic does not inundate the cluster, performance improves. (I explore DB2 Multisystem in more detail later in the chapter.)

To be effective, a shared-nothing cluster requires high-speed communications channels between each machine, or node. To address this issue, IBM designed OptiConnect for OS/400, a fiber-optic communications system that supports data-transfer rates of up to 1 GB per second. To achieve this transfer rate, OptiConnect provides an OS/400 kernel function that supports access to the same transport mechanism that CPUs and I/O subsystems use to transfer data. In so doing, the OptiConnect channel bypasses communications I/O processors and their associated microcode overhead. By letting I/O hardware function as an optical bus extension of a system I/O bus, OptiConnect facilitates direct machine-to-machine communications. When taken together, DB2 Multisystem and OptiConnect make massively parallel processing (MPP) a reality in the AS/400 arena.

64-Bit Architecture

In addition to the performance gains that parallel processing provides, the AS/400 also derives significant benefit from its pure 64-bit architecture. AS/400 servers feature a 64-bit operating system (OS/400), a 64-bit relational database (DB2/400), and up to twelve 64-bit RISC processors (PowerPC). What's more, every software application designed for the AS/400 is a 64-bit application. In contrast, many other servers are based on 32-bit architectures, or a mix of 32-bit and 64-bit technology. For example, servers featuring Intel's 32-bit processors (i.e., Pentium, Pentium Pro, Pentium II) can support only 16- or 32-bit operating systems such as Microsoft Windows 3.1, Windows 95, or Windows NT.[1] Furthermore, third-party applications designed for these systems are similarly restricted to 32-bit performance. Even when servers use a 64-bit processor such as Digital's Alpha, performance still may be constrained by 32-bit operating systems (e.g., Windows NT), 32-bit databases (e.g., Microsoft SQL Server), and/or 32-bit applications. The AS/400's "pure" 64-bit architecture enhances

[1] Intel does not expect to ship a 64-bit CPU until 1999. Redesigning 32-bit applications to fully utilize this 64-bit chip will take many years.

performance because of its impact on three critical areas: addressing, data flow, and computational processing. Let's see why.

The AS/400's address space, or single-level store, contains both main memory and disk space. Because of its 64-bit architecture, the AS/400's address space consists of the total number of bytes that a 64-bit addressing scheme can reference. This number is equal to 2^{64}, or approximately 18.45 million TB! In practical terms, there is no limit to the amount of memory an AS/400 can directly address, which means it can directly address objects on disk even when multiple terabytes of DASD are utilized. In contrast, servers that employ a 32-bit addressing scheme can directly address no more than 4.3 GB of disk storage. This does not mean that 32-bit machines are limited to 4.3 GB hard drives. To be sure, personal computers featuring 8 GB hard drives are becoming common. To address storage beyond 4.3 GB, these machines typically employ a two-part, as opposed to direct, addressing scheme. Because this process requires more resources than a direct addressing scheme, it can hinder performance in 32-bit machines. The AS/400's performance is enhanced as a result of its ability to directly address a virtually unlimited amount of disk storage.

The advantages of 64-bit addressing are not limited to disk storage. The AS/400 also can directly address a virtually unlimited amount of main memory. With IBM's release of V4R1 and the introduction of AS/400e servers, the largest AS/400 model now supports 20 GB of memory, a fivefold increase over prior memory capacity. Memory capacity is a critical determinant of system performance because an inverse relationship exists between memory capacity and physical I/O operations. As the amount of data stored in main memory increases, requisite disk I/O processing decreases, which enhances performance because functions that access disks are orders of magnitude slower than operations accessing main storage. Simply stated, more main memory equates to better performance. Without its 64-bit architecture, the AS/400 could not address vast quantities of main memory directly, and performance would be adversely affected. As is the case with disk storage, 32-bit machines can directly address approximately 4.3 GB of memory. However, because of addressing and other technology constraints, most 32-bit servers feature less than 128 MB of memory.

A 64-bit architecture also has significant benefits in terms of data movement and computational operations. Consider the AS/400's 64-bit, RISC-based PowerPC processors. Like all processors, the PowerPC processor stores data in special structures known as registers. For a computer to process work, data must flow between registers and memory. With its 64-bit architecture, the PowerPC processor can move 64 bits of data in the same amount of time that 32-bit processors can move 32 bits of data. In other words, 64-bit processors move data twice as fast as 32-bit processors, resulting in enhanced performance. Similarly, because 64-bit processors move 64 bits of data at once, they perform operations (e.g., arithmetic, string manipulation) twice as fast as 32-bit processors. To further enhance performance, the PowerPC architecture supports extensions that let it load and store four registers (i.e., 256 bits) in a single CPU clock cycle.

Specialized I/O Processors

To complete this discussion of key factors that enhance AS/400 performance, let me restate what I wrote in Chapter 1 about the AS/400's I/O system. The AS/400 uses specialized, dedicated I/O processors to offload tasks that CPUs traditionally perform. I/O operations, which occur each time the machine communicates with a hardware component such as a disk device or workstation, are one of the most common functions the AS/400 performs. Attached via high-speed, laser-driven fiber-optic buses, AS/400 I/O processors also are responsible for managing printers, communications devices, optical libraries, and the like. The AS/400 supports up to 19 fiber-optic I/O buses. By offloading data-handling tasks from the CPU, the AS/400's I/O system has a truly dramatic impact on system performance.

In data-warehousing applications, I/O operations enable propagation programs to quickly write vast amounts of information to data-warehouse repositories. Similarly, I/O also lets queries retrieve information from data warehouses in a timely manner. Figure 7.7 features an overview of the AS/400 I/O system.

FIGURE 7.7
I/O System Architecture

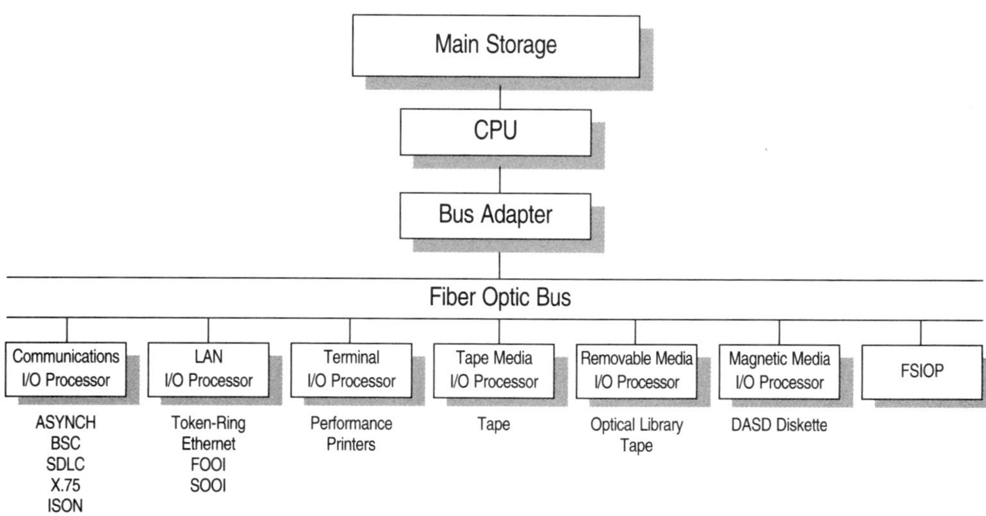

In many ways, AS/400 performance is also intimately related to the scalability and functionality of DB2/400. Let's look more specifically at DB2/400, so you can learn how it enhances query and overall system performance.

DATABASE SCALABILITY AND FUNCTIONALITY

As I noted in Chapter 1, data warehouses employ schema that support intuitive access to information, unlike OLTP applications that feature highly normalized databases. For this reason, OLTP data is typically decoded and denormalized as it is transformed and moved to a data warehouse. In addition, data warehouses often store data gathered from more than one operational system. For these reasons, data warehouses tend to grow quickly, causing database scalability and functionality to take on added significance.

Generally speaking, *scalability* refers to a platform's ability to support growth without requiring substantial modifications to applications. In this light, scalability can describe a platform's capacity to manage an increasing number of transactions, an increasing number of users, an increasing number of devices, and so on. We have already seen that the AS/400 is highly scalable in terms of processing power. Processors can be added as needed to boost performance without changing applications. If need be, up to 32 separate AS/400s also can be linked together to harness the collective processing power of their CPUs. And although this requires DB2 Multisystem for OS/400, existing applications remain unchanged.

In terms of database scalability, the AS/400 is equally impressive. As I discussed in Chapter 1, every AS/400 ships with DB2/400, an industrial-strength, feature-rich, highly scalable relational database that is exceptionally well-suited for data warehousing. Unlike databases such as Oracle, Sybase, and Informix, DB2/400 does not reside on top of an operating system but is tightly integrated with OS/400 and virtually every other major component of the AS/400. Because of this seamless integration, the AS/400 itself manages DB2/400. As long as enough storage is available, a DB2/400 database can grow without IT intervention or changes to applications.

Theoretically, a DB2/400 database can expand to well over 18 million terabytes and still be directly addressed by the system. In practical terms, however, there is a limit to the size of a DB2/400 database. With V4R1, the maximum capacity of a single AS/400 server has been doubled to 1 TB and is expected to increase again in 1998. A single physical file can now hold more than 2 billion records and grow to 248 GB in size. (And as I already mentioned, DB2 Multisystem for OS/400 lets up to 32 AS/400 servers be linked together to support 32 TB of data.) In such an environment, DB2 Multisystem automatically partitions files and spreads them evenly across every machine in a cluster. We can think of this as disk striping across multiple machines. DB2/400 (in conjunction with OS/400) manages partitioning, which is completely transparent to IT personnel. Alternatively, DB2 Multisystem lets us explicitly partition files across multiple machines based on single-field or multi-field keys. By assigning different key values to different machines, we can specify which rows (i.e., records) are stored on particular servers.

In addition to expanding the physical capacity of DB2/400 databases, partitioning lets database operations occur in parallel. For example, DB2 Multisystem lets queries perform insert, update, and delete operations simultaneously on the same file — an extremely advanced parallel-processing function that many other databases do not support. One use for this feature is obvious: Loading data into a data warehouse is a time-consuming process that must be completed in a specific, and often limited, time period (i.e., overnight or during a weekend). Propagation routines that run beyond their allotted processing windows have undermined many data-warehousing projects. DB2 Multisystem and its parallel-processing capabilities can support propagation procedures that move tens of millions of records per hour to AS/400 data warehouses.

Now that we know a single AS/400 can support a 1 TB warehouse and a loosely coupled cluster of AS/400s can support a 32 TB warehouse, let's put these figures into perspective. Sears, the U.S. retailing giant, maintains approximately 4 TB of data in its data warehouse. Unlike Sears, most organizations do not have hundreds of stores, thousands of products, and more than $25 billion in annual revenue. Most organizations are not nearly that large in terms of revenue, locations, or products; and despite the hype surrounding terabyte scalability, few companies will ever require a data warehouse of this magnitude. Figure 7.8, based on research by the META Group, shows the average data-warehouse needs of business by industry. In fact, the needs of most businesses will not exceed the capacity offered by a 150 GB data warehouse. However, it's comforting to know that DB2/400 can capably scale from today's 1 MB data mart to tomorrow's multiple-terabyte data warehouse.

In addition to terabyte scalability, DB2/400 supports a predictive query governor, numerous data-access methods, a query optimizer, and Internet connectivity. Let's examine these facilities — all of which enhance the AS/400 as a data-warehouse server — more closely.

Predictive Query Governor

Unlike query governors in other database products, DB2 for OS/400 Predictive Query Governor can prevent the initiation of a query if it determines that the query's runtime will exceed a specified time limit. Other query governors typically stop a query only *after* a query has run longer than a specified period of time; this non-predictive approach wastes resources because queries can consume significant resources — only to be cancelled.

The AS/400's Predictive Query Governor works closely with the DB2 Query Optimizer to determine whether a query will run beyond a specified time limit. This process occurs in several steps. First, the optimizer examines the query-access plan (an access plan is an AS/400 control structure that describes the

FIGURE 7.8
Data Warehouse Comparison Across Industries

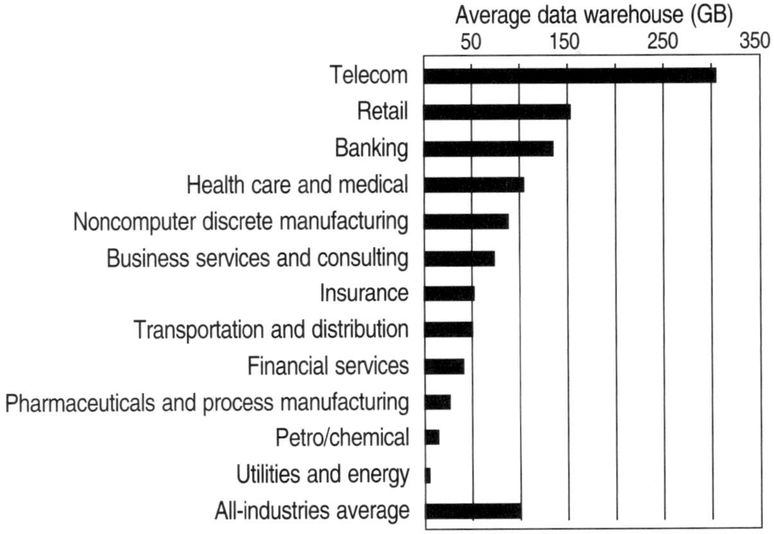

Used with permission of the META Group

actions necessary to satisfy a given query request). As part of this process, the optimizer estimates the query's runtime. Next, it compares the estimated runtime to the specified time limit. If the predicted runtime is less than or equal to the time limit, then the system executes the query. However, if the estimated runtime exceeds the query limit, then a message is sent to the user (for interactive jobs) stating that the query's estimated runtime exceeds the specified time limit. The message, CPA4259, includes the estimated runtime and specified time limit, both in seconds. The user receiving the reply may choose to run or cancel the query (when CPA4529 is sent in batch, the default reply is taken). You can specify the time limit only through the QRYTIMLMT parameter of the CHGQRYA CL command; you cannot use SQL statements to support this function. The syntax for this command is

```
CHGQRYA JOB(999999/USERNAME/JOBNAME) QRYTIMLMT(Number of seconds)
```

In addition to preventing long-running queries from degrading system performance, the Predictive Query Governor also can help you design optimized queries. For example, suppose that you'd like to create a query to perform a given function. You will want to build the most efficient query possible, especially if the query is accessing considerable volumes of data. If you specify a time limit of zero, then the query governor always responds with message CPA4529, which states that the query's runtime will exceed the specified time limit of zero. If you respond with an C (Cancel), the query job will terminate and the Query Optimizer sends tuning messages to the query's job log. You can then examine the job log for guidance in tuning the query. After reviewing the job log, you can adjust the query and repeat the process. In this way, you can design the most efficient query for a given task without ever running a query.

Multiple Data-Access Methods

In conjunction with the AS/400's Licensed Internal Code (LIC), DB2/400 supports a wide variety of data-access methods. LIC is the portion of OS/400 code that operates beneath the AS/400's machine interface (MI). By supporting up to 11 different data-management algorithms, DB2/400 and LIC offer queries a variety of data-access techniques, each tailored to a different situation. DB2/400 Query Optimizer automatically selects the data-access techniques based on its analysis of the query constructs, target data, and overall AS/400 environment (I examine DB2/400 Query Optimizer in more detail in the next section). Now let's look at detailed descriptions of the 11 data-access methods DB2/400 and LIC support, access methods that in turn support the query-intensive workload of data warehouses.

1. *The dataspace scan method.* A *dataspace* is an internal AS/400 object that contains the data in a table. When you use database scan to retrieve data from a table, every row in the table is examined and compared to the selection criteria, and only those rows that match the selection criteria are returned to the calling SQL program or query. Because this method processes every row in a given page, once a page is loaded into memory, that page never needs to be retrieved from disk again. This method minimizes the number of required page I/O operations and thereby enhances performance. Also, because the AS/400's database manager reads every row in a table with this process, the database manager can pre-fetch pages. With pre-fetching, pages are moved from disk to main memory asynchronously, so you can retrieve pages from main memory as soon as processes require access to their contents. As you learned earlier in the chapter, operations that access main memory are much faster than operations that access disk.

   The dataspace scan method is most effective when more than 20 percent of the rows in a table is selected, because every row that fails to meet the selection criteria is still processed. The dataspace scan method also processes deleted records that have not been removed from tables, so be sure that all physical file members this technique accesses are reorganized before you execute the query. You can use the RGZPFM (Reorganize Physical File Member) CL command to remove deleted records.

Alternatively, you can change the REUSEDLT parameter associated with physical files to *YES to free any space allocated to deleted records.

2. *The parallel pre-fetch access method.* This technique is similar to the dataspace scan method, except that it performs I/O processing in parallel. To accomplish this, multiple input streams simultaneously access multiple disk devices to retrieve data from a table. Because this method uses I/O parallel processing, you must initialize the system value QQRYDEGREE or the DEGREE parameter on the CHGQRYA command to allow parallel I/O processing. Otherwise, the query optimizer cannot select the parallel pre-fetch access method. This technique works best when the queried table is spread across multiple disks, when the query is not CPU-intensive, and when there is ample main memory to cache the retrieved data. Generally speaking, 1 MB of main memory also should be available for each input data stream.
3. *The parallel dataspace scan method.* Like the previous technique, this data-access method reduces I/O processing time through parallel pre-fetching. In addition, this method can decompose the dataspace scan processing into discrete tasks that can run in parallel on separate CPUs. Task results are then moved to result buffers, ideally in main memory, and later combined. The parallel dataspace scan method can dramatically reduce query execution times.

   To use the parallel dataspace scan technique, you must have DB2 Symmetric Multiprocessing for OS/400 installed on the system. Furthermore, the query optimizer must be able to select SMP parallel processing through appropriate QQRYDEGREE and/or DEGREE settings. This data-access method is most effective when data is spread across multiple disk devices, when multiple CPUs are available, and when ample storage exists to hold data and results buffers.
4. *The key-selection access method.* Unlike the previous techniques, this method of retrieving data from tables via an index requires keyed-sequence access paths. One example of a DB2/400 structure that generates keyed-sequence access paths is a logical file. Queries that employ the key-selection method read the entire table index from start to end and evaluate any selection criteria that involve key fields. The key-selection method is very efficient when the selection criteria apply mostly to indexed fields, because it accesses the dataspace to retrieve only the rows that meet the selection criteria. Selection criteria that refer to fields outside the index require dataspace data-access operations.

   Query Optimizer chooses the key-selection access method when the query is to retrieve less than 20 percent of the unique key values. This is because every unique key selected from the index results in a random I/O to the dataspace, which is an expensive use of resources. The optimizer also chooses this method if an ORDER BY, GROUP BY, or JOIN operation explicitly directs it to do so.

5. *The parallel key-selection access method.* The parallel key-selection access technique enables parallel processing by first partitioning the possible key values of the index. A separate task on a separate processor then processes each logical partition. In most cases, the tasks will not complete at the same time. When they don't, the parallel key-selection method can further divide partitions that have not yet been processed, maximizing CPU use. As with the parallel dataspace scan method, DB2 Symmetric Multiprocessing for OS/400 must be installed before you can use this method. Similarly, you must ensure the appropriate QQRYDEGREE and/or DEGREE settings so Query Optimizer can select SMP parallel processing. This method is most effective when multiple CPUs and ample main memory are available.
6. *The key-positioning access method.* Like the key-selection access method, this technique requires a keyed-sequence access path. Unlike that method, however, the key-positioning technique processes an index by examining one or more ranges of key values that meet all or some of the selection criteria. All keys in all ranges are read, after which any remaining key selection occurs at the dataspace level. Because it processes fewer rows, the key-positioning method's performance is superior to that of the key-selection method.
7. *The parallel key-positioning access method.* This technique is similar to the key-positioning access method, except that with this method separate tasks executing simultaneously process key ranges. As is the case with all forms of Symmetric Multiprocessing on the AS/400, the query optimizer determines the number of concurrent tasks. If processing capacity is available and no ranges are queued for processing, the system partitions ranges that are being processed. Then, to keep available tasks busy, the tasks process newly created ranges. DB2 Symmetric Multiprocessing for OS/400 must be installed before you can use parallel key positioning. Similarly, you again must ensure the appropriate QQRYDEGREE and/or DEGREE settings so the query optimizer can select SMP parallel processing.
8. *The index-only access method.* You can use this technique in conjunction with any key-selection or key-positioning access method. The primary difference is that the index-only technique causes data to be extracted from the index rather than via a random I/O operation to the dataspace. DB2 Symmetric Multiprocessing for OS/400 must be installed before the system can do index-only processing, and you must ensure that the settings are such that Query Optimizer can select SMP parallel processing. With the release of V4R1, the AS/400 can now use multiple processors at the same time to create or rebuild an index. This functionality provides a considerable

performance boost for ROLAP-based data warehouses, which by design feature many indexes. Parallel indexing on the AS/400 requires DB2 Symmetric Multiprocessing for OS/400.

9. *The parallel-table- or parallel-index-preload access method.* You can use this method with any data-access method to reduce random I/O operations to disk devices. This approach loads table- or index-based data into active memory in parallel (an example of parallel pre-fetching). After the data has been cached in memory, data access can occur without any disk-device I/O operations. The preload process begins as soon as a query is opened, but process control returns to the application before the preload process ends. This lets the application use other access methods independent of the preload processing to fetch rows.
10. *The index-from-index access method.* Using this method, the AS/400's database manager builds a temporary index containing entries for rows that meet the selection criteria. The source of the temporary index is a permanent index. The temporary index is analogous in function to a logical file using select/omit statements; it is built through key positioning on the existing index. Because the temporary index contains entries in the desired sequence for rows that match the selection criteria, access to data via the temporary index is very efficient. Unfortunately, other queries cannot share the temporary index. A potential drawback to this access method is that temporary index creation may require considerable overhead.
11. *The hashing access method.* The AS/400 can also use hashing to access rows in tables. Consider a table that contains a column for last names. With hashing, a formula is applied to these names to derive a unique numeric value for each name; that value is then placed into a structure known as a hash table. To access rows in the table using last names, the formula is applied to the particular last name specified in a query. The resulting hash value for the name provides the exact key to the desired row.

    During the creation of the hash table, every row in a table is scanned only one time, which results in more efficient data access. Furthermore, the hashing access method moves all relevant data from the data space to the hash table so the data does not have to be paged into memory again. DB2/400's hashing algorithm is designed for use by queries that must process data in a grouped (i.e., GROUP BY) or correlated (i.e., JOIN) format; hashing can complement, and in some cases replace, keyed-sequence access paths.

    Because the hash method that DB2/400 employs typically processes rows sequentially, the AS/400's database manager can predict the order of the database-table memory pages needed to process the query. This capability lets the database manager prefetch these pages for efficient I/O functionality and therefore better query performance.

Because it supports such a wide variety of data-access methods, DB2/400 supports the efficient execution of SQL programs and queries. Each access technique is custom tailored to meet the processing needs for queries in a wide range of circumstances. And because data warehousing is query-intensive, it benefits significantly from this variety of data-access techniques.

DB2/400 Query Optimizer

We use queries to retrieve data from DB2/400. And although queries specifically describe what data we are looking for, they do not tell the AS/400 how to access that data. The query-intensive nature of data warehousing makes efficient query-handling an essential server requirement. On the AS/400, this task is left to DB2/400 Query Optimizer, which automatically identifies the most efficient data-access method for a given query using the following processes:

- *Cost Estimation.* During this phase, Query Optimizer evaluates both the query and the current state of the target database. It then calculates implementation costs for all data-access methods that can execute the query. In particular, the optimizer evaluates costs based on these access methods: reading rows directly from the table via database scan, reading rows via an access path using either key selection or key positioning, creating a new access path directly from the dataspace, creating a temporary access path from an existing access path, and finally, using hashing or DB2/400's query sort routine. Query Optimizer evaluates a method only if it meets the necessary conditions that the various DB2/400 data-access methods might require, as I noted above.

  Five components make up the estimated cost of each data-access method, including the start-up cost, the optimization-mode cost, the cost of any access-path builds, the cost of the expected number of page faults that will occur while rows are being read, and the cost of processing the expected number of rows.

  To determine the optimization-mode cost, we can direct the query optimizer toward one of two possible optimization goals: to minimize the time required to retrieve the first buffer of rows from the table, or to minimize the time to run the query assuming that all rows are returned to the calling application. We can specify these optimization goals using the precompile option ALWCPYDTA and the OPTIMIZE FOR *n* ROWS clause.

  Query Optimizer computes the estimated cost of page faults and row processing based on statistics such as table size, row size, index size, and key size. In estimating these costs, the optimizer also considers the impact of each access method and the impact of any relational operators that predicate row selection.

- *Access Plan Validation.* Once it has computed the costs associated with each applicable data-access method, Query Optimizer validates the access plan, which is a set of internal structures that tell SQL how to run an embedded SQL statement most efficiently. Access plans contain information about data and the steps required to extract that data. To determine the best data-access method for the query at hand, the optimizer follows a general set of rules based on various combinations of filters, data-access methods, and indexes.
- *Join and Grouping Operation Optimization.* Query Optimizer also has facilities to optimize both join and grouping operations. For details about these optimization techniques, refer to Chapter 23 of IBM's *DB2 for OS/400 SQL Programming* guide (SC4611-01).

DB2/400 Query Optimizer is an extremely powerful facility that can dramatically enhance the performance of AS/400-based data warehouses. Anytime that APIs, ODBC, Query/400, and the OPNQRYF command access DB2/400, optimization becomes a critical factor. Figure 7.9 represents a high-level schematic of Query Optimizer's interaction with these facilities and DB2/400.

FIGURE 7.9
DB2/400 Query Optimizer

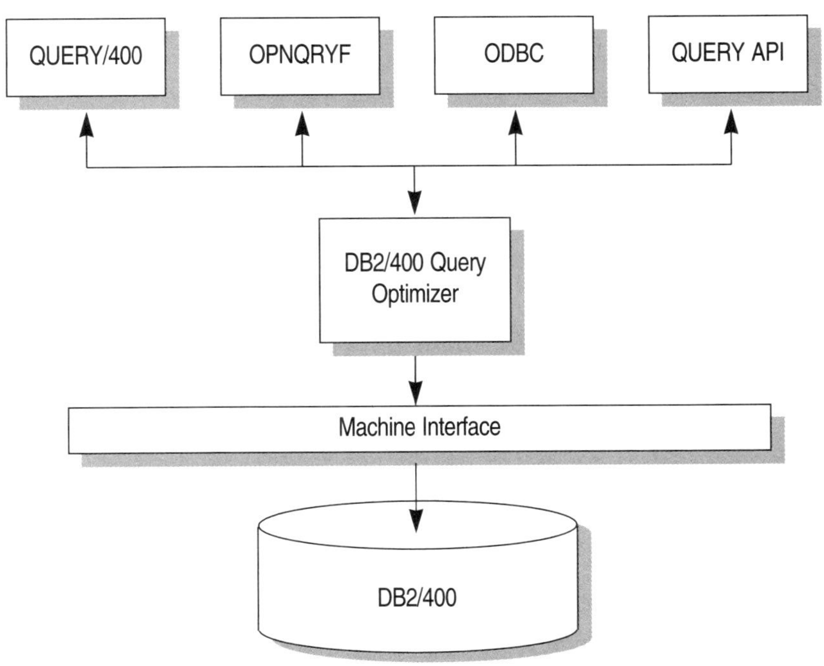

Internet Connectivity

The Internet provides end users with cost-effective access to data located anywhere in the world. To leverage this economical communications infrastructure, the AS/400's Net.Data facility lets remote Web browsers economically access DB2/400 databases. The successor to DB2 WWW, Net.Data directly supports the creation of Web pages that access DB2/400. To use this facility, you must have Internet Connection for AS/400 installed on your AS/400-based data-warehouse server. Internet Connection, which features a host of additional Internet-related facilities, is a no-charge, optional feature of OS/400. Figure 7.10 details the interaction of Net.Data and the Internet in a data-warehousing environment.

FIGURE 7.10
AS/400 Data Warehousing and the Internet

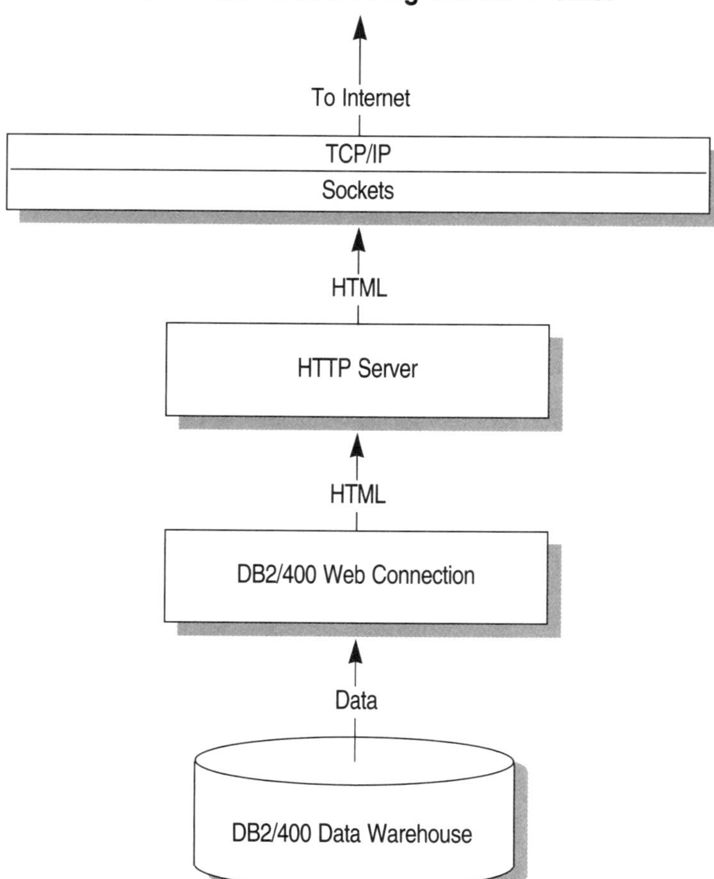

This look at DB2/400 demonstrates that AS/400 servers can easily accommodate large-scale, multiple-terabyte data warehouses. It also shows how the database itself enhances query performance through the use of Predictive Query Governor, advanced data-access methods, and Query Optimizer. Finally, additional DB2/400 facilities support application development, database integrity, and open access via the Internet. All these factors help explain why so many businesses rely on DB2/400 for data warehousing.

Openness

As I discussed in Chapter 1, in a corporate arena where many companies have grown through mergers and acquisitions, data-warehouse servers must be able to connect to and exchange data with a variety of platforms and databases. This functionality is especially critical for organizations that manage infrastructures featuring mainframes, midrange machines, local- and wide-area networks, and powerful workstations. Unfortunately, many such infrastructures include machines from different manufacturers (e.g., IBM, Digital, Hewlett-Packard, Amdahl) and databases from different vendors (e.g., IBM, Sybase, Oracle, Informix, Microsoft). To perform transformational replication in heterogeneous environments, data-warehouse servers must support a wide variety of data-access standards and communications protocols.

The AS/400, through a combination of middleware and database functionality, supports a wide variety of data-access standards and communications protocols. For instance, the AS/400 supports Transmission Control Protocol/ Internet Protocol (TCP/IP), including dynamic routing; Advanced Program-to-Program Communication (APPC); Advanced Peer-to-Peer Networking (APPN); IBM's Distributed Relational Database Architecture (DRDA2); Microsoft's Open Database Connectivity (ODBC); Apple's Data Access Language (DAL); the X/Open Structured Query Language (SQL) Call Level Interface (CLI); and Structured Query Language (SQL) specifications, including ANSI, ISO, and FIPS. The AS/400 also provides Portable Operating Systems Interface for Computing Evironments (POSIX)-compliant operating system services for Unix application vendors. Furthermore, the AS/400 supports transmission protocols such as ANSI X3.135.1992, ISO 9075-1992, and FIPS 127-2 SQL.

In addition to these standards, numerous software applications are available to exploit the AS/400's open capabilities, including transformational replication tools such as IBM's DataPropagator, and DataMirror's Transformation Server.

Extensibility

As I defined it in Chapter 1, extensibility is a platform's ability to accommodate technological advances without disrupting application functionality or necessitating costly upgrades — an important consideration for any server. Data-warehouse servers must protect today's investment as they use tomorrow's technology. As we shall see, the AS/400 is a highly extensible machine.

As I discussed earlier, extensibility is rooted in the AS/400's high-level, technology-independent MI. The MI itself is actually a set of APIs that provides the only way to communicate with AS/400 hardware, as well as some system software. As new technologies come along, additional APIs can be added to the MI. Figure 7.11 provides a high-level view of the MI.

FIGURE 7.11
The Machine Interface (MI)

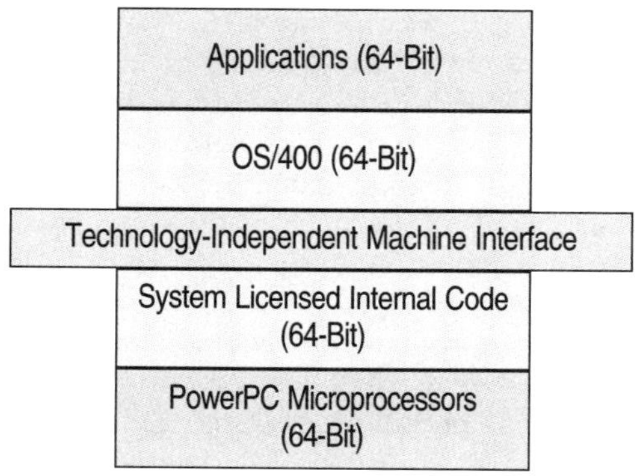

Unlike conventional machine interfaces, the AS/400 MI architecture is not bound to underlying hardware. Largely because of this technology-independent MI, AS/400 customers have never experienced disruptions such as those DOS users have dealt with moving to 32-bit applications. For example, the AS/400 has supported a relatively smooth, painless migration from CISC-based to RISC-based technology. To highlight its extensibility, let's examine how the AS/400 automatically converts a program written on an older CISC-based machine for use on a newer RISC-based model.

When the AS/400 compiles source code, it first creates an intermediate object called a program template, which it then converts into an executable binary object. Unless explicitly deleted, these templates remain with the executable binary objects. Because the format of the program template is dependent upon the MI, and the MI is *not* dependent upon underlying hardware, by deduction, the program template is *not* dependent upon hardware. When applications from a CISC-based AS/400 are transferred to a RISC-based machine, the new machine automatically retranslates the program templates the first time the programs execute. The result is 64-bit binaries optimized for the PowerPC processor. Because of the one-time translation process, users may notice that applications run more slowly the first time they are called on the RISC machine. But this one-time delay is a small price to pay for converting programs to native 64-bit applications.

Because of its technology-independent machine interface, the AS/400 lets existing applications exploit new technology without the need to ever rewrite them. In other words, the AS/400 provides a non-disruptive growth path to the future — a comforting fact for those who invest time and money in AS/400 data warehouses.

Application and Vendor Support

AS/400 performance and functionality are of little consequence if we cannot deliver their benefits to the businesses that use the system. To that end, the AS/400 supports a wide variety of application development languages, including RPG, Cobol, SQL, C++, Java, Smalltalk, and REXX — languages that several thousand software vendors, including independent software vendors (ISVs), have already used to create nearly 30,000 applications.

My focus in the remaining chapters of this book is on 10 applications that have made AS/400 data warehousing a success.

Conclusion

You may notice that common threads run through much of my discussion of the AS/400's components in this chapter. For example, DB2/400 appears in sections regarding parallel processing, data-access methods, the Internet, and scalability. This is because of one of the AS/400's traditional strengths: its integrated nature. No other platform features such a seamless architecture. At the same time, the AS/400 is an open system the effectively supports heterogeneous processing environments.

I also looked at the AS/400 as a data-warehousing server in terms of other key criteria such as performance, scalability, functionality, extensibility, and application support. Its capabilities in these areas account for the AS/400's current status and long-term potential as a highly effective data-warehousing platform.

INTRODUCTION TO SECTION II

Many independent software vendors are actively developing data-warehousing software for the AS/400. Among these many vendors are the following leading companies: Advanced Systems Concepts, Inc., Angoss Software Corporation, Brio Technology, Inc., Business Objects S.A., Carleton Corporation (now part of Apertus Technologies), Coglin Mill Pty. Ltd., Cognos Incorporated, DataMirror Corporation, Datawatch Corporation, Evolutionary Technologies International, Inc., Ferguson Information Systems, Inc., IBM Corporation, Lakeview Technologies, Inc., Logic Works, Inc., Micro-Strategy, Inc., NewGeneration Software, Inc., Olympic amis Ltd., SAMAC, Inc., ShowCase Corporation, Silvon Software, Inc., and Vision Solutions, Inc.

While it is not possible to examine all these vendors' products in detail in the space of this book, an in-depth examination of several leading products can give you a representative idea of the kind and extent of products that are available. In Chapters 8 through 17, I examine comprehensive data-warehousing solutions as well as some tools designed for specific data-warehousing functions. The following companies and products are featured in these chapters:

Company	**Product(s)**
Advanced Systems Concepts, Inc.	SEQUEL
Coglin Mill Pty. Ltd.	RODIN
DataMirror Corporation	Transformation Server for AS/400
Datawatch Corporation	Monarch
Ferguson Information Systems, Inc.	InfoManager
IBM Corporation	DataPropagator Relational Capture and Apply (DPropR/400)
IBM Corporation	Intelligent Miner for AS/400
Olympic amis Ltd.	amis Information Server Suite
ShowCase Corporation	STRATEGY
Silvon Software, Inc.	DataTracker

Using a combination of screen images and text, I have designed the chapters to provide a solid overview of the profiled companies and their products — not to serve as detailed, how-to manuals. Bear in mind that, as always, the most effective way to evaluate products is to use them on a trial basis if you can. In other words, don't let these chapters dissuade you from gaining hands-on experience or seeking customer testimonials.

My decision to exclude certain products from the book was a very difficult one because, without exception, all the companies listed above develop fine software products. But as I said, I simply could not include all of them in the space of this book! I have chosen 10 products as a *representative* sample of available software for the AS/400 data-warehouse market.

To add an element of consistency to these chapters, I use the following example whenever possible to highlight each product's capabilities (To be sure, the example is very simple, and each product can make short work of it.) For each use of this example, assume that the following files are a portion of a normalized sales database. These files contain OLTP data that is to be extracted, transformed, and propagated to a ROLAP-based warehouse repository that end users will analyze. The sample OLTP file layouts for an invoice header, invoice detail, and SKU (product) table file are as follows:

IN001PF (Invoice Header File):

Field Name	Description	Type	Size
INVNUM	Invoice Number	Numeric	6,0
CUSTID	Customer Number	Numeric	9,0
INVMON	Invoice Month	Numeric	2,0
INVDAY	Invoice Day	Numeric	2,0
INVYR	Invoice Year	Numeric	2,0

IN002PF (Invoice Detail File):

Field Name	Description	Type	Size
INVNUM	Invoice Number	Numeric	6,0
ITMNUM	Item Number	Numeric	3,0
SKUID	Product ID Code	Numeric	6,0
INVQTY	Invoice Quantity	Numeric	9,0
UNTPRC	Unit Price	Numeric	6,2

TA001PF (SKU/Product Table):

Field Name	Description	Type	Size
SKUID	Product ID Code	Numeric	6,0
PRDNAM	Product Name	Alpha	10

PRDDSC	Product Description	Alpha	35
PRDCOL	Product Color Code	Alpha	2
PRDSIZ	Product Size Code	Alpha	2
PRDGRP	Product Group Code	Alpha	3
PRDMAT	Product Materials Code	Alpha	3

The transformed transaction-level sales information will first be written to a simple fact table and an associated product-dimension table that comprise part of a larger ROLAP database. You can assume that the fact table and the product dimension table have already been created and are related via a join-logical file. The detailed specifications for the fact and dimension tables follow below.

FACTPF (Sales Fact Table):

Field Name	Description	Type	Size
SKUID	Product ID Code	Numeric	6,0
CUSTID	Customer Number	Numeric	9,0
TIMEID	Time Period ID	Numeric	8,0
INVQTY	Invoice Quantity	Numeric	9,0
INVVAL	Invoice Value	Numeric	11,2

PRODPF (Product Dimension Table):

Field Name	Description	Type	Size
SKUID	Product ID Code	Numeric	6,0
PRDNAM	Product Name	Alpha	10
COLOR	Product Color	Alpha	15
SIZE	Product Size	Alpha	12
GROUP	Product Group	Alpha	25
MATRL	Product Material	Alpha	15

In the following chapters, I explore each product as it is used to perform several tasks based on the product's intended functionality. These tasks include

1. Joining the invoice files by the field INVNUM, and summarizing invoice quantity and sales revenue by SKU.
2. Remapping the field PRDCOL as follows: BL=Blue, BR=Brown,YL=Yellow, BK=Black, WH=White, OR=Orange, RD=Red, GR=Green, and GY=Gray.
3. Writing data to the fact table and dimension table.

4. Designing queries to extract total volume and revenue figures by SKUID.
5. Displaying query results in a table view, as follows:

SKU #	Product Name	Color	Size	Qty Sold	Revenue
102030	RAINCOAT	BROWN	LARGE	43	$4,300
102031	RAINCOAT	BROWN	MEDIUM	10	$1,000
102032	RAINCOAT	BLUE	LARGE	15	$1,500
102033	RAINCOAT	GRAY	SMALL	5	$ 500
103000	UMBRELLA	BLACK	SMALL	12	$ 120
103002	UMBRELLA	RED	SMALL	5	$ 50
103004	UMBRELLA	BLUE	SMALL	23	$ 230
104000	HAT	BLUE	MEDIUM	15	$ 150
104001	HAT	BLACK	X LARGE	10	$ 100
104004	HAT	GRAY	LARGE	22	$ 220
104006	HAT	GRAY	SMALL	5	$ 50
104007	HAT	BROWN	SMALL	16	$ 160
104009	HAT	BROWN	MEDIUM	9	$ 90
105000	BOOTS	BLACK	SMALL	12	$ 600
105001	BOOTS	BLACK	MEDIUM	15	$ 750
105002	BOOTS	BLACK	LARGE	17	$ 850
105003	BOOTS	BLACK	X LARGE	10	$ 500

6. Summarizing and displaying query results by product name in a table (see below) and via graphs and charts.

Product Name	Qty Sold	Revenue
BOOTS	54	2,700.00
HAT	77	770.00
RAINCOAT	73	7,300.00
UMBRELLA	40	400.00

Creating cross-tabular views of sales data, as follows:

	Small	**Medium**	**Large**	**X Large**	**Total**
BOOTS	12	15	17	10	54
HAT	21	24	22	10	77
RAINCOAT	5	10	58	0	73
UMBRELLA	40	0	0	0	40
TOTAL	**78**	**49**	**97**	**20**	**244**

Before we move on to the next section of this book, bear in mind that several of the following products (e.g., Coglin Mill's RODIN, DataMirror's Transformation Server, and IBM's DataPropagator) focus on the extraction, transformation, and propagation of data for data warehouses. Functions such as graphing and charting are beyond the intended purpose of these products. Datawatch Corporation's Monarch, another component product for data-warehousing, focuses on the extraction, transformation, analysis, and propagation of report-based data.

Chapter 8

Advanced Systems Concepts, Inc. and SEQUEL

Company Background

Founded in late 1982, Advanced Systems Concepts, Inc. (ASC), was one of the first productivity-tool developers to focus on the IBM midrange market. Since then, the company's product line has grown to include six AS/400-based products and one PC-based product, including PILOT, a job scheduler; ABSTRACT/PROBE, a documentation and cross-reference tool; STATUS, a resource-tracking and chargeback package; Report Edit Utility (REU), a printer-file-creation tool; Century UpDate, a year-2000 conversion tool; SEQUEL, a data-extraction, transformation, and analysis product; and SEQUEL Viewpoint, an optional PC-based front-end module for SEQUEL.

Privately held ASC is headquartered in Schaumburg, Illinois, where it manages North American sales and product support. The company has approximately 30 employees, and more than 20 distributors and 5,500 customers worldwide. SEQUEL is installed at more than 2,500 customer sites. Recently, ASC entered into a joint marketing and reseller agreement with Brio Technology, Inc., of Palo Alto, California. Under terms of the agreement, ASC offers Brio's BrioQuery as a front-end OLAP tool for SEQUEL-built data warehouses. I'll discuss the synergy of these products later in the chapter.

Product Overview

First offered in 1987 as an alternative to Query and SQL, SEQUEL has evolved into a modular application suite with broad applicability in AS/400-based data warehousing. The product's key strength lies in its ability to access, extract, and transform normalized data stored in operational DB2/400 databases. SEQUEL does not provide support for databases such as Oracle, Sybase, Informix, or SQL Server. SEQUEL features command-driven statements that are syntactically similar to, but more powerful than, standard SQL/400. For example, you can use SEQUEL to update physical files through SEQUEL's exclusive join-update capability. Through its high-level data-manipulation commands, SEQUEL lets programmers quickly and easily access, update, and derive data. This functionality has led to its use as a data-extraction, transformation, and propagation tool for AS/400-based data warehousing.

SEQUEL consists of six native AS/400 components: Kernel, the product's data-access and data-manipulation module; User Interface, a menu-driven, OS/400-based interface for Kernel; Report Writer, a report-generation module;

Tabling, a data-aggregation tool; Charting, a Graphical Data Display Module (GDDM)-based graphing tool; and Auditing, a resource-usage monitor. In addition to these native AS/400 modules, ASC also offers SEQUEL Viewpoint to its customers as an optional SEQUEL component. Available in both 16- and 32-bit versions, Viewpoint provides SEQUEL users with a graphical front-end through which SEQUEL functions are available. In addition, Viewpoint features GUI-based analytic and charting capabilities. Written in Visual Basic, Viewpoint can be used offline to analyze AS/400-based data that has been downloaded to PCs.

In the remainder of this chapter, I examine each module of SEQUEL, as well as Viewpoint, in more detail. Once you've become familiar with these tools, we explore their capabilities through our implementation example. Finally, I examine these products' limitations and strengths relative to data warehousing. During these discussions, I also examine the significance of ASC's recent agreement with Brio Technology, Inc.

Kernel

Kernel is the foundation upon which SEQUEL resides. Designed for IT personnel and advanced end users, Kernel provides a means to flexibly extract, transform, propagate, and analyze AS/400 data. This module serves a dual purpose in data warehousing: 1) it can extract, transform, and write OLTP data to a data warehouse and 2) it can access and manipulate information already stored in a data warehouse.

Kernel can filter DB2/400 data by column (field) and by row (record), and it can join up to 32 physical files. Kernel queries can include multilevel control breaks, aggregate functions (sum, average, minimum, maximum, count), and interactive runtime prompts that can be used to dynamically prompt for input parameters such as customer numbers and date ranges. Through its support of numerous mathematical, date, and substring functions, Kernel also can update field content, change field names, reformat field sizes, translate field values, modify field types, and derive entirely new fields.

In addition to Kernel's extensive data-manipulation capabilities, Kernel-written queries support runtime substitution variables, or parameters, that can be passed from one query to another and that let end users drill up and down through successive layers of data. SEQUEL's user-defined options also can execute OS/400 and user-written commands, as well as application programs. The product respects existing OS/400 object authority and also provides additional library-, file-, and field-level security for both user and group profiles.

User Interface

User Interface provides you with a means to design and execute Sequel queries. To enhance ease-of-use, this module features cursor-sensitive Help, pop-up windows, pull-down menus, a search index, and multilevel hypertext.

New and experienced IT personnel alike can work under one of three chosen assistance levels:

- Basic assistance guides inexperienced users through every step of query construction, including file selection, file-join specifications, field selection, field calculations, record selection, and the like.
- Intermediate assistance presents users with a Source Entry Utility (SEU)-like edit screen and a list of callable prompt screens. This level of Help also supports cut-and-paste, copy, split, mark, and undo editing operations.
- Advanced assistance lets experienced users create and modify queries via a full-screen editor. With this module, users can direct query output to the screen, to formatted report files, to physical files (e.g., in a ROLAP-based data warehouse), and to shared PC folders in dBASE, Excel, Lotus 1-2-3, ASCII, delimited, or merged-text formats.

Report Writer

SEQUEL's Report Writer, which is tightly integrated with Kernel and User Interface, lets IT personnel design AS/400-based reports without programming. End users typically run these reports to retrieve information already stored in warehouse repositories. Report Writer features an on-screen WYSIWYG report painter similar in function to the AS/400 Screen Design Aid (SDA). The product also supports conditional calculations, multilevel subtotals, predefined report templates, runtime prompting, and multilevel sorts. Report Writer is an effective tool for designing simple and complex greenbar reports. Because it is a character-based product, however, Report Writer is not suitable for document-oriented reporting (e.g., text integrated with tables, logos, charts, and other graphics).

The Tabling Module

Using SEQUEL's Tabling module, IT personnel can aggregate and reformat information for online displays, advanced reports, and PC downloads. Like Kernel, this component serves a dual purpose in data warehousing: 1) it can summarize OLTP data for propagation to a warehouse repository (e.g., a fact table), and 2) it can summarize granular information already stored in a data warehouse. Tabling supports conditional logic and mathematical calculations, and it is particularly well suited for rankings, percent of total, and other summary-based analytic models. Tabling's resultant data sets can be printed, viewed on-screen, saved as AS/400 physical files, or downloaded to PC folders in dBASE, Excel, Lotus 1-2-3, ASCII, delimited, or merged-text formats.

The Charting Module

Using SEQUEL's Charting module, IT personnel and end users alike can examine query results graphically on a PC or GDDM-capable color terminal (GDDM is IBM's native AS/400 graphing component). Users also can print graphs locally. The Charting component supports a wide variety of graphs, including line charts, bar charts, scatter diagrams, and pie charts. Tightly integrated with User Interface, the Charting module features a 5250-based actions editor that lets end users adjust axes, legends, tick labels, data labels, colors, margins, symbols, and data elements. This module also can display information from several queries on a single graph. In practice, most organizations that are interested in data warehousing rely on personal computers for viewing graphical information. Despite the effectiveness of the Charting module's 5250-based features, this component has limited appeal in data warehousing.

The Auditing Module

Designed to let you monitor AS/400 system performance, SEQUEL's Auditing Module provides a comprehensive set of inquiries and reports detailing both SEQUEL and system utilization. For SEQUEL jobs, the program tracks access-path usage, file usage, I/O operations, job attributes (number, name, start/end dates, start/end times, etc.), CPU usage, execution parameters, and additional runtime statistics. You can choose to create new aggregate tables or new indices (to improve performance) as a result of this information.

SEQUEL Viewpoint

Offered as an optional component for SEQUEL, Viewpoint lets users create and execute queries, as well as display and graph query results, in a Windows-based GUI environment. In this light, Viewpoint functions as the front-end companion to SEQUEL's back-end components. Through Viewpoint, users also can save query results in AS/400-based physical files or in PC-based spreadsheet, database, and text files such as Lotus 1-2-3, Excel, dBASE, comma-delimited, and the like. Using Viewpoint, you also can examine job logs, maintain library lists, and modify SEQUEL query statements.

In typical Viewpoint implementations, IT personnel create canned queries that end users later execute via icons. For example, a sales icon might execute a SEQUEL query that automatically presents its results on a three-dimensional bar chart. Alternatively, users can download query results directly to a spreadsheet file for further analysis. Advanced end users may also write their own SEQUEL queries.

Implementation Examples

Now that you have a basic understanding of SEQUEL and Viewpoint, let's explore their functionality using our implementation example. To do this most effectively, I have included numerous screen captures of these products as they would be used to perform our sample data-warehousing tasks. For simplicity, let's assume that the data warehouse resides on the same AS/400 as the OLTP database. (In cases where multiple AS/400s are deployed, SEQUEL's FROM clause supports the use of DDM files to copy data from one machine to another.)

In a typical SEQUEL implementation, we first use SEQUEL commands to create and link tables in the data warehouse. Bear in mind that SEQUEL itself does not provide you with a data-warehouse repository. It is a tool for building these repositories; you remain responsible for actually designing the data-warehouse schema. However, once they have been designed, these databases can be created and linked with views using standard SEQUEL commands. After this step is complete, we use SEQUEL to extract, transform, and propagate OLTP data for the data warehouse. The product is well suited for propagation routines that run at specific intervals (e.g., daily, weekly, monthly) or at the end of specific OLTP processes (e.g., to close an accounting period). SEQUEL is not well-suited for net-change propagation based on AS/400 journals because it does not provide direct support for reading journal receivers and extracting data from them. Once a data warehouse has been initialized with information, end users can use SEQUEL Viewpoint to access, analyze, and graph its contents.

After you have populated data warehouses with SEQUEL, end users can use SEQUEL Viewpoint or other ASC-supplied products such as Brio Technology's BrioQuery — a front-end OLAP tool — to analyze and graph data-warehouse information

ASC's recent agreement with Brio Technology is noteworthy. Brio's PC-based OLAP tool, BrioQuery, is a powerful, highly intuitive OLAP, query, charting, and reporting tool designed for end users. With BrioQuery, users can manipulate dimensions using simple drag-and-drop operations. If remote off-line analyses are required, they also can use BrioQuery to analyze data that has been downloaded via ODBC to PCs. In another noteworthy agreement, ASC recently partnered with IBM to provide an AS/400 40S server, SEQUEL, BrioQuery, and Client Access/400 to customers for just under $40,000. This offer is clearly aimed at customers who require low cost, basic data-warehousing functionality.

Getting back to SEQUEL, I had mentioned earlier that we can think of SEQUEL's data-manipulation commands as higher-level, more powerful versions of SQL statements. This functionality provides IT personnel with a very flexible way to transform highly normalized DB2/400-based OLTP data into information suitable for a data warehouse.

The tasks that Figures 8.1 and 8.2 depict, for example, are all that are required to join our sample invoice files and aggregate invoice figures by SKU number.

FIGURE 8.1
Join Tables with SEQUEL

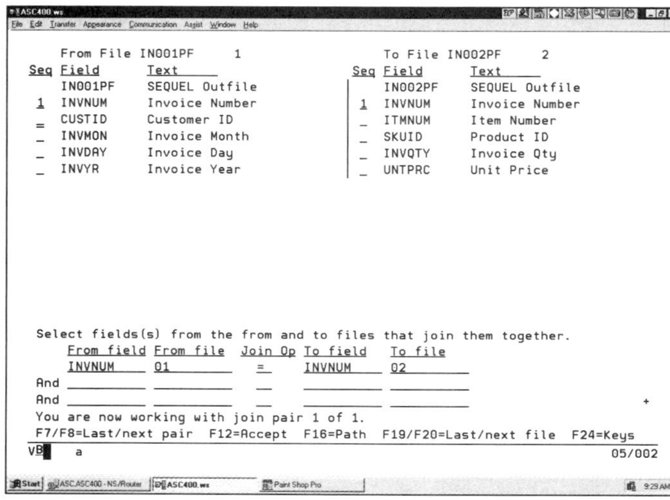

FIGURE 8.2
Aggregating Sales Figures by SKU

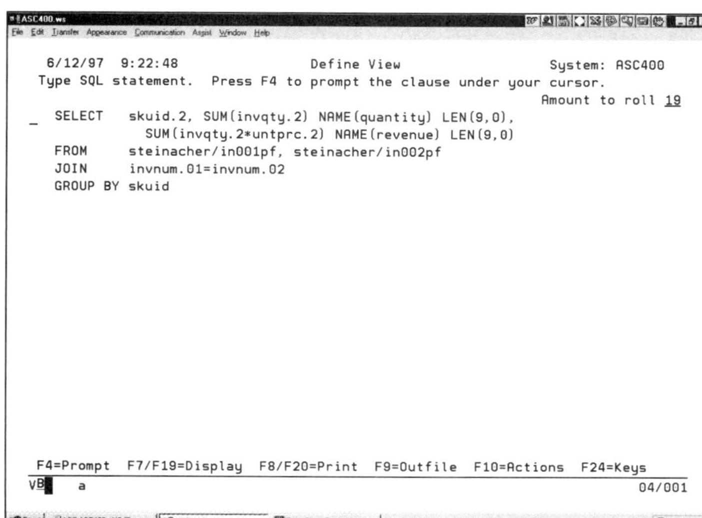

To remap our cryptic color codes, we use SEQUEL to identify all unique color codes in the OLTP database, as Figure 8.3 shows. The results of this operation appear in Figure 8.4.

FIGURE 8.3
Using SEQUEL to Isolate Unique Color Codes

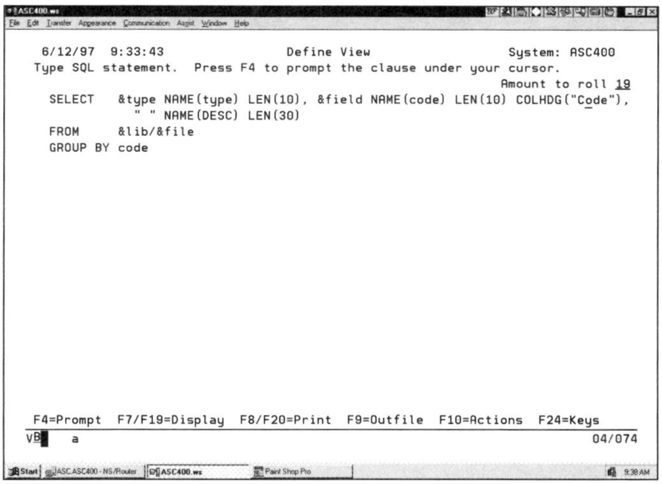

FIGURE 8.4
SEQUEL-Generated Lists of Unique Color Codes

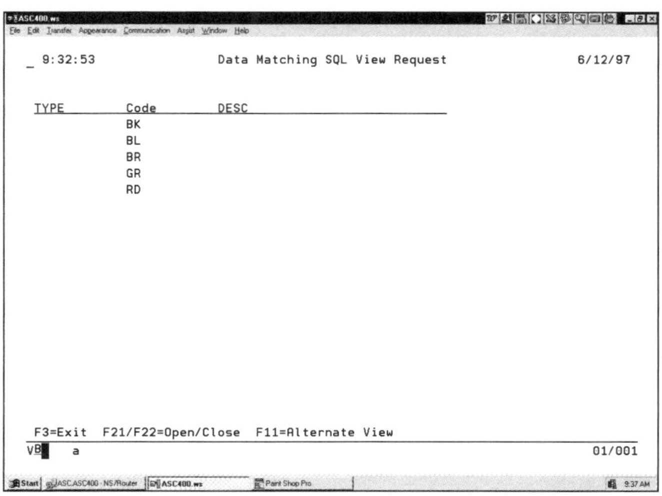

We then use SEQUEL to assign descriptions to color codes, as Figures 8.5 through 8.7 demonstrate. Using similar syntax, we extract detailed information from our OLTP database, transform those details into more meaningful information, and then write it to data-warehouse tables.

FIGURE 8.5
Using SEQUEL to Assign Descriptions to Codes

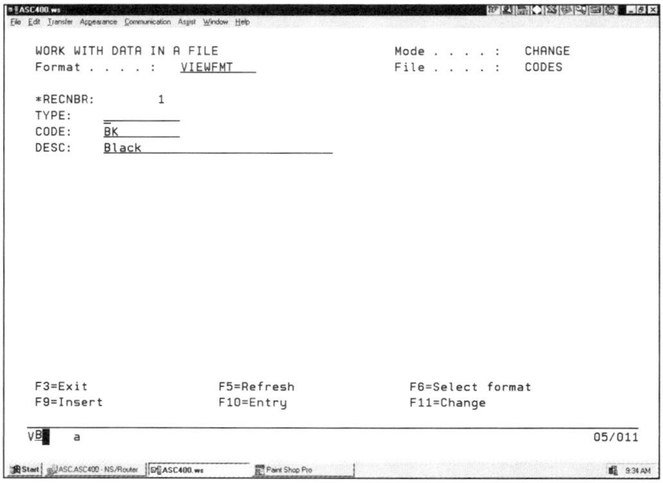

FIGURE 8.6
Executing a View with SEQUEL

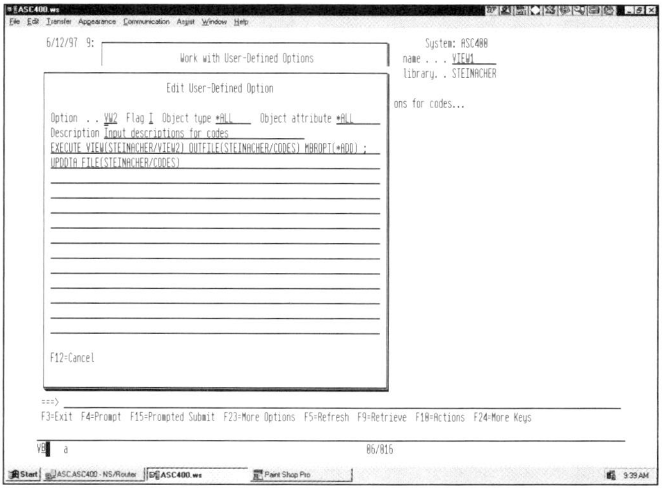

FIGURE 8.7
A SEQUEL Execution Prompt

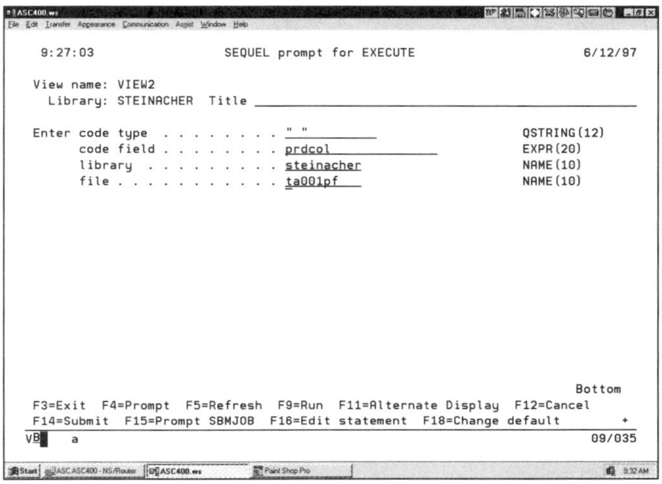

After these tables are created through a process similar to that represented in Figure 8.8, we use SEQUEL to propagate and query the data warehouse.

To summarize sales volume and revenue by SKUID, for example, we create the statement shown in Figure 8.9. Similarly, we use the statement shown in Figure 8.10 (page 133) to retrieve a list of sales figures by SKU, product name, color, and size. To summarize sales figures by product category, the statement represented in Figure 8.11 (page 133) is sufficient. For end users, these statements are assigned to front-end prompt screens.

As stated earlier, SEQUEL Viewpoint provides users with a GUI-based analysis tool and the means to access SEQUEL functionality in an intuitive way. Figure 8.12 (page 134) highlights Viewpoint's View Assist pop-up window.

Figures 8.13 through 8.17 (pages 134–136) detail how we can extract data from several tables in our data warehouse. In addition, we can use the statement in Figure 8.18 (page 137) to generate a simple list (shown in Figure 8.19 on page 138). Figures 8.20 and 8.21 (page 139) highlight the product's graphing capabilities.

FIGURE 8.8
Using SEQUEL to Define a Table

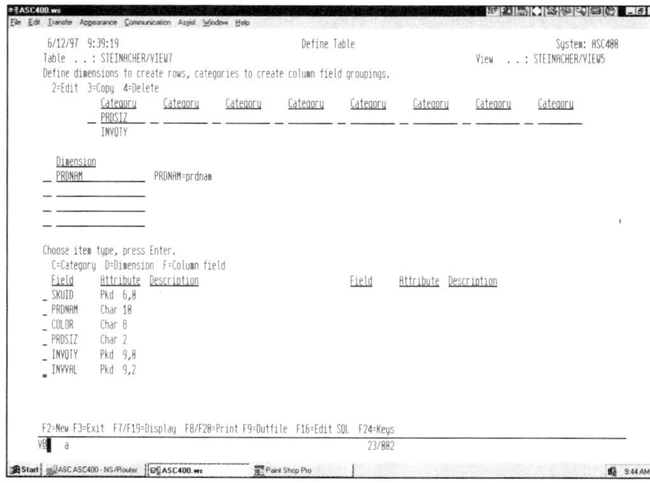

FIGURE 8.9
Summarizing Sales by SKU

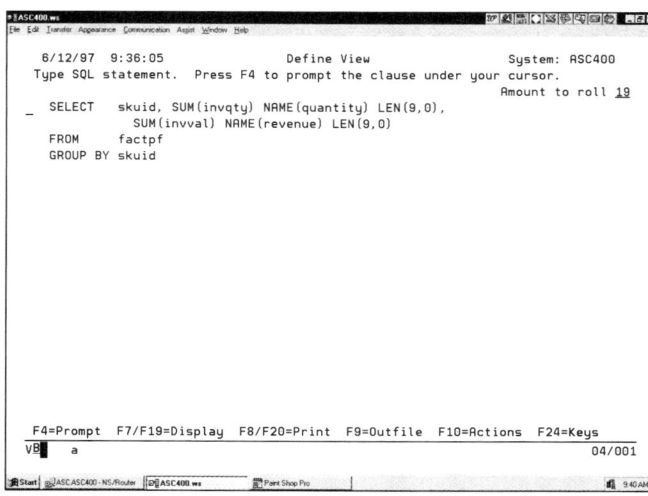

FIGURE 8.10

SEQUEL Statement to Retrieve Data from Fact and Dimension Tables

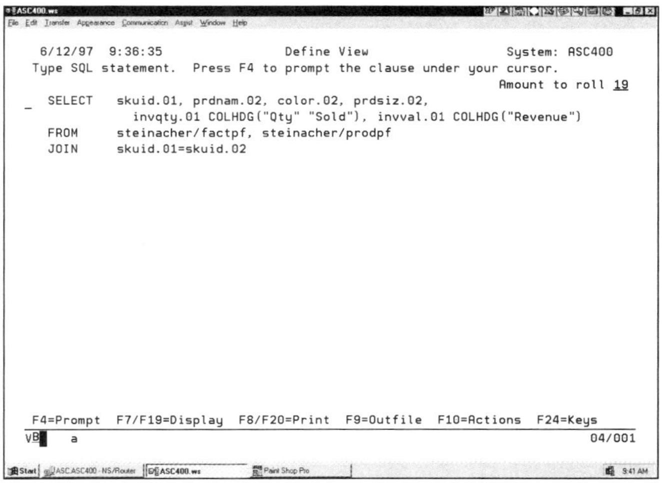

FIGURE 8.11

SEQUEL Statement to Summarize Sales by Product

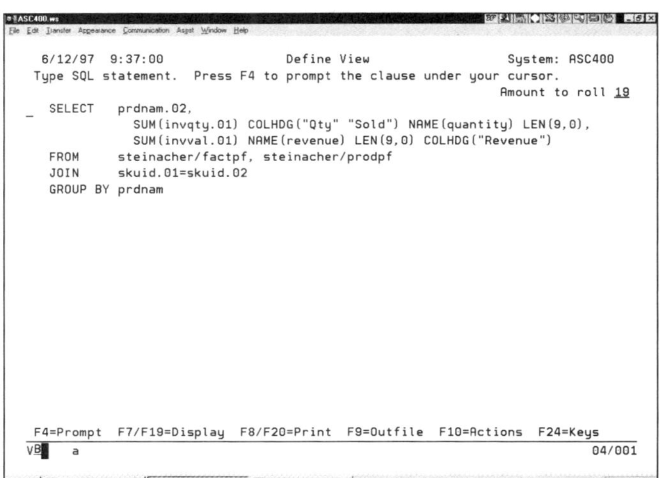

FIGURE 8.12

Using View Assist to Define a Query

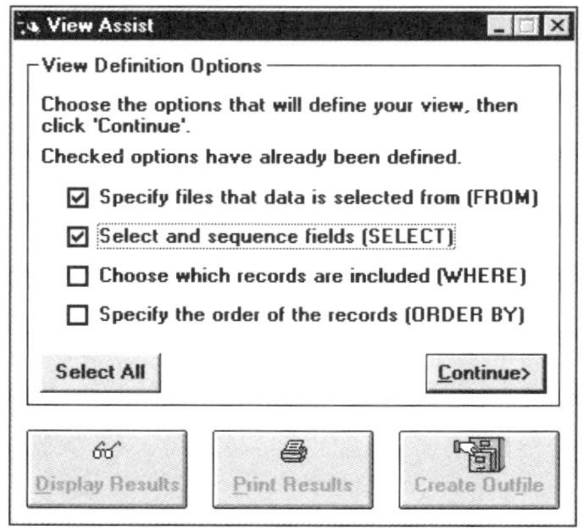

FIGURE 8.13

Using SEQUEL Viewpoint to Select Files

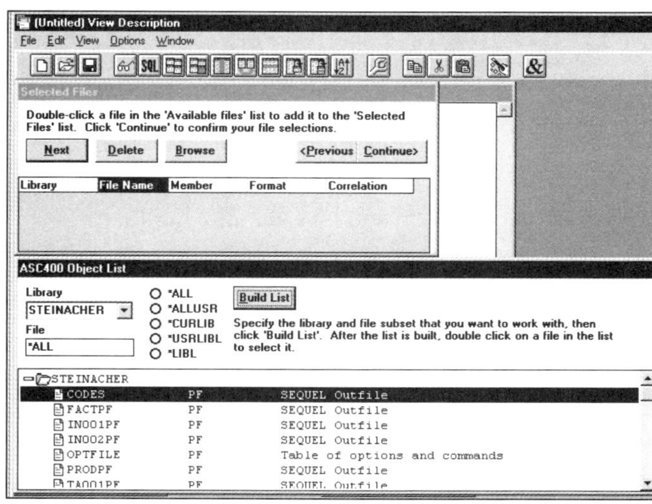

FIGURE 8.14
Viewing Selected File Names with Viewpoint

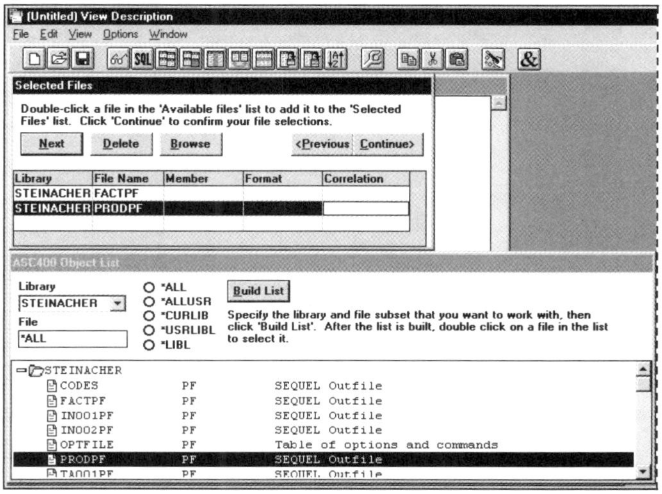

FIGURE 8.15
Using Viewpoint to Join Files

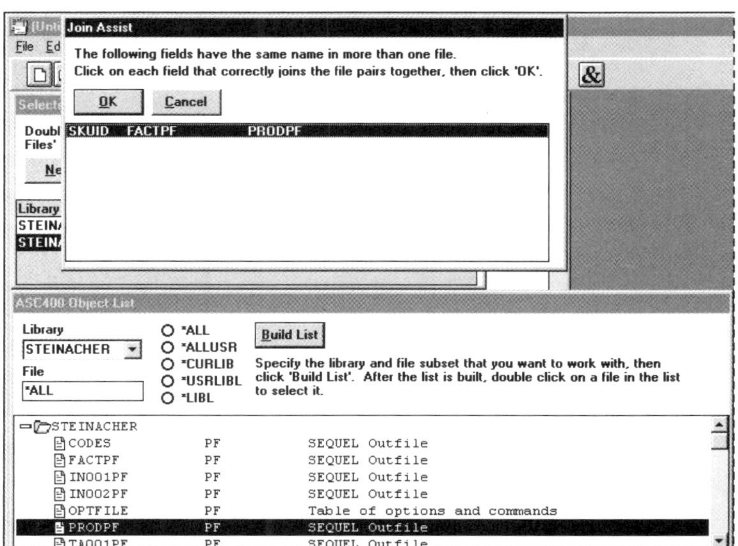

FIGURE 8.16
Viewpoint's View Description Screen

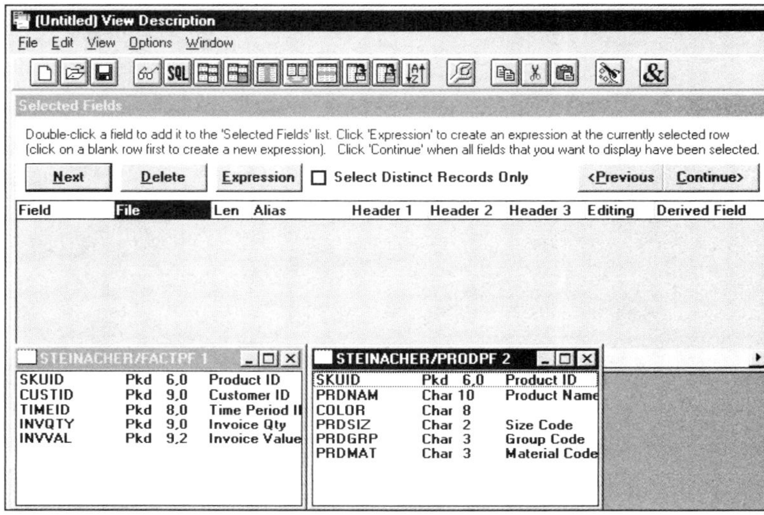

FIGURE 8.17
Deriving Invoice Value

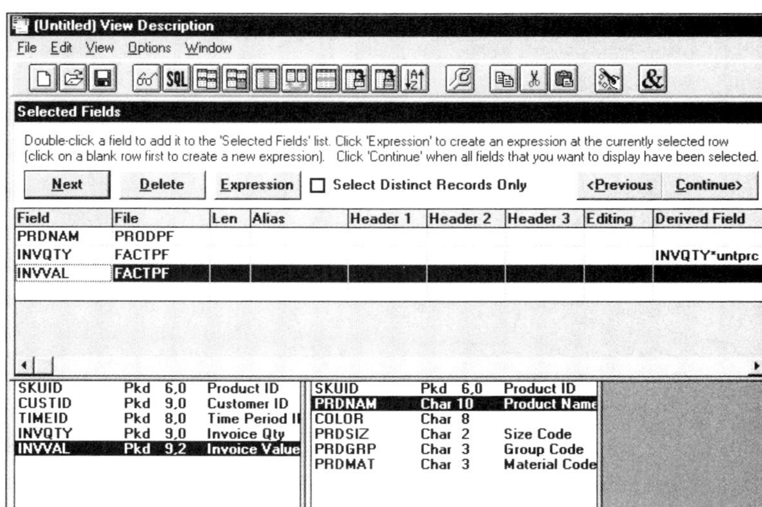

FIGURE 8.18

Statement to Generate Detailed Sales Figures

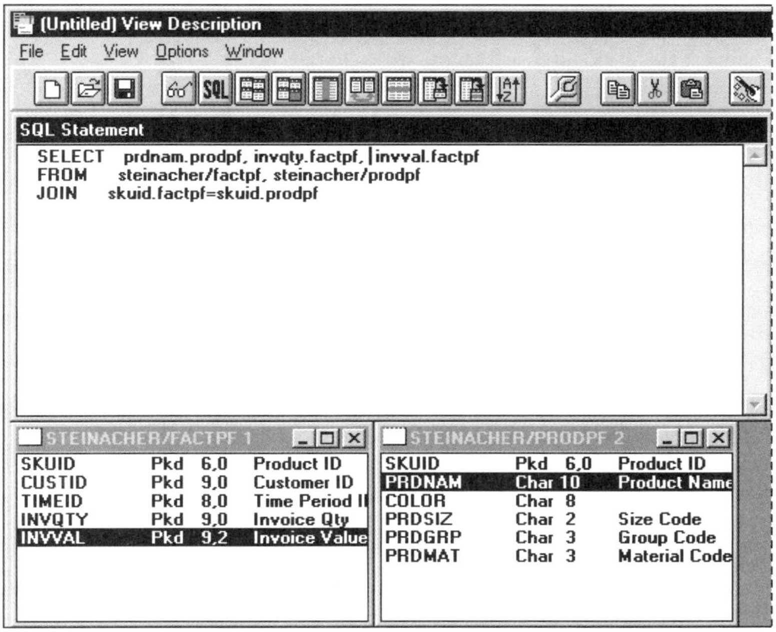

FIGURE 8.19
Detailed Sales Figures

QTEMP/V000000027

File Edit Options Window Help

Product Name	Invoice Qty	Invoice Value
Umbrella	300	7,500.00
Umbrella	200	5,000.00
Umbrella	600	15,000.00
Umbrella	100	2,700.00
Umbrella	300	7,200.00
Boots	300	28,500.00
Boots	500	47,500.00
Boots	300	28,500.00
Boots	600	57,000.00
Boots	200	19,000.00
Raincoat	400	34,800.00
Raincoat	700	60,900.00
Raincoat	100	8,700.00
Hat	200	8,000.00
Hat	100	4,000.00
Hat	800	30,400.00
Hat	200	8,000.00
Hat	800	29,600.00
Hat	400	15,600.00
Hat	500	19,500.00
Raincoat	100	7,500.00
Raincoat	400	30,800.00
Raincoat	100	7,500.00
Raincoat	400	30,400.00
Raincoat	200	15,600.00

FIGURE 8.20
Statement to Group Revenue Figures by Product

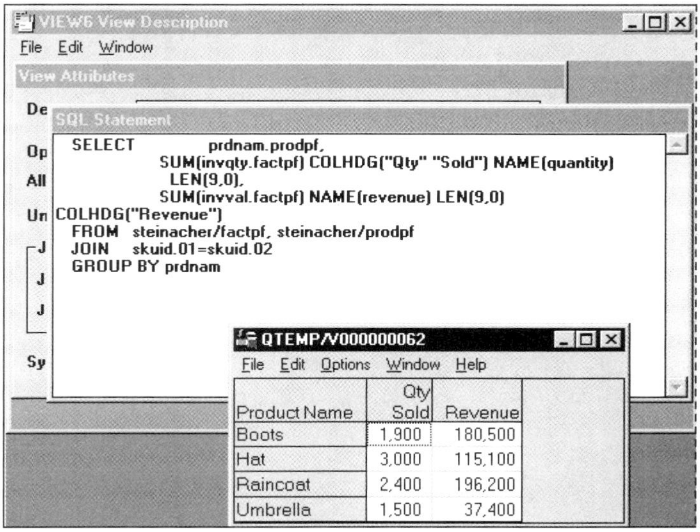

FIGURE 8.21
Using Viewpoint to Graph Revenue by Product

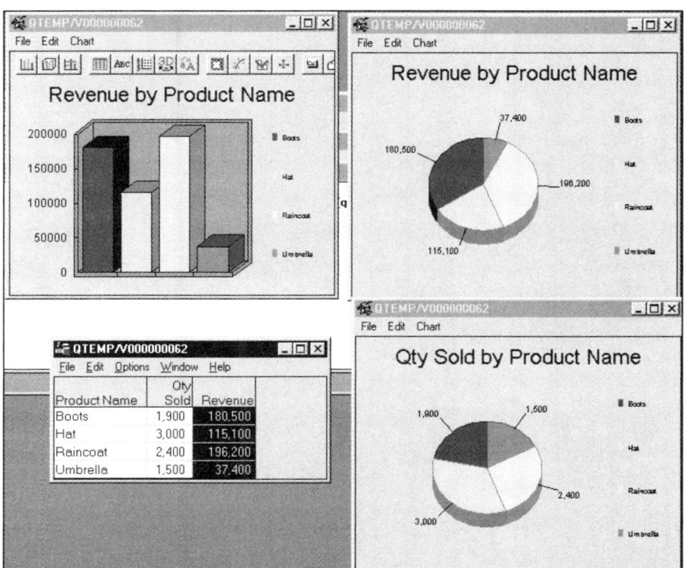

Product Summary and Positioning

In terms of positioning, it's important to note that SEQUEL is not a comprehensive data-warehousing solution. The product does not include a database, so you remain responsible for actually designing and creating data-warehouse repositories such as ROLAP star schema, if necessary. If you feel comfortable with designing data-warehouse schema, SEQUEL provides excellent support for this task. It is also a highly effective transformational replication tool. Using SEQUEL to perform the back-end transformation and propagation tasks, and then using BrioQuery or Viewpoint to analyze the resultant tables, is a very pragmatic, economical way to quickly derive the benefits of data warehousing.

As ASC's agreement with IBM demonstrates, SEQUEL is not aimed at the high end of the AS/400 data-warehousing market. For example, it does not provide EIS functionality or Internet-based data-access tools. For those seeking a way to quickly build basic data warehouses on the AS/400, ASC provides an economical solution.

Chapter 9

Coglin Mill and RODIN

Company Background

Founded in 1985, Coglin Mill Pty. Ltd. is the developer of RODIN, a high-performance, data-extraction, data-transformation, and data-propagation product. A client-server application written in Progress (a 4GL development language), RODIN is currently used to maintain more than 25 large-scale AS/400-based data warehouses. Headquartered in Australia, privately held Coglin Mill has 45 employees and more than 1,000 customers worldwide. The company maintains sales and support offices in Adelaide and Melbourne, Australia, and Rochester, Minnesota. In addition, it maintains relationships with 20 business partners who operate in Los Angeles, San Francisco, New York, Atlanta, St. Louis, Jackson (Mississippi), Toronto, Calgary (Canada), London, Manchester (England), Sydney (Australia), Auckland (New Zealand), Singapore, and Kuala Lumpur. Nine distributors also market RODIN in more than 20 countries throughout the world. In addition to RODIN, Coglin Mill offers MANAGE/400, an AS/400-based menu-maintenance utility, and SUCCESS, an AS/400-based distribution package.

Product Overview

RODIN is not a data warehouse. Rather, it is a specialized application used to define, load, and maintain large-scale, high-volume data warehouses. With RODIN, you can acquire data directly from DB2/400-based OLTP databases or indirectly from external sources provided that a propagation tool and a communications method exists between the source machine and the target AS/400. For example, if source OLTP data is spread across a large wide-area network (WAN) or stored in different databases (e.g., DB2, Oracle, Sybase, Informix), RODIN can be integrated with third-party propagation tolls such as IBM's Data Propagator or Data Mirror's Transformation Server. It also can work together with system-mirroring software such as OMS/400 or MIMIX to effectively move source data from one AS/400 to another.

RODIN can access a variety of AS/400 file structures, including logical files, join-logical files, and both single- and multimember physical files. It can also filter this data by column (field) and by row (record). Once RODIN has isolated source data, it can transform it — update field content, change field names, reformat field sizes, translate field values, modify field types, and derive entirely new fields. The product also supports string manipulation and date arithmetic, and it can update/derive fields using value-translation lists and/or conditional formulae. You also can use RODIN to eliminate duplicate records and to check for referential integrity (i.e., verify that master file records exist for transaction records, and vice versa). The product supports incremental and full-refresh propagation routines.

After it has transformed data and moved it to a primary warehouse repository, RODIN can aggregate and move selected data from the primary repository to one or more data marts, which users then can access by whatever analysis and presentation software they choose, RODIN, which does not include presentation and analysis software, can be integrated with a wide variety of EIS, DDS, OLAP, query, and data-mining tools. For example, users can use Seagate Software's Crystal Reports to design reports based on the data in RODIN databases. Similarly, they can use Platinum Technologies' Forest & Trees to develop EIS applications that access RODIN data. And for multidimensional analyses and/or the conversion of RODIN output files into other PC formats, users will find Datawatch's Monarch quite useful.

RODIN is organized according to its four major functional areas: Data Warehouse, Data Entry, Output Designer, and Output Viewer. Let's examine each of these functions, after which we will be in a better position to look at how RODIN performs our sample data-warehousing tasks.

Data Warehouse

The Data Warehouse component of RODIN lets you introduce important OLTP file structures to the data warehouse. Via this module, critical field and file information is automatically imported into RODIN's metadata management facility — a process that saves you a significant amount of time because you otherwise would have to manually input this information into DDS members to create data-warehouse tables. Data Warehouse also lets you select the keys by which various levels of data are to be stored in the warehouse. In addition, this module lets you define subject-related databases (data sets) that contain related data elements, or fields. Data sets can be summarized or time dependent, and they can contain alpha, numeric, alphanumeric, date, and time fields. Metadata automatically generated from these definitions also maintains the data warehouse and helps users access data in the warehouse.

Data Entry

The Data Entry module is useful when information that is not available electronically must be included in the data warehouse. This module also can be used to create derived data based on information that is already in the data warehouse. For example, you can use Data Entry to create next year's sales budget based on the current year's sales figures. To accomplish these tasks, RODIN generates customized RPG programs. It does not require you to write programs or create SQL/400 statements for these tasks.

Output Designer

A critical component of RODIN, the Output Designer gathers and then exports data from the data warehouse. Suitable for IT personnel and advanced end users, Output Designer lets its users create hard-copy reports (character-based), data marts, and files suitable for interactive browsing. The source for these structures is often the primary data-warehouse repository.

With Output Designer, users can define detail, exception, summary, or tabular reports required for daily, weekly, monthly, or other periodic reporting requirements. Output Designer also can create DB2/400, ASCII, or comma-separated variable files. These files then serve as data sources for desktop and AS/400-based presentation and analysis tools. In addition to EIS, DSS, query, and OLAP products, Output Designer is well-suited as a data source for IBM's leading data-mining application, Intelligent Miner. As we shall see in Chapter 13, Intelligent Miner can use either flat files or DB2/400 files as data sources.

Output Designer is a flexible tool that supports data selection, sequencing, conditioning, highlighting, ranking (single-level and multilevel nested and intersected ranking), calculation, and aggregation operations. It also automatically manages all applicable period calculations (i.e., year-to-date, moving annual average, annual comparisons) based on internal, user-defined calendars. In addition, Output Designer can create multiple-output data sets with a single processing run. Output Designer can also automatically link to external OLTP files (e.g., files that contain codes and their associated descriptions); it does not require those files' structures to be imported into the data warehouse. Finally, Output Designer provides data-set (subject and row) and data-element (column) security to prevent unauthorized access to information.

Output Viewer

RODIN's Output Viewer module can display files generated through the Output Designer facility, which lets reports and other extracted data be viewed online rather than in hard copy. Figure 9.1 illustrates how RODIN's four major functions are accessible via the product's opening menu.

Implementation Example

To effectively convey the functionality of RODIN, this section features numerous screens to illustrate how to use the product to implement our sample problem outlined in the "Introduction to Section II." For simplicity, we assume that the data warehouse resides on the same AS/400 as the OLTP database.

RODIN, through definitions entered via the Data Warehouse menus, automatically generates the tables that comprise our data warehouse. It then processes (i.e., cleanses, filters, reformats) our OLTP data via an internal interface file. RODIN automatically generates RPG programs using the DDS definitions of our OLTP files to accomplish this processing. The RODIN interface technology provides many common transformation routines that can update OLTP

FIGURE 9.1
RODIN's Main Menu

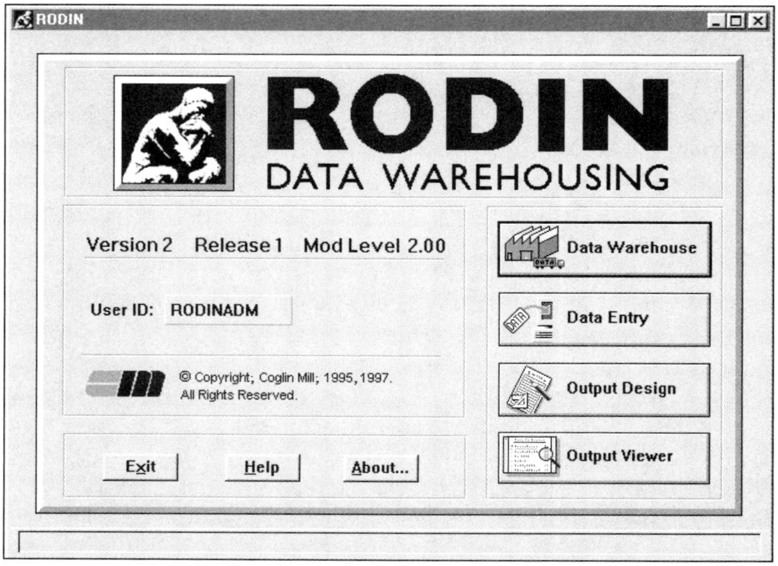

data before it gets to the warehouse. All programs RODIN generates can be modified to accommodate any cleansing, formatting, or validation routines that the product doesn't directly support.

At this point, background server jobs take the data from the standard interface file and propagate it to various subject-related databases (data sets) that have been defined in the data warehouse. RODIN again automatically writes and compiles these server jobs using data-set definitions.

RODIN's data-warehouse update function supports both the initial creation and the incremental loading of data. This update function uses commitment control to ensure the data is recoverable if the system fails during a data-warehouse update procedure. If it encounters validation or data-integrity errors during the update process, RODIN moves a copy of the rejected transaction into an error-recovery file for you to examine later. You can then restart the update function in "error recovery" mode to update these transactions. This recovery process helps ensure data integrity while minimizing required system resources (i.e., the entire propagation process does not have to be rerun).

Figure 9.2 illustrates how our own external OLTP files are introduced to RODIN from an OLTP application called SALES. Our external OLTP files contain data that is propagated to the data warehouse as data elements. A RODIN-generated interface program actually moves this data to the warehouse.

FIGURE 9.2
Using RODIN to Introduce OLTP Tables to the Data Warehouse

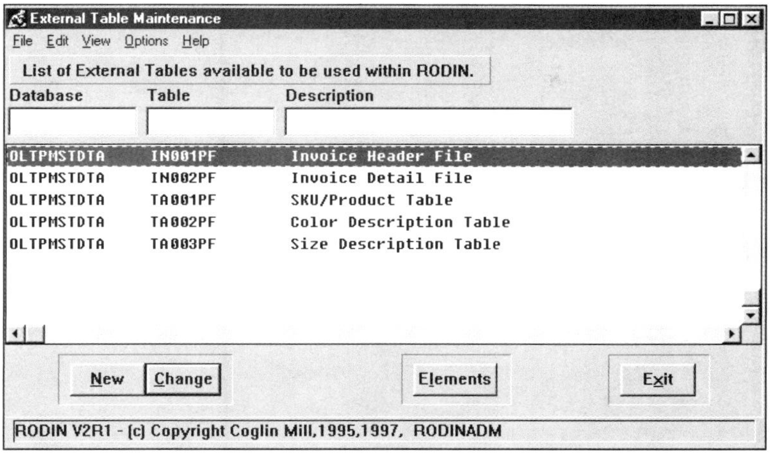

External files typically contain fields that are used as keys, or identifiers, in RODIN data sets.

RODIN lets you add new data to existing data sets and automatically reformats the existing data in the warehouse to the new format. It also supports the creation of new data sets as required.

In Figure 9.3, available OLTP fields are presented for selection. RODIN extracts such information from file specifications (DDS) associated with the OLTP database. Figure 9.4 demonstrates how RODIN field attributes are assigned to INVQTY. When taken together with other fields, this information forms the basis for the RPG interface program. As you can see in Figure 9.4, the name assigned to the extract program in this example is INVOICES.

Data-source definitions form the basis from which RODIN data elements are created. Figure 9.5 (page 147)depicts three data elements defined for our example, including INVPRICE, INVQTY, and INVALUE. In RODIN, a data element can be a field in an external transaction file, an expression over multiple fields and/or multiple external extraction files, a calculation based upon other existing data elements (including literals), data from an external source such as purchased demographic data, or data that we keyed directly into RODIN via the Data Entry function. Data elements can contain alpha, numeric, date, or time data. As you may surmise from Figure 9.5, *external* data elements are extracted directly from the OLTP database while *calculated* data elements are the result of additional processing in RODIN.

FIGURE 9.3

Selecting Available OLTP Files

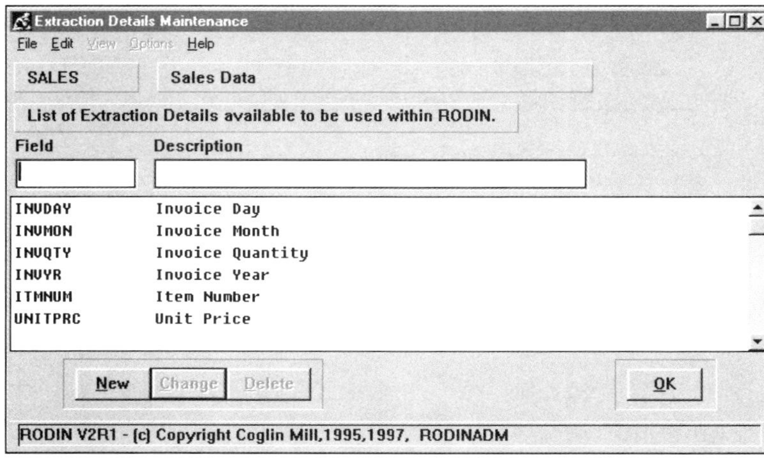

FIGURE 9.4

Assigning RODIN Attributes to Fields

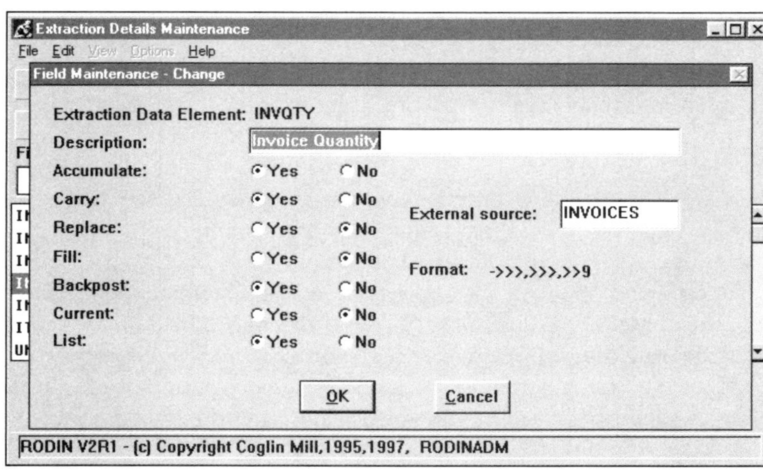

FIGURE 9.5
Defining RODIN Data Elements

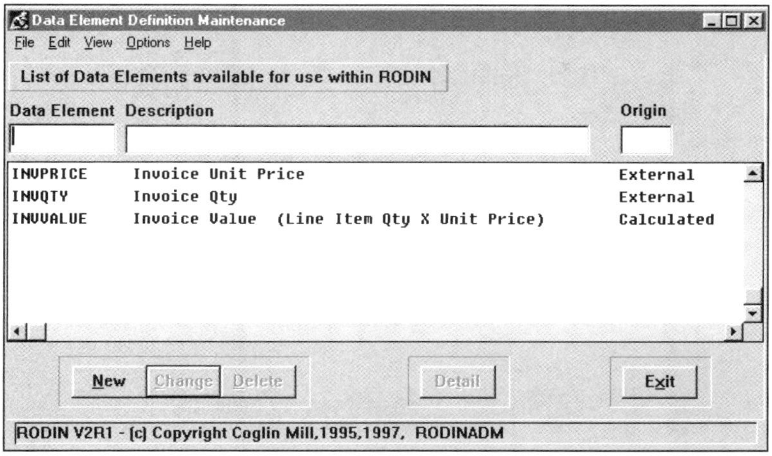

Figure 9.6 depicts the assignment of descriptive text to the data element "Invoice Unit Price." This particular data element is mapped to the OLTP source field UNITPRC in Figure 9.7 (page 148).

Figures 9.8 (page 148) and 9.9 (page 149) illustrate how RODIN's calculation-details maintenance facility derives the field INVVALUE (invoice value).

FIGURE 9.6
Assigning Metadata to a Data Element

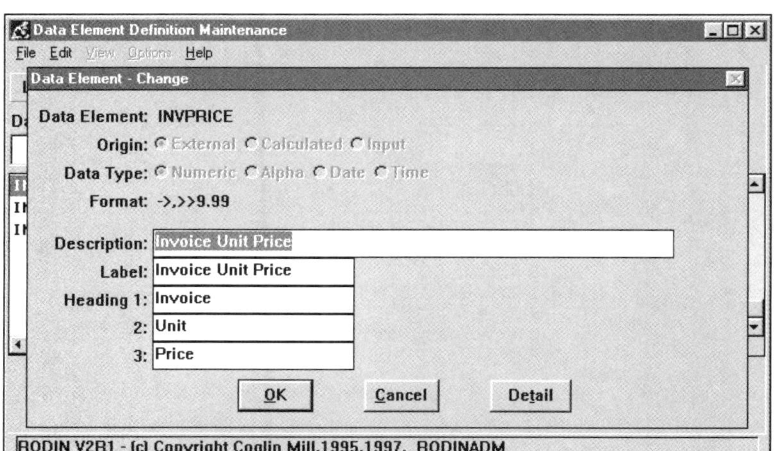

FIGURE 9.7

Mapping an OLTP Field to a RODIN Data Element

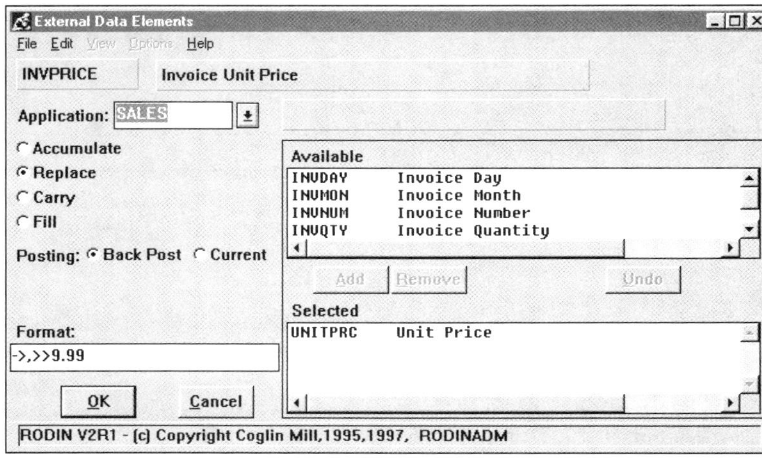

FIGURE 9.8

Defining the Data Element INVVALUE

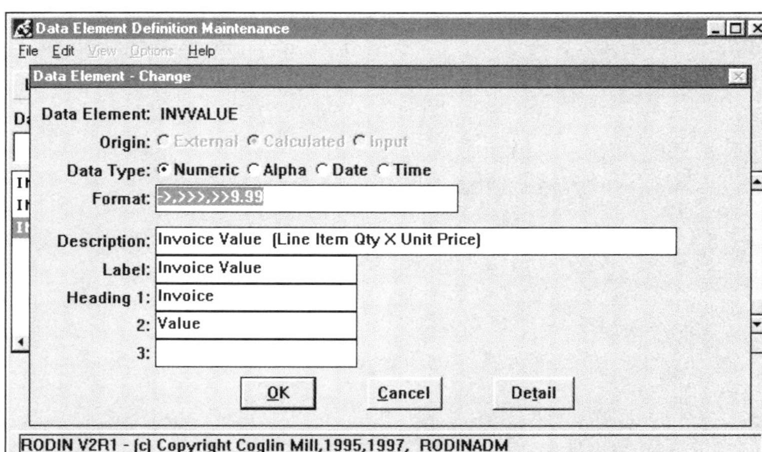

As I mentioned earlier, RODIN can access OLTP files directly in cases where identifiers (i.e., code descriptions) to data sets are required for output (external values). This obviates the need to create parallel master files in the data warehouse. Figure 9.10 shows all the fields in our sample Product Table as they appear in RODIN. RODIN automatically obtained this information through DDS specifications, which make available fields that are relevant to the data

FIGURE 9.9

Specifying Calculation Details for INVVALUE

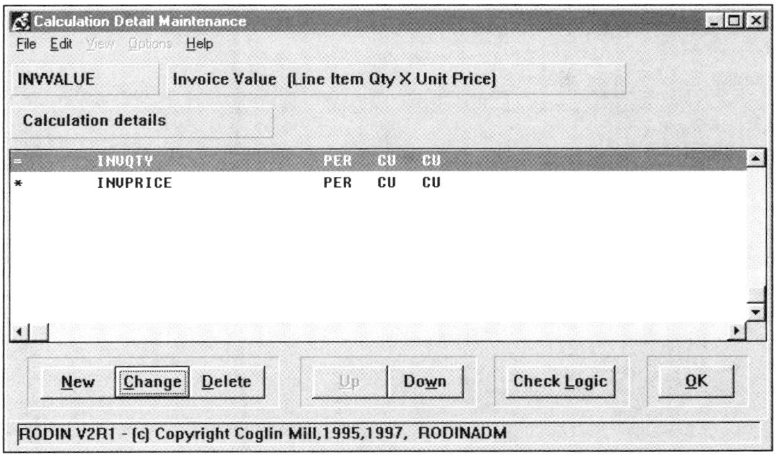

FIGURE 9.10

Introducing the Product Table to the Data Warehouse

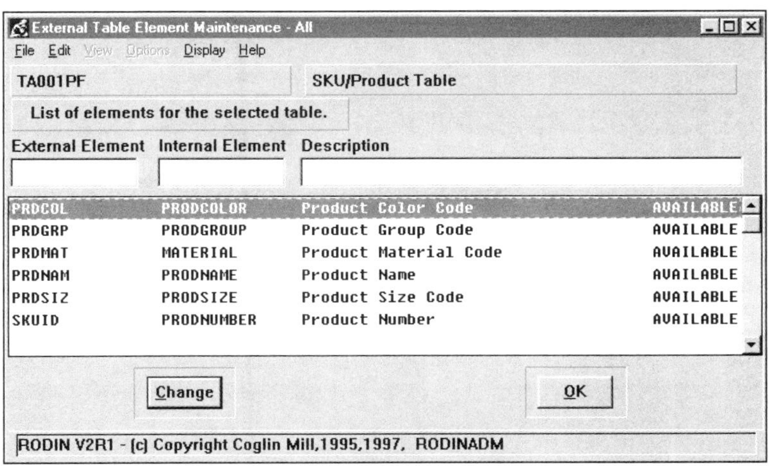

warehouse. These field definitions then become part of the metadata available to end users.

Figure 9.11 (page 150) shows that the Product Color Code is an external value that can be combined with data-warehouse information when output is generated. Similarly, Figure 9.12 (page 150) shows that Product Number is available for both this purpose and for use as an identifier to a data set.

FIGURE 9.11
Assigning Usage Parameters to PRDCOL

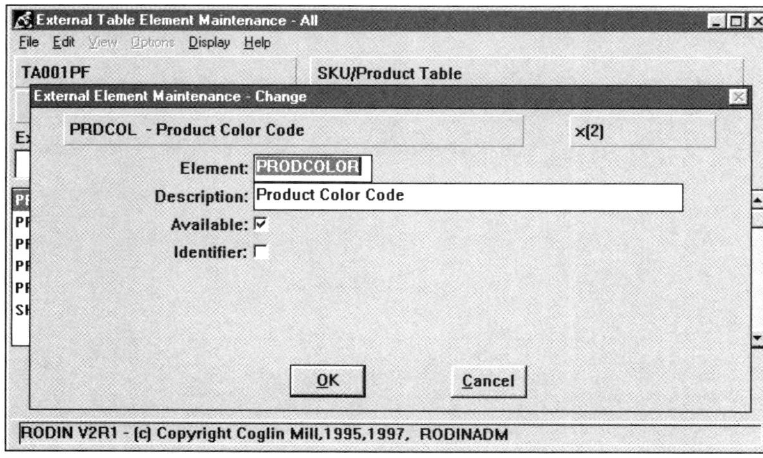

FIGURE 9.12
Assigning Usage Parameters to SKUID

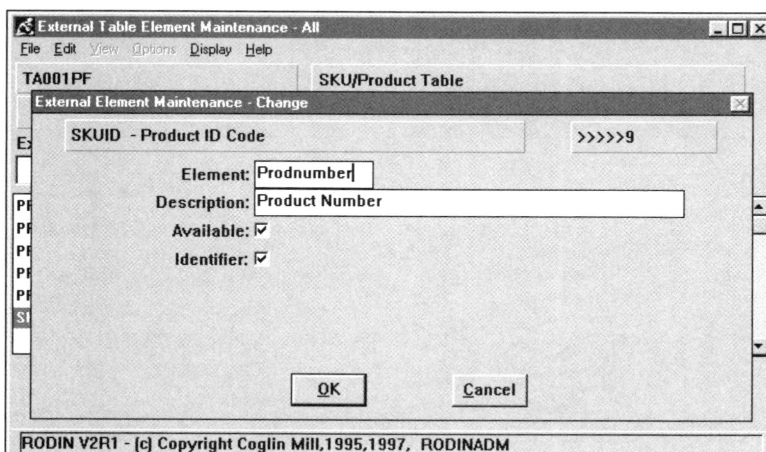

In RODIN, a data set is a collection of one or more data elements stored together in a single "subject oriented" database file with a common level of detail (key) and a common time dimension (period structure). Every RODIN Data Warehouse consists of one or more data sets. Any data set can be used individually or together (if they have common identifiers) to produce any form of output. Each data set in RODIN utilizes a separate DB2/400 physical file.

RODIN includes three types of data sets: A *Detail Data Set* can store transaction-level data, also referred to as non-repeating data, such as invoice line items. In such instances, there is no time dimension because each item is a single occurrence. In a Detail Data Set, there is no summarized data unless the data in a particular data type has already been summarized before being introduced to RODIN. Figure 9.13 depicts a detail data set.

FIGURE 9.13
Detail Data Set

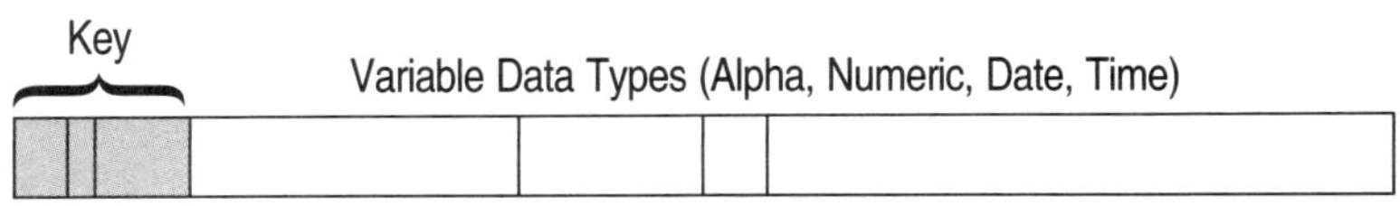

In contrast, a *Summary Data Set* contains time-series data (i.e., net sales value by month for 36 months). Each data type repeats for each period and is referred to as repeating data. Figure 9.14 depicts four data types stored by month for three years. All data for a full year is stored in a single record for storage and processing efficiency.

FIGURE 9.14
Summary Data Set

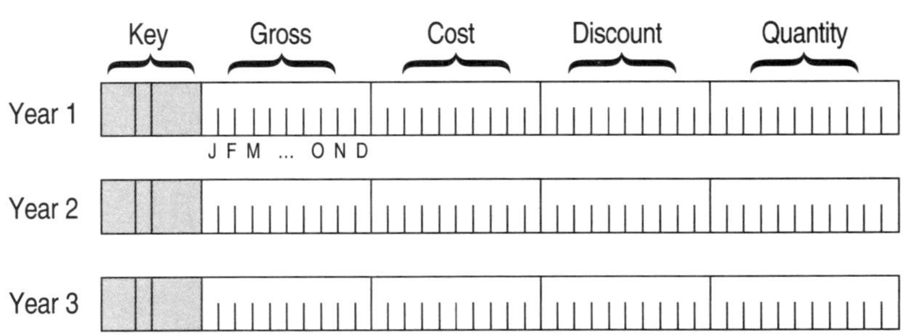

Finally, a *Mixed Data Set* contains both repeating and non-repeating data. Non-repeating data in a Mixed Data Set can store descriptive or master-file data within a Summary Data Set rather than retrieving it from the master files when it is required. Storing data this way improves performance but requires more disk storage. In this scenario, the value of the data is as it was when propagated from the master file. Note that Mixed Data Sets are not recommended for use with constantly changing master files, because if the master file was updated after the propagation process was performed, the data warehouse may use out-of-date information.

So far, we have created two data sets from our sample OLTP data. The first is a Summary Data Set that includes Invoice Qty and Line Item Extended Value by Customer Number and Product Number for 5 years, summarized by month. The second is a Detail Data Set storing Invoice Qty and Line Item Extended Value at Invoice Line Item level (i.e., Product Number within Invoice Number).

As you can see in Figure 9.15, to generate a definition of a data set, we enter several parameters: the data storage type; the period for which data is to be stored; the length of time the data is to be stored; the identifiers (level of detail or key values); the data elements to be stored; required totals, if any; and security access by user or group of users. When we activate the Build button, RODIN generates the database structure (DDS) and the programs (ILE RPG) to create and maintain the data in the specified format.

FIGURE 9.15
Defining a Data Set

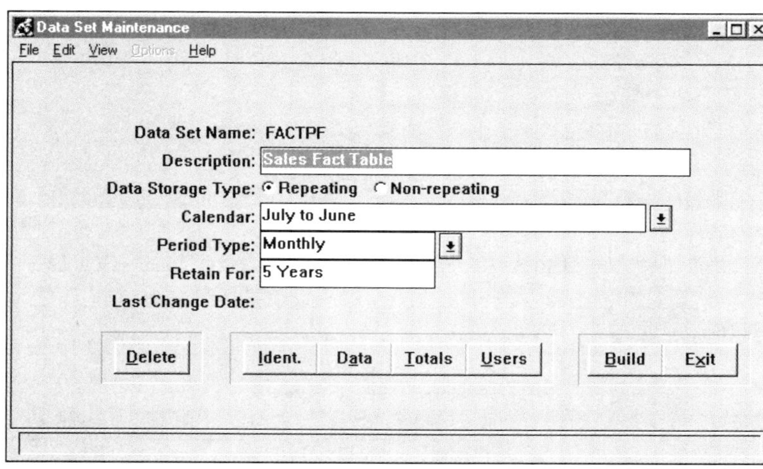

As Figure 9.16 illustrates, the data set FACTPF is keyed by Product Number (from the Invoice Detail file) and Customer Number (from the Invoice Header file). In this case, the data set stores two data elements: Invoice Quantity and Invoice Value. The definitions for these data elements appear in Figures 9.17 and 9.18 (page 154).

This data-set definition creates a file keyed by Product Number, Customer Number, and Year, and contains 24 data fields — Invoice Unit price for months 01 through 12 and Invoice Value for months 01 through 12. Because Product Number is an identifier to this data set, end users can access the

FIGURE 9.16
Selecting Keys for FACTPF

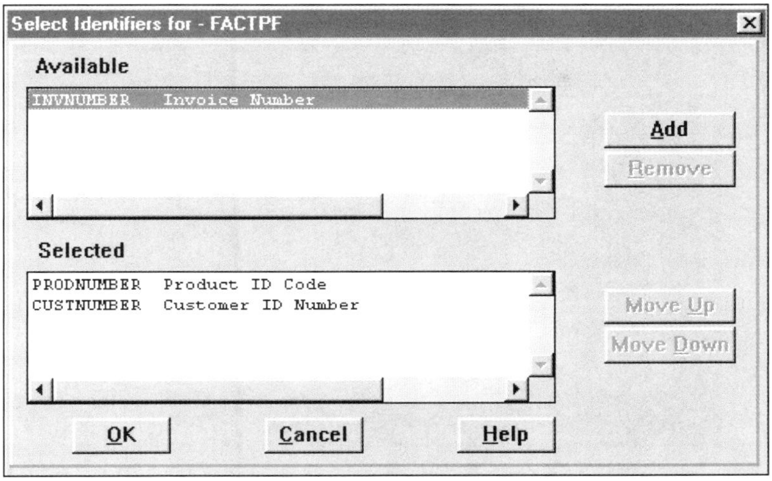

FIGURE 9.17
Further Defining INVQTY

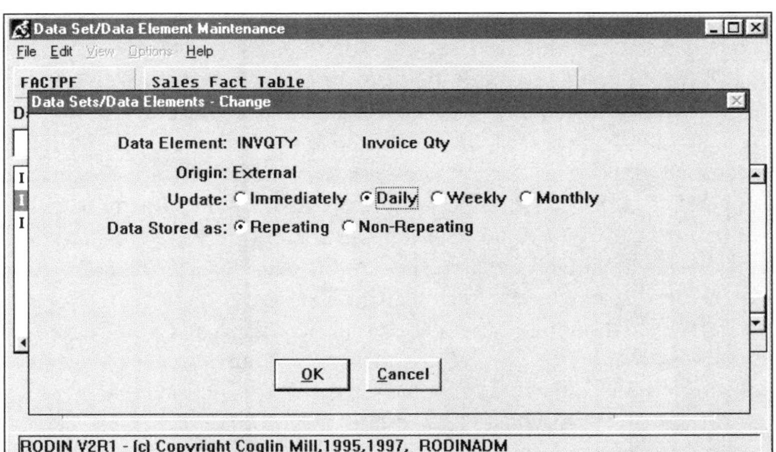

Product Dimension file to retrieve additional product information (i.e., description, color, size) when they use the Output Designer. If they retrieve the color and size code fields from the Product Dimension file, they also can access description tables that store color and size descriptions. In this way, they can bring these details into any form of output that is being created. Happily, these

FIGURE 9.18
Further Defining INVVALUE

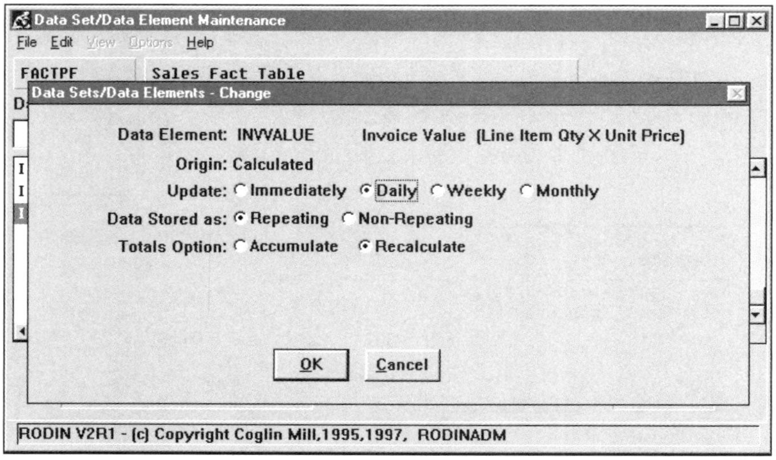

joins are invisible to end users — RODIN metadata simply prompts the fields that are available and lets users select those that are required from the lists.

As I mentioned previously, the second data set summarizes information contained in the Invoice Header and Invoice Detail files. Figures 9.19 through 9.21 depict the creation of a data set called INVOICES. As you see in Figure 9.21 (page 156), this file contains three fields (Invoice Unit Price, Invoice Quantity, and Invoice Value) for each product on each invoice.

Once RODIN has created and initialized a data warehouse, end users and/or IT personnel can begin accessing its contents. The Output Design function lets users design reports, viewable files, and/or export files using a highly intuitive "pallet and canvas" design tool. This function can generate output files such as Comma-Separated Variable files, ASCII text files, or DB2/400 files. In this way, IT personnel can create data marts that are accessible by any EIS, DSS, OLAP, query, or data-mining application. All data elements in all data sets are available to users at all times, within security constraints.

Output Designer supports numerous advanced functions that assist in the physical design of the report or file. In addition, it facilitates the selection, sequencing, and form of the data to be generated, including flexible ranking criteria by column, value, or number (i.e., top 20), as well as "if, then, else" and "and/or" processing logic to select and highlight the required data.

RODIN's Output Designer is tightly integrated with the product's comprehensive metadata facilities. RODIN automatically builds both business and technical metadata at each level of the data warehouse. End users access this data as they learn how and where data is stored. User-defined metadata is available,

FIGURE 9.19
Defining a Data Set Called INVOICES

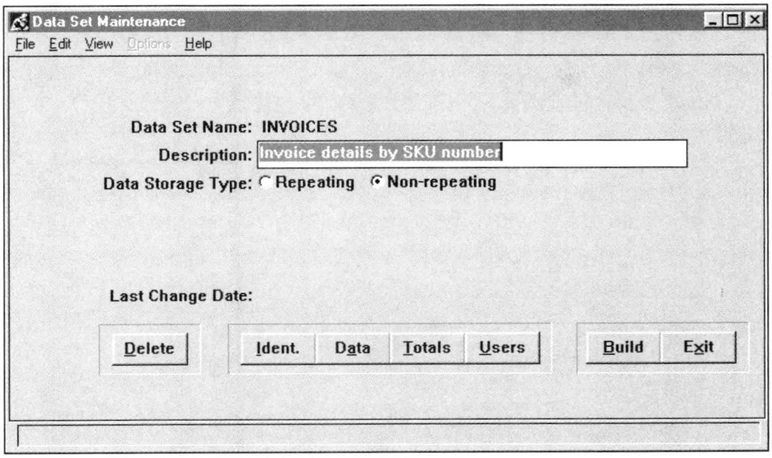

FIGURE 9.20
Introducing OLTP Data to RODIN for Data Set Invoices

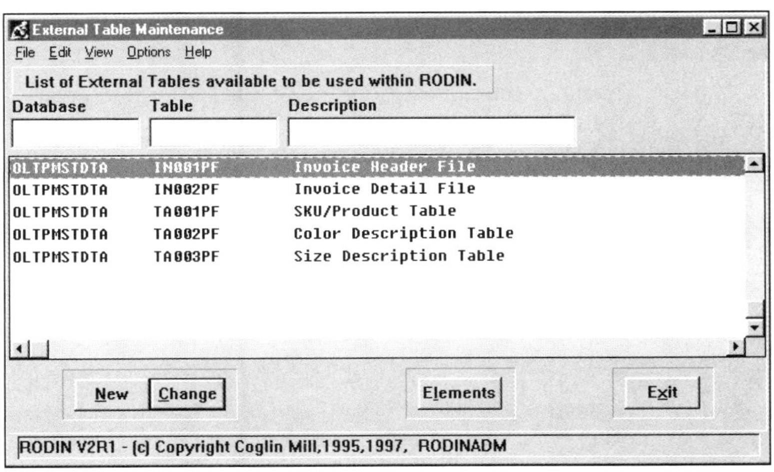

if needed, to further define the data. RODIN metadata alleviates the need for end users to understand underlying database schema. The metadata also helps end users determine what information is stored in the warehouse, and what additional information is accessible from external files.

FIGURE 9.21
Specifying Data Elements for Invoices

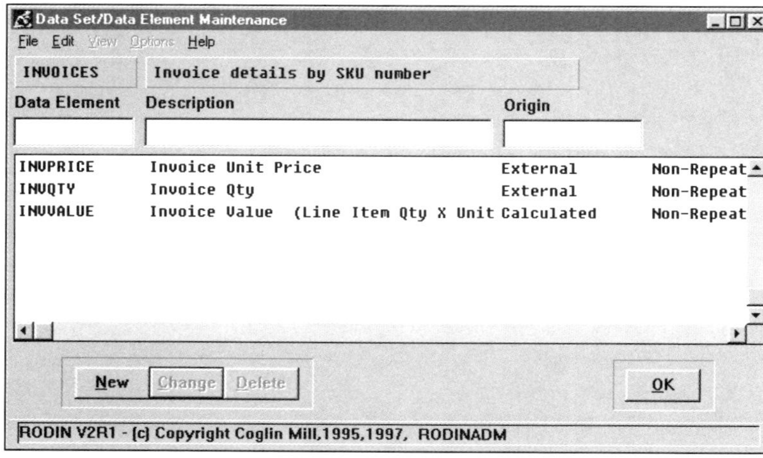

RODIN's metadata is considered "active" in the respect that the data-acquisition, data-warehouse-management, and data-delivery functions are automatically generated by and controlled through the metadata. Any changes to the metadata are subsequently implemented and reflected throughout the data warehouse.

For our first output exercise, let's use the Output Designer to create a report that summarizes Product sales by individual SKU#. We input the specifications that appear in Figure 9.22 by selecting required elements and dropping them on the "canvas" in required locations. Afterward, we press the Build button to generate RPG programs that produce the output upon request. Figure 9.23 illustrates how the report appears when we examine it via the interactive Output Viewer.

Now let's create a cross-tab report to summarize product sales by product name and size, as depicted by the format in Figure 9.24 (page 158). In this case, columns are defined as Calculations that apply "if" logic to determine whether the item belongs to the correct size group for each column. This logic appears in the Property Sheet illustrated in Figure 9.25 (page 158). Figure 9.26 (page 159) depicts the results as we see them through the Output Viewer.

Now let's produce a report that summarizes Product sales by Product Name. We use sequencing to produce the output in descending Invoice Sales Value order. Figures 9.27 through 9.29 (pages 159–160) depict the creation of this report, while Figure 9.30 (page 161) illustrates how the data appears when we view it interactively.

FIGURE 9.22

Using Output Designer to Define a Detail Report

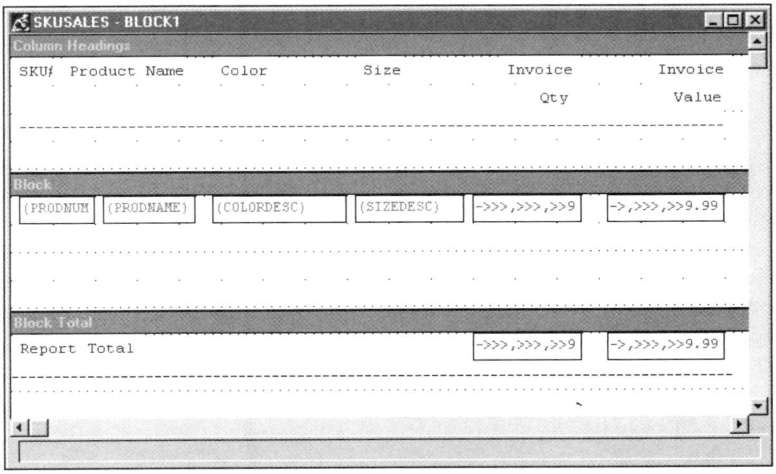

FIGURE 9.23

Viewing a Report Online

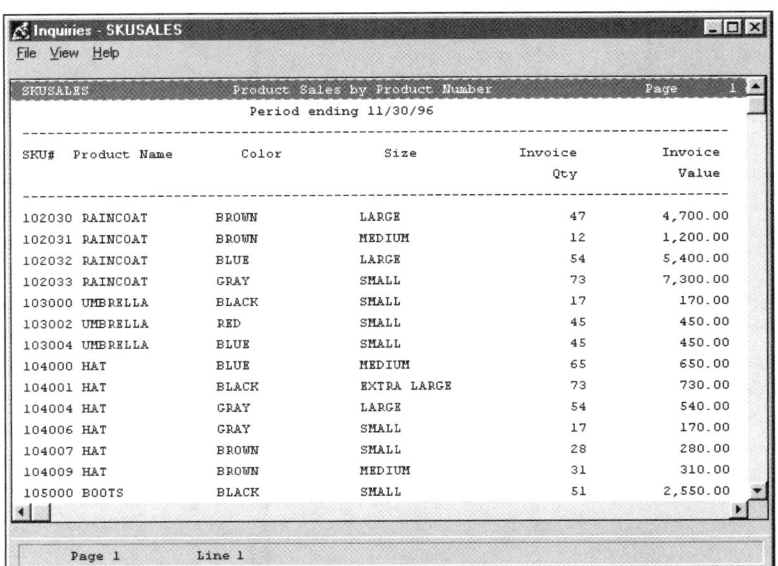

FIGURE 9.24
Defining a Cross-Tab Report

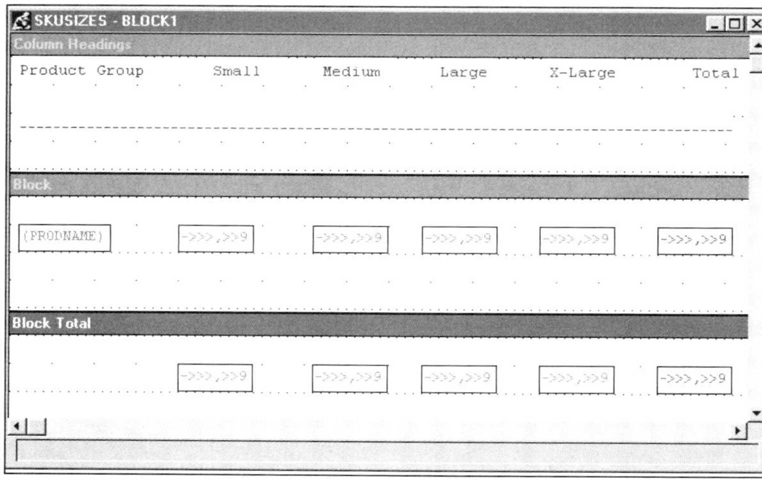

FIGURE 9.25
Grouping Data for a Cross-Tab Report

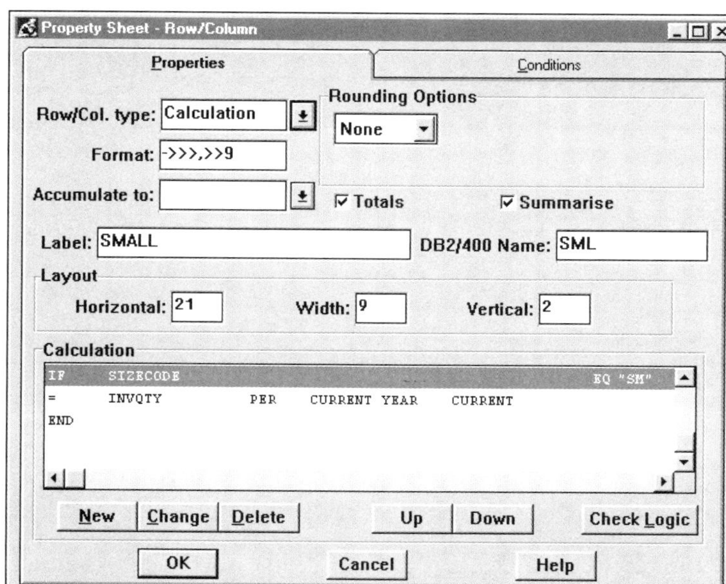

FIGURE 9.26
Viewing a Cross-Tab Report Online

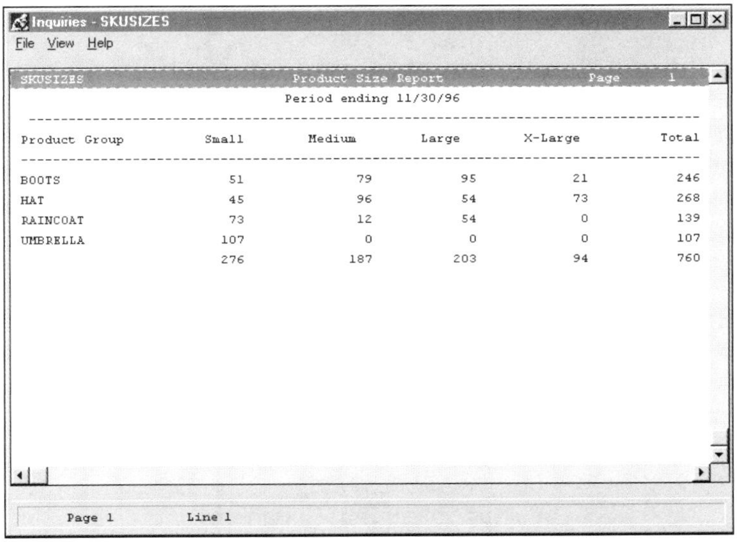

Product Group	Small	Medium	Large	X-Large	Total
BOOTS	51	79	95	21	246
HAT	45	96	54	73	268
RAINCOAT	73	12	54	0	139
UMBRELLA	107	0	0	0	107
	276	187	203	94	760

FIGURE 9.27
Designing the Format

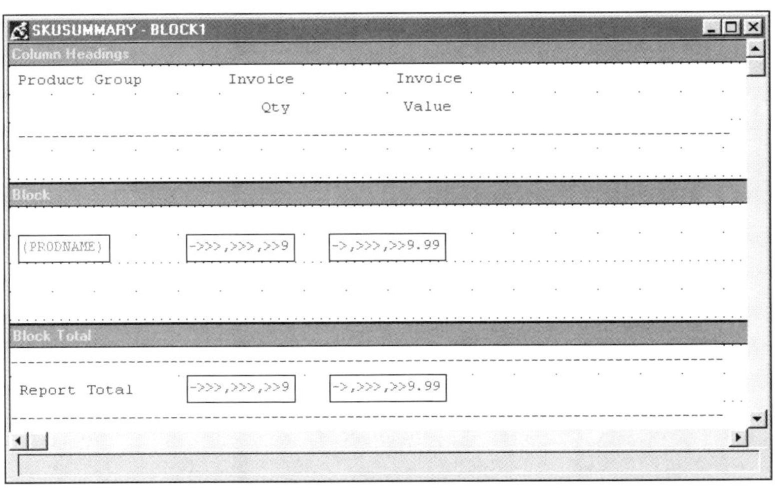

FIGURE 9.28
Specifying a Summary

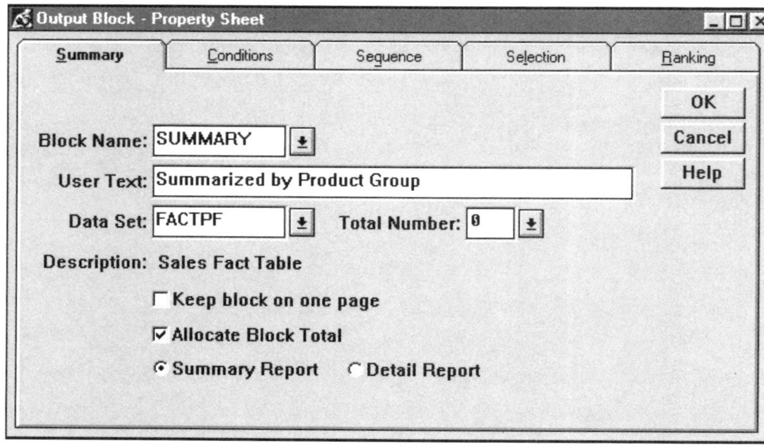

FIGURE 9.29
Specifying Sort Sequence

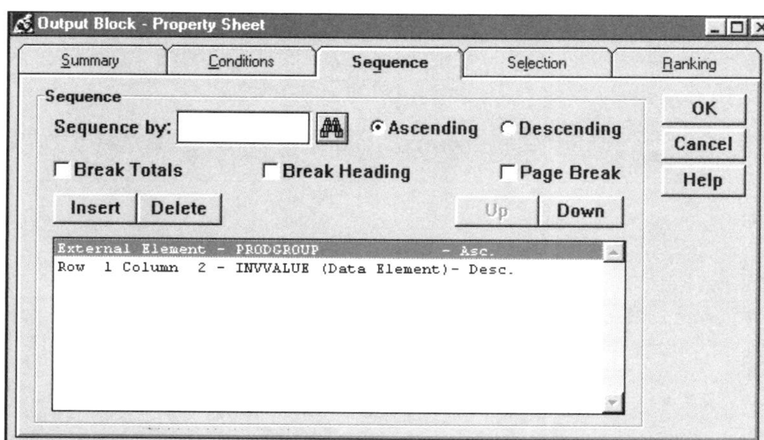

FIGURE 9.30
Viewing the Report Online

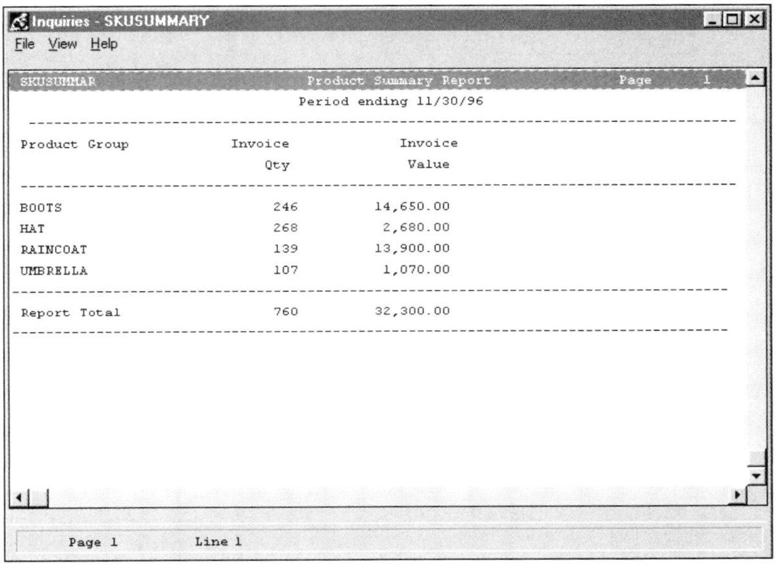

PRODUCT SUMMARY AND POSITIONING

RODIN is a tool used to define, populate, and maintain large-scale, enterprise-wide, DB2/400-based data warehouses. It does not include a database per se. Furthermore, it is not intended to function as a comprehensive data-warehousing solution because it does not include presentation and analysis software.

RODIN's greatest strength is rooted in its creation of RPG programs to perform all data-acquisition and data-management tasks. In contrast to other data-propagation products, RODIN does not require you to write SQL statements or external programs to transform data. And because it generates RPG code, RODIN processes data more efficiently and more flexibly than higher-level, SQL/400-based replication products such as IBM's DataPropagator and DataMirror's Transformation Server.

RODIN fully supports and exploits the AS400's parallel-processing capabilities during both data-load and data-extract processing, and is thus a highly scalable solution that can capably manage an SMP-enabled multi-terabyte data warehouse. To put its capabilities into context, let's look at some performance benchmarks.

In tests conducted at IBM's Teraplex Center on a 12-way model 650 AS/400, RODIN loaded 100-byte records into a data warehouse at the rate of 45 million records per hour. It also loaded 500-byte records at a rate of 38 million per hour and 2,000-byte records at a rate of 11 million per hour. Associated hourly gigabyte rates were 5, 19, and 22, respectively. These tests were conducted without journaling, as would be the case during an initial load process. No cleansing processes were performed during these tests. However, after adding extensive cleansing processes to the test procedures, load rates declined by a mere 5 to 15 percent. At a cost of $50,000 for entry-level servers to $250,000 for 12-way machines, RODIN is not for everybody. However, for large organizations that must acquire, transform, move, and manage significant volumes of data for their data warehouse, RODIN makes a lot of sense. And when you compare the cost of AS/400 programmers to RODIN's price, it is often difficult to justify the creation of homegrown data-management software.

Chapter 10

DataMirror Corporation and Transformation Server for AS/400

Company Background

DataMirror Corporation, founded in 1993, develops software to extract, transform, and synchronize data across numerous homogeneous and heterogeneous databases and platforms. Headquartered in Markham, Ontario, Canada, DataMirror has annual revenues of approximately $20 million and more than 420 customers worldwide. A publicly traded company listed on the Toronto Stock Exchange, DataMirror also maintains regional sales and support offices in San Francisco; Dallas; Canton, Connecticut; and Chicago. The company services customers in the United Kingdom and Ireland through an office located outside London. A variety of distribution channels also markets DataMirror products in Australia, South America, and continental Europe. DataMirror maintains alliances with Brio Technology, Digital, Ernst & Young, Hewlett-Packard, IBM, JD Edwards, Microsoft, Olympic amis, Oracle, Sun, and Sybase.

Transformation Server for AS/400, DataMirror's flagship product for the AS/400 market, is designed to access, transform, and replicate S/36, S/38, and AS/400 data files. The product can move data across multiple AS/400s or from one database to another on a single machine. DataMirror also develops versions of Transformation Server that replicate data among Oracle databases on HP 9000, RS/6000, and Sun computers, between DB2/400 and Oracle on these same systems, and to both Oracle and Microsoft SQL Server databases on Windows NT-based PCs. Additional versions of the product replicate DB2/400 data from and to Microsoft SQL Server databases residing on Pentium- and Alpha-based Windows NT Servers. While DataMirror's strategic goal for the Transformation Server product line is to transform and replicate data across any database on any platform, this chapter focuses solely on the transformation and movement of DB2/400 data in a homogenous AS/400 environment.

In addition to Transformation Server, DataMirror sells ObjectMirror, a real-time object-mirroring application used to replicate AS/400 objects to one or more failsafe target systems.

Product Overview

A comprehensive transformation and replication product, Transformation Server for AS/400 can access a variety of file structures, including both single- and multimember physical files. To reduce network traffic, the product filters source data by column (field) and by row (record). Once Transformation Server has filtered data, it transforms that data into meaningful information suitable for a data warehouse. The product can update field content, change field names, reformat field sizes, translate field values, modify field types, and derive entirely new fields directly or through value-translation lists. Programmers also can bolster these functions with external, callable programs referred to as user exits. Although Transformation Server has fairly comprehensive data-transformation capabilities, you will find it necessary to utilize user exits from time to time.

Transformation Server replicates data asynchronously, does not require two-phase commits, and can refresh warehouse repositories on a net-change basis periodically or in real time. The product also supports full-copy database replenishment. In the case of net-change propagation, Transformation Server examines journaled transactions and propagates only those data elements that have changed. It can propagate DB2/400 data on a single AS/400, from one AS/400 to another, or from one AS/400 to multiple target AS/400s. The program also can distribute information in a cascading fashion and consolidate data from numerous AS/400s onto a single target machine.Transformation Server works with both SNA and TCP/IP communications protocols and can be installed on any AS/400 running V2R2 or later. Unlike Coglin-Mill's RODIN, or IBM's Data-Propagator/400 (which I examine in Chapter 13), Transformation Server for AS/400 is not yet available with a GUI interface. However, DataMirror is actively working to address this issue.

For several key reasons, Transformation Server has been widely embraced as an effective data-transformation and warehouse-propagation tool:

- As a menu-based application, Transformation Server does not require programming skills to install, administer, or use. Any IT professional (e.g., programmers, system administrators, systems analysts) with rudimentary knowledge of DB2/400 can effectively use this product to transform and replicate data. Additionally, all menu options are available as commands and can be included in CL programs to automate administration and use of the product.
- Transformation Server automates tasks that would otherwise require SQL, RPG, or COBOL code to accomplish. As you will see later in this chapter, it lets you manipulate and update data using intuitive, English-like phrases.
- Transformation Server lets you rapidly distribute DB2/400 data throughout an enterprise. Because this product obviates the need to write and test complicated programs, you can implement warehouse applications in less time.

Implementation Example

To use Transformation Server effectively, you must perform four main tasks. These include

1. The definition of one or more target systems.
2. The selection of files, records, and fields to be propagated.
3. The definition and association of target files with source files.
4. The initiation of a propagation schedule.

To effectively convey Transformation Server's functionality, this chapter includes numerous screen captures that illustrate how we can use the product to propagate our sample invoice data to a data warehouse residing on a separate AS/400.

Defining Target Systems

In Transformation Server parlance, a target system does not necessarily refer to an additional physical AS/400 upon which a data warehouse resides. Rather, target systems are logical definitions that reside on AS/400s that contain source data for data warehouses. These logical target systems provide a way to group together related files that must remain synchronized during transformation and propagation processes; these groups can then be processed and transferred to additional AS/400s independently of one another. For example, one logical target system might include a number of sales files while another consists of numerous inventory files. In the case of a data warehouse, Transformation Server can propagate both groups of files to the same physical target AS/400, and it can do so with different frequencies. For instance, it can transfer inventory data to the warehouse continually throughout the day, while it propagates sales information one time each evening. Transformation Server's target systems facilitate this functionality.

To define a target system, we select option 2 (Work with Target Systems) from the DataMirror Source System Menu in Figure 10.1 to execute the Work with Target Systems command that appears in Figure 10.2.

After we press F6 at this command prompt, we are asked to input the target system name and description on the Add Target System screen shown in Figure 10.3 (page 167). In this case, we have opted to create a target system called DATAWHSE. Notice that the bottom portion of the Add Target System screen includes a section entitled Communication Type. Parameters in this section of the screen specify the physical address of the target AS/400, as well as the applicable communications protocol.

After we have entered the information on this screen, the Work with Target Systems command (shown in Figure 10.4 on page 167) reflects the addition of a new target system.

FIGURE 10.1
DataMirror Source System Menu

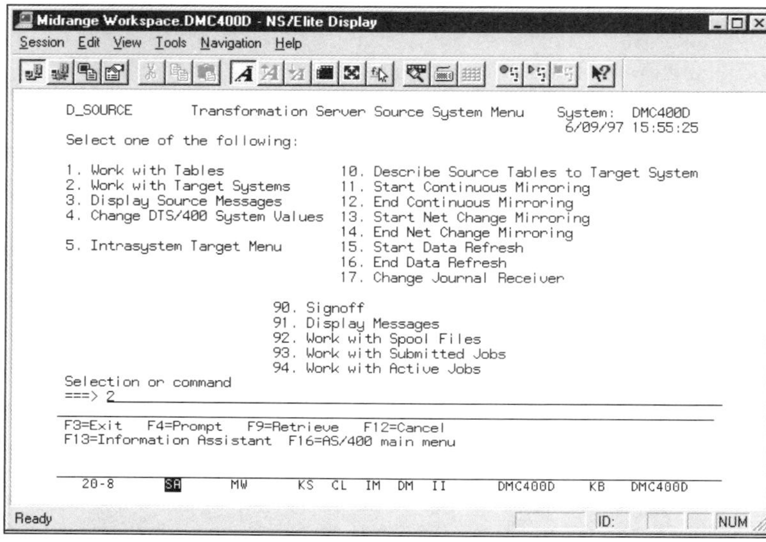

FIGURE 10.2
Work with Target Systems Screen

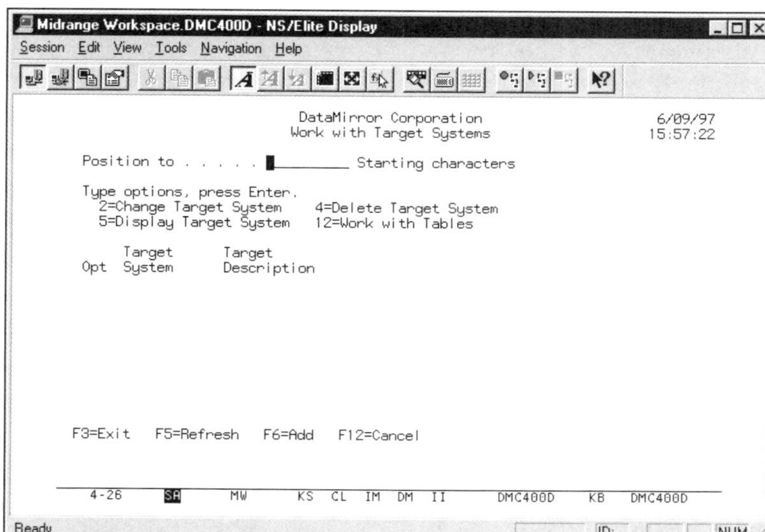

FIGURE 10.3

Add Target System Screen

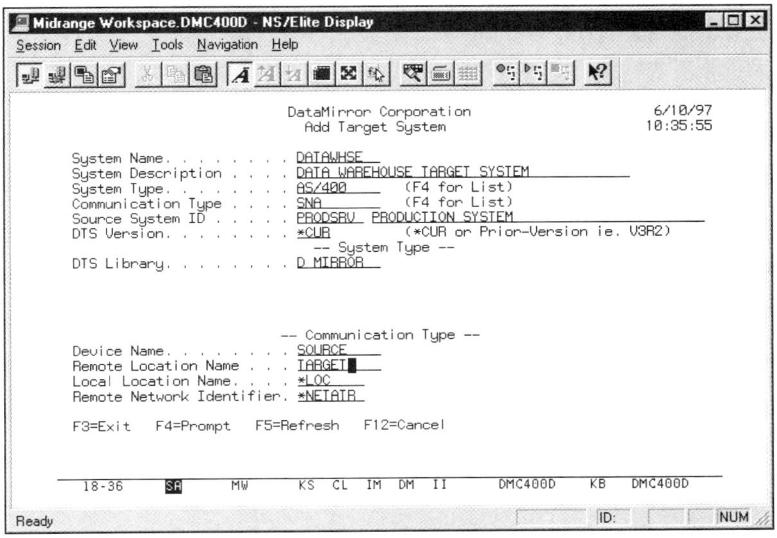

FIGURE 10.4

Work with Target Systems Screen, Option 12

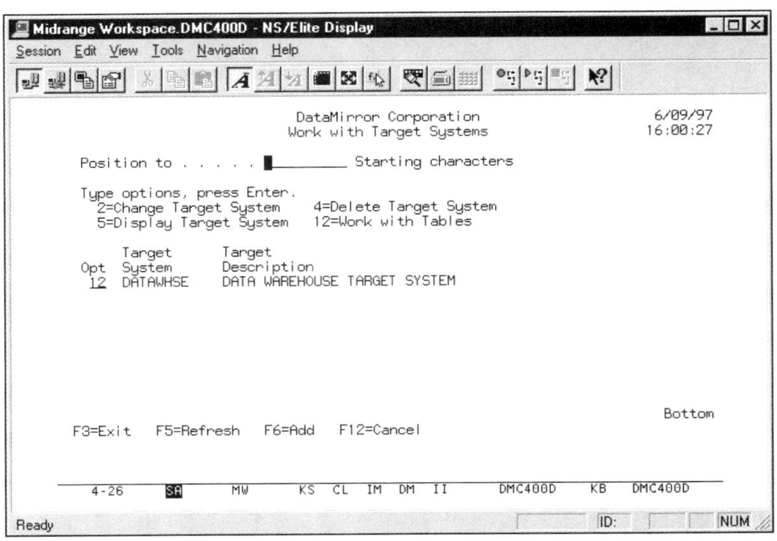

Selecting Source Data

After we have defined one or more logical target systems on the source AS/400, we then select files, records, and fields for transformation and propagation to the data warehouse. To add a file to Transformation Server, we select option 1 (Work with Tables) from the Source System Menu shown in Figure 10.5.

FIGURE 10.5
Source System Menu, Option 1

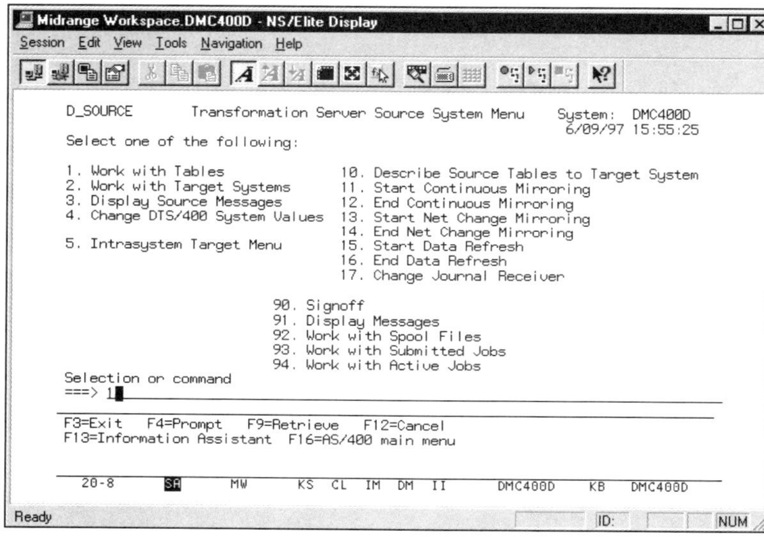

The DataMirror Work with Tables screen then displays a list of all files previously added to Transformation Server. As Figure 10.6 illustrates, files have not yet been added at this point.

To actually add files (or tables), we press F6 to invoke the Add Table command prompt, shown in Figure 10.7. In this case, we have specified the invoice header file IN001PF and its corresponding library. When we add a file to Transformation Server with the Add Table command, the file's field names and attributes are automatically added to Transformation Server's metadata repository.

FIGURE 10.6
Work with Tables Screen

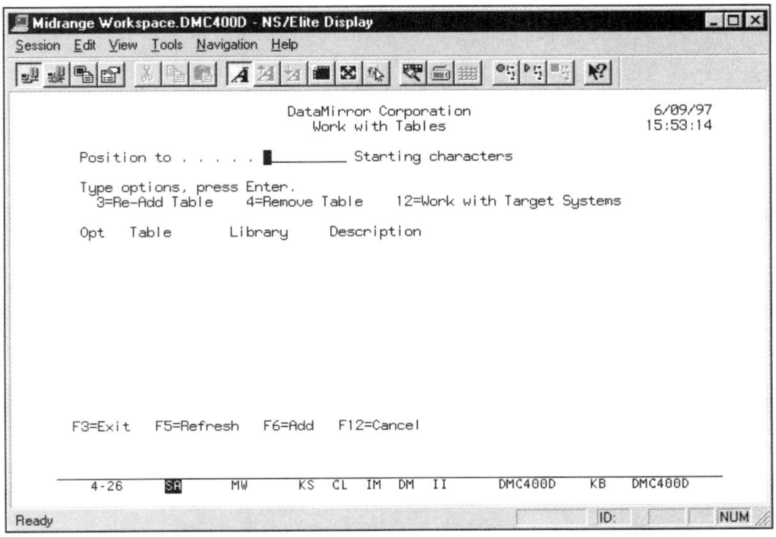

FIGURE 10.7
Add Table Screen

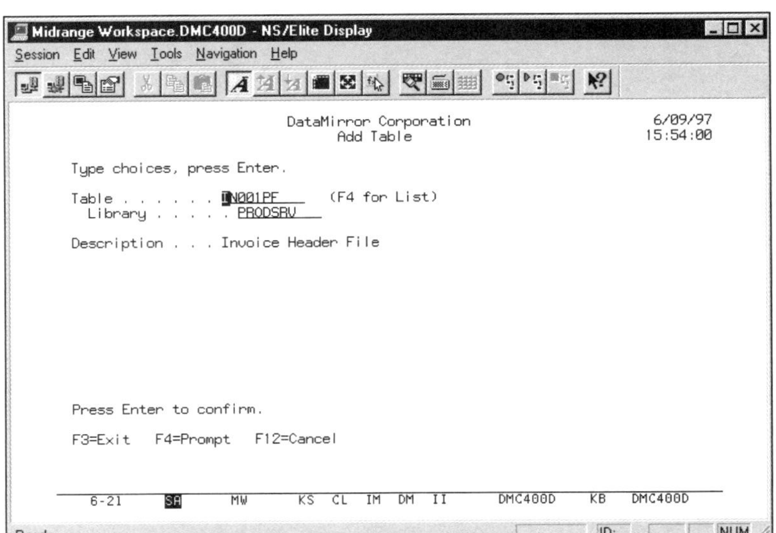

The product also lets us add multiple files in a single step, whether via wild-card characters or by specifying an entire library. Figure 10.8 shows the Work with Tables command after we have added the product file TA001PF to Transformation Server.

FIGURE 10.8
Work with Tables Screen, Product File TA001PF Added

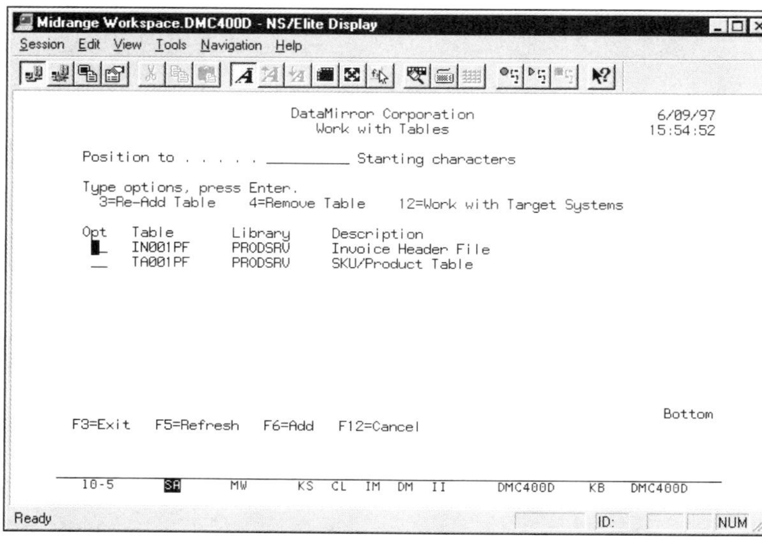

Once we have added files to Transformation Server, we can propagate these files to other databases and machines. To select the invoice header file IN001PF, we invoke the Work with Tables (By Target) command, shown in Figure 10.9.

After we select this file by entering a 1 to the left of the file name, Transformation Server presents us with its Select Target screen, as Figure 10.10 demonstrates. We can select the type of update processing (either uniquely keyed or via relative record number) to be used in replicating data to the target table. As you can see, we can opt to replicate data by choosing option 1 or option 3, which transmits the entire contents of the selected file to a specified table on the target system. On this screen, we also can elect to replicate data through mirroring.

FIGURE 10.9
Work with Tables (by Target) Screen, Option 1

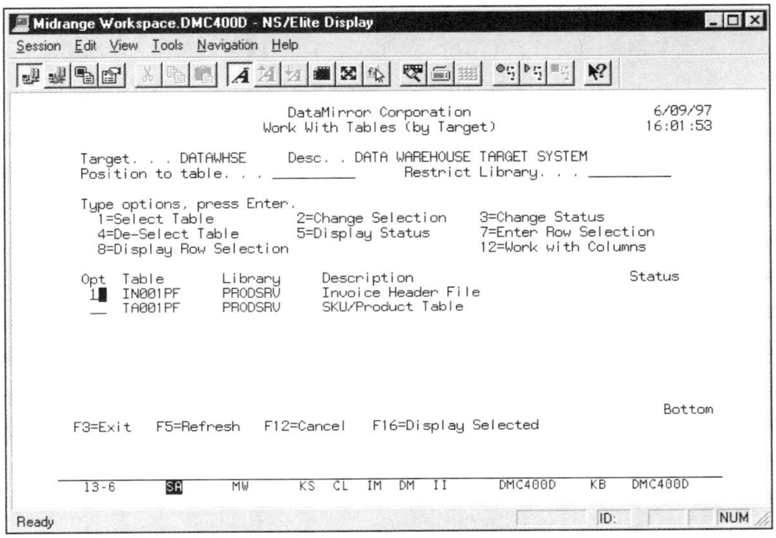

FIGURE 10.10
Select Target Screen, Option 1

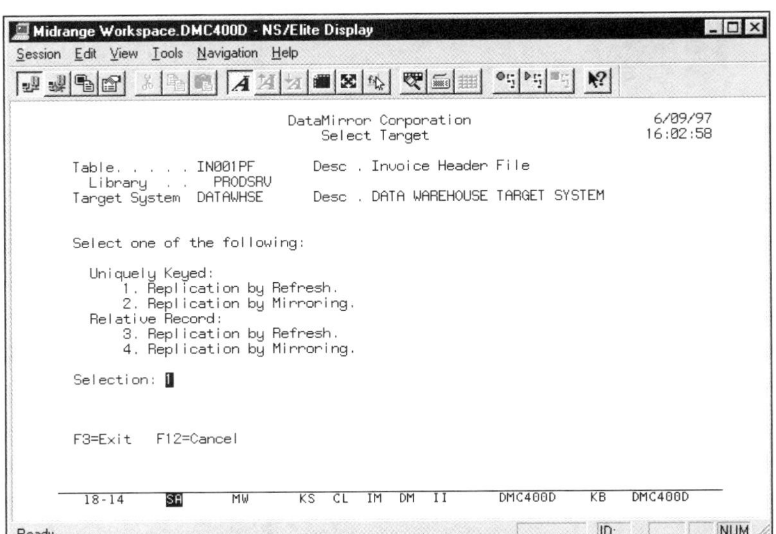

After we specify the desired replication method for IN001PF, the Work with Tables (by Target) screen reappears, as shown in Figure 10.11. Notice that the status of file IN001PF has been updated to IDLE, which means that the table has been selected for replication but has not yet been activated. (In a later step, we change the status of this file from IDLE to RFSH (refresh) to actually activate the propagation process.) At this point, we input 12 (Work with Columns) to the left of the file IN001PF to specify field-selection criteria.

FIGURE 10.11
Work with Tables (by Target) Screen, Option 12

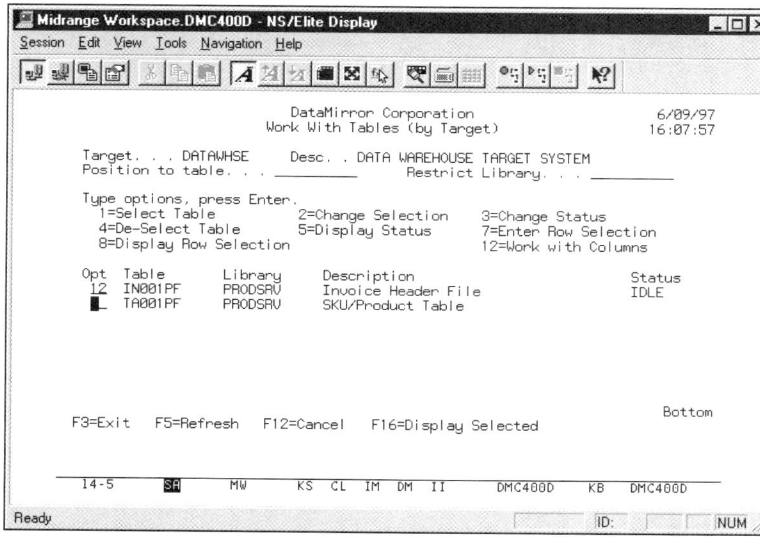

The Work with Columns screen in Figure 10.12 lets us choose fields by entering a 1 next to each field to be propagated. Alternatively, we can select F9 to include all fields, after which we can use a 4 to de-select individual fields. Unfortunately, Transformation Server does not support the dynamic linking of multiple files at source in the reviewed release. This limitation may require us to create join-logical files or a DataMirror User Exit to accomplish that task. However, the next release of Transformation Server for AS/400, scheduled for general availability in late 1997 or early 1998, will support joins. (This new functionality will be added to the screen previously shown in Figure 10.11.)

FIGURE 10.12
Work with Columns Screen

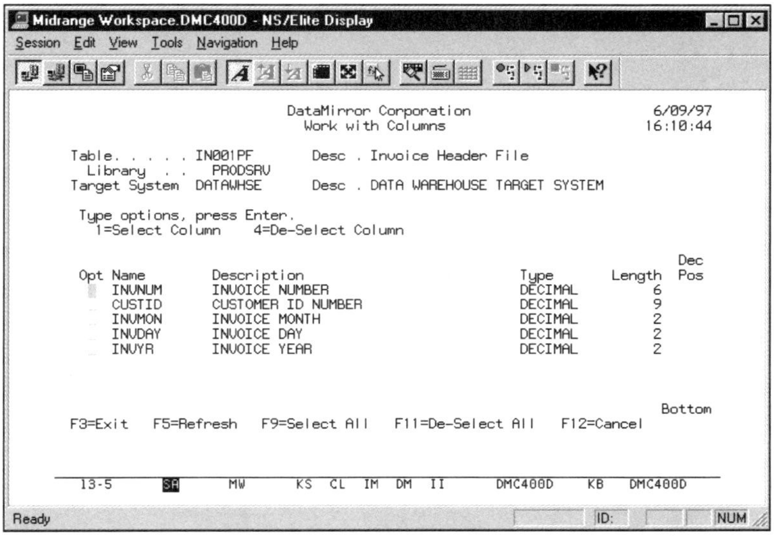

After we select file TA001PF, the Work with Tables (by Target) command appears as shown in Figure 10.13 on the following page. As you can see, the status of both IN001PF and TA001PF is now IDLE.

As we saw in Chapter 3, the capability to select particular fields (i.e., columns) for propagation to a data warehouse is a key feature of any replication product. With column selection, only pertinent fields are transferred to the data warehouse, thereby reducing network traffic and the associated communications overhead. Furthermore, we can leave confidential information behind in source files for security or other reasons.

After we specify logical target systems and define source data to be propagated to the warehouse, we must describe source tables to the target AS/400. We use option 10 (Describe Source Tables to Target System) on the Source System Menu, shown in Figure 10.14 (page 174), to send data description specifications (DDS) to the target AS/400. Figure 10.15 (page 175) depicts the Start DataMirror (STRDTAMIR) command that we invoke to describe source files to the target machine. In this case, because the "Describe source to target" parameter has been initialized to *ONLY, we have opted to send only metadata to the target system.

FIGURE 10.13

Work with Tables (by Target) Screen, IN001PF and TA001PF IDLE

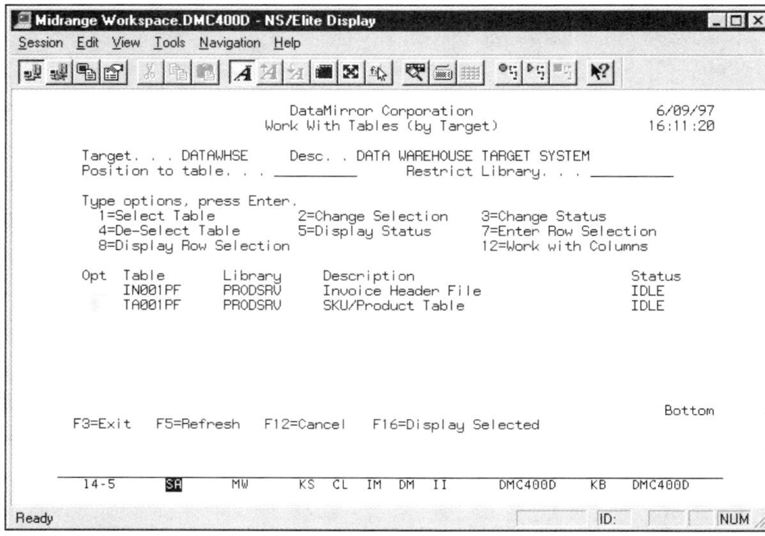

FIGURE 10.14

Source System Menu, Option 10

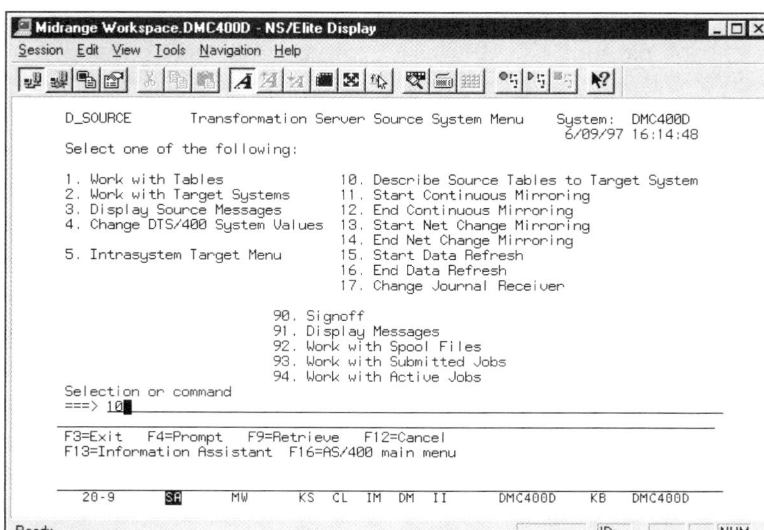

FIGURE 10.15

Start DataMirror (STRDTAMIR) Command Screen

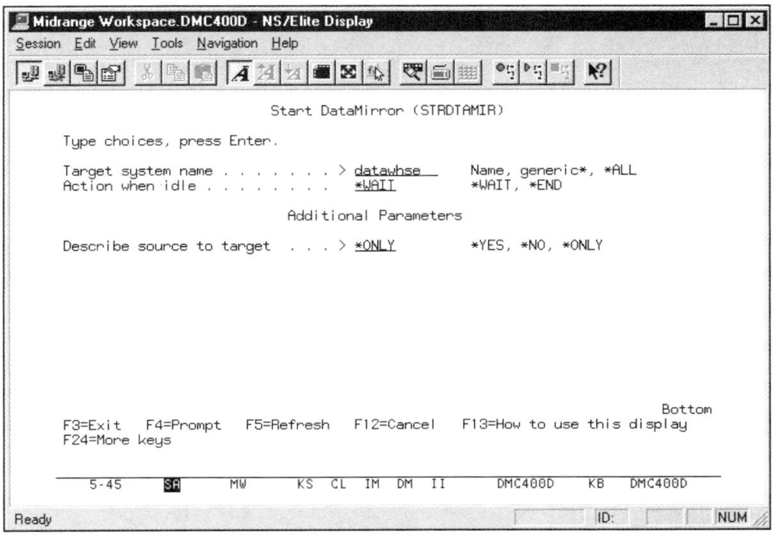

The process of describing source tables to the target machine saves us considerable time. Without this functionality, we would have to manually rekey DDS on the target system. After this step, we sign on to the target machine to actually define the target database (i.e., data warehouse).

Defining Target Tables

Let's now assume that we have signed on to the target AS/400. To define files on the target AS/400, we'll select option 1 (Work with Tables) from the DataMirror Target System Menu, as shown in Figure 10.16 (page 176). This option lets us choose source files, as the Work with Source Tables command in Figure 10.17 (page 176) shows. For example, to assign IN001PF to a target table, we input a 1 to the left of IN001PF. This step causes the Assign Target Table screen to appear (shown in Figure 10.18 on page 177). As you can see, we can assign IN001PF to either an existing file on the target machine via option 1 or to a new table on the target machine via option 2. When we choose option 2, we have complete flexibility in designing the layout of the target table when Transformation Server creates it. In this example, we selected option 1 (Assign to Existing Table).

Figure 10.16
DataMirror Target Systems Menu

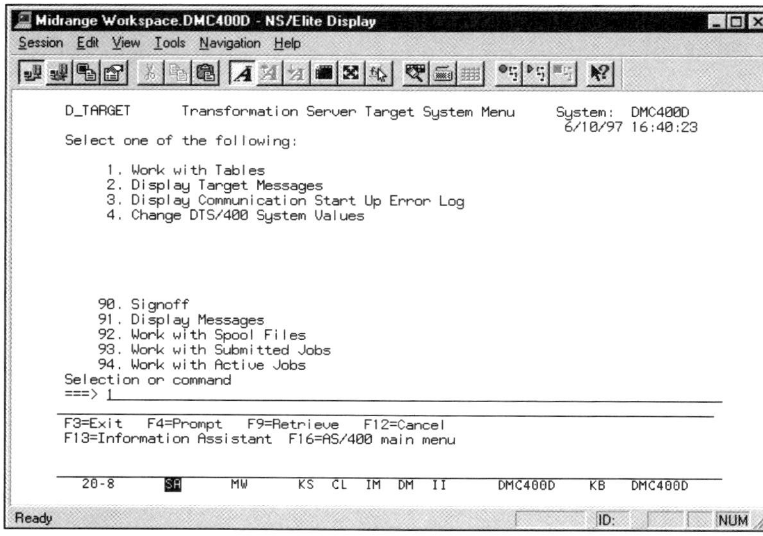

Figure 10.17
Work with Source Tables Screen, Option 1

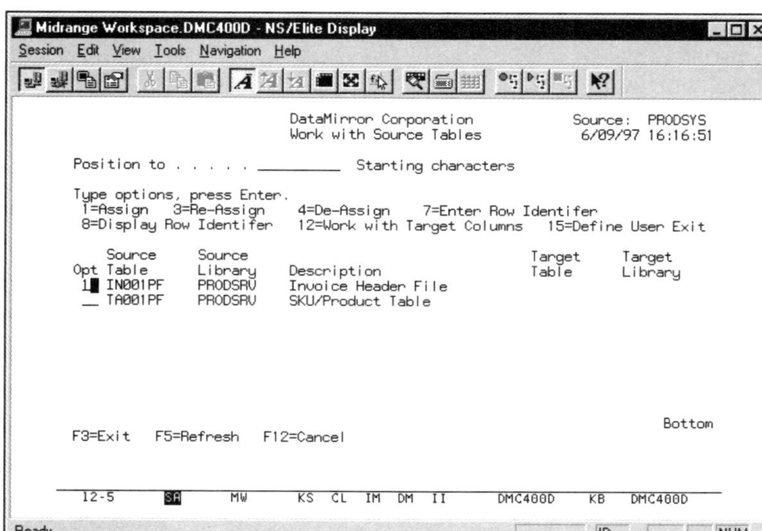

FIGURE 10.18
Assign Target Table Screen

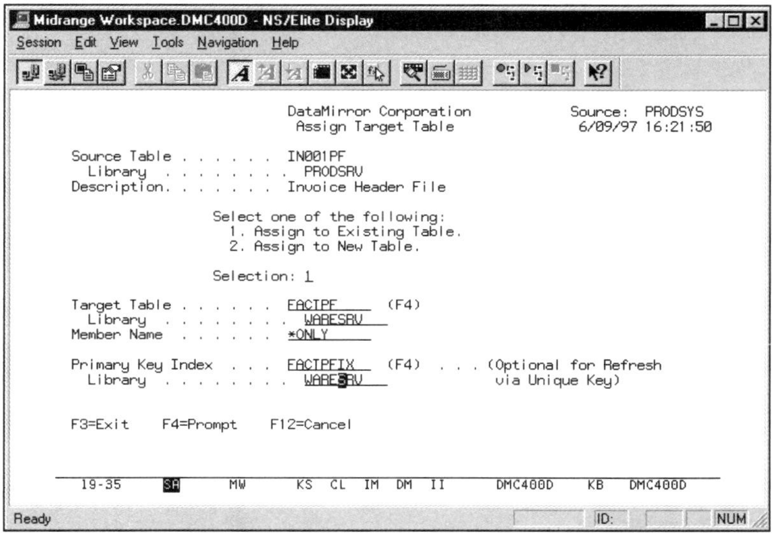

At this point, we can define the structure of target fields (i.e., columns) on the target machine. The Work with Target Columns screen shown in Figure 10.19 (page 178) on the following page lets us derive new expressions. On this screen, Transformation Server also displays the source fields of target fields if the field names are consistent across the files. In Figure 10.19, we have selected the field TIMEID by inputting a 7 so the field can be populated via a derived expression.

Transformation Server lets us quickly create complex transformation routines with user exits. Figure 10.20 (page 178) illustrates how we use a user exit (i.e., a user-defined program expression) to propagate the values from the source fields INVMON, INVDAY, and INVYR to TIMEID.

For fields defined as type DATE, Transformation Server provides a date-conversion function (%TODATE) that we can use to generate new century-compliant fields. Figure 10.21 (page 179) shows the Work with Target Columns screen after the derived expression for TIMEID has been created. To reflect this fact, the source column entry for the TIMEID field has been initialized with the keyword *DERIVED. Note that once Transformation Server has defined a target file, the file cannot be modified. If modifications become necessary, we must delete the existing target file and create a new one.

FIGURE 10.19
Work with Target Columns Screen, Option 7 for TIMEID

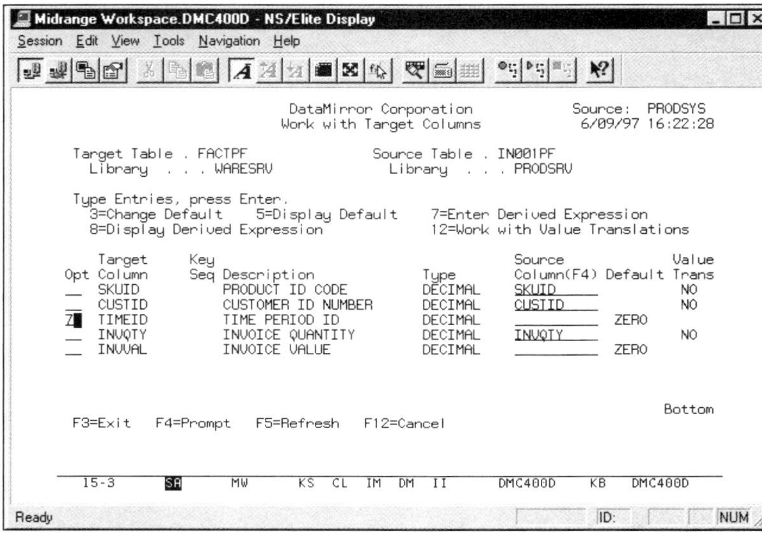

FIGURE 10.20
Enter Derived Expression Screen

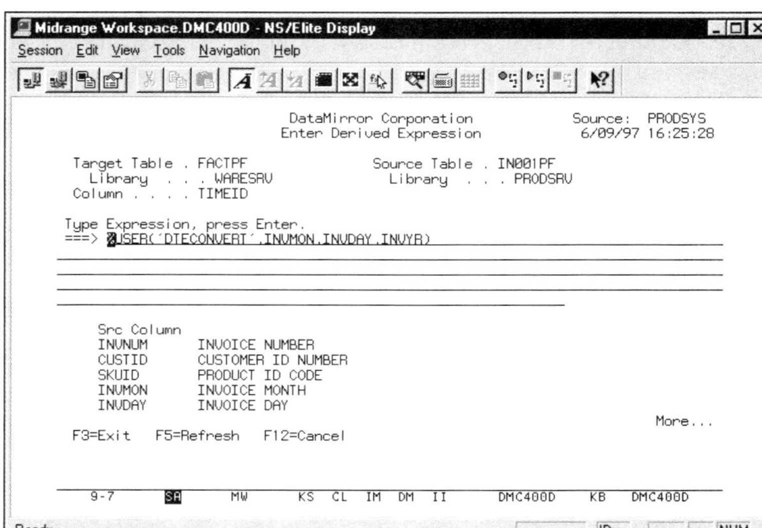

FIGURE 10.21

Work with Target Columns Screen, TIMEID Expression Derived

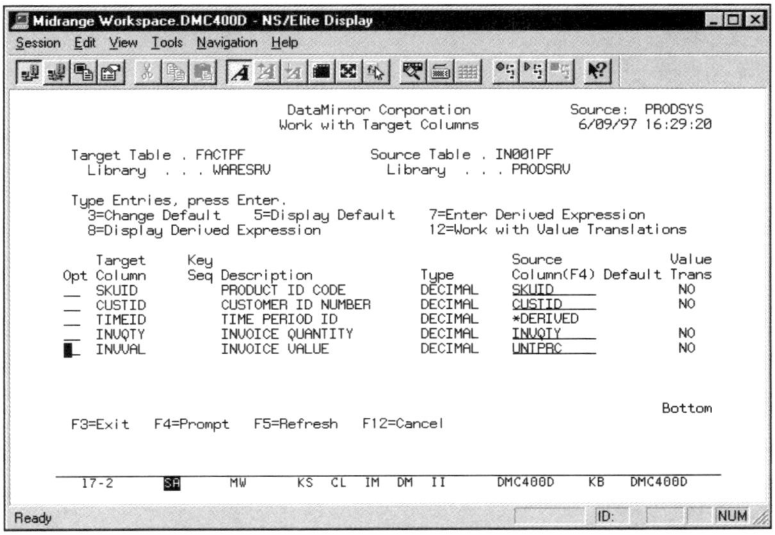

To further illustrate Transformation Server's transformation functionality, we map the field PRDCOL (product color) in TA001PF to a target field called COLOR in target table PRODPF. We assign the file TA001PF to file PRODPF using the same method we used above. In this situation, however, we do not use a derived expression. Rather, we employ a value-translation list to assign color names to color codes. To create a value-translation list for the field COLOR, we input a 12 to the left of the field, as Figure 10.22 (page 180) demonstrates. This action invokes the Work with Value Translations screen shown in Figure 10.23 (page 180). To assign specific field values to codes, we invoke the Add Value Translation command by pressing F6 at this screen. Figure 10.24 (page 181) illustrates the assignment of Blue to the code BL. Figure 10.25 (page 181) depicts the completed color-value-translation list.

FIGURE 10.22
Work with Target Columns Screen, Option 12 for COLOR

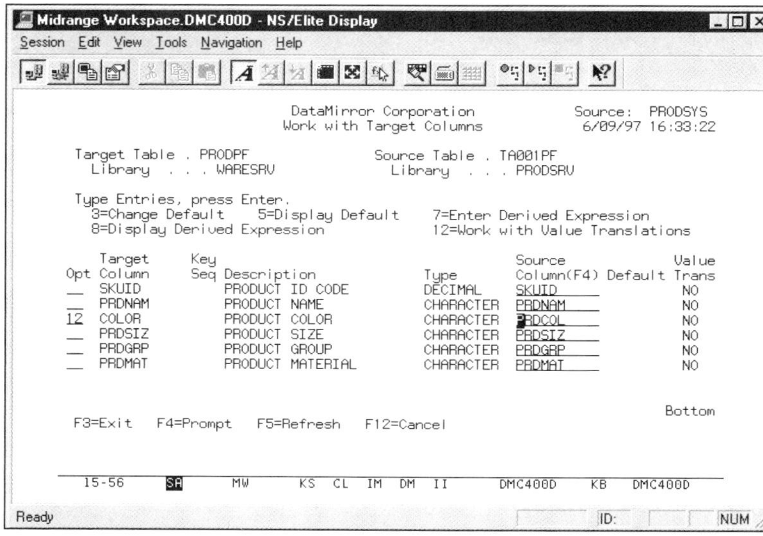

FIGURE 10.23
Initial Work with Value Translations Screen

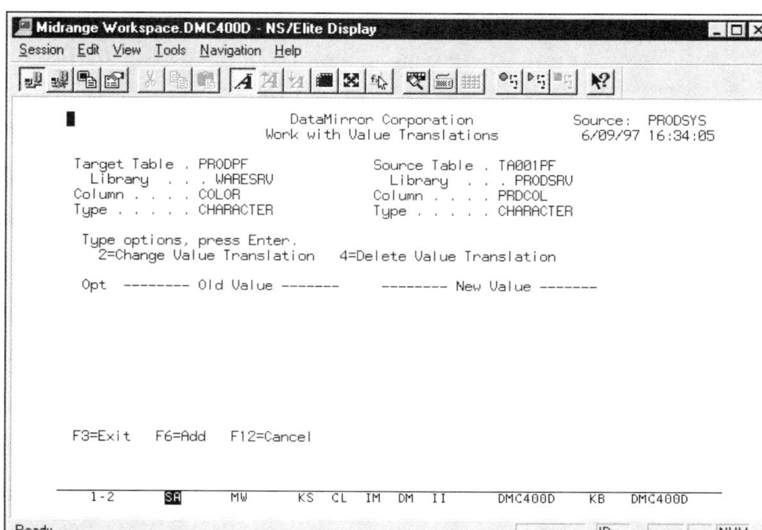

FIGURE 10.24
Add Value Translation Screen

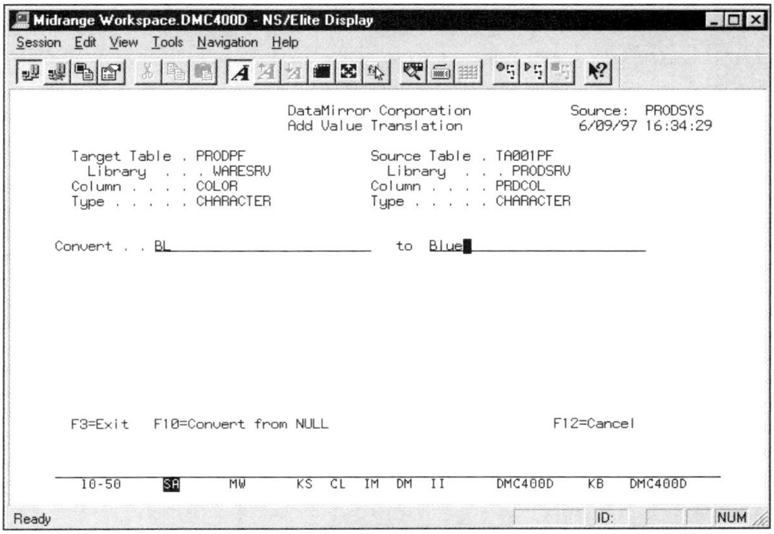

FIGURE 10.25
Completed Work with Value Translations Screen

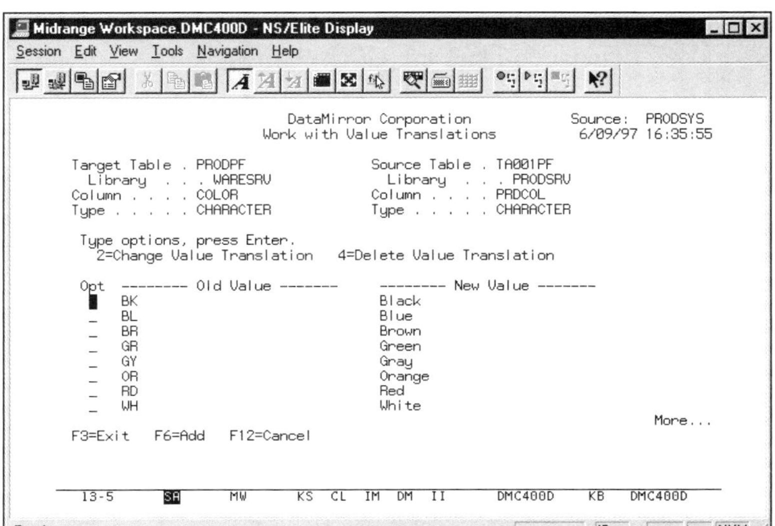

As a final step on the target system, let's assign a summarization program to appropriate fields. In this instance, let's assume we have written a program called SUMUPDATE in a language such as RPG or Cobol. The purpose of this program is to aggregate data by keys. Figures 10.26 and 10.27 illustrate how to invoke the user-exit assignment process for a program called SUMUPDATE.

FIGURE 10.26
Work with Source Tables Screen, Option 15

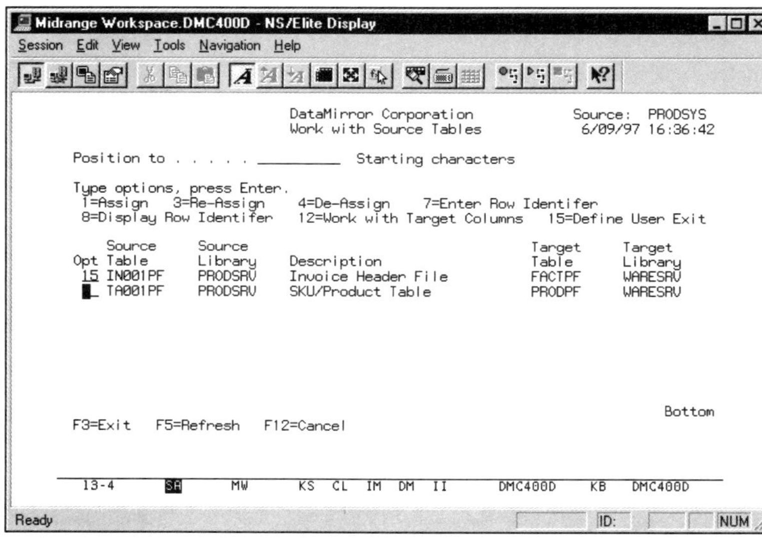

FIGURE 10.27
Change User Exit Definition Screen for Program SUMUPDATE

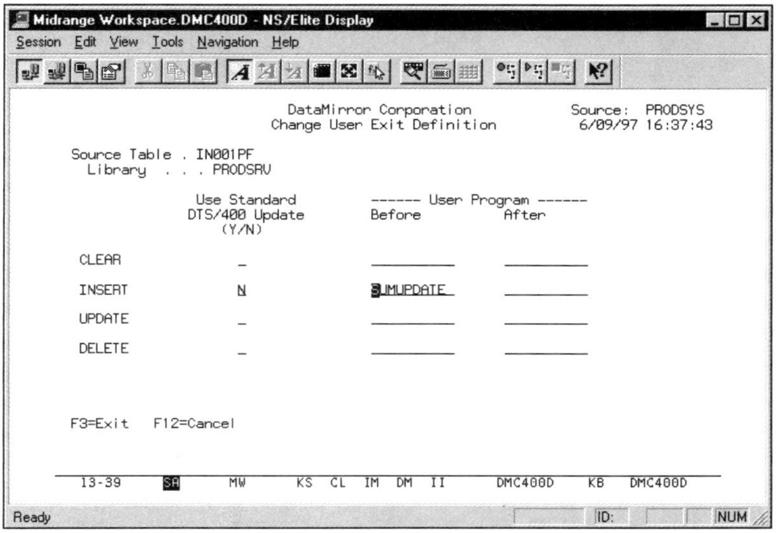

At this point, we have completed the target system administration processes. To actually begin the replication process, we return to the source system. When we use the Replication By Refresh Method, as in this example, we must change the status of each source file from IDLE to RFSH (refresh). To perform this process, we select option 2 (Work with Target Systems) on the Source System Menu, followed by option 12 (Work with Tables by Target). After we complete these two steps, we input option 3 (Change Status) next to each file, as shown in Figure 10.28 (page 184). Figure 10.29 (page 184) illustrates how we actually change the status of each file to Refresh.

FIGURE 10.28

Work with Tables (by Target) Screen, Option 3

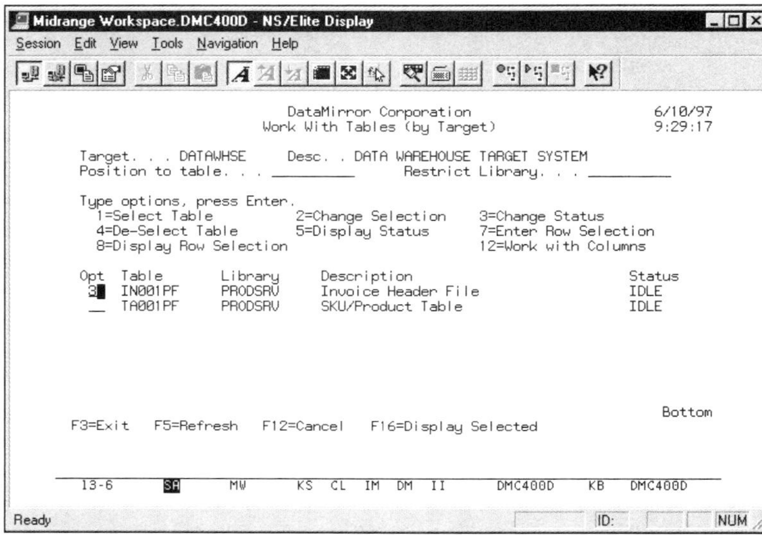

FIGURE 10.29

Change Status Screen, Refresh Option

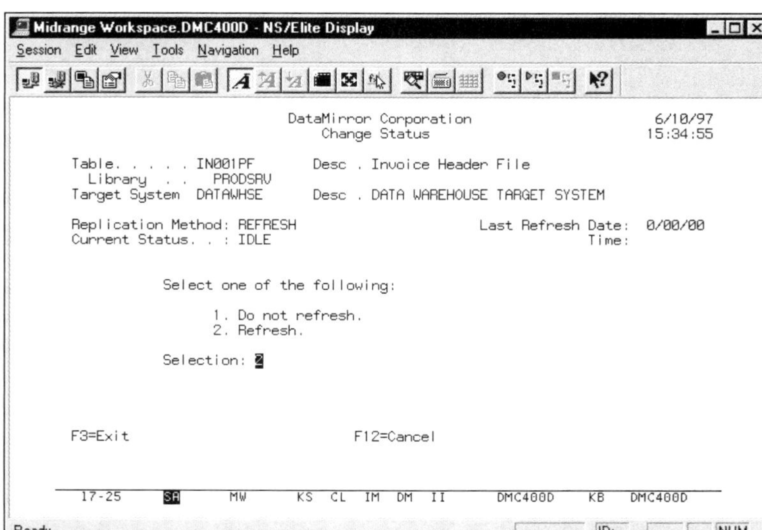

Choosing a Propagation Schedule

The final step in our data-warehouse propagation example is to initiate the replication process. In this example, we are using refresh propagation to load the data warehouse. From the Source System Menu (Figure 10.30), we select option 15 (Start Data Refresh), which invokes the Start Data Refresh command shown in Figure 10.31 on the following page.

FIGURE 10.30

Source System Menu, Option 15

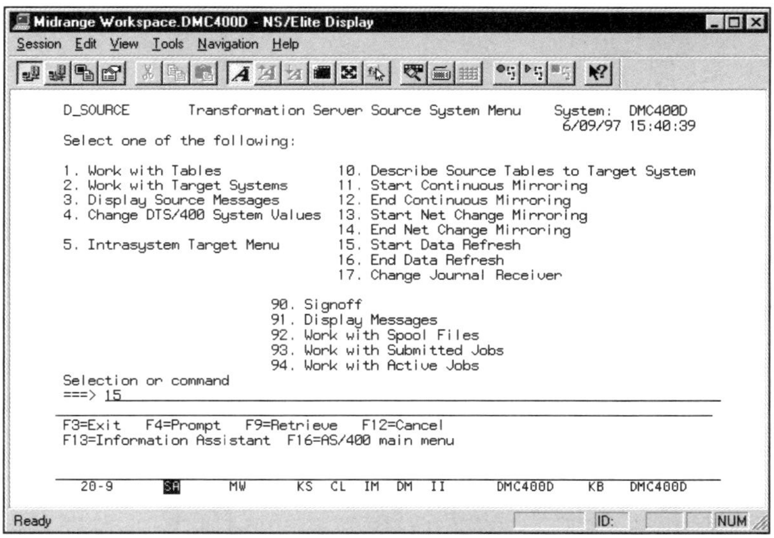

We input the target system name DATAWHSE in the Target System Name prompt, after which the replication procedure is submitted to batch. Transformation Server is now ready to maintain the target file on either a full-refresh or net-change basis. Be aware that refresh procedures that access large files require significant system resources to execute. The Start Data Refresh command, which we also can execute from a scheduling system such as Robot/400 or from within a user-defined CL program, has the following syntax:

```
STRDTARSH <target system name> <tables to refresh>
```

In cases where we want to employ continuous mirroring, we select option 11 on the Source System menu or invoke the STRDTAMIR command with an "Action When Idle" parameter value of *WAIT. To begin net-change mirroring, we select option 13 on the Source System menu or invoke the STRDTAMIR command with an "Action When Idle" parameter of *END. Because mirroring

FIGURE 10.31
Start DataRefresh (STRDTARSH) Screen

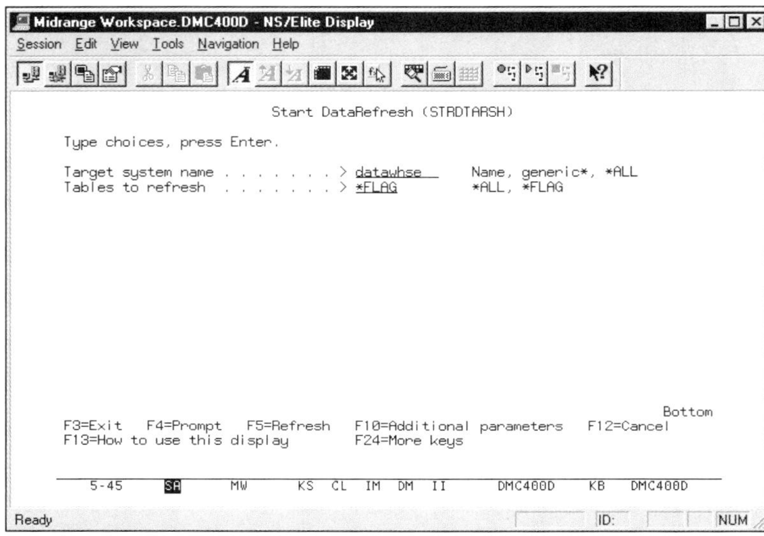

maintains data-warehouse repositories as changes occur in the operational database, it has less of an impact on system resources than full refreshes do. The syntax of the STRDTAMIR command is

```
STRDTAMIR <target system name> <action when idle>
```

Transformation Server performs change propagation through the use of AS/400 journals. If the files we select for mirroring are already journaled, Transformation Server uses the existing journal receivers. If the files are not journaled, the product automatically initiates the journaling process and performs all journal maintenance tasks. When we initiate changes to the status of files, it is important to note that journal entries for any given table/target combination system are considered valid candidates for propagation from the time the status changes to ACTV (Active) on the Work with Table Targets screen on the source.

PRODUCT SUMMARY AND POSITIONING

DataMirror's Transformation Server for AS/400 focuses on the acquisition, transformation, and replication of DB2/400-based OLTP data for DB/400-based data warehouses. The product itself is not a data warehouse; rather, it is a tool that can be used to create, populate, and maintain data-warehouse repositories. You remain responsible for designig the schema for these reposetories, and for integrating the repositories with presentation and analysis tools.

Many of the functions Transformation Server performs can be accomplished through a combination of SQL, RPG, and/or COBOL programming. However, given the product's ease-of-use and its price of $3,250 to $29,800, such efforts are difficult to justify in light of the scarcity and cost of programming manpower. Furthermore, the manual creation of propagation routines to move data from journal receivers to databases on a net-change basis requires programming skills that are beyond the means of many AS/400 shops.

As an application that can move data across systems without requiring you to manually create and send/receive DDM files, Transformation Server is well-suited for use with distributed OLTP or distributed data-warehousing applications. However, as an SQL-based product, Transformation Server does not offer the flexibility to manipulate large volumes of data as freely or efficiently as Coglin Mill's RODIN. Of course, flexibility and power have a price. That is, RODIN requires more time to install and learn than Transformation Server does.

Your affinity for DataMirror Transformation Server will depend largely on the amount of data you must move, the degree to which you must transform that data, and the number of AS/400s you must access for that data.

Chapter 11

Datawatch Corporation and Monarch

Company Background

Founded in 1981, Datawatch Corporation develops a variety of client- and server-based applications for Windows 3.1, Windows 95, and Windows NT. In addition, Datawatch offers Monarch, its flagship business-intelligence product, to the IBM midrange market through partnerships with several AS/400 software companies. Datawatch's products include Monarch, a PC-based product that lets users access, analyze, transform, and replicate data in spooled (e.g., report) files; Monarch ES, a Windows NT Server-based report-archival system featuring front-end capabilities similar to those found in Monarch; Redwing, a Windows-based product that lets users extract data from Adobe portable document files; and Q-Support, a Windows-based Help desk and asset-management package.

Headquartered in Wilmington, Massachusetts, Datawatch is publicly held (NASDAQ:DWCH) and had annual revenue in 1997 of $32 million. The company has approximately 150 employees and more than 25,000 customers worldwide. Datawatch manages North American sales and support through its head office in Wilmington, and maintains additional offices in the United States, Canada, and Europe. Monarch, its multidimensional data-analysis tool, has sold more than 160,000 copies since its introduction in 1991. Major software resellers throughout the world market the product, which is available in English, German, French, and Japanese language editions.

To integrate Monarch functionality with AS/400-based spooled output, Datawatch maintains partnerships with AS/400 software companies such as Business Computer Design (BCD), Inc.; Momentum Utilities Pty. Ltd.; Enable-Soft, Inc.; ETi Solutions, Inc.; and Vanguard Systems, Inc. Outside the AS/400 arena, Datawatch has additional partnerships with more than 25 software and consulting enterprises including Eastman Software, Inc., (formerly Wang Software) and Insci Corporation.

Product Overview

With the exception of Monarch, every product featured in this book is designed to access, transform, and manipulate information stored in databases. Monarch, however, is designed to perform these functions using data stored in formatted spooled files. Because of this critical difference, you might find it helpful to review the sidebars "Spooled Files" (page 192) and "Report Mining" (page 193) before you read more about Monarch and how it works.

[1]1998 revenue included sales of Apple-based product lines that were sold in November 1997.

Monarch has two uses in data warehousing. First, it lets IT personnel and end users transform detailed, report-based data into more meaningful information without programming. This data can then be uploaded to data warehouses. Second, as I mentioned earlier, the package lets users perform sophisticated, multidimensional analyses on downloaded spooled files. A schematic overview of Monarch's functionality appears in Figure 11.1.

FIGURE 11.1
Monarch Overview

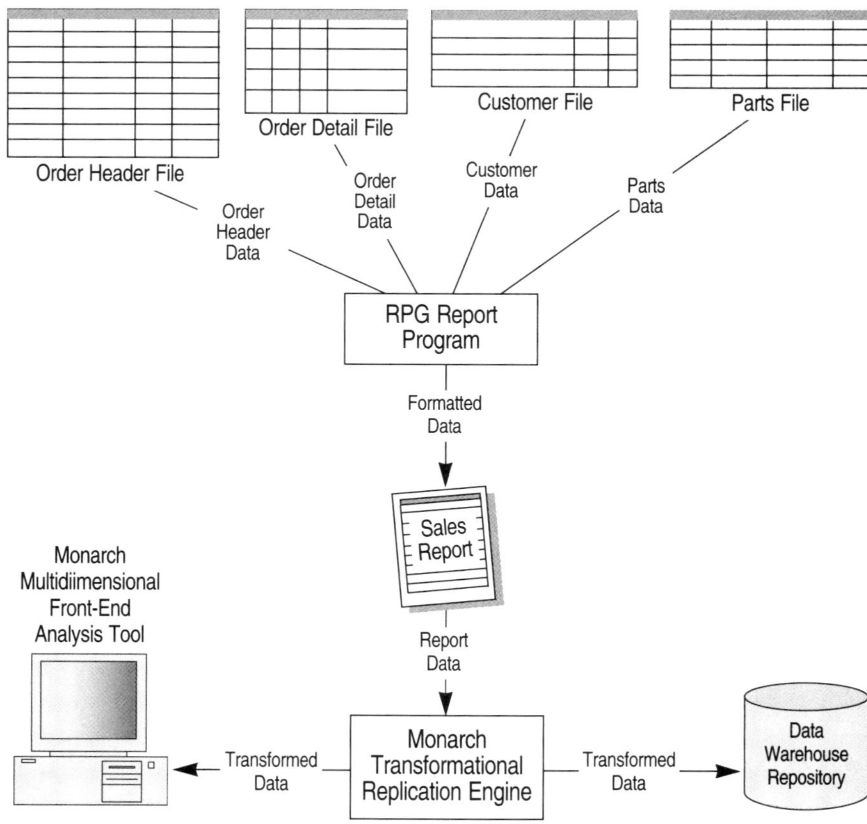

A client-based application coded in Visual C++, Monarch features a multidimensional analysis engine, a charting component, a custom-designed GUI interface, and plug-ins for popular Web browsers such as Netscape Navigator and Microsoft Explorer. With the exception of its browser software, Monarch's components are tightly integrated and are not available separately. Monarch technology, available in 16- and 32-bit versions, is licensed to AS/400 software developers who have augmented it with spooled-file management capabilities. As a client-based application, Monarch processes spooled files that have been downloaded to an AS/400 folder, a PC-based server, or a local hard disk. To populate DB2/400-based data warehouses, data is first extracted from the downloaded spooled file, transformed using Monarch's highly intuitive interface, exported in ASCII format, then uploaded back into DB/400 files on the AS/400.

A multidimensional analysis engine that can process any ASCII text file lies at the heart of Monarch's many features. Using Monarch's analytic capabilities, end users can filter data by field and by record. They also can sort, subtotal, graph, and export data to PC applications such as Lotus, Excel, dBASE, and Paradox. Monarch's analysis engine also supports date arithmetic, string manipulation, conditional logic, statistical functions, and mathematical operations. End users can use these functions to derive new fields, rename fields, modify field attributes, translate field values, convert dates, and so on. Monarch's analysis engine also can simultaneously extract information from multiple instances of a single report — a feature that enables trend analysis because it lets you examine multiple instances of a report (e.g., monthly sales reports) over time. Monarch also lets users create multidimensional charts and graphs via its graphics component. End users can then drill up and down through these graphical depictions of information. They also can view graphs, associated tables, and the underlying report in side-by-side windows. With Monarch's browser plug-in, the Monarch Report Explorer, users can also view spooled files over the Internet or corporate intranets. Report Explorer is available as a standalone report viewer.

Implementation Example

To use Monarch effectively, we must perform three functions: download a spooled file, extract data from the spooled file, and analyze the extracted data. We have modified our sample sales data and written it to an AS/400 printer file (e.g., a spooled file) called IN001RF.

To download IN001RF from the AS/400 to a personal computer, we used Spool-Explorer/400, a spooled-file management package that Business Computer Design, a Datawatch business partner, has developed. (BCD licenses Monarch technology and augments it with spooled-file management capabilities. It offers this technology to AS/400 customers as its EZ-Pickin's product).

Figure 11.2 (page 194) depicts an output queue as viewed through BCD's Spool-Explorer/400, a GUI-based product that lets you manage spooled files (e.g., download, delete, print, move, save). In addition, you can place Spool-Explorer/400 commands into CL programs to automate the download process (spooled files are automatically copied from the AS/400 to local drives after the report has executed). Monarch can then be called automatically, at which point any predefined extraction and analysis processes can execute — a feature particularly useful for processing large reports. For example, suppose a vice

Spooled Files

AS/400 spooled files are special structures designed to store report data and the control information needed to format and print that data on paper. As with AS/400 physical and logical files, data description source (DDS) members specify the structure of spooled files. Unlike physical and logical files, spooled files typically consist of multiple, unique record formats whose function is to print header, footer, detail, and summary information.

Conceptually, spooled files share two striking similarities with data-mart repositories: First, both structures are maintained by programs that transform raw OLTP data into meaningful information. And while a data-mart maintenance procedure accesses numerous normalized files to write transformed data to a database, a report program accesses normalized files and writes transformed data to an externally described printer file. And second, both spooled files and data marts are designed for specific departments or purposes; they do not contain enterprise-wide data culled from a variety of OLTP applications.

There are also two major differences between spooled files and data marts: First, spooled files do not feature intuitive GUIs (paper is a static medium and, as such, does not readily support advanced analyses). Data marts, on the other hand, let end users access their contents via GUI interfaces. Second, the structure of spooled files does not adhere to advanced database schema such as the ROLAP star or snowflake designs. In this context, spooled files are more closely related to flat files.

president in a marketing organization wants to see multidimensional graphs of sales data each morning. If a lengthy sales report already exists with this information, we can have it run nightly and download automatically to the vice president's PC, where Monarch can then process it. In this scenario, the vice president arrives each morning and clicks on an icon to view sales graphs, not aware that the graphs originated from a report file on the AS/400. Spool-Explorer/400 recognizes all applicable AS/400 object and user-profile security specifications.

For the remainder of this chapter, let's assume that IN001RF has been downloaded to a PC-based server and that Monarch will interactively analyze the file's contents.

Figure 11.3 (page 194) shows Monarch's opening screen after IN001RF has been opened. As you can see, the screen closely resembles a hard-copy report. Monarch recognizes print control codes and displays spooled files as they would appear when printed. Once a report has been opened, we must identify the lines in the report (i.e., records) that contain valuable information. This process is called *trapping* and is illustrated in Figure 11.4 (page 195). Typically, we first trap detail lines, then heading and footer lines. Figure 11.4 demonstrates how we trapped detail records in IN001RF. In this case, we used a trap to identify all detail lines that have numeric characters in positions 9 through 14 (i.e., the invoice number).

Report Mining

Report mining describes processes whereby raw data is extracted from spooled files, transformed into valuable information, then analyzed directly or propagated to data-warehouse repositories. Report mining can deliver significant benefit to the data warehousing arena in two ways: First, it lets spooled files be used as intermediate data sources for warehouses. Remember that data in spooled files is created by extraction, transformation, and propagation processes (e.g., report programs) that already exist in an OLTP application. What's more, these processes generate information that is of particular interest to end users; otherwise, the report programs would not have been written in the first place. Rather than create new processes to extract and transform OLTP data from databases, you can often use spooled files as sources of information for data warehouses. A second benefit of report mining is that it lets end users perform multidimensional analyses directly on downloaded spooled files — without support from you.

While report mining provides the analytic functionality we find in many data-warehousing solutions, there are several reasons we should not consider it a replacement for data warehouses:

- Report-mining products do not yet support sophisticated online analytical processing (end users who analyze large volumes of data require advanced OLAP functionality).
- Reports occasionally contain minor inaccuracies such as inappropriate rounding algorithms. In these cases, it is preferable to extract data for a data warehouse directly from an OLTP data source.
- We cannot use report mining to simultaneously analyze data from a variety of different reports. For example, we cannot easily compare data from a sales report to data from a bookings report unless the reports have similar formats.

These issues notwithstanding, report mining is an economical and pragmatic way to quickly enable multidimensional analysis at the desktop. In addition, report mining gives IT personnel who don't have an in-depth knowledge of OLTP database schema a way to transform and move OLTP data into data warehouses.

After isolating records in the sales report, we must define fields. Because we simply drag the cursor over data that comprises a field, this process is very intuitive.

Figure 11.5 (page 195) illustrates how we created the "customer" field. The area in black represents the field as the cursor movement defined it. In this case, we assigned the name "customer" to the field using Monarch's Field Properties dialog box. Monarch automatically defines all other field attributes (e.g., type, length). In addition to character and numeric fields, the product recognizes 90 different date formats. For numeric fields, Monarch assigns the appropriate number of decimal places as well. Monarch also recognizes and

FIGURE 11.2
BCD's Spool-Explorer/400

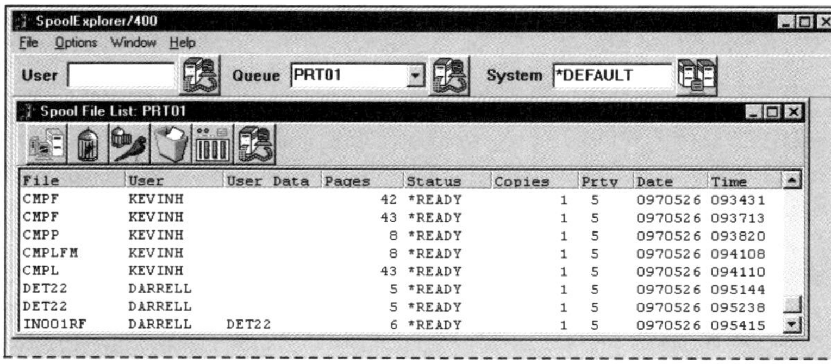

FIGURE 11.3
Using Monarch to View a Downloaded Report

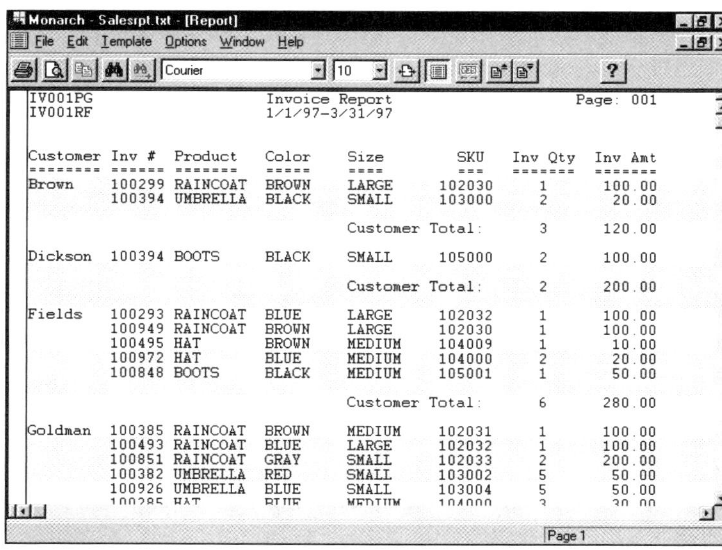

accounts for special characters and codes that appear on accounting reports, including cr, dr, (), and negative signs to the left and right of numbers.

Figure 11.6 (page 196) shows the Trap Definition screen after we have defined additional detail fields. Monarch has facilities to verify that user-defined field boundaries are wide enough to encompass data throughout a spooled file. The product also can simultaneously trap multiple detail, header, and footer lines.

FIGURE 11.4

Trapping Detail Lines in a Report

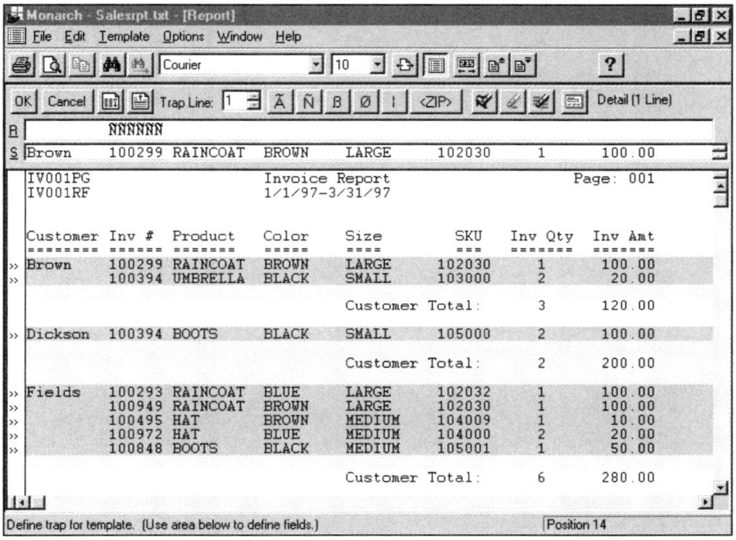

FIGURE 11.5

Defining a Field Called CUSTOMER

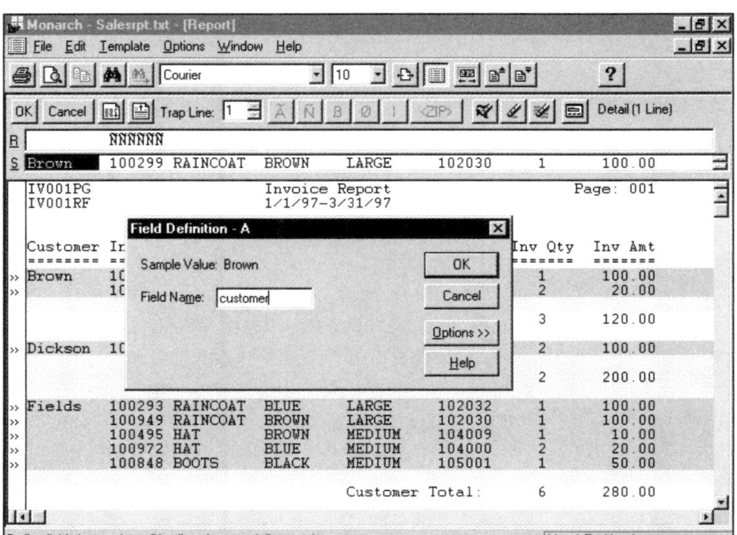

FIGURE 11.6

Monarch's Report Window After Defining Multiple Fields

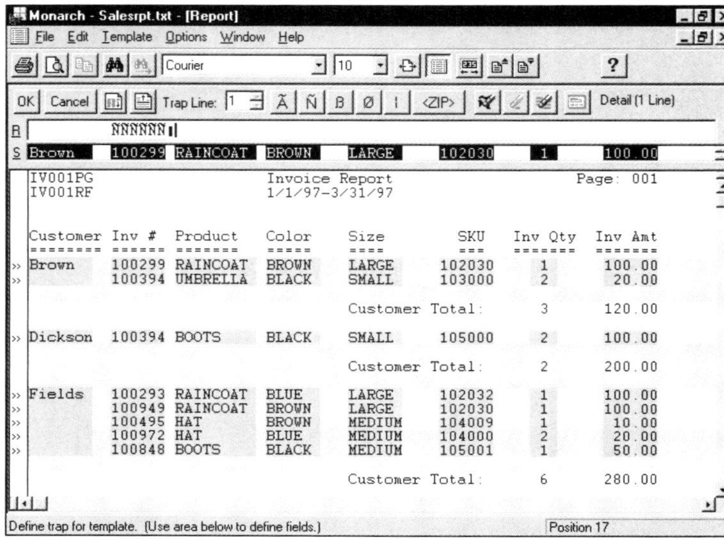

Figure 11.7 shows how IN001RF's detail lines appear in Monarch's table window. The table window is the heart of Monarch's analysis engine — end users can use more than 40 functions to analyze and transform data in Monarch tables. These functions support string manipulation, mathematical operations, date arithmetic, field conversions (e.g., character to date, numeric to character), conditional logic, and so on. Users also can use these functions to derive entirely new fields. Figure 11.8 shows how we can define a new field, while Figure 11.9 (page 198) illustrates how we can change an existing field.

To summarize data, we can use Monarch's Summary Definition dialog box to specify dimensions and associated values. Figure 11.10 (page 198) illustrates the specification of a four-dimensional summary based on SKU, product name, color, and size. Figure 11.11 (page 199) shows the resultant summary table.

Once we have defined a multidimensional summary in Monarch, we can click a drill-up or dill-down icon to automatically collapse or expand the summary table by one dimension. In this way, we can quickly drill through many levels of aggregate data. Figure 11.12 (page 199) illustrates the invocation of Monarch's "drill up" function, while Figure 11.13 (page 200) shows the resulting summary table. As you can see, the size dimension no longer appears in the table.

FIGURE 11.7
Monarch's Table Window

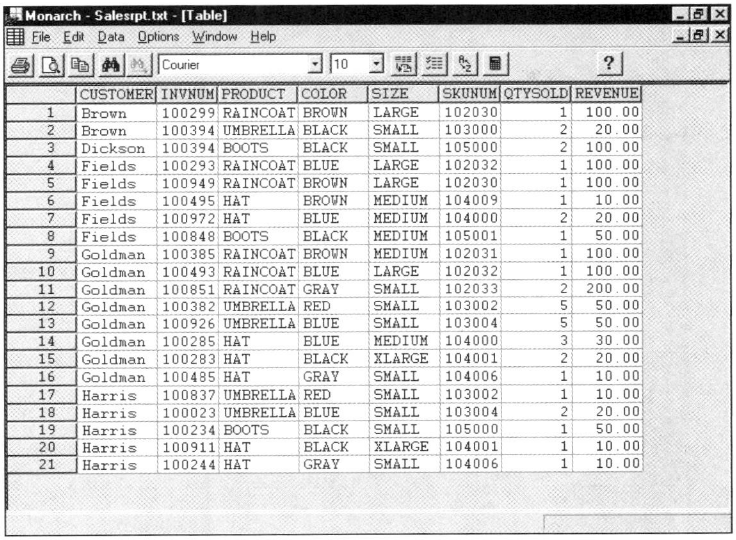

	CUSTOMER	INVNUM	PRODUCT	COLOR	SIZE	SKUNUM	QTYSOLD	REVENUE
1	Brown	100299	RAINCOAT	BROWN	LARGE	102030	1	100.00
2	Brown	100394	UMBRELLA	BLACK	SMALL	103000	2	20.00
3	Dickson	100394	BOOTS	BLACK	SMALL	105000	2	100.00
4	Fields	100293	RAINCOAT	BLUE	LARGE	102032	1	100.00
5	Fields	100949	RAINCOAT	BROWN	LARGE	102030	1	100.00
6	Fields	100495	HAT	BROWN	MEDIUM	104009	1	10.00
7	Fields	100972	HAT	BLUE	MEDIUM	104000	2	20.00
8	Fields	100848	BOOTS	BLACK	MEDIUM	105001	1	50.00
9	Goldman	100385	RAINCOAT	BROWN	MEDIUM	102031	1	100.00
10	Goldman	100493	RAINCOAT	BLUE	LARGE	102032	1	100.00
11	Goldman	100851	RAINCOAT	GRAY	SMALL	102033	2	200.00
12	Goldman	100382	UMBRELLA	RED	SMALL	103002	5	50.00
13	Goldman	100926	UMBRELLA	BLUE	SMALL	103004	5	50.00
14	Goldman	100285	HAT	BLUE	MEDIUM	104000	3	30.00
15	Goldman	100283	HAT	BLACK	XLARGE	104001	2	20.00
16	Goldman	100485	HAT	GRAY	SMALL	104006	1	10.00
17	Harris	100837	UMBRELLA	RED	SMALL	103002	1	10.00
18	Harris	100023	UMBRELLA	BLUE	SMALL	103004	2	20.00
19	Harris	100234	BOOTS	BLACK	SMALL	105000	1	50.00
20	Harris	100911	HAT	BLACK	XLARGE	104001	1	10.00
21	Harris	100244	HAT	GRAY	SMALL	104006	1	10.00

FIGURE 11.8
Deriving a New Field Called UNITPRICE

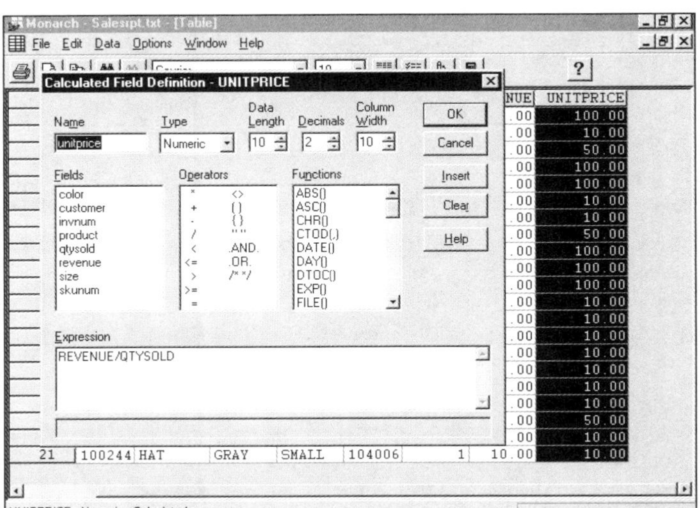

FIGURE 11.9
Changing Attributes of Field REVENUE

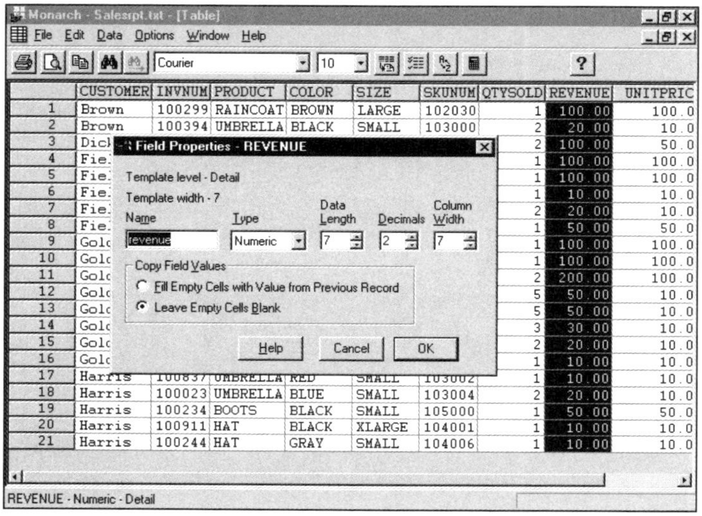

FIGURE 11.10
Using Monarch to Define a Four-Dimensional Summary

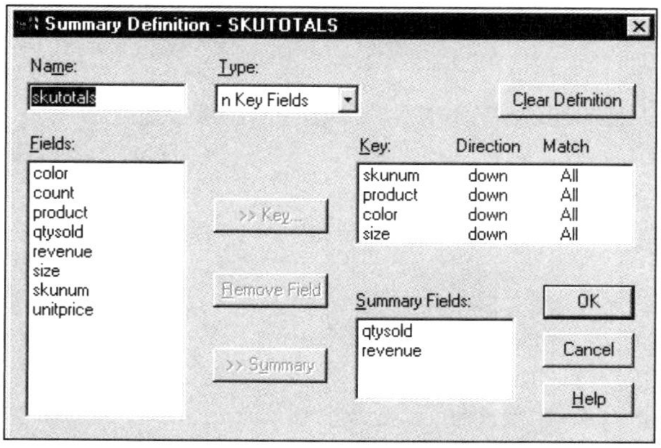

We also can use Monarch's summary feature to create different slices of data. For example, Figure 11.14 (page 200) shows sales revenue per product. To support data visualization, Monarch also lets us create a variety of graphs and charts below or alongside summary tables.

Figure 11.15 (page 201) shows a bar chart next to the product summary. If they are displayed, Monarch charts and graphs change dynamically as we drill

FIGURE 11.11
Viewing the Four-Dimensional Summary

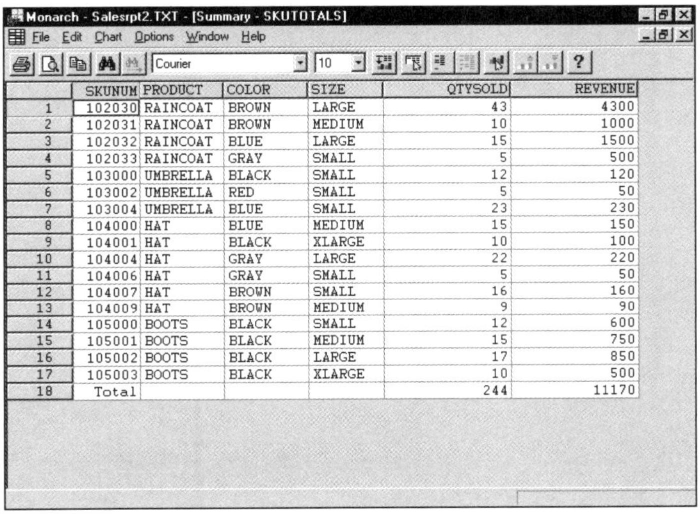

	SKUNUM	PRODUCT	COLOR	SIZE	QTYSOLD	REVENUE
1	102030	RAINCOAT	BROWN	LARGE	43	4300
2	102031	RAINCOAT	BROWN	MEDIUM	10	1000
3	102032	RAINCOAT	BLUE	LARGE	15	1500
4	102033	RAINCOAT	GRAY	SMALL	5	500
5	103000	UMBRELLA	BLACK	SMALL	12	120
6	103002	UMBRELLA	RED	SMALL	5	50
7	103004	UMBRELLA	BLUE	SMALL	23	230
8	104000	HAT	BLUE	MEDIUM	15	150
9	104001	HAT	BLACK	XLARGE	10	100
10	104004	HAT	GRAY	LARGE	22	220
11	104006	HAT	GRAY	SMALL	5	50
12	104007	HAT	BROWN	SMALL	16	160
13	104009	HAT	BROWN	MEDIUM	9	90
14	105000	BOOTS	BLACK	SMALL	12	600
15	105001	BOOTS	BLACK	MEDIUM	15	750
16	105002	BOOTS	BLACK	LARGE	17	850
17	105003	BOOTS	BLACK	XLARGE	10	500
18	Total				244	11170

FIGURE 11.12
Drilling Up One Layer in the Summary

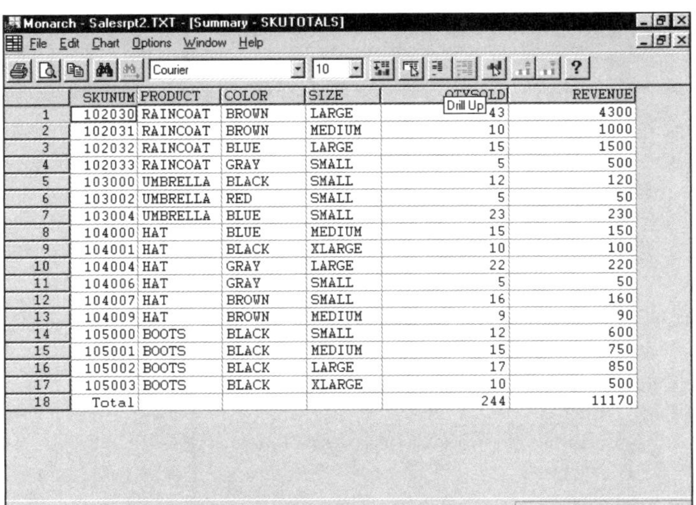

	SKUNUM	PRODUCT	COLOR	SIZE	QTYSOLD	REVENUE
1	102030	RAINCOAT	BROWN	LARGE	43	4300
2	102031	RAINCOAT	BROWN	MEDIUM	10	1000
3	102032	RAINCOAT	BLUE	LARGE	15	1500
4	102033	RAINCOAT	GRAY	SMALL	5	500
5	103000	UMBRELLA	BLACK	SMALL	12	120
6	103002	UMBRELLA	RED	SMALL	5	50
7	103004	UMBRELLA	BLUE	SMALL	23	230
8	104000	HAT	BLUE	MEDIUM	15	150
9	104001	HAT	BLACK	XLARGE	10	100
10	104004	HAT	GRAY	LARGE	22	220
11	104006	HAT	GRAY	SMALL	5	50
12	104007	HAT	BROWN	SMALL	16	160
13	104009	HAT	BROWN	MEDIUM	9	90
14	105000	BOOTS	BLACK	SMALL	12	600
15	105001	BOOTS	BLACK	MEDIUM	15	750
16	105002	BOOTS	BLACK	LARGE	17	850
17	105003	BOOTS	BLACK	XLARGE	10	500
18	Total				244	11170

through various levels of aggregate information. We also can choose to view graphs and charts without corresponding summary tables.

FIGURE 11.13

Viewing the Resultant Three-Dimensional Summary

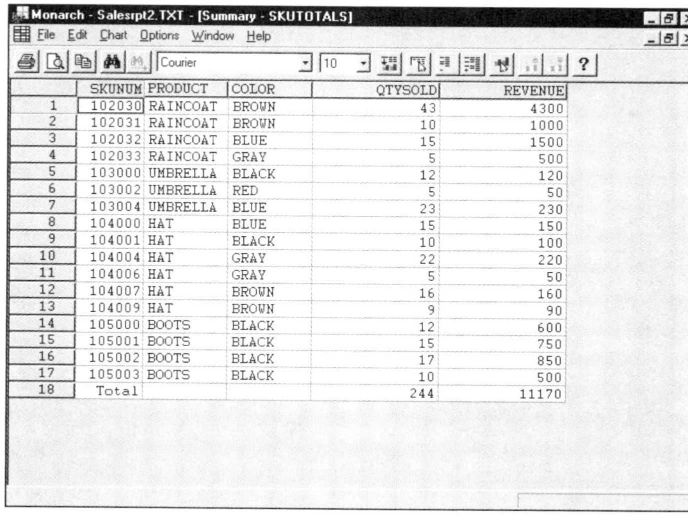

	SKUNUM	PRODUCT	COLOR	QTYSOLD	REVENUE
1	102030	RAINCOAT	BROWN	43	4300
2	102031	RAINCOAT	BROWN	10	1000
3	102032	RAINCOAT	BLUE	15	1500
4	102033	RAINCOAT	GRAY	5	500
5	103000	UMBRELLA	BLACK	12	120
6	103002	UMBRELLA	RED	5	50
7	103004	UMBRELLA	BLUE	23	230
8	104000	HAT	BLUE	15	150
9	104001	HAT	BLACK	10	100
10	104004	HAT	GRAY	22	220
11	104006	HAT	GRAY	5	50
12	104007	HAT	BROWN	16	160
13	104009	HAT	BROWN	9	90
14	105000	BOOTS	BLACK	12	600
15	105001	BOOTS	BLACK	15	750
16	105002	BOOTS	BLACK	17	850
17	105003	BOOTS	BLACK	10	500
18	Total			244	11170

FIGURE 11.14

Viewing Revenue by Product

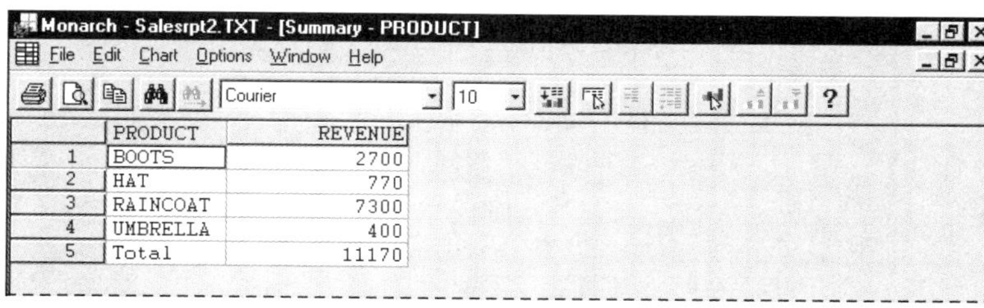

	PRODUCT	REVENUE
1	BOOTS	2700
2	HAT	770
3	RAINCOAT	7300
4	UMBRELLA	400
5	Total	11170

Additionally, Monarch's summary feature supports the creation of cross-tabular data views. Figure 11.16 depicts the definition of such a summary, while Figure 11.17 (page 202) shows the resulting table.

With Monarch, we also have the option to save all extraction, summary, and charting definitions in a reusable template, or model, file. We can then apply these models to future instances of a given report. By using models, end users do not have to redefine extraction and transformation rules each time they run a report. As you have seen, we used Monarch to effectively transform a spooled file into a simple data mart.

FIGURE 11.15
Graphing Revenue by Product

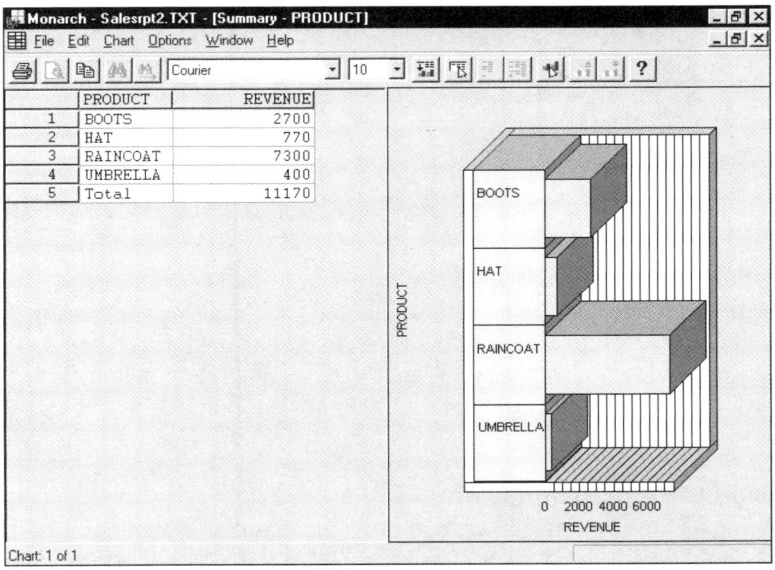

FIGURE 11.16
Defining a Cross-Tabular Summary

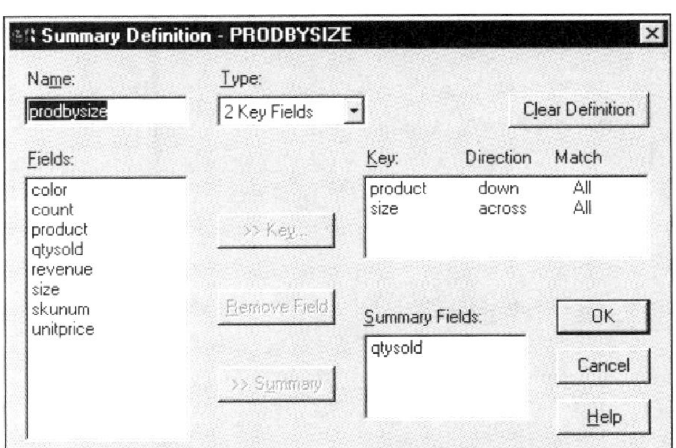

We also can use Monarch to electronically distribute downloaded spooled files together with any associated models. To do this, we create specialized files known as portable reports. A portable report contains one or more spooled files and any associated model specifications. We also can encrypt, compress, and password-protect portable reports. Because of an effective 10:1

FIGURE 11.17
Viewing the Resultant Cross-Tabular Summary

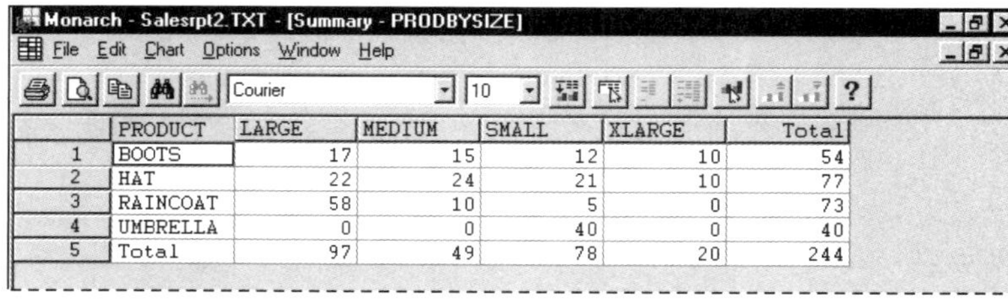

	PRODUCT	LARGE	MEDIUM	SMALL	XLARGE	Total
1	BOOTS	17	15	12	10	54
2	HAT	22	24	21	10	77
3	RAINCOAT	58	10	5	0	73
4	UMBRELLA	0	0	40	0	40
5	Total	97	49	78	20	244

compression algorithm, portable reports are well suited for distribution via the Internet, intranets, CD-ROMs, and the like. A 2,000-page AS/400 report, for example, requires approximately 400K of storage after Monarch has compressed it. To use portable reports, recipients must have Monarch or the Monarch Report Explorer, and they must know the portable report's password if one has been assigned.

PRODUCT SUMMARY AND POSITIONING

According to the Gartner Group, corporate data centers generate more than 600 billion pages of hard copy each year. Given this volume, report mining is obviously an extremely useful function. Much like OLTP databases, reports are a potential gold mine of business intelligence. And like data-warehousing analysis tools, Monarch lets end users analyze reports as they would a data-warehouse repository, thus leveraging previous investments in hard-copy reporting systems.

Monarch is not a data warehouse. Rather, it is a transformational replication tool that can be used to propagate report-based data to data warehouses. As such, Monarch is a valuable complement to more traditional database replication products such as Coglin-Mill's RODIN, DataMirror's Transformation Server, and IBM's DataPropagator.

However, despite its utility, Monarch does not facilitate metadata management, nor can it access databases. What's more, Monarch does not support OLAP functionality, nor can it present information to users via advanced, EIS-style interfaces. However, Monarch does let end users quickly and easily analyze report-based data, and it also lets IT personnel propagate report-based data to data warehouses. At approximately $300 per copy, it is a highly economical, useful complement to traditional data warehouses.

Chapter 12

Ferguson Information Systems, Inc. and InfoManager

Company Background

Ferguson Information Systems, Inc. (FIS), established in 1995, is the North American marketing and support organization for InfoManager OY of Helsinki, Finland. InfoManager OY, founded in 1987, is a software-development concern that specializes in AS/400-based applications. InfoManager OY's principal product is InfoManager, an AS/400-based data-warehousing product. This chapter focuses on FIS and InfoManager.

Privately-held FIS employs 25 people and maintains offices in Atlanta, Cincinnati, Dallas, and Sacramento. The company has partnerships with IBM in the United States, Hyatt Technology in Canada, and GCC IBS SA in Mexico. It also maintains partnerships with several health-care, banking, and insurance firms. FIS has North American distribution rights for InfoManager. InfoManager is currently installed at more than 300 sites worldwide and marketed in 15 countries through a variety of distribution channels.

Product Overview

Originally an AS/400-based EIS development tool, InfoManager has been bolstered with data-warehousing functionality. The product's Gateway module can be used to extract data from a number of sources, including single- and multi-member DB2/400 files, flat files, ASCII files, comma-separated files, and spooled files. After you transform this data using InfoManager's built-in support for consolidations, filters, conversion tables, and classifications, the data is loaded into DB2/400-based data repositories. InfoManager's database adheres to the ROLAP star schema. After InfoManager's database has been initialized, end users equipped with its presentation, analysis, and report-writing software can access and examine data

InfoManager is a modular software package that consists of up to four components, including InfoManager Server, a multipurpose module for creating and populating data warehouses; InfoManager Client, a PC-based presentation and analysis module; InfoManager Connect, an optional interface that lets third-party PC products access the InfoManager data warehouse; and InfoManager Planner, an optional budgeting, forecasting, and reporting tool for use with leading spreadsheet products. A detailed description of these components follows.

InfoManager Server

InfoManager Server is a 5250-based software module that lets you define and create data-warehouse repositories that are well-suited for use as data marts. Server also lets you perform basic extraction, transformation, and data-propagation tasks. In terms of transformational replication, Server can filter DB2/400 data by column (field) and by row (record); it also can update field content, change field names, reformat field sizes, translate field values, modify field types, and derive entirely new fields. Server also maintains a comprehensive metadata repository that lets InfoManager dynamically update dimensions and hierarchies in the data warehouse. The metadata itself can be extracted directly from DDS source members in your OLTP applications. In addition, the product supports both incremental, partial, and full-refresh data propagation. In terms of security, Server lets you define user- and application-specific data-access rights.

InfoManager Client

Available in 16- and 32-bit versions, InfoManager Client is a PC-based module that supports OS/2, Windows 3.1, Windows 95, and Windows NT operating systems. End users can use Client to query, analyze, and graph information stored in the InfoManager data warehouse. True to its roots as an EIS tool, Client also lets you create advanced interfaces and graphics for executives who have little hands-on computer experience. InfoManager Smart Screens and Presentations enable this functionality. Smart Screens uses maps, warning lights, text indicators, and other advanced EIS-style graphics to direct end users to areas that warrant attention. InfoManager presentations contain sets of graphs and reports that end users require regularly (e.g., for monthly reporting requirements). Figures 12.1 and 12.2 depict two EIS-style screens created with InfoManager. In Figure 12.1, a map of the world presents sales figures to executives, while Figure 12.2 features a simple-to-use menu interface. With Client's traffic-light feature, end users also can view data in tabular form and, if they choose, can color-code rows and columns based on mathematical conditions. These spreadsheet-like structures let end users quickly identify situations that require attention.

FIGURE 12.1
An InfoManager Smart Screen

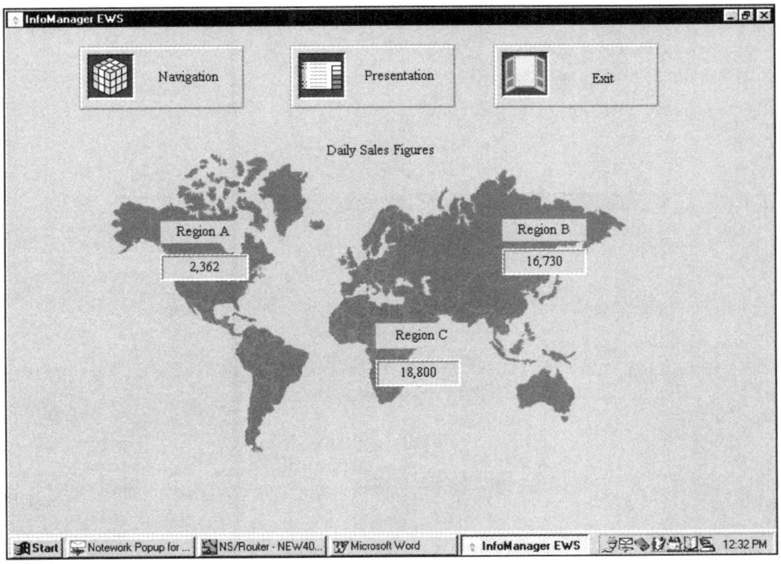

FIGURE 12.2
An EIS Menu Designed with InfoManager

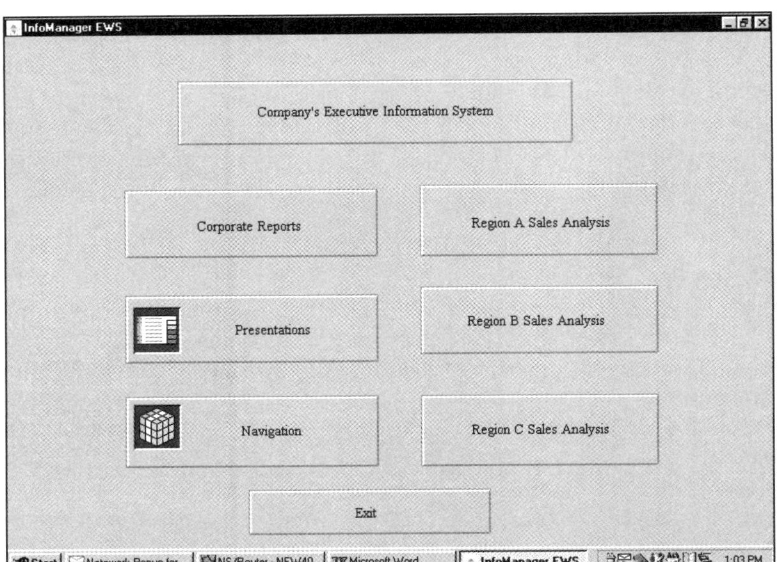

Additionally, InfoManager's Client module features a comprehensive graphing facility that supports more than 75 predefined charts. Figure 12.3 depicts the opening menu to Client's charting functions. Once data is loaded into an InfoManager data repository, end users can use these charts to drill up and down through various dimensions of information.

FIGURE 12.3
Client's Charting Menu

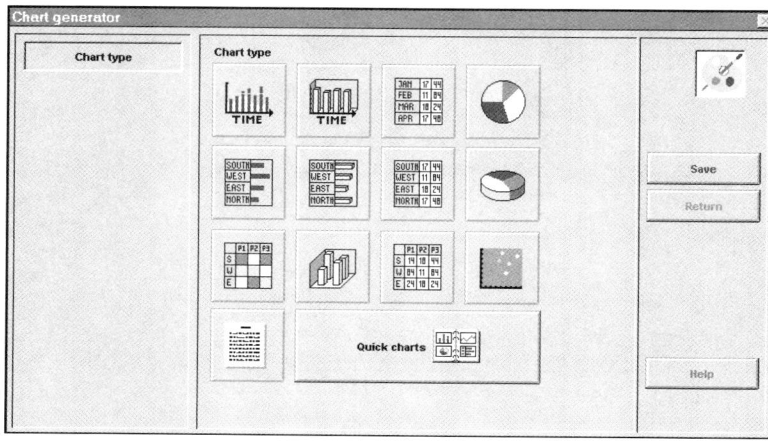

They also can save charts and graphs in presentations. Presentations serve two purposes: First, end users can group related charts and graphs together, and second, they can download these charts and graphs to personal computers. When these items are downloaded, InfoManager Client copies both the charts and their underlying data to local hard disks. Downloaded presentations can be used to support off-line analyses. InfoManager also tracks the date of each download. Figure 12.4 details the opening screen for three sample InfoManager presentations.

InfoManager Connect

Unlike Server and Client, Connect is an optional module whose main purpose is to provide a way to extract data from InfoManager's DB2/400-based data repositories for use in PC-based applications such as Excel. Connect lets you automatically update existing spreadsheet files with information from the data warehouse. Connect also generates Smart Book interfaces for Excel users. In addition, it can distribute PC-based report files to local, remote, and mobile users.

FIGURE 12.4
Opening Screen for Presentations

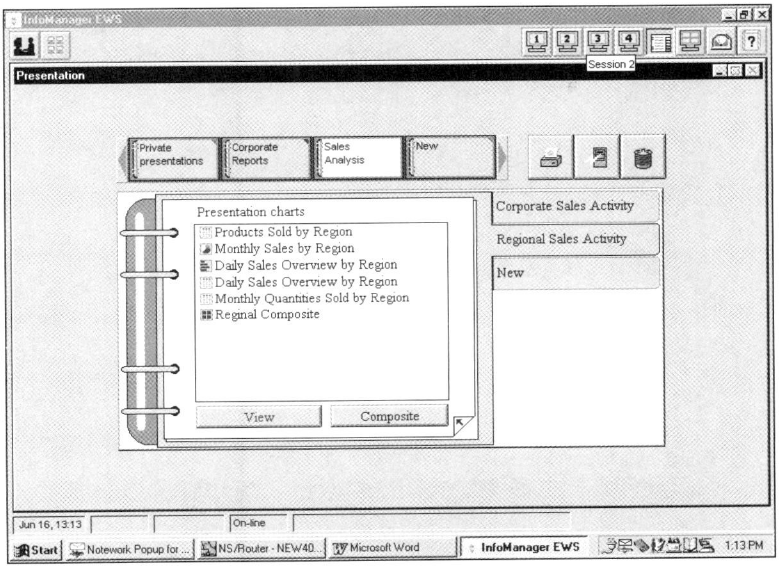

InfoManager Planner

Another optional module, InfoManager's Planner is designed specifically for budgeting, forecasting, and financial-reporting applications. Using Excel-based templates, end users can analyze information in the data warehouse. After they have made changes to the data, they can load the updated information back into the data warehouse. Planner can maintain several versions of the same financial plan, and it is designed to support currency conversions and overhead allocations as well.

IMPLEMENTATION EXAMPLE

To illustrate the functionality of InfoManager, this section features several screen captures of the product as we would use it to perform our sample data-warehousing tasks. For the sake of simplicity, let's assume that the data warehouse resides on the same AS/400 as the OLTP database. For distribution across multiple AS/400s or other advanced propagation needs, we can integrate InfoManager with third-party products such as IBM's DataPropagator or DataMirror's Transformation Server for AS/400.

Figure 12.5 (page 208) shows the main menu of InfoManager's 5250-based Server module. Using options from this menu, we can create multidimensional databases that are well-suited for use as data marts.

FIGURE 12.5
InfoManager Server Main Menu

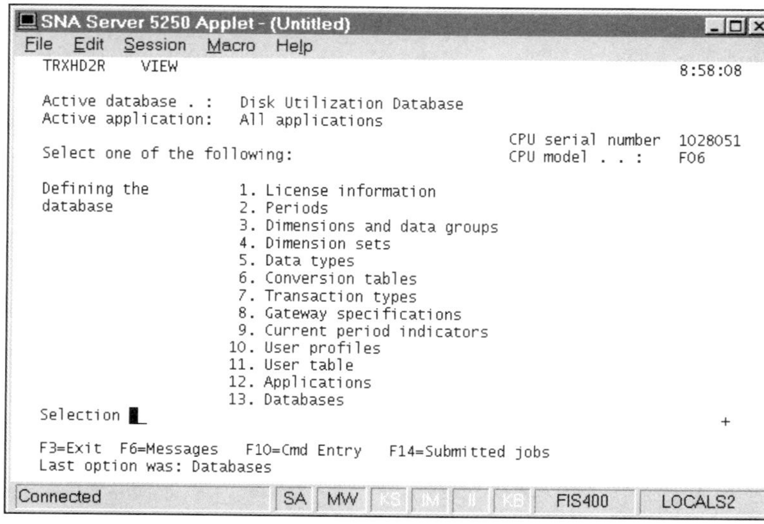

After we use a series of 5250 screens to create the data-warehouse database, we define applicable time periods for the warehouse. InfoManager has four predefined periods integrated throughout its databases, including day, week, month, and calendar year, and we can add as many other time periods to the warehouse as necessary. (InfoManager does not consider time period a separate dimension, because it is integrated throughout the InfoManager data warehouse.) After we establish time periods, we create applications within the data warehouse. We use these applications to uniquely identify different groups of end users for security purposes. Next, we establish *dimensions* (both hierarchical and single-level dimensions) in the warehouse. We then define the various combination of dimensions that might exist for analyses — a time-consuming process that requires careful planning.

These structures, referred to as *dimension sets*, define the order in which drill-down and drill-up operations can be executed. Once we have established dimensions and dimension sets, we can establish links between OLTP database elements and the data warehouse. Referred to as *data-group mappings*, these structures support the data-extraction process. We then establish data-transformation routines that typically use derived fields and look-up tables. After we create transformation routines, we can define transactions to actually update the data warehouse. As you might infer from all these steps, the process of creating InfoManager databases is complex, so new customers should take advantage of FIS's training and consulting services.

Once data has been loaded into the warehouse, end users can use InfoManager's default charts and the Chart Generator to create new charts and graphs. Figures 12.6 through 12.9 detail the product's Chart Generator screens. Using these screens, we can create several charts using our sample sales data.

FIGURE 12.6
Chart Generator's Navigation Definition Screen

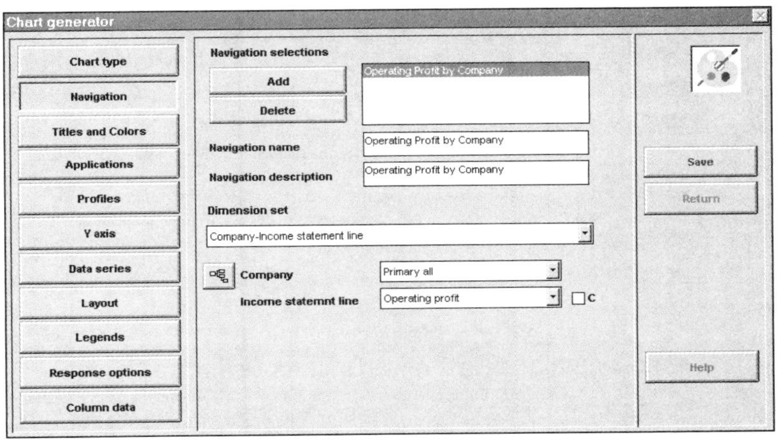

FIGURE 12.7
Chart Generator's Navigation Y-Axis Definition Screen

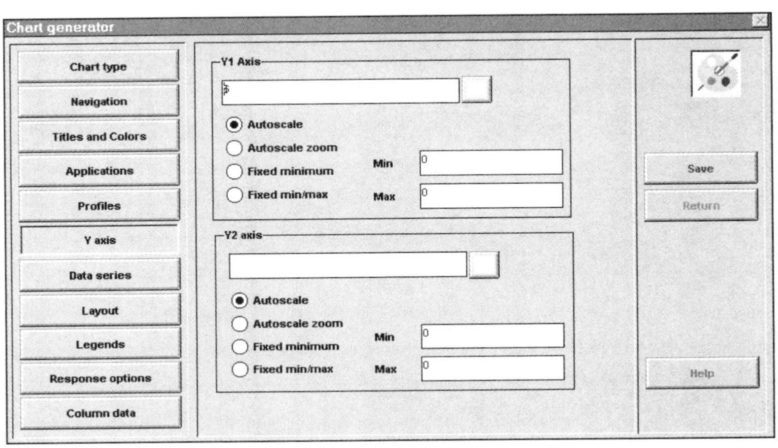

FIGURE 12.8
Chart Generator's Data Series Definition Screen

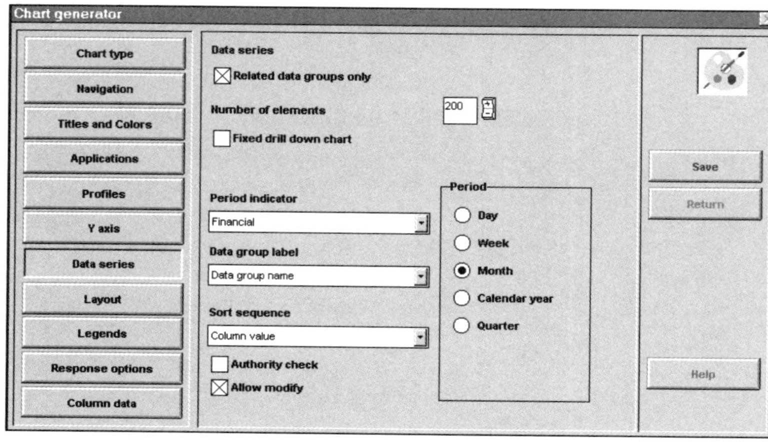

FIGURE 12.9
Chart Generator's Response Options Definition Screen

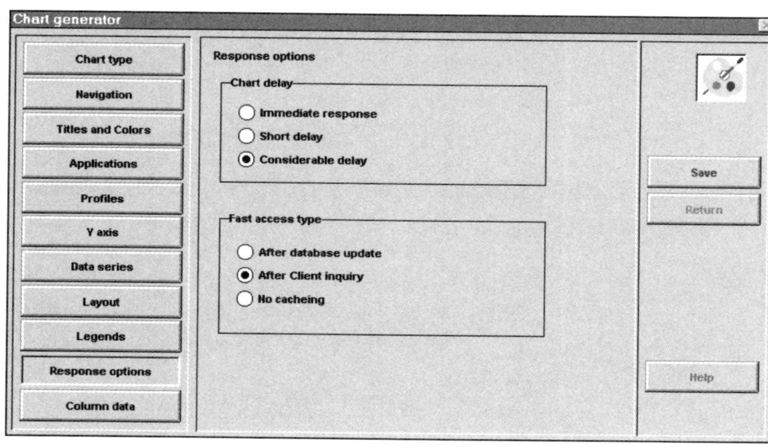

Figure 12.10 depicts a horizontal bar graph of sales by product category, while Figure 12.11 on the following page illustrates how end users can use InfoManager to drill down into data.

End users also can perform drill-down operations on tables, as shown in Figure 12.12 (page 212). Figure 12.13 (page 212) highlights InfoManager's traffic-light feature. Notice that a 22-percent variance has been computed and flagged in the right-most column.

FIGURE 12.10
Graphical Depiction of Daily Sales by Product

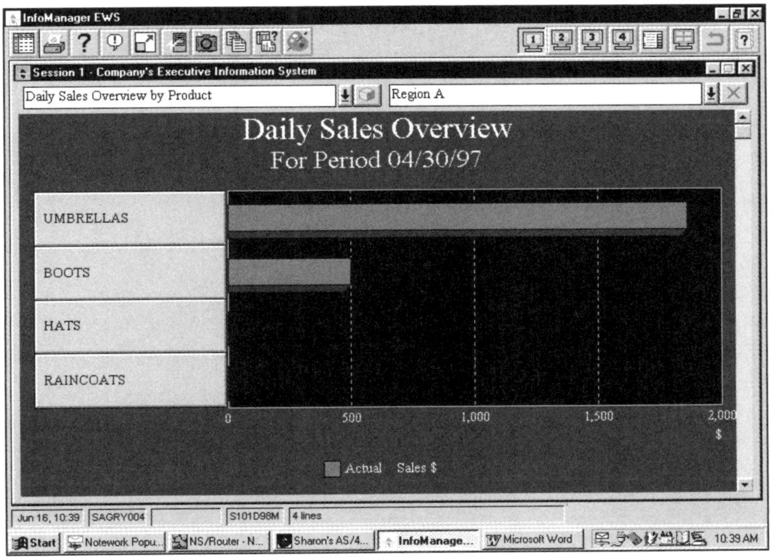

FIGURE 12.11
Sales Graph with Drill-Down Options

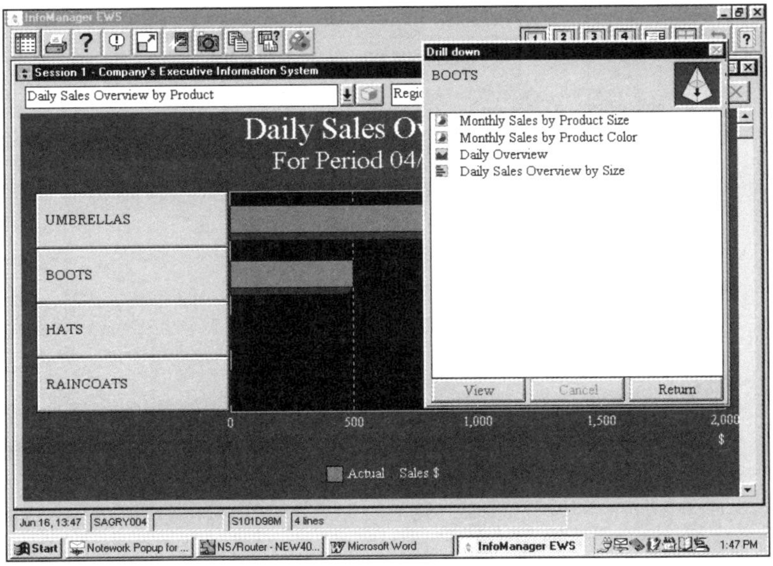

FIGURE 12.12
Sales Table with Drill-Down Options

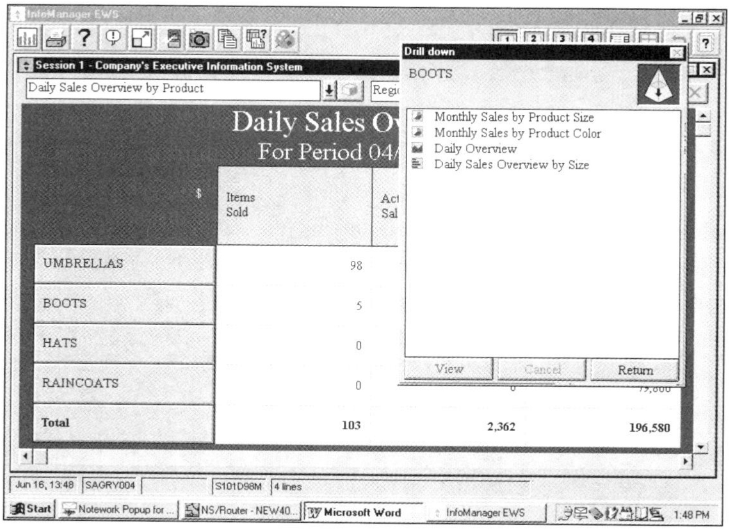

FIGURE 12.13
Using Colors to Flag a Variance

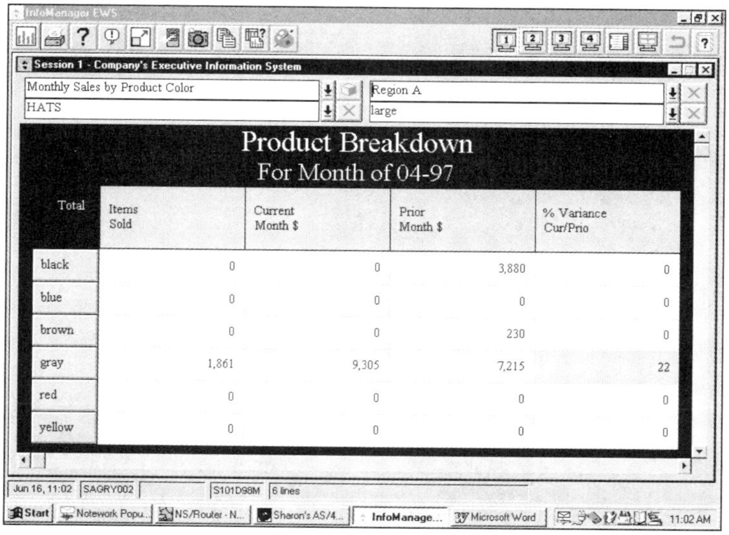

A numeric cross-tabular display consisting of product categories and sizes appears in Figure 12.14. I have used InfoManager's traffic-light graphics to show the same cross-tabular display in Figure 12.15 (page 214). Instead of highlighting certain figures by color, I have chosen clouds to denote situations that require attention. InfoManager lets end users display up to four different charts on a single screen.

FIGURE 12.14

Cross-Tabular View of Sales by Product and Size

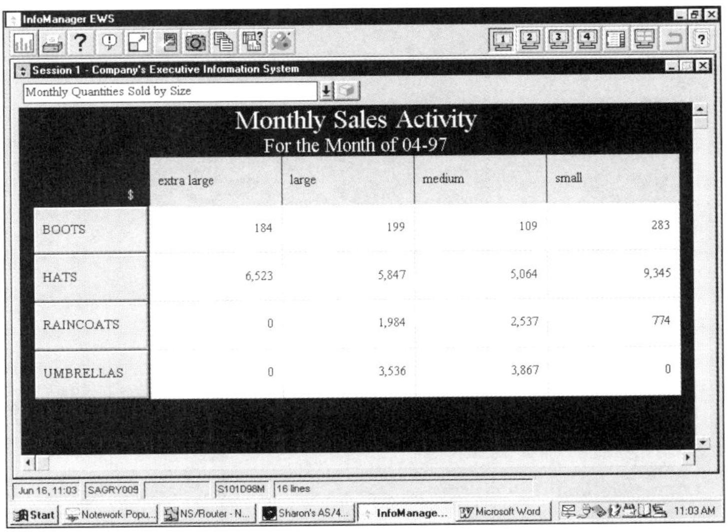

FIGURE 12.15

Using Clouds to Highlight Situations that Require Attention

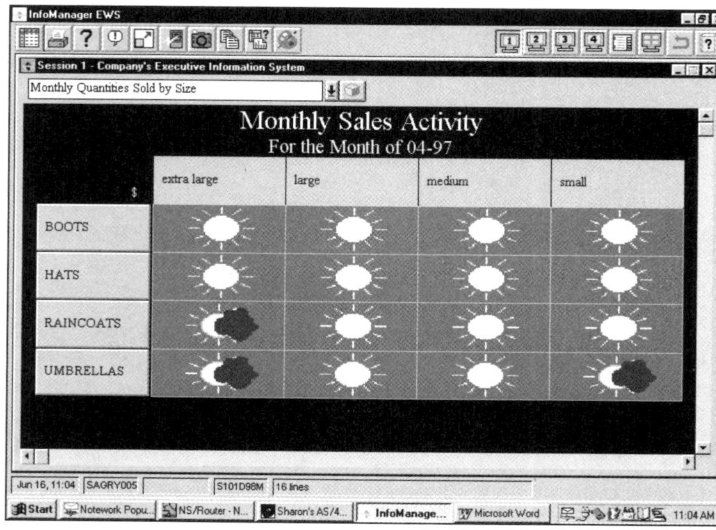

PRODUCT SUMMARY AND POSITIONING

InfoManager is an integrated data-warehousing product that is well-suited for environments with multiple data marts. From dimensions that you specify via 5250 screens, InfoManager creates data repositories that adhere to the star schema. The specification of these dimensions, and especially their interrelationships, requires careful planning. However, it does eliminate the need to manually design and build your data-warehouse repositories. For end users, InfoManager features a consistent, integrated GUI.

InfoManager has traditionally been targeted at health care, banking, and insurance organizations, so solutions that are tailored for these industries are available. Another of InfoManager's strengths is rooted in its history as an advanced presentation tool. InfoManager holds extra appeal for companies interested in EIS-style presentation support. Using PC clients, the product facilitates both sophisticated multidimensional analyses and the advanced presentation of data via unique Smart Screens and Presentations.

A concurrent five-user license for the complete InfoManager data warehouse is available for $35,000 and includes the Connect product; additional user licenses cost $1,000 each. Annual maintenance fees are 15 percent of the purchase price. The fee for one week of optional FIS training is approximately $6,000 for most IT departments. Because the definition and creation of InfoManager databases can be complex, I highly recommend this training.

Chapter 13

IBM Corporation and DataPropagator Relational Capture and Apply

Company Background[1]

With fiscal 1996 revenues in excess of $75 billion, IBM Corporation is the world's largest provider of computer hardware, software, and consulting services. IBM's hardware sales include AS/400 midrange computers, RS/6000 workstations, S/390 mainframes, Aptiva desktop personal computers, and ThinkPad notebook computers, as well as a variety of network, communications, and storage devices. The company's software offerings include database products, operating systems, and other applications. IBM also offers service, software, equipment leasing, financing and maintenance. Headquartered in Armonk, New York, publicly held IBM (NYSE:IBM) offers service and support in more than 140 countries.

In addition to in-house development of OS/400 and DB2/400, IBM supports third-party AS/400 application development through its Partners In Development (PID) program. To bolster the development of AS/400-based data warehouses, IBM maintains partnerships with software companies such as Angoss Software, Brio Technologies, Business Objects, Carleton (which has been purchased by Apertus Technologies), Coglin Mill, Cognos, DataMirror, Evolutionary Technologies International, Ferguson Information Systems, Lakeview Technologies, Logic Works, MicroStrategy, New-Generation Software, Olympic amis, SAMAC, ShowCase, Silvon, and Vision Solutions. In addition to business partnerships with consulting firms such as Price Waterhouse and Naviant (formerly MRJ), IBM designs data-mining applications for numerous industries, including insurance; distribution; banking, finance, and securities; government; health care; manufacturing; petroleum; and finally, utilities and energy.

IBM also develops data-warehousing applications and tools, including DataPropagator, a family of transformational replication products designed to move data across various DB2 databases (including DB2/400); DataGuide, a set of products designed to store technical metadata extracted from multiple platforms; DataJoiner, a utility designed to extract data from non-DB2 data sources; Intelligent Decision Server, a LAN-based solution designed to distribute business analysis across an enterprise; Neural Network Utility (NNU), a visual development environment designed to support data mining via artificial neural networks (ANNs); and Intelligent Miner, a multiplatform data-mining

[1]Because Chapters 13 and 14 each focus on IBM products, the "Company Background" section provides the same information in each chapter.

solution. This chapter explores the applicability of DataPropagator Relational Capture and Apply (or DPropR/400) in an AS/400-based data-warehousing environment.

Product Overview

An important member of IBM's data-replication family, DPropR/400 is a comprehensive replication tool designed specifically for the AS/400. In heterogeneous environments, we can use additional IBM products (discussed below) in conjunction with DPropR/400 to transform and replicate data across platforms and other databases.

To properly position DPropR/400 within IBM's lineup of replication software, let's briefly examine its components and functionality in terms of heterogeneous replication, followed by an in-depth examination of DPropR/400 in a homogenous AS/400 environment.

DPropR/400 itself consists of three core AS/400-based components, including an Administration component, a Capture component, and an Apply component. We look at DPropR/400 Administrator more closely later in the chapter.

To replicate AS/400 data across platforms, your system must have both DataJoiner and an administration tool. For example, you can accomplish replication to or from Oracle, Sybase, Informix, or SQL Server (as well as other databases that support ODBC) using a combination of DPropR/400, DataPropagator for OS/2, and DataJoiner.

In Unix, MVS, or OS/2 environments, the DataPropagator Capture and Apply components are separate products. In Unix environments, Capture functionality is supported for IBM's AIX; Apply functionality is supported for AIX, HP-UX, and Solaris. In MVS environments, DataPropagator NonRelational Version 2 provides asynchronous update replication for IMS to MVS DB2 and from MVS DB2 to IMS. DataRefresher, another member of the IBM DataPropagator family, runs on MVS and supports full-refresh propagation from sources such as VSAM, IMS, and PSDS. In addition, DataJoiner for AIX enables replication to and from Oracle, Sybase, and other ODBC-compliant data sources.

Finally, two options are available for data replication with Lotus Notes. The AS/400 Integration Enhanced Pak for Lotus Notes lets you initiate replication between DB2/400 and Lotus Notes running on the Integrated PC server. OS/400 V3R2, V3R7, and V4R1 currently support this functionality. In environments that use a dedicated Notes server, Notes Pump release 2.1 introduced support for DPropR/400.

In the remainder of this chapter, I focus on DB2/400-based data propagation using DPropR/400.

Introduced in February of 1995 on V3R1 of OS/400, DPropR/400 supports both single- and multimember physical files (on the source AS/400), and it can ilter source data by column (field) and by row (record). Designed for IT personnel, DPropR/400 replicates data asynchronously and can periodically refresh warehouse repositories on a full-refresh or net-change basis. In the case of net-change propagation, DPropR/400 examines journaled transactions and, as we shall see, uses a unique architecture to propagate modified data elements to target files. DB2/400 data can be propagated on a single AS/400, from one AS/400 to another, or from one AS/400 to multiple AS/400s. The product also supports cascading replication and can consolidate data from numerous AS/400s onto a single target machine. DPropR/400 requires V3R1 (or above) and supports both SNA and TCP/IP communications protocols.

In creating DPropR/400, IBM took a unique approach to product design. Instead of building a new transformation engine for DPropR/400, IBM provides users with command-driven prompts that accept standard SQL statements. In this way, DPropR/400 leverages SQL and its support for transformational processing and other forms of data manipulation. For example, it uses standard SQL statements to filter rows and to aggregate data according to keys. In addition, DPropR/400 uses SQL functionality to join multiple tables on the source machine. Similarly, target AS/400s use SQL union capabilities to consolidate multiple versions of a production file into a single file (many-to-one propagation). Through DPropR/400's support of user exits, SQL or stored procedures can be executed immediately before or after the replication of changed data.

Freed from the constraints of building a new data-transformation engine, IBM focused its design efforts on back-end transaction consistency and data recovery. This focus is most apparent in DPropR/400's use of an intermediate staging area to support commitment control. After reading journal entries for registered production files, DPropR/400 writes these changes (either *before*, *after*, or *both* images) to staging tables. These changes are then managed via commitment control on the source AS/400 and are not eligible for propagation to the target AS/400 until the associated commitment boundary has been reached. In addition to staging data, DPropR/400 also maintains control information in additional relational tables. Together, the staging and control data let DPropR/400 support rollback recovery; this functionality ensures data integrity on the target AS/400.

By integrating the transformational power of SQL with a robust, integrity-driven approach to data replication, DPropR/400 lets you quickly transform and distribute DB2/400 data across multiple AS/400s. Because DPropR/400 obviates the need to write and test complicated programs, you can implement data warehouses with this product in less time and for less money than with manual processes.

Main Processes

As I mentioned earlier, three main processes are necessary to transform and move information into a data warehouse with DPropR/400. During Administration, you define the replication process. Afterward, the Capture process records database changes in DPropR/400's staging area, while the Apply process updates target files with data stored in staging tables. Let's take a closer look at each of these processes.

Administration

Through DPropR/400's Administration component, you use either OS/400 Control Language (CL) commands or DataPropagator's Administration Tool to register source files, create subscriptions, and control the Capture and Apply processes. In DPropR/400, the term *registration* refers to a process whereby source tables are made available for propagation. A source table need only be registered one time without regard to the number of target machines that may eventually receive data from it. Additionally, there is no need to manually define source-table attributes to target machines. A *subscription* in DPropR/400 actually defines a replication request and also establishes relationships between registered source tables and their associated target tables.

During the Administration process, IT personnel must define three server roles (control server, data server, and copy server) and three user roles (administrator, registrar, and subscriber). The control server contains the actual subscription definitions, while the data server stores the source files and intermediate staging and control tables. The copy server contains the target database.

Administrators are IT personnel who grant authorities to users who are classified as either registrars or subscribers. Typically, one individual (i.e., the security officer) in a company is tasked with administrative responsibility for DPropR/400. In addition to managing authorities, administrators also manage the actual replication jobs.

Registrars are responsible for registering source files and fields in DPropR/400 and for granting authorities to subscribers who may use the source data.

Finally, subscribers create subscriptions based on the registered files. Subscriptions contain all the information required to propagate data, including the name of the registered file, fields that comprise the target files and their relationship to source fields, the type of copy (i.e., refresh or update), and the frequency of the copy (e.g., every 15 minutes). Subscribers are responsible for transforming source data, so they should be familiar with SQL. An unlimited number of subscribers and registrars can be defined in an environment, though in practice it is not uncommon to see one individual serving in both roles.

Capture

Residing on the data (source) server, the Capture process monitors database transactions, records database changes, updates the staging table with journal entries, and records commitment-control information for every transaction. For each registered source file, the Capture process uses one staging file (referred to as the Change Data table) and two control files (the Pruning Control table and the Critical Selection table) to manage transactional processing. DPropR/400 automatically creates these files during the registration of source files. Change

Data tables store unapplied changes derived from insert, update, and delete operations run against the related source files. To prevent the Change Data tables from growing to unmanageable sizes, DPropR/400's Apply process stores data in the Pruning Control tables to indicate when data can be removed from the associated Change Data tables. To maximize performance, the Change Data tables should be reorganized on a regular basis to actually remove deleted records. The purpose of the Critical Section file is to synchronize the Capture and Apply processes. In addition to these specialized intermediate tables, DPropR/400 also maintains a single Unit of Work table that stores information about committed data for all registered source files. Capture's pruning process also maintains this file, which should be reorganized regularly.

Apply

DPropR/400's Apply component processes subscriptions. As part of this process, it accesses registered files (for full-refresh propagation) or intermediate staging files (for change propagation) on the data server and copies data to the target files. The Apply process itself normally runs on the copy server; however, in a push scenario, it can be located on the data server. In the case of net-change propagation, the Apply process joins the appropriate Change Data table with the Unit of Work table to propagate only committed changes to the target database.

Implementation Example

Now that you have a high-level overview of DPropR/400's components and processes, let's examine how we can use the product to implement our simple data-warehousing example.

Figures 13.1 through 13.7 demonstrate how we can use DPropR/400 to perform the first step in our implementation example (i.e., the summarization of invoice data from two related files). In Figure 13.1, I used DPropR/400's ADDDPRCAPE command to register a previously created view for files IN001PF and IN002PF. I specified a join-logical file called IN001N2LF, which must be created outside of DPropR/400, in the "Base file" parameter of the command. Because this registration will be used for full refreshes only, I set the "Capture columns" parameter to *NONE. With this specification, changes are not captured for this source view, and therefore no staging table environment is created. The "Library for control files" parameter specifies the location of the registration control files. The default value *BASFILE is the same library as the source table/view that is being registered. We use the "Capture relative record number" parameter when no column in the source table uniquely identifies each source record. This parameter, when set to *YES, lets DPropR/400 use the relative record number of the source table as the key to the target table. The "Record images" parameter specifies the changes to be captured. This parameter instructs DPropR/400 to capture *before*, *after*, or *both* images of any change made to the source table. When registering for net-change replication, we must specify *BOTH here. You should note that when you want to use net-change propagation, *BOTH images should be specified in the STRJRNPF command, regardless of whether you will capture *before*, *after*, or *both* images with the capture process.

FIGURE 13.1
Registering the Join View IN001N2LF

```
                     Add DPR Capture Entry (ADDDPRCAPE)

 Type choices, press Enter.

 Base file  . . . . . . . . . . . > IN001N2LF
   Library  . . . . . . . . . . . >   INVOICEDB    Name
 Library for control files  . . .   *BASFILE      Name, *BASFILE
 Base type  . . . . . . . . . . .   *USERTABLE     *USERTABLE, *CONSISTENT...
 Allow full refresh . . . . . . .   *YES           *YES, *NO
 Text 'description' . . . . . . .   *NONE

 Capture columns  . . . . . . . .   *NONE
               + for more values
 Capture relative record number     *NO            *YES, *NO
 Record images  . . . . . . . . .   *AFTER         *AFTER, *BEFORE, *BOTH



                                                                        Bottom
 F3=Exit   F4=Prompt   F5=Refresh   F12=Cancel   F13=How to use this display
 F24=More keys
```

Our next task is to create the subscription to the view using DPropR/400's ADDDPRAPYE command. This CL command is run on the target AS/400. In Figure 13.2, I specified IN001N2LF in library INVOICEDB as the base file. The target table for this subscription is AGGRBYSKU in library INVOICEDB. In the "Target type" parameter, I specified *BASEAGR, which means that SQL column functions will be used to aggregate the source table during the Apply process. In the "Data server" parameter, I specified the relational database (RDB) name where the base file is registered. In this case, it is defined locally, so I used the keyword *LOCAL. In the "Activate subscription" parameter, I specified *YES so that DPropR/400 can run this subscription when it is created. Had I specified *NO, the subscription would be disabled and DPropR/400's Apply procedure would not recognize it as a serviceable subscription. In the Priority parameter, I specified 1 to denote that this subscription has the highest priority.

FIGURE 13.2
Associating IN001N2LF with Target File AGGRBYSKU

```
                         Add DPR Apply Entry (ADDDPRAPYE)

 Type choices, press Enter.

 User . . . . . . . . . . . . . .   *CURRENT      Name, *CURRENT
 Target file  . . . . . . . . . . > AGGRBYSKU
   Library  . . . . . . . . . . . >   INVOICEDB   Name
 Base file  . . . . . . . . . . . > IN001N2LF
   Library  . . . . . . . . . . . >   INVOICEDB   Name
 Data server  . . . . . . . . . . > *LOCAL
 Activate subscription  . . . . .   *YES          *YES, *NO
 Target type  . . . . . . . . . . > *BASEAGR      *POINTINTIME, *CONSISTENT...
 Priority . . . . . . . . . . . .   1             1-999

                                                                       More...
 F3=Exit   F4=Prompt   F5=Refresh   F12=Cancel   F13=How to use this display
 F24=More keys
```

As I mentioned earlier, this propagation procedure is not designed for net-change replication. If I want to aggregate changes from the source view and then store the aggregated results in the target table, I would first modify the source view's registration to accommodate change capture. I would then change the keyword of the "Target type" parameter on the ADDDPRAPYE command to *CHANGAGR. This parameter directs the Apply process to perform the aggregation of the captured changes.

The capability to aggregate changes is one of DPropR/400's most powerful features. Change aggregation is useful in many instances — for example, to sum the sales quantity and revenue at each branch of our fictitious department store at the end of each day.

Figures 13.3 through 13.7 (pages 222–224) highlight additional features of the ADDDPRAPYE command. For example, in the "SQL statement" prompt shown in Figure 13.3, I can specify SQL statements that are to execute before Apply processes the subscription. To enable user exit functionality, I can specify SQL statements that call stored procedures. At the "Server to run on" prompt, I specify the RDB name.

In Figure 13.4, you will notice that an SQL statement can also be executed after Apply processes the subscription. As before, this statement can be a call to a stored procedure. We use the "Row selection expression" parameter to specify a column on which to perform the grouping function. In this example, I've entered SKUID. The "Row selection expression" parameter corresponds to SQL clauses that can be added to a SELECT statement. I've specified (0=0) in Figure 13.4 because the WHERE clause is implied.

FIGURE 13.3
DPropR/400's Run Before SQL Prompt

```
                      Add DPR Apply Entry (ADDDPRAPYE)

Type choices, press Enter.

SQL to run before:
  SQL statement . . . . . . . . _ *NONE

  Server to run on . . . . . . .
  Allowed SQL states . . . . . .   ______         00000-FFFFF, *NONE
               + for more values   ______
               + for more values _

                                                                 More...
F3=Exit   F4=Prompt   F5=Refresh   F12=Cancel   F13=How to use this display
F24=More keys
```

FIGURE 13.4
DPropR/400's Run After SQL Prompt

```
                      Add DPR Apply Entry (ADDDPRAPYE)

Type choices, press Enter.

SQL to run after:
  SQL statement . . . . . . . . _ *NONE

  Server to run on . . . . . . .
  Allowed SQL states . . . . . .   ______         00000-FFFFF, *NONE
               + for more values   ______
               + for more values _
Row selection expression . . . . > '(0=0) GROUP BY SKUID'

Source columns . . . . . . . . . > SKUID
               + for more values

                                                                 More...
F3=Exit   F4=Prompt   F5=Refresh   F12=Cancel   F13=How to use this display
F24=More keys
```

In Figure 13.5, I specified *NONE for "Key columns" and *NO for "Unique key" to denote that no key will be used in the aggregated target table. In the "Target columns" prompt, I could have renamed columns in the target table to make them more meaningful. In using the default keyword *COLUMN, I directed DPropR/400 to simply use the names of the columns from the registered source.

FIGURE 13.5
Specifying That Target File Has No Keys

```
                    Add DPR Apply Entry (ADDDPRAPYE)

Type choices, press Enter.

Key columns . . . . . . . . . . > *NONE
               + for more values
Unique key . . . . . . . . . . . > *NO             *YES, *NO
Target columns:                   _
  Column . . . . . . . . . . . .   *COLUMN
  New column . . . . . . . . . .
               + for more values _

                                                                More...
F3=Exit   F4=Prompt   F5=Refresh   F12=Cancel   F13=How to use this display
F24=More keys
```

In Figure 13.6, I show how we use SQL statements to aggregate data. In this case, I used the SUM column function to aggregate revenue figures that are first derived by multiplying invoice quantity by unit price. Figure 13.6 highlights two key points of DPropR/400. First, the package really requires its users to have a working knowledge of SQL. Second, DPropR/400's power and flexibility are limited only by the degree to which its users can use SQL.

In Figure 13.7, I show how we use the ADDDPRAPYE command to define the interval during which the subscription will run. By specifying 1 for Number and *DAY for Interval, I am telling DPropR/400 to run the aggregation against the base table one time per day. I left the "Create target file" prompt to its default of *YES so that the subscription process creates the target file automatically. I also left the "Check target file format" parameter to its default of *YES. This parameter, which is examined when an existing target table is specified, directs the subscription process to identify discrepancies between the source columns and the target columns. It is ignored when the target table does not exist. I specified *NO in the "Add DPR capture entry" parameter because this target table will not serve as a source for additional replication. We set this parameter to *YES when we want cascading replication to occur.

FIGURE 13.6
Deriving Total Quantity Sold and Total Revenue

```
                    Add DPR Apply Entry (ADDDPRAPYE)

 Type choices, press Enter.

 Calculated columns:
   Column . . . . . . . . . . . . > SUMINVQTY
   Expression . . . . . . . . . . > 'SUM(INVQTY)'


   Column . . . . . . . . . . . . > REVENUE
   Expression . . . . . . . . . . > 'SUM(INVQTY*UNTPRC)'


               + for more values _
 Run mode . . . . . . . . . . . .   *OPTIMISTIC   *ADD, *REPLACE...
 Iterations . . . . . . . . . . .   *NOMAX        1-10, *NOMAX, *NONE

                                                                More...
 F3=Exit   F4=Prompt   F5=Refresh   F12=Cancel   F13=How to use this display
 F24=More keys
```

FIGURE 13.7
Directing Subscription to Run Once Daily

```
                    Add DPR Apply Entry (ADDDPRAPYE)

 Type choices, press Enter.

 Interval between iterations:
   Number . . . . . . . . . . . . > 1              1-60
   Interval . . . . . . . . . . .   *DAY           *WEEK, *DAY, *HOUR, *MIN
               + for more values _
 Expiration date  . . . . . . . .   *PERM          Date, *PERM
 Create target file . . . . . . .   *YES           *YES, *NO
 Check target file format . . . .   *YES           *YES, *NO
 Add DPR capture entry  . . . . . > *NO            *YES, *NO



                                                                 Bottom
 F3=Exit   F4=Prompt   F5=Refresh   F12=Cancel   F13=How to use this display
 F24=More keys
```

Step two of our implementation example requires us to remap color codes with more descriptive text. To perform this task, we first create a value-translation table (PRDCOLOR) that contains each color code and its associated value. We perform this task outside DPropR/400 because the product lacks an effective value-translation facility.[2] Next, TA001PF (our product/SKU attributes table) is joined to PRDCOLOR (as you may recall, TA001PF contains the color codes for our products). We then register the joined view of products and colors using DPropR/400's ADDDPRCAPE command, as shown in Figure 13.8.

FIGURE 13.8

Registering the Join View TA001WCOLORLF

```
                        Add DPR Capture Entry (ADDDPRCAPE)

 Type choices, press Enter.

 Base file  . . . . . . . . . . . > TA001WCOLORLF
   Library  . . . . . . . . . . . >   INVOICEDB    Name
 Library for control files  . . .   *BASFILE       Name, *BASFILE
 Base type  . . . . . . . . . . .   *USERTABLE     *USERTABLE, *CONSISTENT...
 Allow full refresh . . . . . . .   *YES           *YES, *NO
 Text 'description' . . . . . . .   *NONE

 Capture columns  . . . . . . . . > *NONE
                + for more values
 Capture relative record number     *NO            *YES, *NO
 Record images  . . . . . . . . .   *AFTER         *AFTER, *BEFORE, *BOTH




                                                                     Bottom
 F3=Exit   F4=Prompt   F5=Refresh   F12=Cancel   F13=How to use this display
 F24=More keys
```

As in Figure 13.1, I specified *NONE in the "Capture columns" parameter here to denote that we are using full-refresh replication.

Our next task is to create the subscription to the join view called TA001WCOLORLF. Figures 13.9 through 13.11 (pages 226–227) illustrate this process. Once again, I used DPropR/400's ADDDPRAPYE command.

In Figure 13.9, I specified table PRODPF in library INVOICEDB in the "Target file/Library" prompt. In the "Target type" parameter, I specified *USERCOPY to denote that columns that exist in the target table match the source table for this subscription. Again, we could easily enhance this scenario to propagate changes to the target table, which is useful if we want to perform an initial full refresh of the target table followed by incremental updates. Of course, our choice of a full refresh or an initial refresh followed by incremental updates depends on the volume of data that is replicated. Large tables that are updated constantly (e.g., order or invoice tables) are good candidates for change

[2]In practice, this lack is usually not an issue. Required code tables (e.g., for colors in this example) would most likely exist in the OLTP database. Associated values for codes in these tables can easily be brought into DPropR/400 via a join file. However, as previously mentioned, join files must be created outside of DPropR/400.

FIGURE 13.9
Associating TA001WCOLORLF with Target File PRODPF

```
                    Add DPR Apply Entry (ADDDPRAPYE)

Type choices, press Enter.

User . . . . . . . . . . . . . .   *CURRENT      Name, *CURRENT
Target file  . . . . . . . . . . > PRODPF
  Library  . . . . . . . . . . . >   INVOICEDB   Name
Base file  . . . . . . . . . . . > TA001WCOLORLF
  Library  . . . . . . . . . . . >   INVOICEDB   Name
Data server  . . . . . . . . . . > *LOCAL
Activate subscription  . . . . .   *YES          *YES, *NO
Target type  . . . . . . . . . . > *USERCOPY     *POINTINTIME, *CONSISTENT...
Priority . . . . . . . . . . . .   1             1-999

                                                                      More...
F3=Exit   F4=Prompt   F5=Refresh   F12=Cancel   F13=How to use this display
F24=More keys
```

propagation, while small tables with relatively static data (e.g., state or country code tables) are good candidates for full-refresh propagation.

In Figure 13.10, I specified the "Key column" parameter. For a *USERCOPY type, the Apply process requires a unique key so that follow-up updates can be applied to the appropriate row. In Figure 13.11, I directed DPropR/400 to keep the subscription interval at once daily. However, I changed the "Create target file" parameter to *NO because the file has already been created. Again, I set the "Add DPR capture entry" parameter to *NO, because we will not use this target table in a cascading replication scheme.

Step three of our implementation example calls for us to write data to the sales fact table and product dimension table. To do this, I used the registration I already created for table IN001NLF, so I won't show the registration screens again. I do have to create another subscription to the view IN001N2LF, however, and the following screens illustrate how to do this.

In Figure 13.12 (page 228), I specified IN001N2LF to be the "Base file" in Base Library INVOICEDB, while the "Target file" is FACTPF in Target Library INVOICEDB. For simplicity, assume that this table has already been created. I specified *USERCOPY in the "Target type" parameter to denote that columns that exist in the target table match the source table for this subscription.

In Figure 13.13 (page 228), I specified the columns from the source registration that will be included in our target table. In this case, I did not make any modifications to the columns.

FIGURE 13.10
Using DPropR/400 to Specify a Key

```
                         Add DPR Apply Entry (ADDDPRAPYE)

 Type choices, press Enter.

 Key columns . . . . . . . . . . > SKUID
               + for more values
 Unique key . . . . . . . . . . .  *YES          *YES, *NO
 Target columns:                 _
   Column . . . . . . . . . . . .  *COLUMN
   New column . . . . . . . . . .
               + for more values _
 Calculated columns:             _
   Column . . . . . . . . . . . .  *NONE
   Expression . . . . . . . . . .



               + for more values _
 Run mode . . . . . . . . . . . .  *OPTIMISTIC   *ADD, *REPLACE...
 Iterations . . . . . . . . . . .  *NOMAX        1-10, *NOMAX, *NONE
                                                                More...
 F3=Exit   F4=Prompt   F5=Refresh   F12=Cancel   F13=How to use this display
 F24=More keys
```

FIGURE 13.11
Directing Subscription to Run Once Daily

```
                         Add DPR Apply Entry (ADDDPRAPYE)

 Type choices, press Enter.

 Interval between iterations:    _
   Number . . . . . . . . . . . .  1             1-60
   Interval . . . . . . . . . . .  *DAY          *WEEK, *DAY, *HOUR, *MIN
               + for more values _
 Expiration date  . . . . . . . .  *PERM         Date, *PERM
 Create target file . . . . . . > *NO            *YES, *NO
 Check target file format . . . .  *YES          *YES, *NO
 Add DPR capture entry  . . . . . > *NO          *YES, *NO







                                                                 Bottom
 F3=Exit   F4=Prompt   F5=Refresh   F12=Cancel   F13=How to use this display
 F24=More keys
```

FIGURE 13.12
Associating IN001N2LF with Target File FACTPF

```
                    Add DPR Apply Entry (ADDDPRAPYE)

Type choices, press Enter.

User . . . . . . . . . . . . . .   *CURRENT      Name, *CURRENT
Target file  . . . . . . . . . . > FACTPF
  Library  . . . . . . . . . . . >   INVOICEDB   Name
Base file  . . . . . . . . . . . > IN001N2LF
  Library  . . . . . . . . . . . >   INVOICEDB   Name
Data server  . . . . . . . . . . > *LOCAL
Activate subscription  . . . . .   *YES          *YES, *NO
Target type  . . . . . . . . . . > *USERCOPY     *POINTINTIME, *CONSISTENT...
Priority . . . . . . . . . . . .   1             1-999

                                                                    More...
F3=Exit   F4=Prompt   F5=Refresh   F12=Cancel   F13=How to use this display
F24=More keys
```

FIGURE 13.13
Specifying Columns from Source File for Target File

```
                    Add DPR Apply Entry (ADDDPRAPYE)

Type choices, press Enter.

Source columns . . . . . . . . . > SKUID
                                 > PRDNAM
                                 > COLOR
               + for more values > PRDSIZ
Key columns  . . . . . . . . . . > *NONE
               + for more values
Unique key . . . . . . . . . . . > *YES          *YES, *NO
Target columns:                   _
  Column . . . . . . . . . . . .   *COLUMN
  New column . . . . . . . . . .
               + for more values _

                                                                    More...
F3=Exit   F4=Prompt   F5=Refresh   F12=Cancel   F13=How to use this display
F24=More keys
```

In Figure 13.14, I created two new columns for our target fact table. The first column is a calculated value INVVAL that is derived by multiplying INVQTY by UNTPRC. The Column parameter names the expression. The second new column, TIMEID, is a time-stamp field that is initialized to zero with the Expression parameter.

FIGURE 13.14

Creating Two New Columns in the Target File

```
                        Add DPR Apply Entry (ADDDPRAPYE)

Type choices, press Enter.

Calculated columns:
  Column . . . . . . . . . . . . > INVVAL
  Expression . . . . . . . . . . > '(INVQTY*UNTPRC)'



  Column . . . . . . . . . . . . > TIMEID
  Expression . . . . . . . . . . > 0



              + for more values _
Run mode . . . . . . . . . . . .   *OPTIMISTIC    *ADD, *REPLACE...
Iterations . . . . . . . . . . .   *NOMAX         1-10, *NOMAX, *NONE

                                                                More...
F3=Exit   F4=Prompt   F5=Refresh   F12=Cancel   F13=How to use this display
F24=More keys
```

In Figure 13.15, I registered the product dimension table PRODLF. To do this, I specified PRODLF to be the "Base file" in Base Library INVOICEDB. Because this registration is for full refreshes only, I specified the "Capture columns" parameter as *NONE. I accepted default values for the other parameters.

FIGURE 13.15

Registering PRODLF for Full Refreshes

```
                       Add DPR Capture Entry (ADDDPRCAPE)

Type choices, press Enter.

Base file  . . . . . . . . . . . > PRODLF
  Library  . . . . . . . . . . . >   INVOICEDB    Name
Library for control files  . . .   *BASFILE       Name, *BASFILE
Base type  . . . . . . . . . . .   *USERTABLE     *USERTABLE, *CONSISTENT...
Allow full refresh . . . . . . .   *YES           *YES, *NO
Text 'description' . . . . . . .   *NONE

Capture columns  . . . . . . . . > *NONE
              + for more values
Capture relative record number     *NO            *YES, *NO
Record images  . . . . . . . . .   *AFTER         *AFTER, *BEFORE, *BOTH




                                                                 Bottom
F3=Exit   F4=Prompt   F5=Refresh   F12=Cancel   F13=How to use this display
F24=More keys
```

Next, we must subscribe to the join view PRODLF. The following screens show how we can use this process to extract total volume and revenue by SKUID from PRODLF (you may recall that PRODLF is a pre-existing file that joins the sales fact table to the product dimension table).

In Figure 13.16, I specified PRODLF as the "Base file" in Base Library INVOICEDB. The "Target file" is AGGRBYSKU2 in Target Library INVOICEDB.

FIGURE 13.16

Associating PRODLF with Target File AGGRBYSKU2

```
                      Add DPR Apply Entry (ADDDPRAPYE)

 Type choices, press Enter.

 User . . . . . . . . . . . . . .     *CURRENT     Name, *CURRENT
 Target file  . . . . . . . . . . > AGGRBYSKU2
   Library  . . . . . . . . . . . >   INVOICEDB    Name
 Base file  . . . . . . . . . . . > PRODLF
   Library  . . . . . . . . . . . >   INVOICEDB    Name
 Data server  . . . . . . . . . . > *LOCAL
 Activate subscription  . . . . .   *YES           *YES, *NO
 Target type  . . . . . . . . . . > *BASEAGR       *POINTINTIME, *CONSISTENT...
 Priority . . . . . . . . . . . .   1              1-999







                                                                       More...
 F3=Exit   F4=Prompt   F5=Refresh   F12=Cancel   F13=How to use this display
 F24=More keys
```

Again, I specified *BASEAGR in the "Target type" prompt to denote that SQL column functions will be used to manipulate the contents of the base table for this subscription.

In Figure 13.17, I used the "Row selection" parameter to specify a column on which to perform the grouping function. In this example, I had to choose SKUID. Again, I used the (0=0) specification because the WHERE clause of the SQL statement is implied.

To specify the aggregation conditions for the target table, I again used SQL syntax. Figure 13.18 illustrates how SQL's SUM column function summarizes the figures for total volume and total revenue.

To perform the multikey data extraction process called for in step five of the implementation example, I created another subscription to PRODLF. In it, I created a target table to hold the results of the extraction. Figure 13.19 (page 232) illustrates how I created the subscription with "Target file" AGGRBYSKU3, while Figure 13.20 (page 232) demonstrates my specifications of PRDNAM, COLOR, and PRDSIZ in the grouping clause to make these columns part of the target table.

FIGURE 13.17

Grouping Data by SKUID

```
                         Add DPR Apply Entry (ADDDPRAPYE)

 Type choices, press Enter.

 SQL to run after:
   SQL statement . . . . . . . .   *NONE


   Server to run on . . . . . . .
   Allowed SQL states . . . . . .                00000-FFFFF, *NONE
                + for more values
                + for more values _
 Row selection expression . . . . > '(0=0) GROUP BY SKUID'


 Source columns . . . . . . . . . > SKUID
                + for more values

                                                                    More...
 F3=Exit   F4=Prompt   F5=Refresh   F12=Cancel   F13=How to use this display
 F24=More keys
```

FIGURE 13.18

Deriving Total Quantity Sold and Total Revenue

```
                         Add DPR Apply Entry (ADDDPRAPYE)

 Type choices, press Enter.

 Calculated columns:
   Column . . . . . . . . . . . . > TOTVOLUME
   Expression . . . . . . . . . . > 'SUM(INVQTY)'


   Column . . . . . . . . . . . . > REVENUE
   Expression . . . . . . . . . . > 'SUM(INVVAL)'


                + for more values _
 Run mode . . . . . . . . . . . .   *OPTIMISTIC   *ADD, *REPLACE...
 Iterations . . . . . . . . . . .   *NOMAX        1-10, *NOMAX, *NONE

                                                                    More...
 F3=Exit   F4=Prompt   F5=Refresh   F12=Cancel   F13=How to use this display
 F24=More keys
```

FIGURE 13.19

Associating PRODLF with Target File AGGRBYSKU3

```
                        Add DPR Apply Entry (ADDDPRAPYE)

Type choices, press Enter.

User . . . . . . . . . . . . . .   *CURRENT      Name, *CURRENT
Target file  . . . . . . . . . . > AGGRBYSKU3
  Library  . . . . . . . . . . . >   INVOICEDB   Name
Base file  . . . . . . . . . . . > PRODLF
  Library  . . . . . . . . . . . >   INVOICEDB   Name
Data server  . . . . . . . . . . > *LOCAL
Activate subscription  . . . . .   *YES          *YES, *NO
Target type  . . . . . . . . . . > *BASEAGR      *POINTINTIME, *CONSISTENT...
Priority . . . . . . . . . . . .   1             1-999

                                                                     More...
F3=Exit   F4=Prompt   F5=Refresh   F12=Cancel   F13=How to use this display
F24=More keys
```

FIGURE 13.20

Specifying a Multikey Aggregation

```
                        Add DPR Apply Entry (ADDDPRAPYE)

Type choices, press Enter.

SQL to run after:
  SQL statement  . . . . . . . .   *NONE


  Server to run on . . . . . . .
  Allowed SQL states . . . . . .                 00000-FFFFF, *NONE
                + for more values
                + for more values
Row selection expression . . . . > '(0=0) GROUP BY SKUID, PRDNAM, COLOR, PRDSIZ

                                                                     More...
F3=Exit   F4=Prompt   F5=Refresh   F12=Cancel   F13=How to use this display
F24=More keys
```

In Figure 13.21, I specified "Source columns" such as SKUID to be included in the target table. As before, I used the SUM function of SQL to compute TOTVOLUME and REVENUE in Figure 13.22.

FIGURE 13.21
Specifying Columns from Source File for Target File

```
                          Add DPR Apply Entry (ADDDPRAPYE)

Type choices, press Enter.

SQL to run after:
  SQL statement . . . . . . . .   *NONE


  Server to run on . . . . . . .
  Allowed SQL states . . . . . .                00000-FFFFF, *NONE
             + for more values
             + for more values _
Row selection expression . . . .  *ALL


Source columns . . . . . . . . . > SKUID
                                 > CUSTID
             + for more values > INVQTY
                                                                More...
F3=Exit   F4=Prompt   F5=Refresh   F12=Cancel   F13=How to use this display
F24=More keys
```

FIGURE 13.22
Deriving Total Quantity Sold and Total Revenue

```
                          Add DPR Apply Entry (ADDDPRAPYE)

Type choices, press Enter.

Calculated columns:
  Column . . . . . . . . . . . . > TOTVOLUME
  Expression . . . . . . . . . . > 'SUM(INVQTY)'



  Column . . . . . . . . . . . . > REVENUE
  Expression . . . . . . . . . . > 'SUM(INVVAL)'


             + for more values _
Run mode . . . . . . . . . . . .  *OPTIMISTIC    *ADD, *REPLACE...
Iterations . . . . . . . . . . .  *NOMAX         1-10, *NOMAX, *NONE

                                                                More...
F3=Exit   F4=Prompt   F5=Refresh   F12=Cancel   F13=How to use this display
F24=More keys
```

Finally, to compute total volume and total revenue per product that step six of the implementation example requires, I created another DPropR/400 subscription. Figure 13.23 illustrates how I once again selected PRODLF as the base table. For the target table, I specified AGGRBYPRDNM in library INVOICEDB. Figures 13.24 and 13.25 illustrate how to specify the row-selection criteria and SQL SUM function, respectively, as in earlier examples.

FIGURE 13.23
Associating PRODLF with Target File AGGRBYPRDN

```
                        Add DPR Apply Entry (ADDDPRAPYE)

 Type choices, press Enter.

 User . . . . . . . . . . . . . .   *CURRENT      Name, *CURRENT
 Target file  . . . . . . . . . . > AGGRBYPRDN
   Library  . . . . . . . . . . . >   INVOICEDB   Name
 Base file  . . . . . . . . . . . > PRODLF
   Library  . . . . . . . . . . . >   INVOICEDB   Name
 Data server  . . . . . . . . . . > *LOCAL
 Activate subscription  . . . . .   *YES          *YES, *NO
 Target type  . . . . . . . . . . > *BASEAGR      *POINTINTIME, *CONSISTENT...
 Priority . . . . . . . . . . . .   1             1-999

                                                                    More...
 F3=Exit   F4=Prompt   F5=Refresh   F12=Cancel   F13=How to use this display
 F24=More keys
```

PRODUCT SUMMARY AND POSITIONING

IBM's DPropR/400 is a database-driven product designed for robust, high-integrity data transformation and propagation applications. Like Coglin Mill's RODIN and DataMirror's Transformation Server, DPropR/400 is not a data warehouse; rather, it is a tool used to create, populate, and maintain data-warehouse repositories. Once data has been moved to the warehouse, we would use other products to analyze the data.

IBM clearly focused its DPropR/400 development effort on propagation. The product's use of staging files and commitment control make it especially well-suited for sites that require high-integrity, all-or-none data replication. The product does not feature proprietary support for transformational processing; instead, it relies on SQL's data-manipulation capabilities. DPropR/400 seamlessly integrates the power and flexibility of SQL with its core strength in propagation, so it is very well suited for IT personnel with SQL experience.

DPropR/400 is available on a per-processor basis and costs from $1,350 to $8,000. Of course, you can accomplish many of the functions DPropR/400

FIGURE 13.24
Grouping Data by PRDNAM

```
                        Add DPR Apply Entry (ADDDPRAPYE)

  Type choices, press Enter.

  SQL to run after:
    SQL statement . . . . . . . .   *NONE



    Server to run on . . . . . . .
    Allowed SQL states . . . . . .          00000-FFFFF, *NONE
                  + for more values
                  + for more values _
  Row selection expression . . . . > '(0=0) GROUP BY PRDNAM'



  Source columns . . . . . . . . . > PRDNAM
                  + for more values
                                                                More...
  F3=Exit   F4=Prompt   F5=Refresh   F12=Cancel   F13=How to use this display
  F24=More keys
```

FIGURE 13.25
Deriving Total Quantity Sold and Total Revenue

```
                        Add DPR Apply Entry (ADDDPRAPYE)

  Type choices, press Enter.

  Calculated columns:
    Column . . . . . . . . . . . . > TOTVOLUME
    Expression . . . . . . . . . . > 'SUM(INVQTY)'



    Column . . . . . . . . . . . . > REVENUE
    Expression . . . . . . . . . . > 'SUM(INVVAL)'



                  + for more values _
  Run mode . . . . . . . . . . . .   *OPTIMISTIC   *ADD, *REPLACE...
  Iterations . . . . . . . . . . .   *NOMAX        1-10, *NOMAX, *NONE
                                                                More...
  F3=Exit   F4=Prompt   F5=Refresh   F12=Cancel   F13=How to use this display
  F24=More keys
```

performs using a combination of SQL and RPG or COBOL programming. However, given the product's cost, such efforts are difficult to justify given the relatively high cost of programmers. As I've mentioned several times, programming is an expensive, time-consuming, error-prone process. Furthermore, the manual creation of propagation routines to move data from journal receivers to databases on a net-change basis requires programming skills that are beyond the means of many AS/400 shops.

ADDENDUM: WINDOWS 95/NT CLIENT

A Windows 95/NT client tool for DPropR/400 called AS/400 Data Propagator Administrator Tool can be requested. Available at no cost, this GUI component is a plug-in for Client Access/400 Operations Navigator. To introduce you to this feature of DPropR/400, I've included here screen captures that represent the steps required to perform our sample data-warehousing tasks. For details concerning the actual DPropR/400 processes that are taking place, refer to the main body of this chapter.

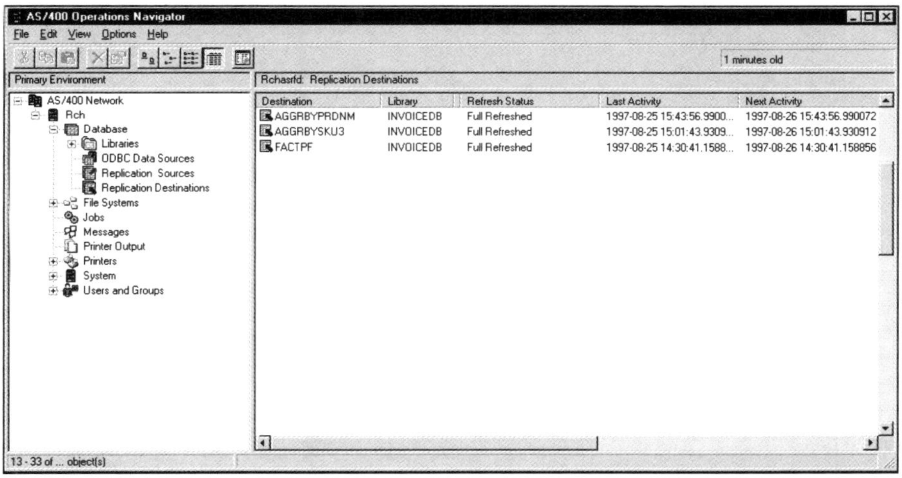

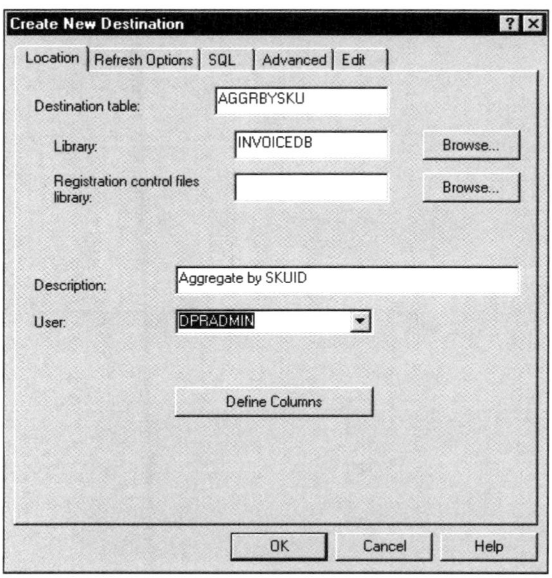

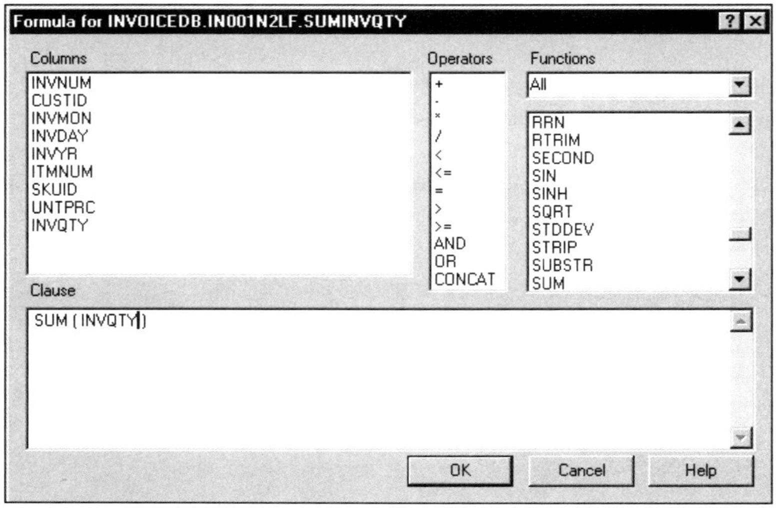
Formula for INVOICEDB.IN001N2LF.SUMINVQTY
Columns
INVNUM
CUSTID
INVMON
INVDAY
INVYR
ITMNUM
SKUID
UNTPRC
INVQTY
Operators
+
-
*
/
<
<=
=
>
>=
AND
OR
CONCAT
Functions
All
RRN
RTRIM
SECOND
SIN
SINH
SQRT
STDDEV
STRIP
SUBSTR
SUM
Clause
SUM (INVQTY)
OK
Cancel
Help

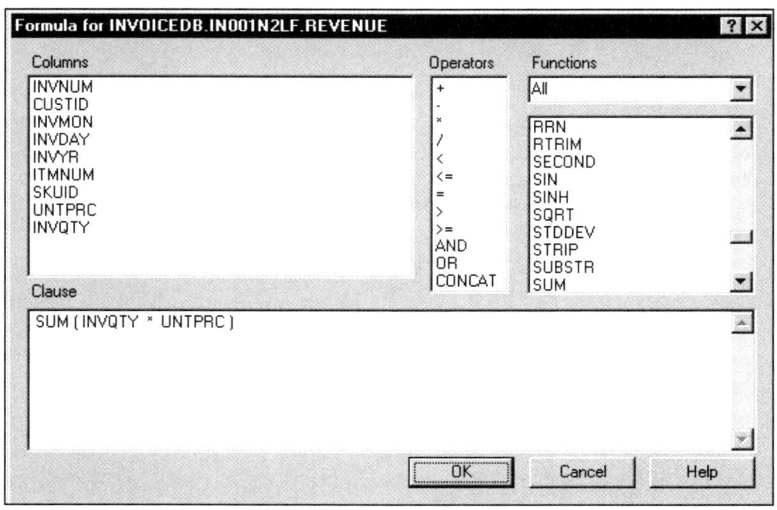
Formula for INVOICEDB.IN001N2LF.REVENUE
Columns
INVNUM
CUSTID
INVMON
INVDAY
INVYR
ITMNUM
SKUID
UNTPRC
INVQTY
Operators
+
-
*
/
<
<=
=
>
>=
AND
OR
CONCAT
Functions
All
RRN
RTRIM
SECOND
SIN
SINH
SQRT
STDDEV
STRIP
SUBSTR
SUM
Clause
SUM (INVQTY * UNTPRC)
OK
Cancel
Help

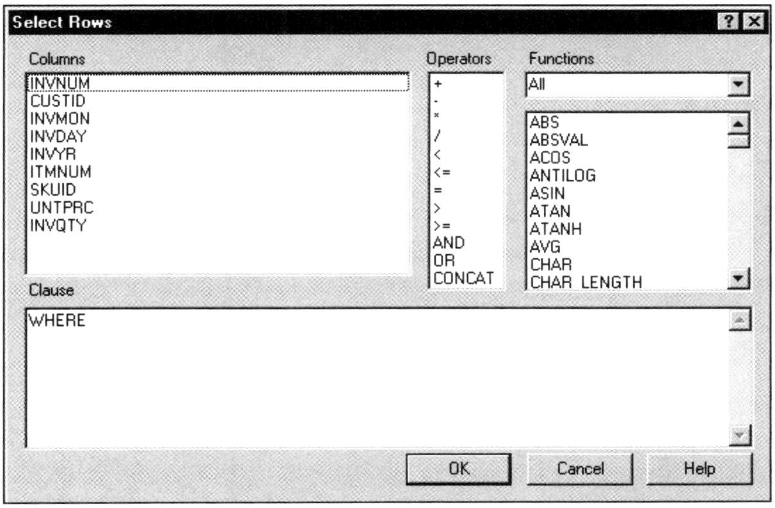
Select Rows
Columns
INVNUM
CUSTID
INVMON
INVDAY
INVYR
ITMNUM
SKUID
UNTPRC
INVQTY
Operators
+
-
*
/
<
<=
=
>
>=
AND
OR
CONCAT
Functions
All
ABS
ABSVAL
ACOS
ANTILOG
ASIN
ATAN
ATANH
AVG
CHAR
CHAR_LENGTH
Clause
WHERE
OK
Cancel
Help

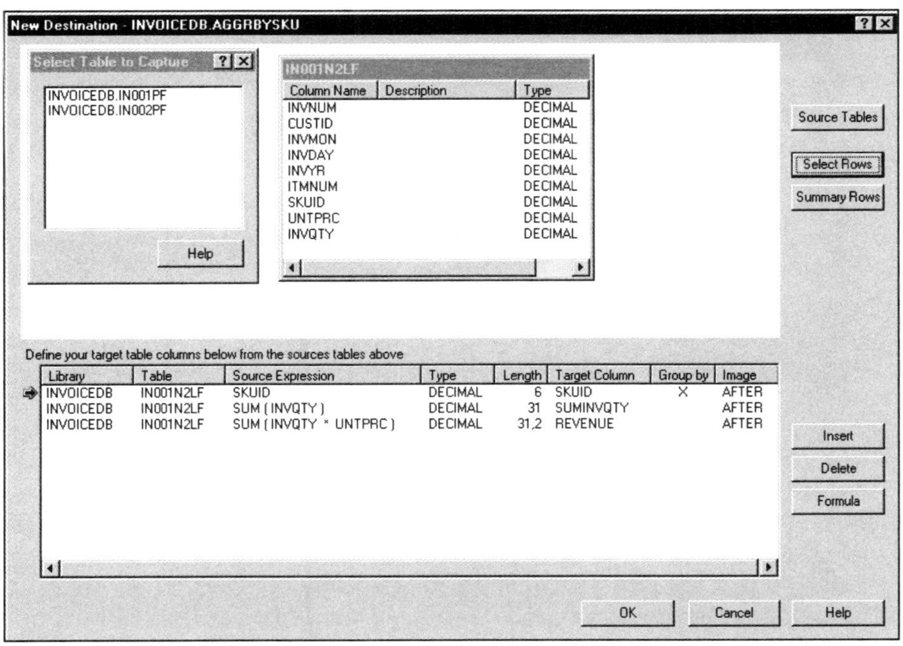
New Destination - INVOICEDB.AGGRBYSKU
Select Table to Capture
INVOICEDB.IN001PF
INVOICEDB.IN002PF
Help
IN001N2LF
Column Name
Description
Type
INVNUM DECIMAL
CUSTID DECIMAL
INVMON DECIMAL
INVDAY DECIMAL
INVYR DECIMAL
ITMNUM DECIMAL
SKUID DECIMAL
UNTPRC DECIMAL
INVQTY DECIMAL
Source Tables
Select Rows
Summary Rows
Define your target table columns below from the sources tables above
Library | Table | Source Expression | Type | Length | Target Column | Group by | Image
INVOICEDB | IN001N2LF | SKUID | DECIMAL | 6 | SKUID | X | AFTER
INVOICEDB | IN001N2LF | SUM (INVQTY) | DECIMAL | 31 | SUMINVQTY | | AFTER
INVOICEDB | IN001N2LF | SUM (INVQTY * UNTPRC) | DECIMAL | 31,2 | REVENUE | | AFTER
Insert
Delete
Formula
OK
Cancel
Help

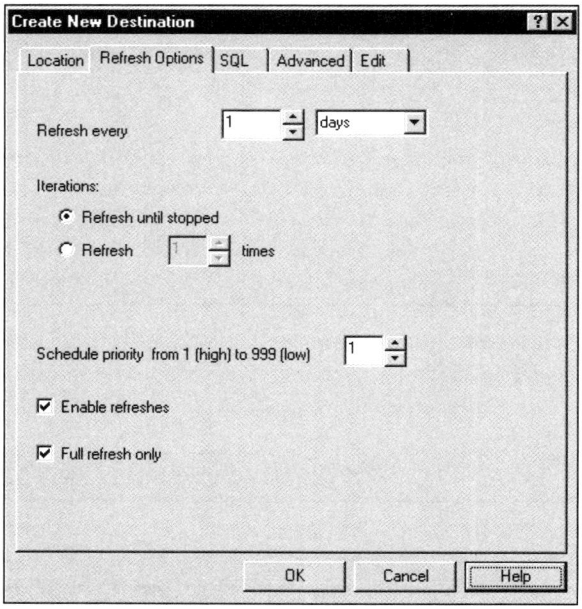
Create New Destination
Location
Refresh Options
SQL
Advanced
Edit
Refresh every
1
days
Iterations:
Refresh until stopped
Refresh
1
times
Schedule priority from 1 (high) to 999 (low)
1
Enable refreshes
Full refresh only
OK
Cancel
Help

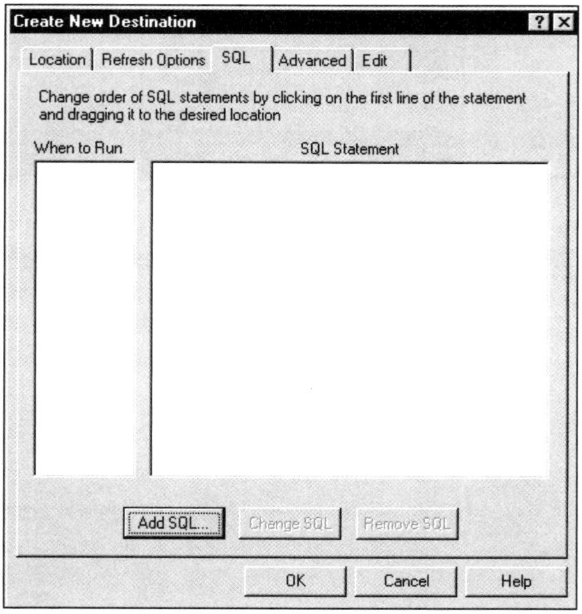
Create New Destination
Location
Refresh Options
SQL
Advanced
Edit
Change order of SQL statements by clicking on the first line of the statement and dragging it to the desired location
When to Run
SQL Statement
Add SQL...
Change SQL
Remove SQL
OK
Cancel
Help

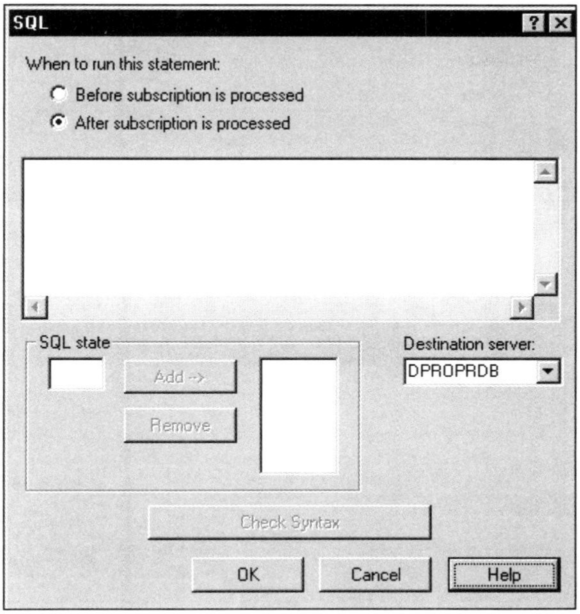
SQL
When to run this statement:
Before subscription is processed
After subscription is processed
SQL state
Add -->
Remove
Destination server:
DPROPRDB
Check Syntax
OK
Cancel
Help

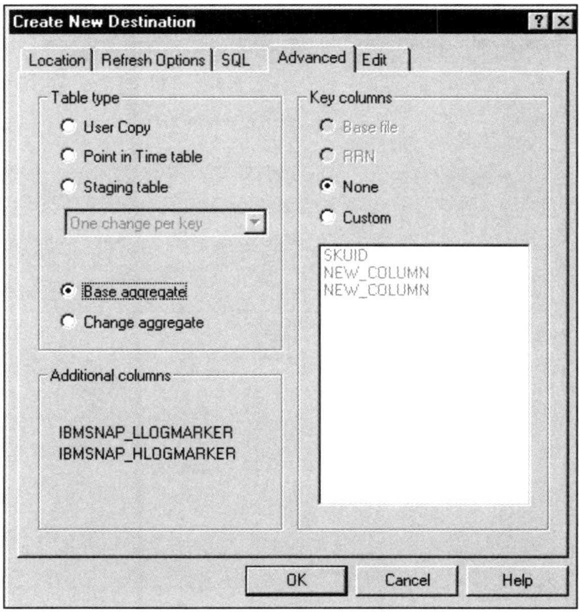
Create New Destination
Location
Refresh Options
SQL
Advanced
Edit
Table type
User Copy
Point in Time table
Staging table
One change per key
Base aggregate
Change aggregate
Key columns
Base file
RRN
None
Custom
SKUID
NEW_COLUMN
NEW_COLUMN
Additional columns
IBMSNAP_LLOGMARKER
IBMSNAP_HLOGMARKER
OK
Cancel
Help

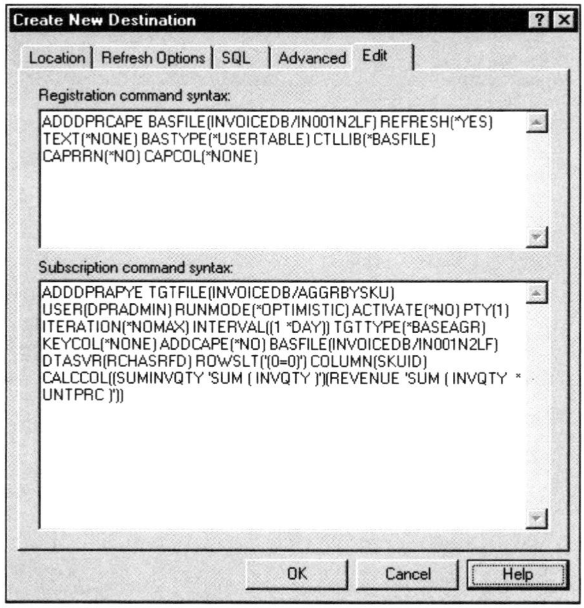
Create New Destination
Location
Refresh Options
SQL
Advanced
Edit
Registration command syntax:
ADDDPRCAPE BASFILE(INVOICEDB/IN001N2LF) REFRESH(*YES)
TEXT(*NONE) BASTYPE(*USERTABLE) CTLLIB(*BASFILE)
CAPRRN(*NO) CAPCOL(*NONE)
Subscription command syntax:
ADDDPRAPYE TGTFILE(INVOICEDB/AGGRBYSKU)
USER(DPRADMIN) RUNMODE(*OPTIMISTIC) ACTIVATE(*NO) PTY(1)
ITERATION(*NOMAX) INTERVAL((1 *DAY)) TGTTYPE(*BASEAGR)
KEYCOL(*NONE) ADDCAPE(*NO) BASFILE(INVOICEDB/IN001N2LF)
DTASVR(RCHASRFD) ROWSLT('(0=0)') COLUMN(SKUID)
CALCCOL((SUMINVQTY 'SUM (INVQTY)')(REVENUE 'SUM (INVQTY *
UNTPRC)'))
OK
Cancel
Help

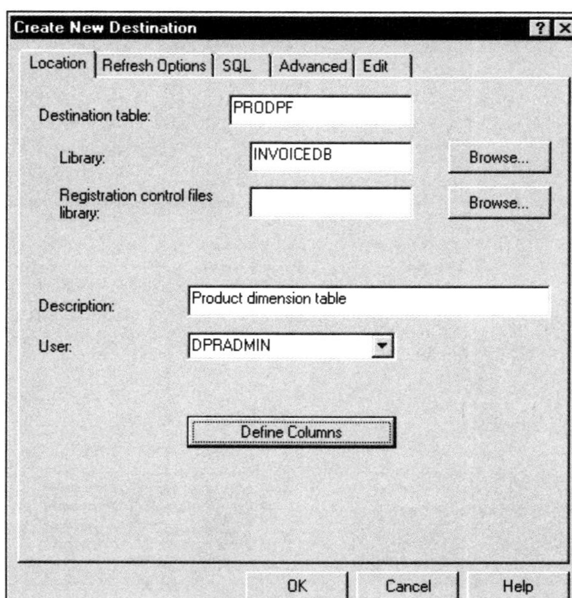
Create New Destination
Location
Refresh Options
SQL
Advanced
Edit
Destination table:
PRODPF
Library:
INVOICEDB
Browse...
Registration control files library:
Browse...
Description:
Product dimension table
User:
DPRADMIN
Define Columns
OK
Cancel
Help

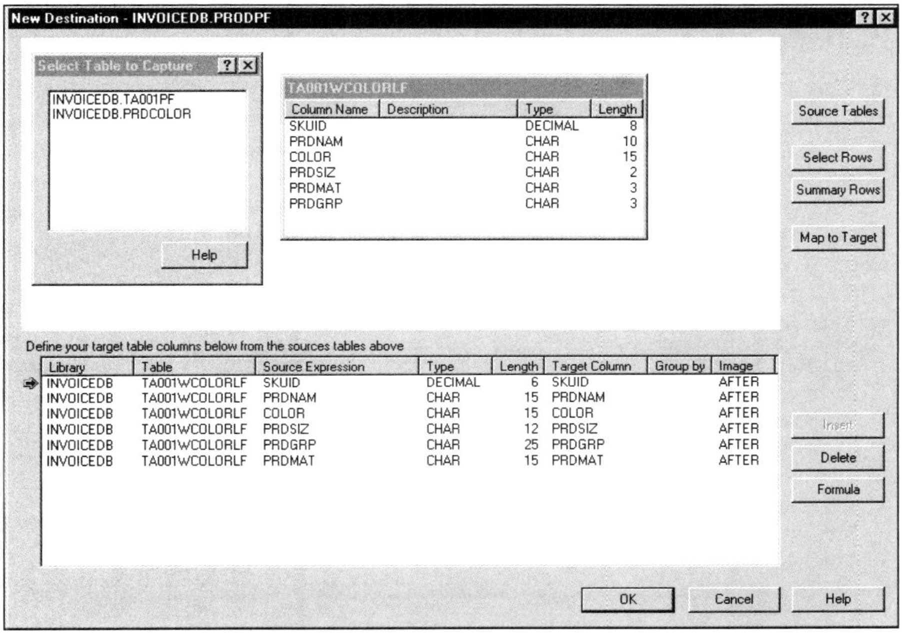
New Destination - INVOICEDB.PRODPF
Select Table to Capture
INVOICEDB.TA001PF
INVOICEDB.PRDCOLOR
Help
TA001WCOLORLF
Column Name | Description | Type | Length
SKUID DECIMAL 8
PRDNAM CHAR 10
COLOR CHAR 15
PRDSIZ CHAR 2
PRDMAT CHAR 3
PRDGRP CHAR 3
Source Tables
Select Rows
Summary Rows
Map to Target
Define your target table columns below from the sources tables above
Library | Table | Source Expression | Type | Length | Target Column | Group by | Image
INVOICEDB TA001WCOLORLF SKUID DECIMAL 6 SKUID AFTER
INVOICEDB TA001WCOLORLF PRDNAM CHAR 15 PRDNAM AFTER
INVOICEDB TA001WCOLORLF COLOR CHAR 15 COLOR AFTER
INVOICEDB TA001WCOLORLF PRDSIZ CHAR 12 PRDSIZ AFTER
INVOICEDB TA001WCOLORLF PRDGRP CHAR 25 PRDGRP AFTER
INVOICEDB TA001WCOLORLF PRDMAT CHAR 15 PRDMAT AFTER
Insert
Delete
Formula
OK
Cancel
Help

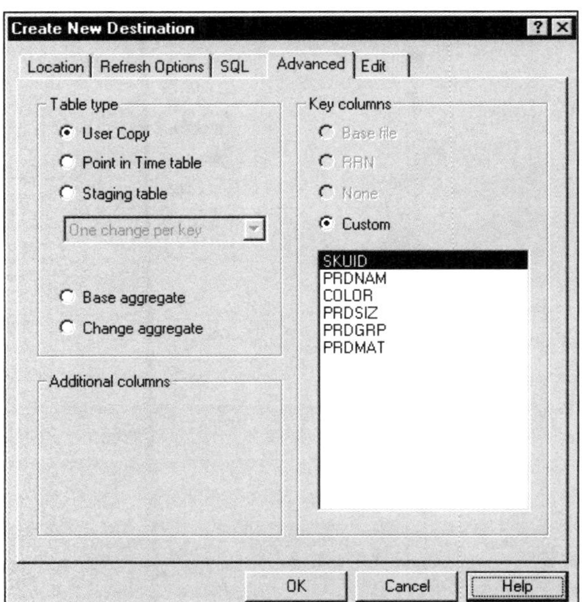
Create New Destination
Location
Refresh Options
SQL
Advanced
Edit
Table type
User Copy
Point in Time table
Staging table
One change per key
Base aggregate
Change aggregate
Additional columns
Key columns
Base file
RRN
None
Custom
SKUID
PRDNAM
COLOR
PRDSIZ
PRDGRP
PRDMAT
OK
Cancel
Help

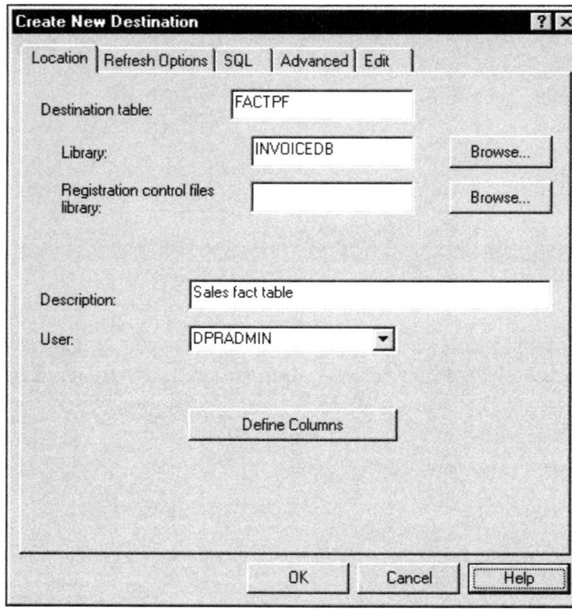
Create New Destination
Location
Refresh Options
SQL
Advanced
Edit
Destination table:
FACTPF
Library:
INVOICEDB
Browse...
Registration control files library:
Browse...
Description:
Sales fact table
User:
DPRADMIN
Define Columns
OK
Cancel
Help

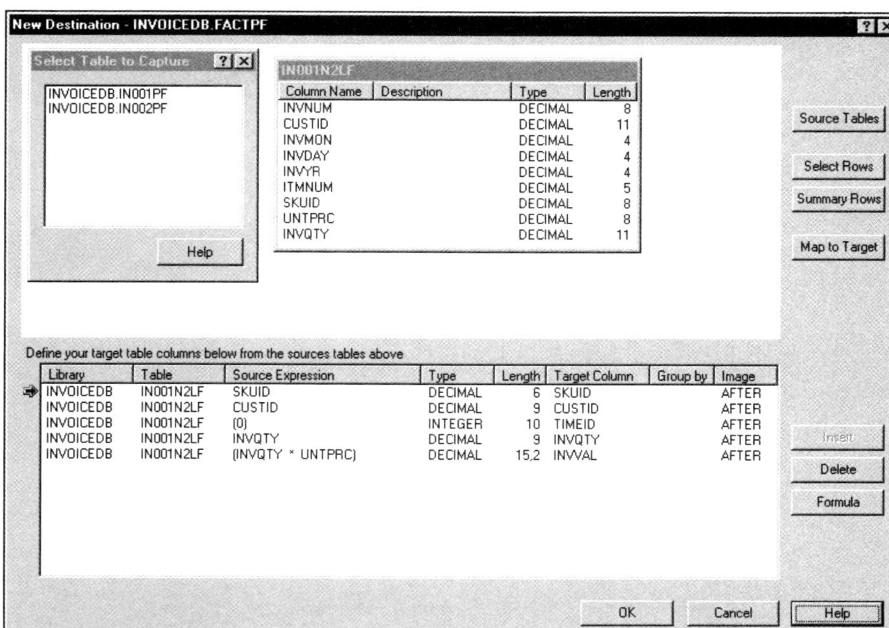
New Destination - INVOICEDB.FACTPF
Select Table to Capture
INVOICEDB.IN001PF
INVOICEDB.IN002PF
Help
IN001N2LF
Column Name
Description
Type
Length
INVNUM DECIMAL 8
CUSTID DECIMAL 11
INVMON DECIMAL 4
INVDAY DECIMAL 4
INVYR DECIMAL 4
ITMNUM DECIMAL 5
SKUID DECIMAL 8
UNTPRC DECIMAL 8
INVQTY DECIMAL 11
Source Tables
Select Rows
Summary Rows
Map to Target
Define your target table columns below from the sources tables above
Library
Table
Source Expression
Type
Length
Target Column
Group by
Image
INVOICEDB IN001N2LF SKUID DECIMAL 6 SKUID AFTER
INVOICEDB IN001N2LF CUSTID DECIMAL 9 CUSTID AFTER
INVOICEDB IN001N2LF (0) INTEGER 10 TIMEID AFTER
INVOICEDB IN001N2LF INVQTY DECIMAL 9 INVQTY AFTER
INVOICEDB IN001N2LF (INVQTY * UNTPRC) DECIMAL 15,2 INVVAL AFTER
Insert
Delete
Formula
OK
Cancel
Help

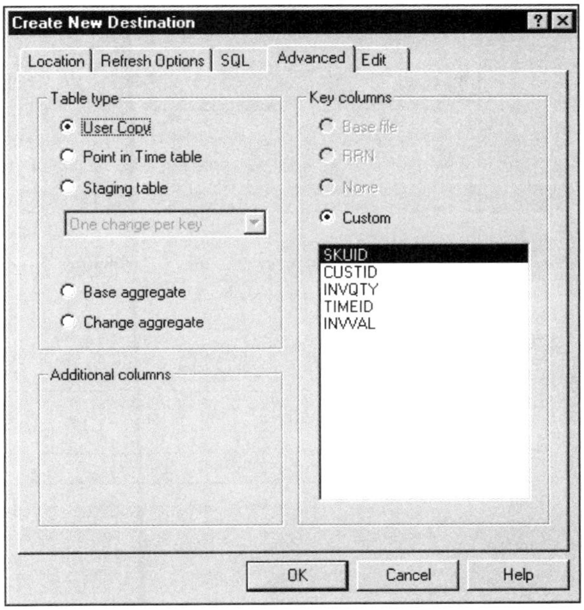
Create New Destination
Location
Refresh Options
SQL
Advanced
Edit
Table type
User Copy
Point in Time table
Staging table
One change per key
Base aggregate
Change aggregate
Additional columns
Key columns
Base file
RRN
None
Custom
SKUID
CUSTID
INVQTY
TIMEID
INVVAL
OK
Cancel
Help

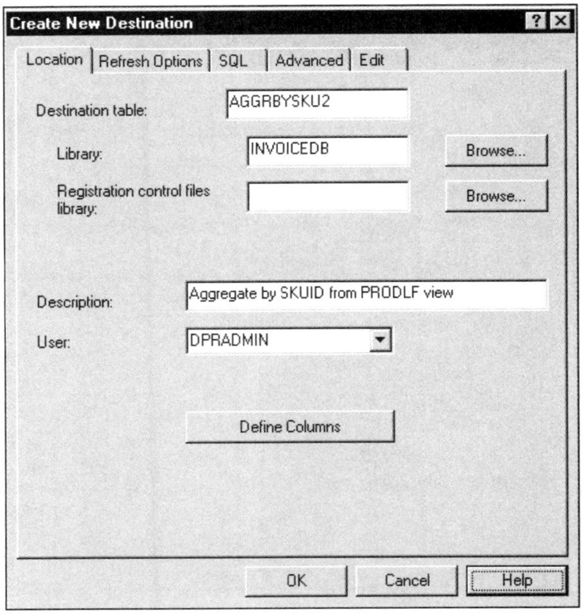
Create New Destination
Location
Refresh Options
SQL
Advanced
Edit
Destination table:
AGGRBYSKU2
Library:
INVOICEDB
Browse...
Registration control files library:
Browse...
Description:
Aggregate by SKUID from PRODLF view
User:
DPRADMIN
Define Columns
OK
Cancel
Help

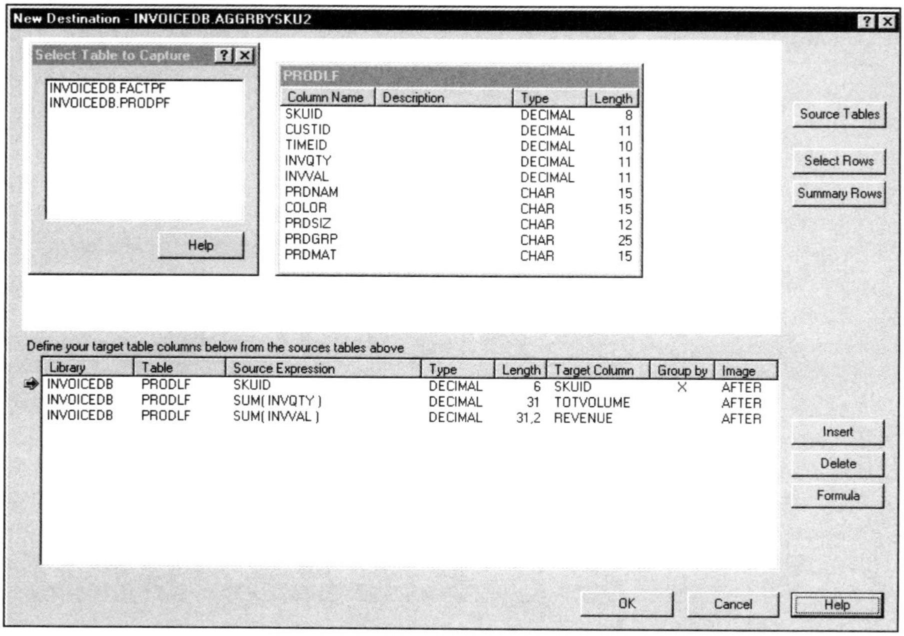
New Destination - INVOICEDB.AGGRBYSKU2
Select Table to Capture
INVOICEDB.FACTPF
INVOICEDB.PRODPF
Help
PRODLF
Column Name Description Type Length
SKUID DECIMAL 8
CUSTID DECIMAL 11
TIMEID DECIMAL 10
INVQTY DECIMAL 11
INVVAL DECIMAL 11
PRDNAM CHAR 15
COLOR CHAR 15
PRDSIZ CHAR 12
PRDGRP CHAR 25
PRDMAT CHAR 15
Source Tables
Select Rows
Summary Rows
Define your target table columns below from the sources tables above
Library Table Source Expression Type Length Target Column Group by Image
INVOICEDB PRODLF SKUID DECIMAL 6 SKUID X AFTER
INVOICEDB PRODLF SUM(INVQTY) DECIMAL 31 TOTVOLUME AFTER
INVOICEDB PRODLF SUM(INVVAL) DECIMAL 31,2 REVENUE AFTER
Insert
Delete
Formula
OK
Cancel
Help

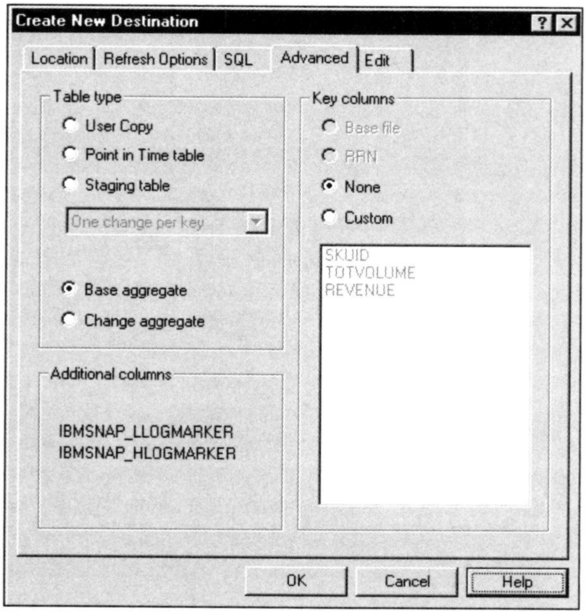
Create New Destination
Location
Refresh Options
SQL
Advanced
Edit
Table type
User Copy
Point in Time table
Staging table
One change per key
Base aggregate
Change aggregate
Key columns
Base file
RRN
None
Custom
SKUID
TOTVOLUME
REVENUE
Additional columns
IBMSNAP_LLOGMARKER
IBMSNAP_HLOGMARKER
OK
Cancel
Help

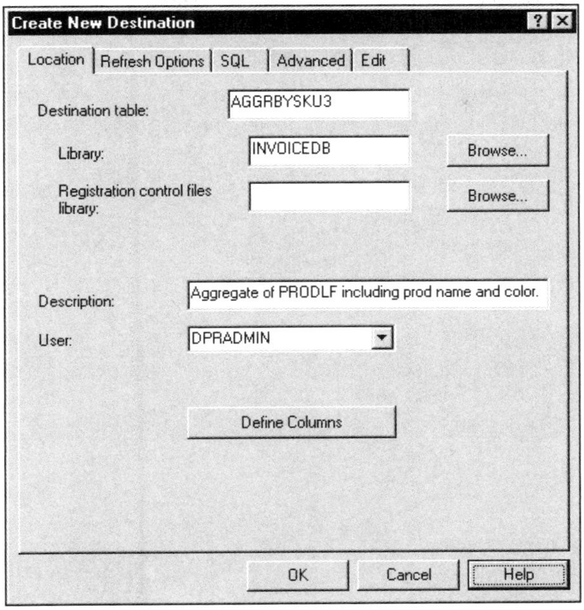
Create New Destination
Location
Refresh Options
SQL
Advanced
Edit
Destination table:
AGGRBYSKU3
Library:
INVOICEDB
Browse...
Registration control files library:
Browse...
Description:
Aggregate of PRODLF including prod name and color.
User:
DPRADMIN
Define Columns
OK
Cancel
Help

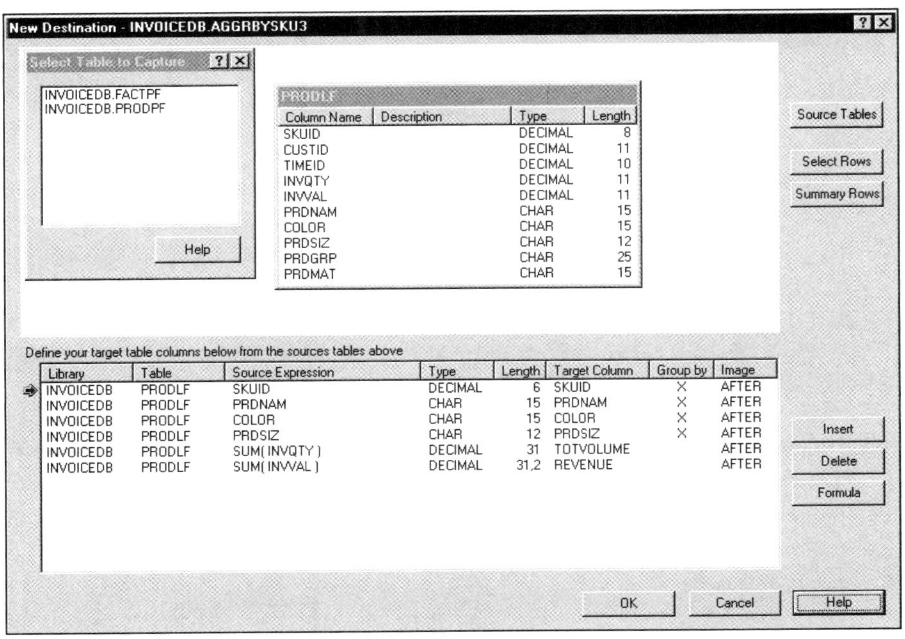
New Destination - INVOICEDB.AGGRBYSKU3
Select Table to Capture
INVOICEDB.FACTPF
INVOICEDB.PRODPF
Help
PRODLF
Column Name Description Type Length
SKUID DECIMAL 8
CUSTID DECIMAL 11
TIMEID DECIMAL 10
INVQTY DECIMAL 11
INVVAL DECIMAL 11
PRDNAM CHAR 15
COLOR CHAR 15
PRDSIZ CHAR 12
PRDGRP CHAR 25
PRDMAT CHAR 15
Source Tables
Select Rows
Summary Rows
Define your target table columns below from the sources tables above
Library Table Source Expression Type Length Target Column Group by Image
INVOICEDB PRODLF SKUID DECIMAL 6 SKUID X AFTER
INVOICEDB PRODLF PRDNAM CHAR 15 PRDNAM X AFTER
INVOICEDB PRODLF COLOR CHAR 15 COLOR X AFTER
INVOICEDB PRODLF PRDSIZ CHAR 12 PRDSIZ X AFTER
INVOICEDB PRODLF SUM(INVQTY) DECIMAL 31 TOTVOLUME AFTER
INVOICEDB PRODLF SUM(INVVAL) DECIMAL 31,2 REVENUE AFTER
Insert
Delete
Formula
OK
Cancel
Help

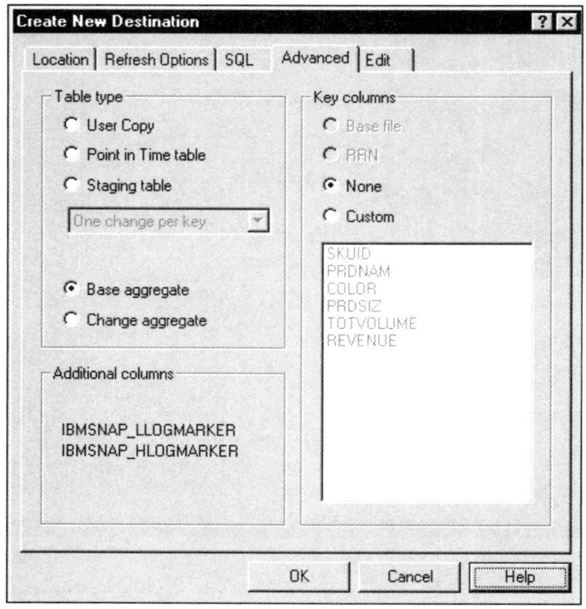
Create New Destination
Location
Refresh Options
SQL
Advanced
Edit
Table type
User Copy
Point in Time table
Staging table
One change per key
Base aggregate
Change aggregate
Additional columns
IBMSNAP_LLOGMARKER
IBMSNAP_HLOGMARKER
Key columns
Base file
RRN
None
Custom
SKUID
PRDNAM
COLOR
PRDSIZ
TOTVOLUME
REVENUE
OK
Cancel
Help

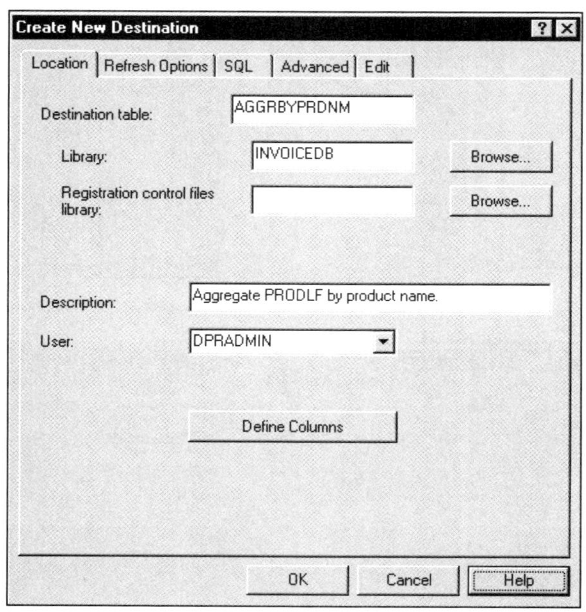
Create New Destination
Location
Refresh Options
SQL
Advanced
Edit
Destination table:
AGGRBYPRDNM
Library:
INVOICEDB
Browse...
Registration control files library:
Browse...
Description:
Aggregate PRODLF by product name.
User:
DPRADMIN
Define Columns
OK
Cancel
Help

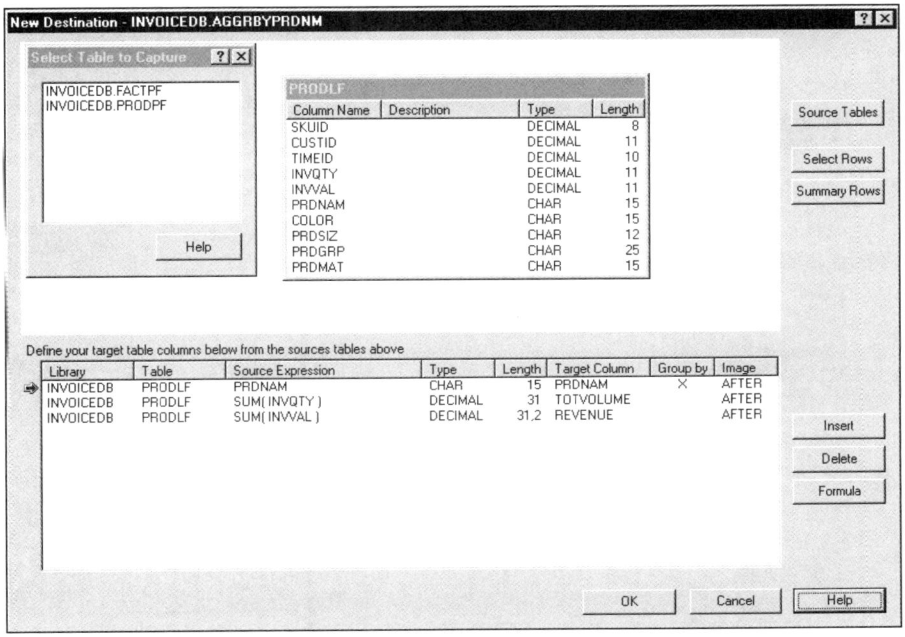
New Destination - INVOICEDB.AGGRBYPRDNM
Select Table to Capture
INVOICEDB.FACTPF
INVOICEDB.PRODPF
Help
PRODLF
Column Name | Description | Type | Length
SKUID DECIMAL 8
CUSTID DECIMAL 11
TIMEID DECIMAL 10
INVQTY DECIMAL 11
INVVAL DECIMAL 11
PRDNAM CHAR 15
COLOR CHAR 15
PRDSIZ CHAR 12
PRDGRP CHAR 25
PRDMAT CHAR 15
Source Tables
Select Rows
Summary Rows
Define your target table columns below from the sources tables above
Library | Table | Source Expression | Type | Length | Target Column | Group by | Image
INVOICEDB PRODLF PRDNAM CHAR 15 PRDNAM X AFTER
INVOICEDB PRODLF SUM(INVQTY) DECIMAL 31 TOTVOLUME AFTER
INVOICEDB PRODLF SUM(INVVAL) DECIMAL 31,2 REVENUE AFTER
Insert
Delete
Formula
OK
Cancel
Help

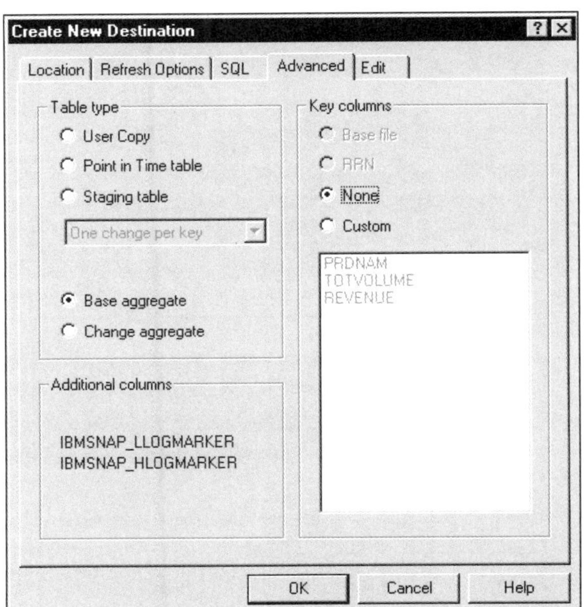
Create New Destination
Location
Refresh Options
SQL
Advanced
Edit
Table type
User Copy
Point in Time table
Staging table
One change per key
Base aggregate
Change aggregate
Key columns
Base file
RRN
None
Custom
PRDNAM
TOTVOLUME
REVENUE
Additional columns
IBMSNAP_LLOGMARKER
IBMSNAP_HLOGMARKER
OK
Cancel
Help

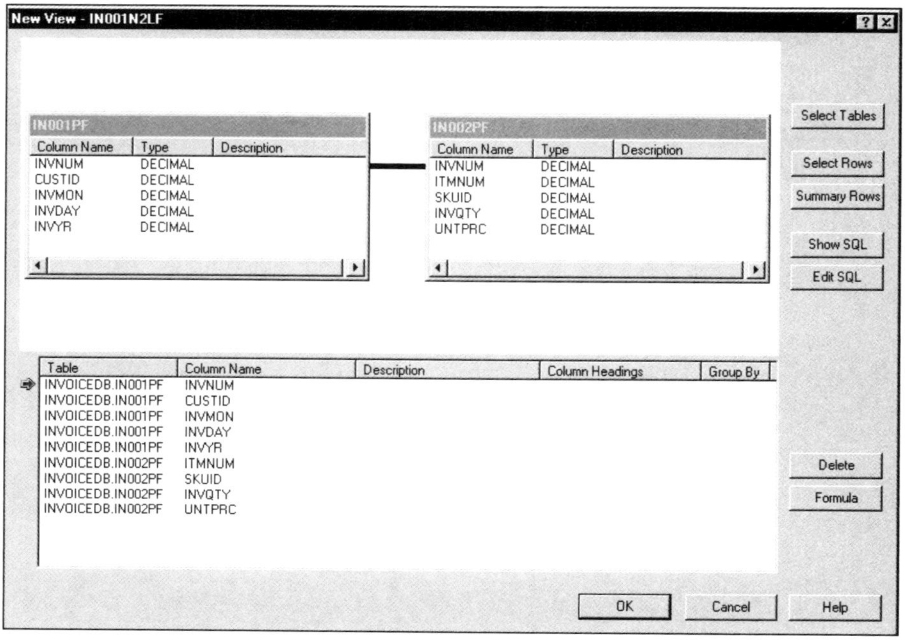
New View - IN001N2LF
IN001PF
Column Name | Type | Description
INVNUM DECIMAL
CUSTID DECIMAL
INVMON DECIMAL
INVDAY DECIMAL
INVYR DECIMAL
IN002PF
Column Name | Type | Description
INVNUM DECIMAL
ITMNUM DECIMAL
SKUID DECIMAL
INVQTY DECIMAL
UNTPRC DECIMAL
Select Tables
Select Rows
Summary Rows
Show SQL
Edit SQL
Table | Column Name | Description | Column Headings | Group By
INVOICEDB.IN001PF INVNUM
INVOICEDB.IN001PF CUSTID
INVOICEDB.IN001PF INVMON
INVOICEDB.IN001PF INVDAY
INVOICEDB.IN001PF INVYR
INVOICEDB.IN002PF ITMNUM
INVOICEDB.IN002PF SKUID
INVOICEDB.IN002PF INVQTY
INVOICEDB.IN002PF UNTPRC
Delete
Formula
OK
Cancel
Help

Chapter 14

IBM Corporation and Intelligent Miner for AS/400

Company Background[1]

With fiscal 1996 revenues in excess of $75 billion, IBM Corporation is the world's largest provider of computer hardware, software, and consulting services. IBM's hardware sales include AS/400 midrange computers, RS/6000 workstations, S/390 mainframes, Aptiva desktop personal computers, and ThinkPad notebook computers, as well as a variety of network, communications, and storage devices. The company's software offerings include database products, operating systems, and other applications. IBM also offers service, software, equipment leasing, financing and maintenance. Headquartered in Armonk, New York, publicly held IBM (NYSE:IBM) offers service and support in more than 140 countries.

In addition to in-house development of OS/400 and DB2/400, IBM supports third-party AS/400 application development through its Partners In Development (PID) program. To bolster the development of AS/400-based data warehouses, IBM maintains partnerships with software companies such as Angoss Software, Brio Technologies, Business Objects, Carleton (which has been purchased by Apertus Technologies), Coglin Mill, Cognos, DataMirror, Evolutionary Technologies International, Ferguson Information Systems, Lakeview Technologies, Logic Works, MicroStrategy, New-Generation Software, Olympic amis, SAMAC, ShowCase, Silvon, and Vision Solutions. In addition to business partnerships with consulting firms such as Price Waterhouse and Naviant (formerly MRJ), IBM designs data-mining applications for numerous industries, including insurance; distribution; banking, finance, and securities; government; health care; manufacturing; petroleum; and finally, utilities and energy.

IBM also develops data-warehousing applications and tools, including DataPropagator, a family of transformational replication products designed to move data across various DB2 databases (including DB2/400); DataGuide, a set of products designed to store technical metadata extracted from multiple platforms; DataJoiner, a utility designed to extract data from non-DB2 data sources; Intelligent Decision Server, a LAN-based solution designed to distribute business analysis across an enterprise; Neural Network Utility (NNU), a visual development environment designed to support data mining via artificial

[1]Because Chapters 13 and 14 each focus on IBM products, the "Company Background" section provides the same information in each chapter.

neural networks (ANNs); and Intelligent Miner, a multiplatform data-mining solution. In this chapter, I examine Intelligent Miner (Version 1) for AS/400.

Product Overview

Intelligent Miner for AS/400 is a comprehensive data-mining application featuring technology culled from IBM research centers in the United States, Germany, and England. Available for OS/400 since December of 1996, Intelligent Miner supports six data-mining techniques that can be used to analyze information in DB2/400 databases as well as flat (or stream) files. In addition to its core competency in data mining, Intelligent Miner provides support for the transformation of source data and the visualization of output results.

Designed for IT personnel, Intelligent Miner requires OS/400 V3R7 (or later) and at least one CD-ROM-equipped Windows 95/NT client. Partly because of its extensive use of advanced graphics, the product does not support terminal devices. The product's graphics include duplex bar charts, histograms, pie charts, line graphs, tree structures, and subcharts that can be ordered by statistical significance. Intelligent Miner's functionality can be integrated with third-party application programs via published APIs. Intelligent Miner is also available for RS/6000 and S/390 computers.

In nearly all instances, IT personnel have to prepare input data before Intelligent Miner's algorithms can process it. In cases when input data exists in DB2/400 files, Intelligent Miner provides support for 18 common data-transformation tasks, or processing functions. These functions, which run in batch and are based upon SQL, can be used to join multiple files, filter fields, derive new fields, encode missing field values, change the case of text fields, map field values using look-up tables, filter records, split records, summarize records, generate random samples of data, execute external SQL statements, and group records into quantiles. *Quantiles* are sets of cut-off points used to divide a population of records into smaller groups, each of which contains an equal number of records (to the extent possible). For example, *quartiles* are values that divide a group of records into four equal groups, while quintiles are values that divide a group of records into five equal groups. Quartiles and quintiles are simply two different quantiles. Data sets that have been transformed by Intelligent Miner's processing functions are referred to as *output data sources* and can be either DB2 tables or views.

Once data has been transformed, you can analyze it using one or more data-mining techniques. You can use these techniques to discover associations, sequential patterns, similar time sequences, and clusters. In addition, you can predict both classifications and values.

Intelligent Miner ships with three sample data-mining bases. A data-mining base is a repository of metadata that details input data, output data, mining run settings, and mining results. Because data mining requires large volumes of transaction-level data, our implementation example is not well-suited for this product. Therefore, we will use sample data provided with Intelligent Miner to explore the product's functionality.

Implementation Example

To use Intelligent Miner, you first select transaction-level data for mining, transform that data, execute data-mining functions, and then interpret the results. Figures 14.1 and 14.2 (page 254) illustrate how we open a mining base with Intelligent Miner, while Figure 14.3 (page 254) shows how we choose various processing functions. Finally, Figure 14.4 (page 255) illustrates how we open a particular data-mining technique. The following sections demonstrate these respective techniques.

Figure 14.1
Opening a Mining Base

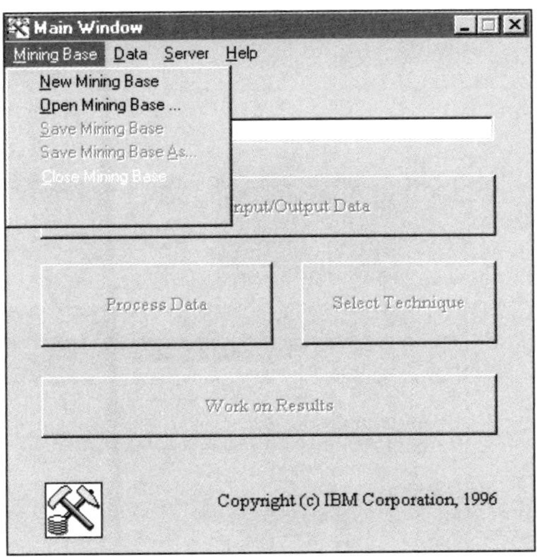

Discovering Associations

Through statistical analysis, Intelligent Miner can identify associations that exist between items within the space of a single event, or transaction. An event is defined as a discrete, identifiable activity that may vary in duration. Shopping trips, airline flights, and periods of stock trading are examples of events that have undergone associative analyses.

Market-basket analysis is one common application for associative data mining because retailers often want to know which products are commonly purchased together. Products bought in tandem are typically placed far apart in stores, causing customers to walk around, view more goods, and possibly

FIGURE 14.2
Selecting a Mining Base

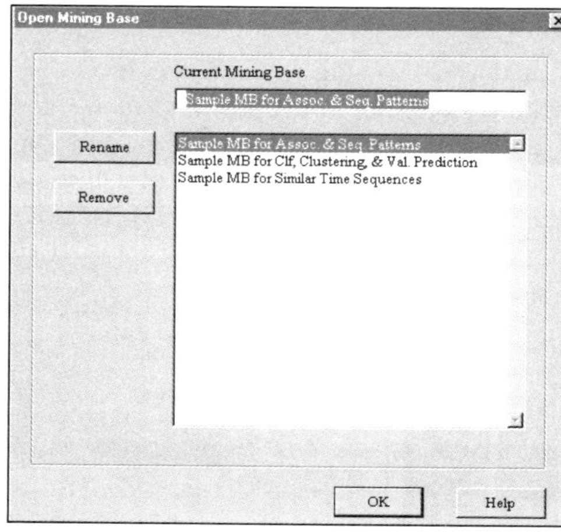

FIGURE 14.3
Selecting a Transformation Function

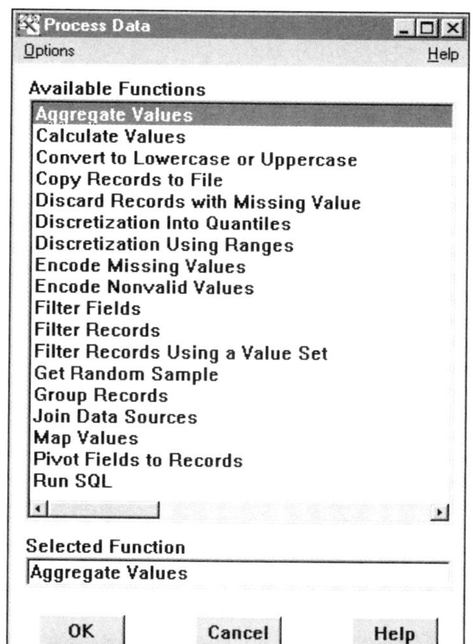

FIGURE 14.4
Selecting a Data-Mining Technique

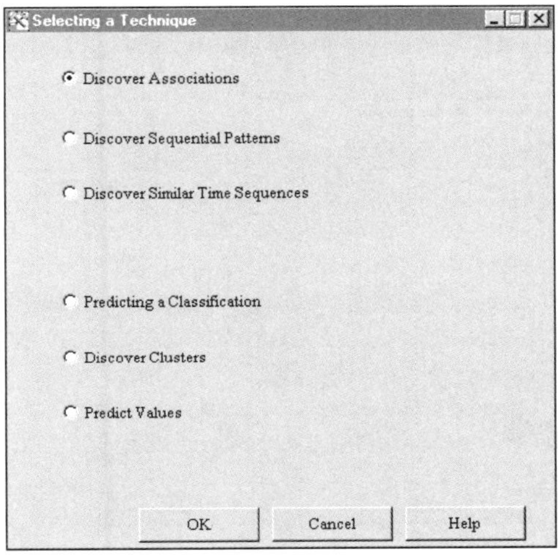

make additional purchases. Using detailed sales data, perhaps collected via cash-register scanners, Intelligent Miner can determine how often various products are purchased together. For example, suppose sales information pertaining to 10,000 shopping trips has been collected and stored in a DB2/400 file. Referring again to Figure 14.4, we select Discover Associations to analyze the shopping data. Figure 14.5 (page 256) demonstrates how file and field names are specified for the actual associative data-mining run.

Let's suppose that an association between gouda cheese and crackers has been discovered. Intelligent Miner can express such associations (i.e., rules), as well as support factors and confidence levels, via English-like phrases. Figure 14.6 (page 256) illustrates how associations appear in a condensed format, while Figure 14.7 (page 257) shows the same information in complete sentences. In this example, the confidence factor of 80 percent means that, on average, 8 of 10 gouda cheese buyers will also buy crackers during the same shopping trip. The support factor of 2.996 percent means that gouda cheese was purchased during 2.996 percent of sampled shopping trips. Again, a shopping trip is considered one discrete event, or transaction.

Intelligent Miner also computes summary figures that describe each data-mining run. An example of one such summary appears in Figure 14.8 (page 257). The summary window includes information such as the total number of transactions, number of items, maximum items per transaction, average items per transaction, total number of sequences, and the minimum support factor.

FIGURE 14.5
Specifying Fields for an Associative Analysis

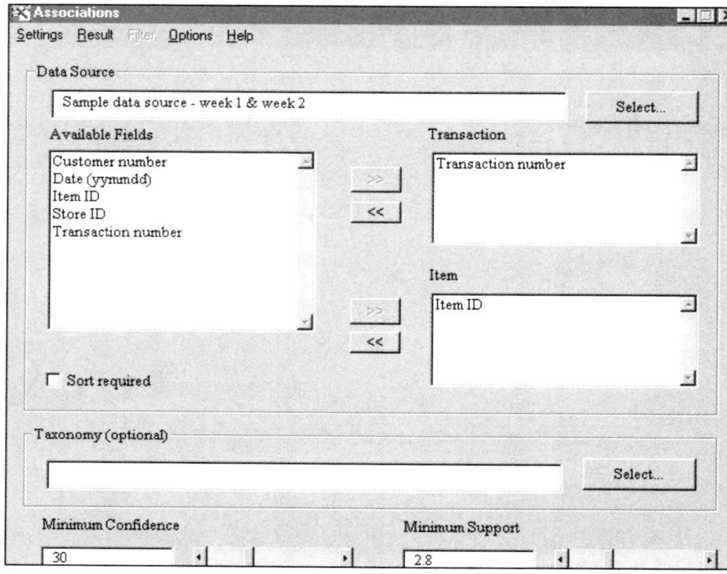

FIGURE 14.6
Associations Expressed in Condensed Format

File View Sort Filter Format

Support	Confidence	Type	Lift	Rule		
2.996	80.0	+	8.5	[Gouda Cheese]	==>	[Crackers]
2.996	32.0	+	8.5	[Crackers]	==>	[Gouda Cheese]
3.371	60.0	+	7.6	[Orange juice]	==>	[Brandy]
3.371	42.9	+	7.6	[Brandy]	==>	[Orange juice]
5.243	48.3	+	2.8	[Puzzle (1000 p.)]	==>	[Toy car]
7.491	43.5	+	2.5	[Toy car]	==>	[Cream]
7.491	42.6	+	2.5	[Cream]	==>	[Toy car]
5.243	30.4	+	2.8	[Toy car]	==>	[Puzzle (1000 p.)]
3.745	100.0	+	5.4	[Detergent]	==>	[Lemonade]
2.996	100.0	+	19.1	[Mineral water] AND [Antifreeze]	==>	[Soap A]
2.996	100.0	+	8.6	[Lemonade] AND [Soap A]	==>	[Mineral water]
2.996	100.0	+	8.6	[Antifreeze] AND [Soap A]	==>	[Mineral water]
2.996	80.0	+	4.4	[Mineral water] AND [Soap A]	==>	[Lemonade]
2.996	80.0	+	15.3	[Antifreeze]	==>	[Soap A]
2.996	80.0	+	6.9	[Antifreeze]	==>	[Mineral water]
2.996	80.0	+	21.4	[Mineral water] AND [Soap A]	==>	[Antifreeze]
2.996	80.0	+	4.4	[Antifreeze]	==>	[Lemonade]
3.745	71.4	+	6.1	[Soap A]	==>	[Mineral water]
3.745	66.7	+	5.7	[Apple juice]	==>	[Mineral water]
2.996	66.7	+	12.7	[Mineral water] AND [Lemonade]	==>	[Soap A]
3.371	64.3	+	10.7	[Soap A]	==>	[Toilet paper]
2.996	61.5	+	5.3	[Colour slide film]	==>	[Mineral water]

FIGURE 14.7
Associations Expressed in Full Sentences

File View Sort Filter Format

When a customer buys Gouda Cheese then the customer also buys Crackers in 80.0% of cases.
This pattern is present in 2.996% of transactions.

When a customer buys Crackers then the customer also buys Gouda Cheese in 32.0% of cases.
This pattern is present in 2.996% of transactions.

When a customer buys Orange juice then the customer also buys Brandy in 60.0% of cases.
This pattern is present in 3.371% of transactions.

When a customer buys Brandy then the customer also buys Orange juice in 42.9% of cases.
This pattern is present in 3.371% of transactions.

When a customer buys Puzzle (1000 p.) then the customer also buys Toy car in 48.3% of cases.
This pattern is present in 5.243% of transactions.

When a customer buys Toy car then the customer also buys Cream in 43.5% of cases.
This pattern is present in 7.491% of transactions.

FIGURE 14.8
Summary Statistics for a Data-Mining Run

Association Rules - Database Statistics	
Number of Transactions =	267
Number of Items =	80
Maximum Items per Transaction =	26
Average Items per Transaction =	3.73034
Total number of Rules =	39
Total number of LargeItemSets =	76
Minimum Support =	2.800
Minimum Confidence =	30.0

Intelligent Miner lets users specify minimum support factors for data-mining runs. This is useful because associations with higher support factors are deemed more relevant than ones with lower support factors. By isolating patterns with relatively high support factors, Intelligent Miner can isolate potentially significant patterns in less time. Intelligent Miner also lets users specify a minimum confidence factor. The higher the confidence level, the stronger the relationship between the two items. However, the lower the confidence level, the more relationships the user can expect to uncover.

Discovering Sequential Patterns

Intelligent Miner can also identify sequential patterns that exist between items related to one another over multiple events, or transactions. To discover sequential patterns, users follow the same basic steps as those illustrated in the preceding association example. The key differences, of course, are the chosen data-mining technique and the input data source. In this case, you select *sequential patterns* and the input data source consists of data collected from *multiple* events. To identify sequential patterns in customer spending, several shopping trips are examined over time. For example, Intelligent Miner may determine that when customers purchase charcoal for a BBQ, there is an 87.5 percent chance that they will purchase scouring pads within one month. In this case, you would most likely filter transactional data by invoice date to ensure that Intelligent Miner's analysis is limited to desired time frames. Sequential patterns are expressed along with support factors, and Intelligent Miner lets you specify minimum support levels for sequential mining runs. The current version of Intelligent Miner expresses the results of sequential pattern analyses in a format similar to that depicted in Figure 14.9.

FIGURE 14.9
Results of Sequential Pattern Analysis

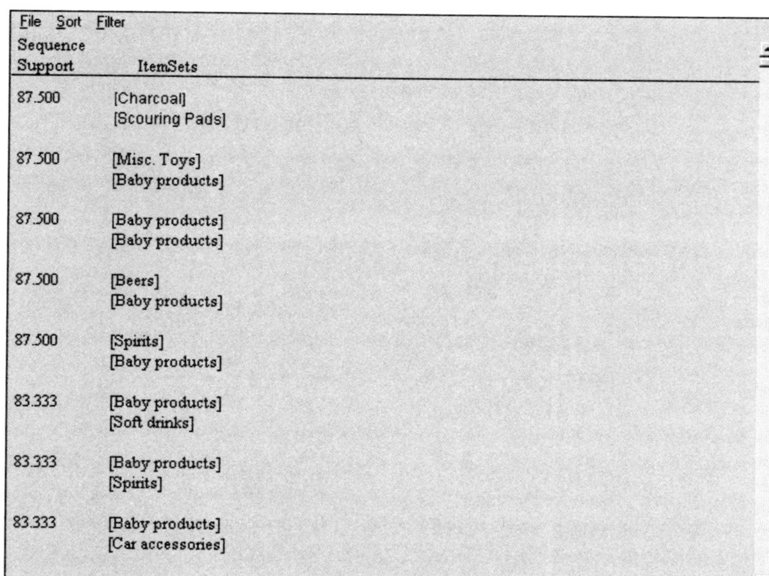

Discovering Similar Time Sequences

In addition to sequential patterns, you also can use Intelligent Miner to identify similar time sequences in data. Similar time sequences refer to patterns that apply to multiple items in a population. It is not necessary to execute a sequential-patterns exercise before the discovery of similar time sequences. One use for similar-time-sequence discovery might be the identification of stocks whose share prices have moved in tandem over time. Intelligent Miner expresses the results of similar-time-sequence analyses via a scrollable list of pairs of related items. The list denotes all pairs that exhibit similar sequences. Below the list box, a pair of line graphs highlights the associated data.

Predicting Classifications

You also can use Intelligent Miner to classify items (i.e., records) in a population (i.e., database) based on classifications of similar items. For example, suppose a department store differentiates customers according to their credit histories. A customer who has defaulted on credit-card payments may be classified in the store's database as a bad credit risk, and a customer who has never missed a payment may be classified as a good credit risk. When these classes are presented to Intelligent Miner along with associated attributes such as salary, age, marital status, and gender, the product can classify credit-card applicants.

Intelligent Miner can execute classification routines using both tree-induction and neural-network algorithms. Either method can be used to classify databases. Figure 14.10 (page 260) illustrates how users select a specific algorithm. Generally speaking, Intelligent Miner's tree-induction algorithm processes data more quickly than the neural-network algorithm and is easier to understand. However, the neural-network algorithm is more effective for classifying data contained in numerous fields, especially numeric fields, because tree induction attempts to force every record into a category, even in cases when insufficient justification exists about which category is appropriate. The neural-network algorithm, through an additional category dubbed "unknown," helps reduce the number of errors, or misses, in classification.

To predict classifications, you let Intelligent Miner first examine the input data source in "training mode." In this phase, the product identifies relationships between various combinations of attributes (e.g., salary, age, marital status, gender) and classes (e.g., bad credit risk, good credit risk). These rules are then applied to additional samples of data in "test mode." These additional samples of data should contain data for which classifications are known. In this way, you can evaluate the accuracy of the model that was derived in training mode as it classifies data in test mode. Figure 14.11 (page 260) demonstrates how you can view rules through a tree-like graphic when you use the tree-induction algorithm to classify data. By clicking on various nodes on the graphic, users can view underlying conditional formulae responsible for

FIGURE 14.10

Selecting an Algorithm End Mode for a Classification Run

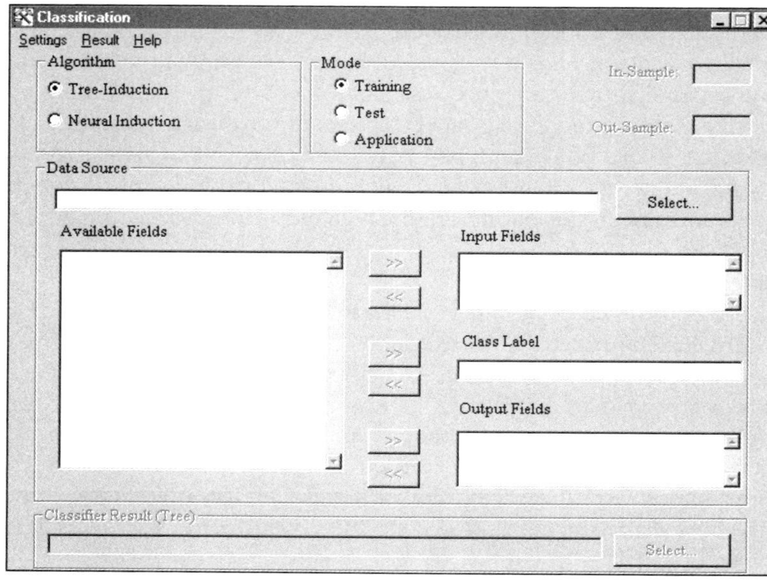

FIGURE 14.11

Graphical Depiction of a Tree Induction Model

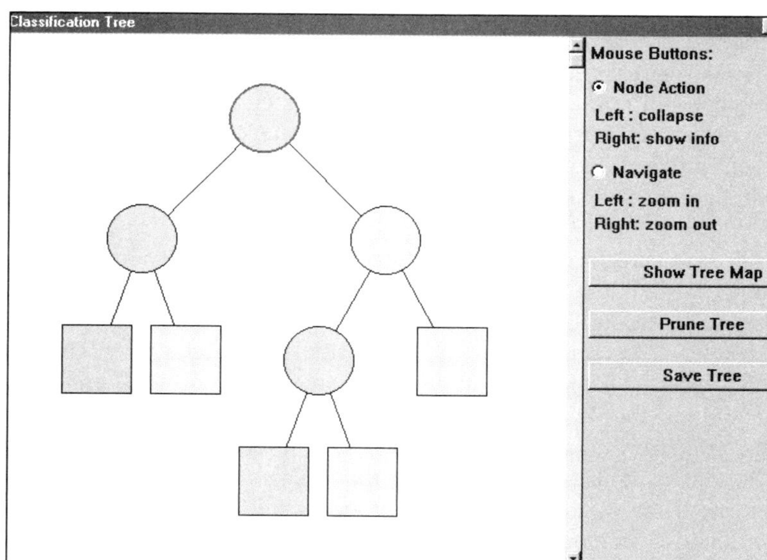

moving data down the tree. After a test run has been completed, analysts who are familiar with the underlying business model should examine the results to evaluate whether the resulting classifications makes sense. If they do not, the input data source may have to be modified (i.e., clarification of attributes). Both training and test runs are then executed again. Once the output classifications make sense in test mode, users can run Intelligent Miner in "application mode." It is during this phase that Intelligent Miner applies the derived classification rules to the target population. You can view the final results of classification runs via a bar graph of attribute distributions. This graph shows only the number of records that were assigned to each category based on threshold values in each of the attributes. Intelligent Miner's bar graphs do not show what values were assigned to specific records.

Discovering Clusters

Intelligent Miner also has the capability to partition populations into clusters of similar items. We can think of clusters as mutually exclusive, trait-based classes. We often use clusters in classification algorithms. The essential difference between classification and clustering routines is that in the case of classification routines, users already know the various groups that exist in a population. These users want to uncover the rules that determine which class particular records will fall into. In the case of clustering, users are more interested in discovering which attributes distinguish one resulting class from another.

Intelligent Miner ships with two clustering routines. Using statistical analysis, its Demographic Clustering Algorithm automatically determines the optimal number of clusters for a population. To do this, the algorithm conducts a field-by-field examination of each record (i.e., item) in a database (i.e., population) and then creates clusters that maximize the similarity between items in each cluster while minimizing their differences. Intelligent Miner also includes a neural-network clustering algorithm that is more effective for clustering continuous data and data comprised of records with many fields. Both algorithms let you specify the number of clusters to be created as well as the number of training passes to be conducted on the input data source. As with the classification technique, you must choose a specific algorithm before a clustering run can commence.

Intelligent Miner displays cluster results through a unique image consisting of histograms and pie charts. Histograms represent numerical fields such as age and weight, while pie charts represent non-numeric, categorical data such as marital status, gender, or age group. IT personnel and end users alike can drill into individual histograms and pie charts to examine underlying details via subcharts. Figure 14.12 (page 262) illustrates how the results of a clustering run might appear. In this instance, a fictitious insurance company's policy-holder database was partitioned by attributes such as gender, marital status, age, and commute distance. The left side of the graphic shows what proportion of the data set was placed in that particular cluster. On the right side, numbers running consecutively from zero act as cluster identification labels. The histograms and pie charts associated with a particular cluster depict the six attributes deemed most significant to the composition of that cluster. Attributes themselves appear in order of significance from left to right. In addition, the histograms and pie charts reflect the possible values (i.e., male, female) for their associated attributes (i.e., gender) as well as the distribution of those values across items in the associated cluster. In the case of pie charts, the inner circle shows the distribution of values for that particular cluster, while the outer circle shows the distribution of values in the entire data set. In the case of histograms, the bars outlined in red show the distribution of values within that particular cluster, while the gray bars show the distribution of values within the entire data set (see inset in Figure 14.12).

FIGURE 14.12
Graphical Depiction of a Clustering Run's Results

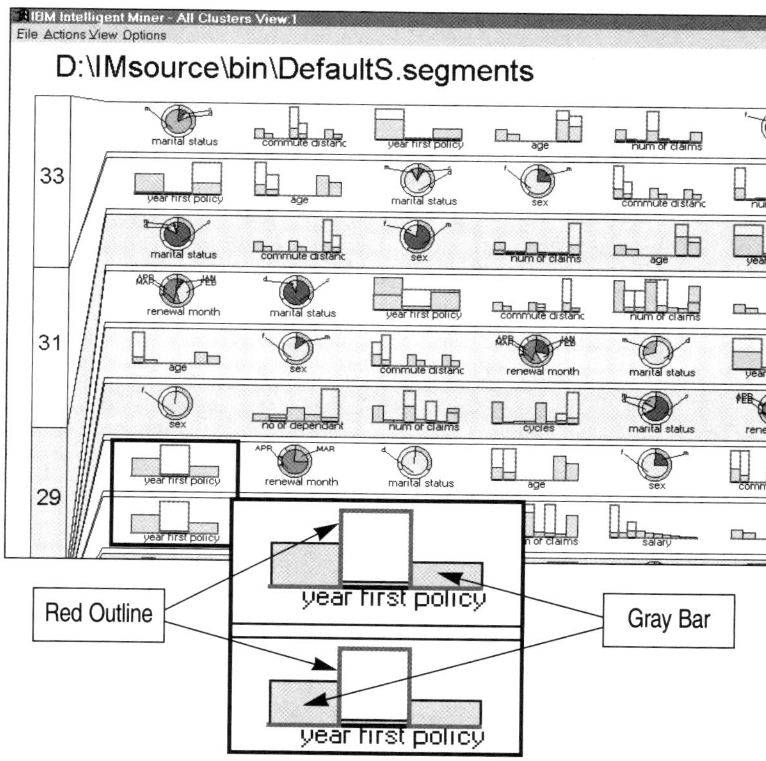

There are many uses for clustering. The banking and insurance industries, for example, use clustering routines to define classes based on income, marital status, age, education, gender, credit history, and a host of other traits. They then use these classes as a basis for assigning risk, which in turn determines loan fees and policy premiums. In the advertising world, clustering techniques are the mainstay of market-segmentation algorithms. Target marketing, of course, would not be possible without the proper identification of market segments. Market segments, or classes, group individuals who share common purchasing profiles. One example of effective target marketing is the inclusion of customer-specific ads in credit-card statements.

Predicting Values

You also can use Intelligent Miner to generate predictive data models. Using a mathematical process known as the Radial Basis Function (RBF) technique, Intelligent Miner considers a user-specified field's values and then attempts to relate each value to the values of associated fields. A model is then created that can be used to predict the value of the key field based upon the values of associated fields. Predicting values is also known as *scoring*.

Let's look again at an example I used in Chapter 6. Suppose that a particular house with four bedrooms, two baths, one fireplace, and three acres of property was recently sold for $300,000. Suppose further that a neighboring house with three bedrooms, one bath, two fireplaces, and four acres of land sold for $325,000. Intelligent Miner can examine many such sales and then generate a model that describes the relationship between selling price and the number of rooms, fireplaces, and acres associated with each property. A real-estate agency can then use this predictive model to set prices for houses new to the market. In actual analyses, RBF algorithms can examine hundreds or even thousands of different attributes.

Product Summary and Positioning

For companies with large volumes of transaction-level data, as well as significant financial and computing resources, Intelligent Miner makes sense. This product has the potential to shed new light on critical operational and strategic issues.

In this first release, it is apparent that Intelligent Miner's techniques and algorithms were not developed together. Nowhere is this more apparent than in the product's interface. Intelligent Miner's GUI needs improvement. In particular, the result screens are inconsistent across techniques and are, in some cases, fairly difficult to understand. According to IBM, the next release of Intelligent Miner will have a more intuitive, consistent interface.

Interface issues not withstanding, bear in mind that Intelligent Miner's data-mining technology is what really matters. On this front, there is widespread agreement both inside and outside IBM that the product's techniques and algorithms are among the world's finest. And I'll take an ugly right answer over a beautiful wrong one any day. To be sure, IBM invested considerable resources in the development of Intelligent Miner's underlying techniques and algorithms.

As we saw in Chapter 6, data mining requires transaction-level data. Although summarized data may be useful in some cases, summaries tend to mask subtle patterns in data. Because of this, Intelligent Miner customers should be prepared to create denormalized versions of significant portions of their operational databases. As one would surmise, the denormalization of operational databases requires both DASD and horsepower. Those customers who dedicate one or more AS/400 servers to data warehousing are in the best position to fully utilize Intelligent Miner.

And finally, keep in mind that data mining is not a plug-and-play application. Users must understand the principles of data mining as well as Intelligent Miner's particular techniques and algorithms. Of course, these users must also understand their own business model as well as that of the industry in which it operates. For additional fees, IBM offers technical and business consulting services to support Intelligent Miner in the AS/400 arena. Intelligent Miner itself is available for a one-time charge of $15,000 to $42,000, depending upon AS/400 model. Optional monthly maintenance fees are also available for an additional $210 per month.

Chapter 15

Olympic amis Limited and amis V8

Company Background

Previously Cap Gemini Application Products International Ltd., Olympic amis Ltd. was founded in 1997 by former Cap Gemini employees. A division of Olympic Resources and Services Ltd., Olympic amis employs approximately 60 people and maintains offices in Dublin, Ireland; London and Manchester, England; Johannesburg, South Africa; and Chicago. The company also has partnerships with software developers, distributors, and consulting firms including Aspect (Australia), Cap Gemini (worldwide), Commercial Software Services (Hong Kong, Malaysia), DataMirror (Canada), Data Systemfin (Argentina), Estimulo (Portugal), Polygon (Hungary), Silverlake Systems (Malaysia), Trentisa (Spain), and Turning Point (UK, USA). Cap Gemini Sogeti, headquartered in France, is the former parent of Cap Gemini Application Products.

Olympic Resources, the parent of Olympic amis Ltd., was founded in 1988. Consisting of eight divisions, Olympic Resources provides managerial, financial, and IT consulting services to the insurance, finance, and banking industries. Outside the private sector, the company provides services to numerous governmental agencies. In addition to consulting, Olympic Resources develops AS/400-based back-office and underwriting software for the Lloyds and General Insurance markets. These packages include Nucleus, Visual Writer and Ipacri. Olympic Resources employs more than 150 people and has annual revenues of approximately $23 million.

Olympic amis Ltd.'s principal product is amis V8. Olympic amis' software is now installed at more than 550 sites worldwide.

Product Overview

Originally a DB2/400-based multidimensional modeling tool, amis V8 has developed into a comprehensive data-warehousing solution. In addition to facilitating construction of both primary warehouse repositories and relational OLAP (ROLAP) data marts, amis V8 provides front-end presentation, analysis, and report-writing tools for end users. Figure 15.1 (page 266) features a high-level overview of the amis V8 architecture.

amis V8 is a modular data-warehousing solution consisting of six components: amis Quester, a metadata-management facility for maintaining primary data-warehouse repositories; amis OLAP, a multidimensional modeling tool for maintaining amis data marts; amis Connect, the facility through which DB2/400-based data is propagated to amis data marts; amis Desktop, a Windows-based query, presentation, and analysis tool; amis Desktop Developer, an open interface

FIGURE 15.1
Overview of amis V8 Architecture

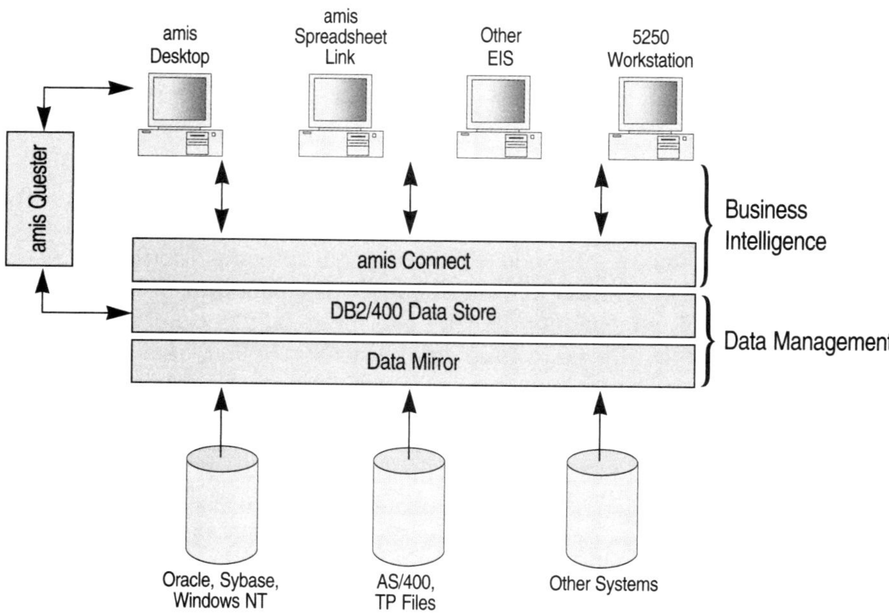

©Olympic amis Limited

for third-party access to the amis data warehouse; and finally, amis Spreadsheet Link, an open interface for spreadsheet-based access to the amis data warehouse. A detailed description of each amis V8 component follows.

amis Quester

amis Quester's primary function is to propagate DB2/400-based data to primary warehouse repositories. Using amis Quester, you can access logical files, join files, and multimember physical files. The product also can join multiple physical files and filter data by column (field) and by row (record). Through its support of mathematical, date, and substring functions, Quester performs basic transformational replication tasks. The product is not designed to extract information on a net-change basis from journal receivers. For organizations that require such functionality, or in environments with heterogeneous databases, a third-party replication product is a good companion for amis Quester.

A flexible query and reporting tool, amis Quester also facilitates end-user access to amis primary warehouse repositories and to DB2/400-based operational (OLTP) databases. Quester's comprehensive metadata repository, or data dictionary, enables access to these data stores. Quester's data dictionary stores field names, field aliases, field definitions, file names, file aliases, and rules used to derive warehouse information. A 5250 interface or a custom-designed C++ Windows client program invokes Quester's functionality. The client program is available in both 16- and 32-bit versions.

amis OLAP

amis OLAP is the foundation of amis V8. Through specifications input by IT personnel, amis OLAP builds relational OLAP data marts. With amis Connect, you can maintain these data marts directly from OLTP databases or through a primary warehouse repository. The OLTP database approach is known as a two-tiered architecture because this method maintains two levels of data: the OLTP database and one or more data marts. The primary-repository approach is referred to as a three-tiered architecture because it maintains three layers of data: the OLTP database, the primary warehouse repository, and one or more data marts.

Using dimensions you specify, amis OLAP automatically creates physical and logical files designed to hold varying levels of aggregate data. These databases are designed to support multidimensional analyses that employ such functions as drilling, slicing, dicing, and so on. amis OLAP supports an unlimited number of consolidation levels, as well as multiple versions of the same data elements (e.g., forecasted amounts, budgeted amounts, variances). Of course, as more levels of data are added to the schema, load times and associated resource requirements will increase. amis OLAP also features facilities through which users can interactively maintain data (i.e., currency conversion rates) in the data mart.

amis Connect

amis Connect provides the mechanism through which DB2/400-based data is propagated to amis data marts. Tightly integrated with amis OLAP, amis Connect supports direct access to OLTP databases (i.e., a two-tiered architecture) and to primary warehouse repositories (i.e., a three-tiered architecture). It also includes facilities that support basic data-transformation functions. amis Connect does not move data to primary warehouse repositories.

amis Desktop

Programmed in C++ and available in 16- and 32-bit versions, amis Desktop provides end users with an intuitive user interface through which they can access amis warehouses (as well as OLTP databases). Used to interactively query DB2/400-based information, amis Desktop supports spreadsheet, graphing, and OLAP functionality. To facilitate remote analyses, the product lets users download subsets of AS/400 data to personal computers. amis Desktop also includes five worksheet templates designed to present information in predefined ways. You can use these templates to conduct ranking analyses, year-to-date analyses, exception reporting, historical (i.e., trend) analyses, and variance analyses. End users are free to customize all amis Desktop worksheets.

amis Desktop Developer

amis Desktop Developer, an optional module, features application programming interfaces (APIs) for amis data marts. IT personnel who want to develop their own customized interfaces with third-party products (e.g., Visual Basic, Forest & Trees) would use Desktop Developer.

amis Spreadsheet Link

A C++ application available in both 16- and 32-bit versions, amis Spreadsheet Link facilitates data transfer between the amis warehouse and spreadsheet packages such as Lotus 1-2-3 and Microsoft Excel. End users can then use these packages to manipulate, report on, and otherwise analyze information downloaded from the AS/400-based data warehouse. They also can use Spreadsheet Link to upload spreadsheet data to the amis warehouse.

Implementation Example

To effectively convey the functionality of amis V8, this section features numerous screen captures of the product as we use it to perform our sample data-warehousing tasks. For simplicity, let's assume that the data warehouse resides on the same AS/400 as the OLTP database.

Figure 15.2 depicts how our sample invoice files are joined using amis Connect's join function. As you can see, amis Connect provides a GUI interface through which we can specify the target files, join fields, and join operations. Figure 15.3 illustrates how we can use amis Connect's Data function to select the field INVQTY from the invoice detail file. This field is later propagated to our sales fact table.

Figure 15.4 (page 270) demonstrates how amis Connect's Item function lets us select the product SKU field for the product dimension table in our data warehouse. Figure 15.5 (page 270) depicts how we select the field INVMON using the amis Connect's DataSet function.

If we choose, we can use invoice month to determine the period for which invoice quantity and value figures are associated. In amis, an item typically describes a variable such as a quantity or value. A data set, on the other hand, commonly relates multiple occurrences of an item across time. At this point, we have joined the invoice files in our sample OLTP database and demonstrated how various data elements in those files can be selected for use in our data warehouse. Now let's create the sales fact table for our data warehouse.

Figure 15.6 (page 271) depicts the first step in creating the fact table with amis Quester. As you can see, I have chosen the invoice files as sources for the sales fact table. Figure 15.7 (page 271) displays the fields from the invoice

FIGURE 15.2

Using amis V8 to Join the Invoice Files

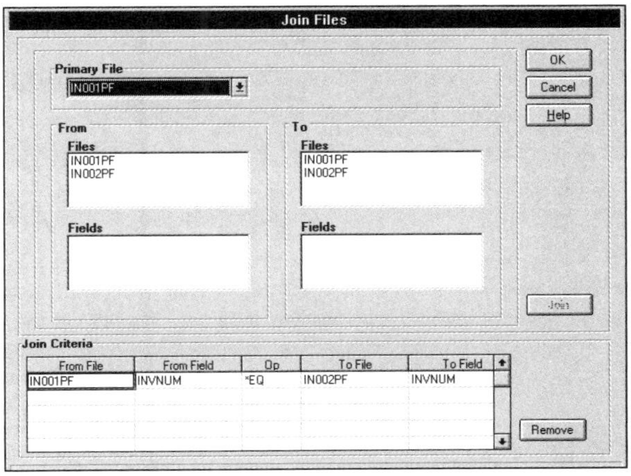

FIGURE 15.3

Using amis' Data Function to Select INVQTY

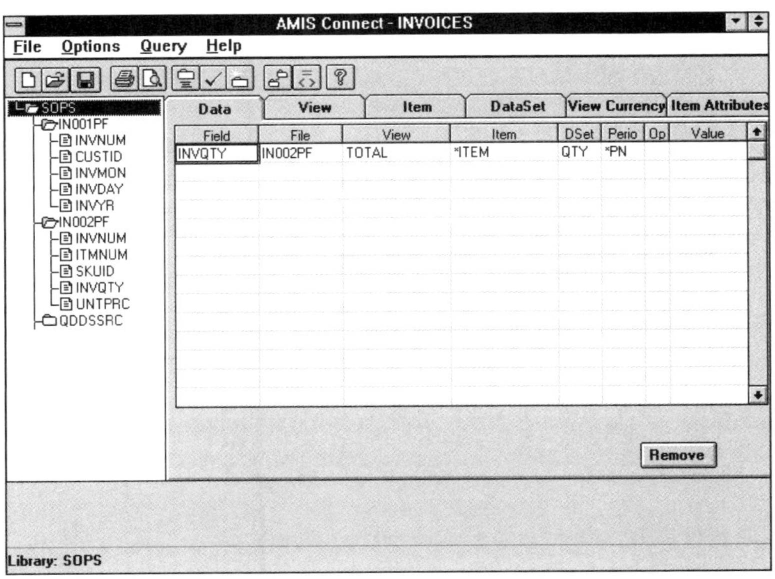

detail file that are available for use in the fact table. As you can see, several field names are gray and several field names are black. Gray denotes fields that have been selected for the fact table.

FIGURE 15.4

Using amis' Item Function to Select SKUID

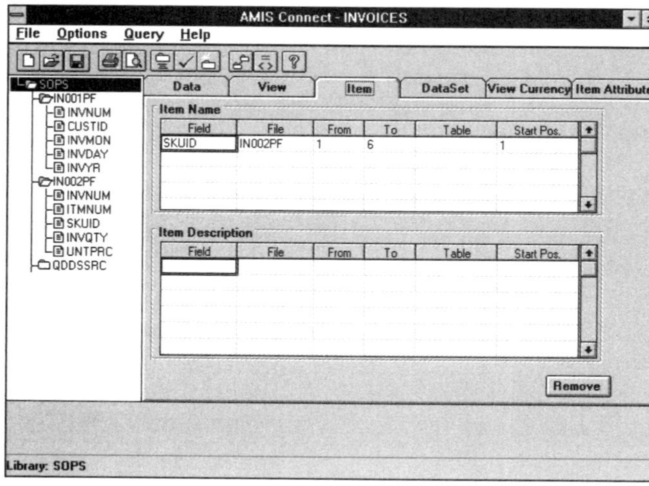

FIGURE 15.5

Using amis' DataSet Function to Select INVMON

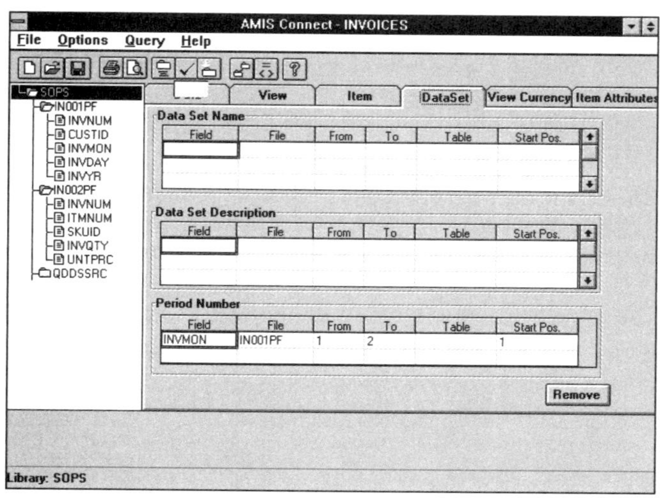

Figure 15.8 (page 272) lists those fields from the invoice header file that have been made available for the fact table.

Figure 15.9 (page 272) depicts amis Quester's Sequencing function, which maintains the level of detail in the sales fact table. To transform data or to

FIGURE 15.6
Selecting Source Files for the Sales Fact Table

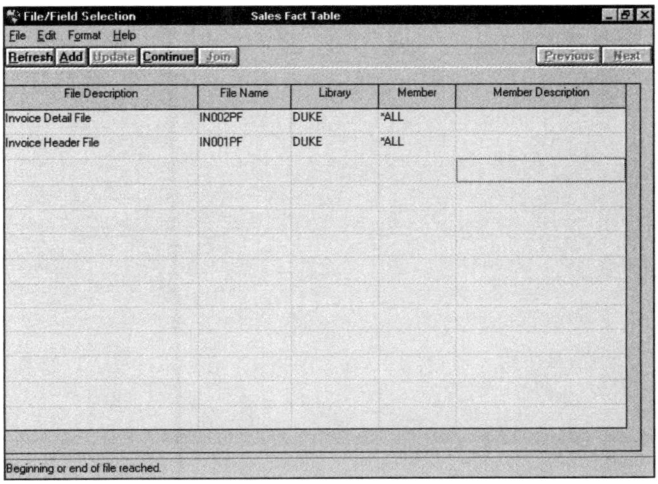

FIGURE 15.7
Invoice Detail Fields Available for the Sales Fact Table

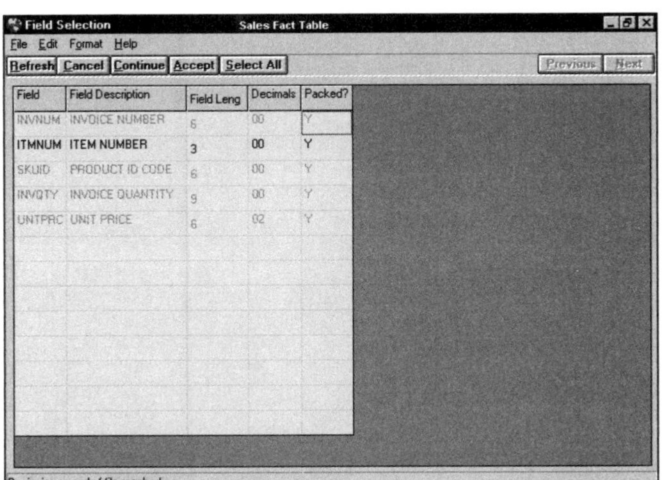

derive new fields in target files such as our fact table, amis provides a calculation function, as shown in Figure 15.10 (page 273). In this instance, the invoice value field is derived using a simple mathematical expression.

FIGURE 15.8
Invoice Header Fields Available for the Sales Fact Table

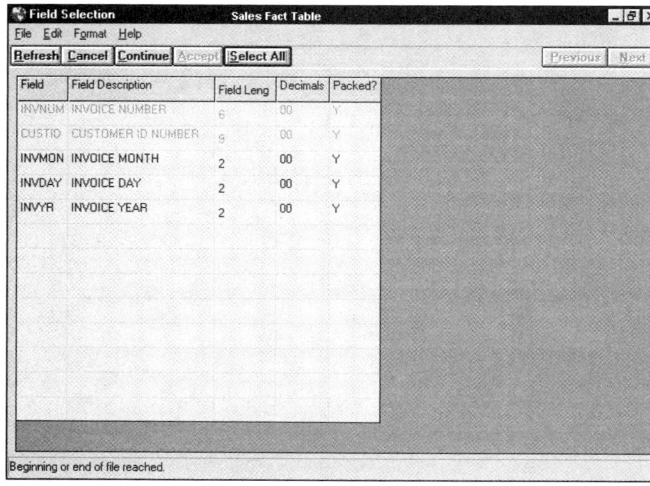

FIGURE 15.9
Using amis Quester to Sequence Data

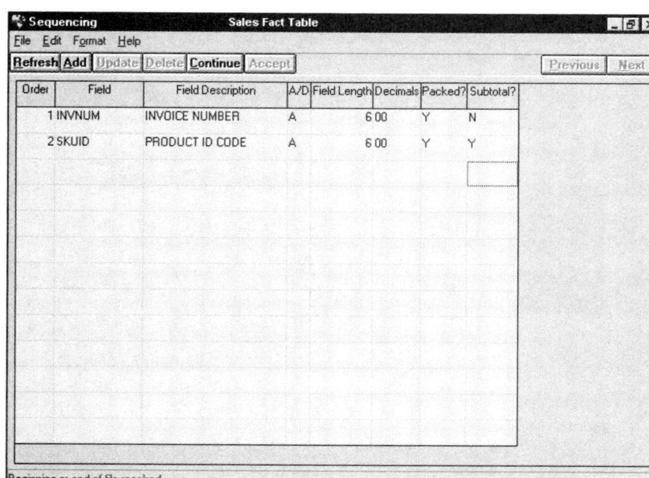

To order fields in the fact table, we use amis Quester's Summary Preformat function, as Figure 15.11 demonstrates. In essence, this screen represents a high-level version of a data description specification (DDS) for the fact table.

FIGURE 15.10
Using amis Quester to Derive a Field

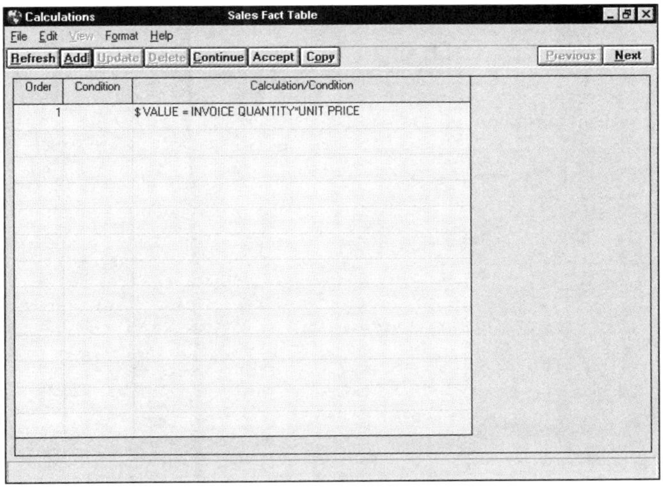

FIGURE 15.11
Formatting the Sales Fact Table

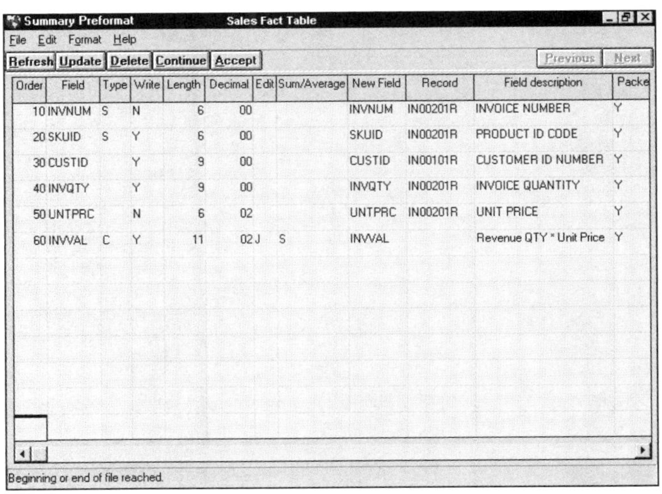

amis Quester uses specifications from the Summary Preformat screen to create files such as our fact table.

Next, we use amis Quester to set up an inquiry screen that accesses product attributes in TA001PF using the SKUID field. Figure 15.12 depicts

FIGURE 15.12
Using amis Quester to Introduce TA001PF to the Warehouse

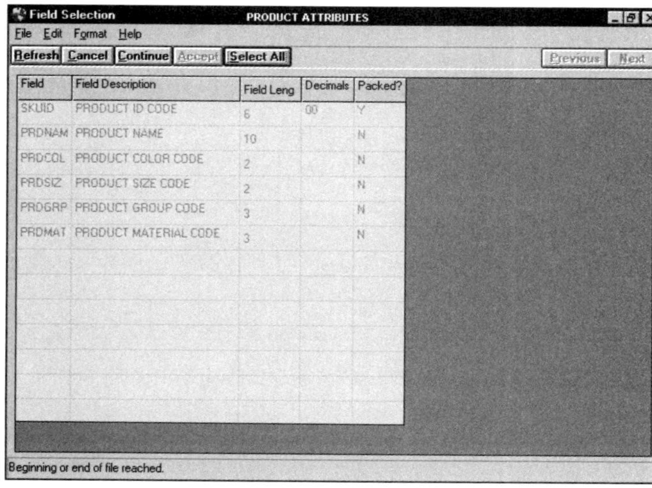

FIGURE 15.13
Formatting the Product Attributes Table

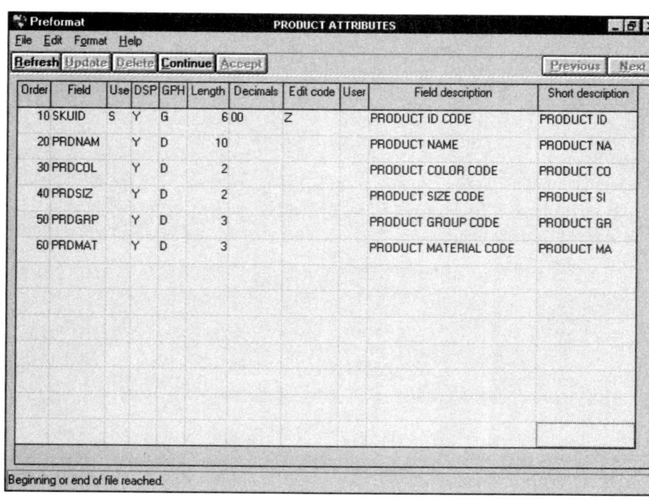

Quester's Field Selection screen as it lists all fields in TA001PF. Figure 15.13 illustrates how the Preformat function works to order selected fields for the product attributes inquiry. In Figure 15.14, Quester's Client/Server defaults screen customizes the inquiry. In this case, we set the application type parameter to 1 to indicate a single record inquiry result. Finally, Figure 15.15 illustrates how product attributes are displayed for an input SKUID value. amis Quester also can access product attributes in batch mode for propagation to data warehouse files.

FIGURE 15.14
Customizing Processing Options for an Inquiry

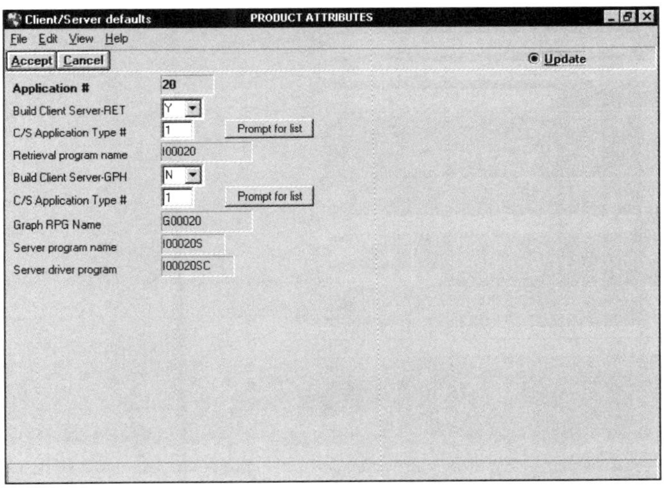

FIGURE 15.15
Layout for the Product Attributes Inquiry Screen

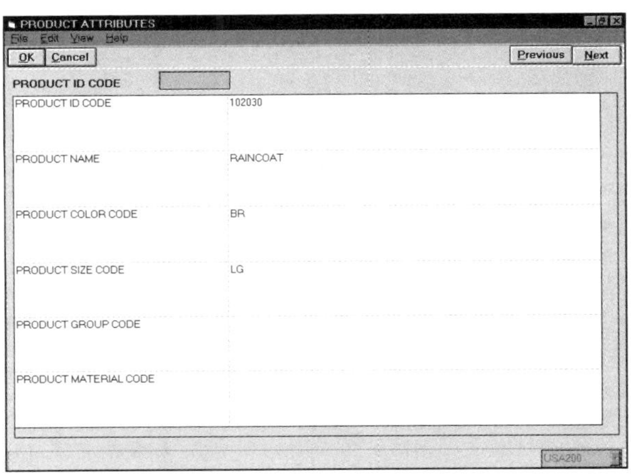

Let's take a look at how we can use amis Quester to create and populate the product dimension file. Figure 15.16 illustrates how we use amis Quester's Field Selection screen to select fields for the product dimension file.

FIGURE 15.16

Selecting Fields for the Product Dimension File

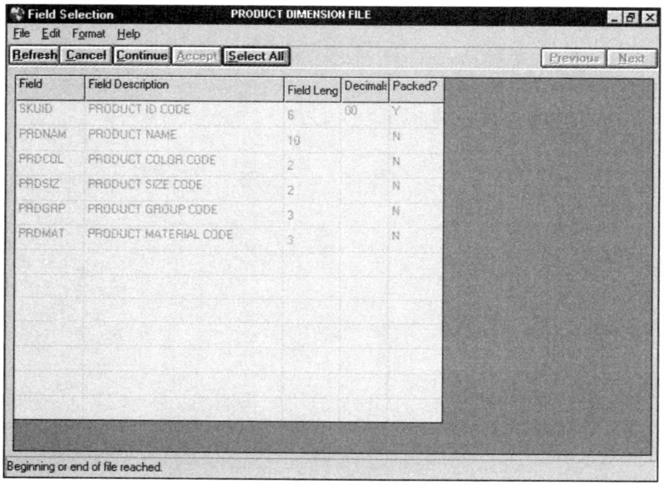

Using amis Quester's Calculation function as shown in Figure 15.17 and 15.18, we can input conditional statements to map product colors to associated codes, which lets the actual color names be stored in the product dimension file.

Figure 15.19 (page 278) illustrates how the Summary Preformat screen lets us order fields in the product dimension file. amis Quester uses these specifications to create the product dimension file for our data warehouse.

We also can use amis Quester to create an interactive maintenance routine for our product dimension file. Figure 15.20 (page 278) depicts how we use amis Quester's Field Selection screen to select fields for this maintenance procedure.

Figure 15.21 (page 279) illustrates how the procedure is set up for processing by SKUID values. Figure 15.22 (page 279) shows how we use amis Quester's Preformat screen to determine the placement of fields on the maintenance screen, and Figure 15.23 (page 280) demonstrates Quester's Client/Server Defaults screen initialized for the update process. In this case, we have selected the application number parameter from a pop-up window that lists amis' various update modes. We have chosen option 1 (for single record maintenance) for this scenario. As you can see, we could have used a multiple-record (i.e., subfile) processing method to maintain the product dimension file. Finally, Figure 15.24 (page 280) illustrates how we can use amis Quester to maintain a product dimension record.

FIGURE 15.17
Mapping Color Codes to Descriptions

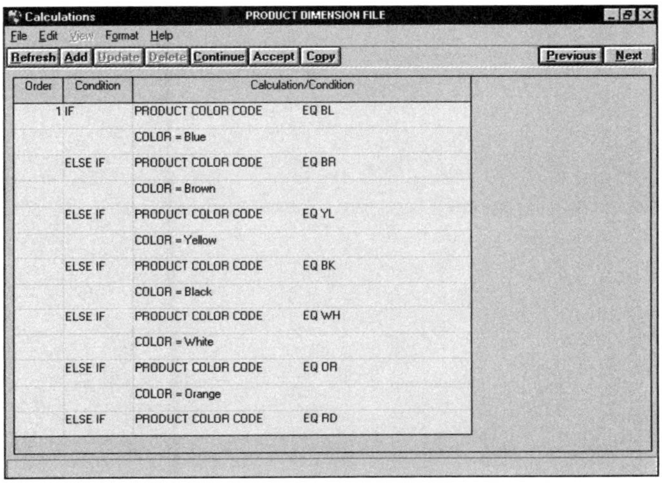

FIGURE 15.18
Mapping Color Codes and Size Codes to Descriptions

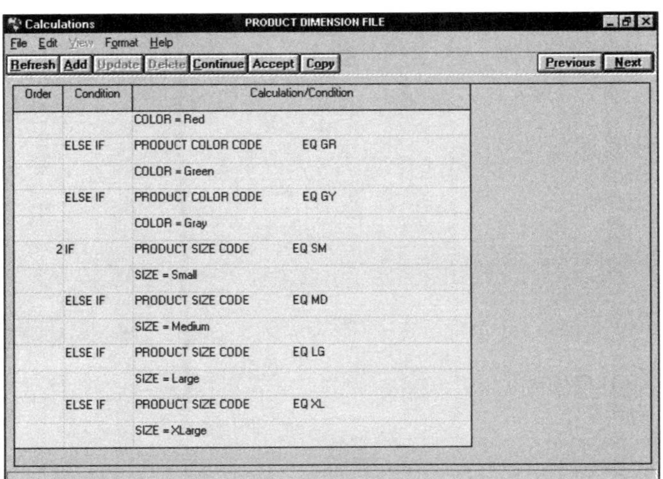

FIGURE 15.19

Formatting the Product Dimension File

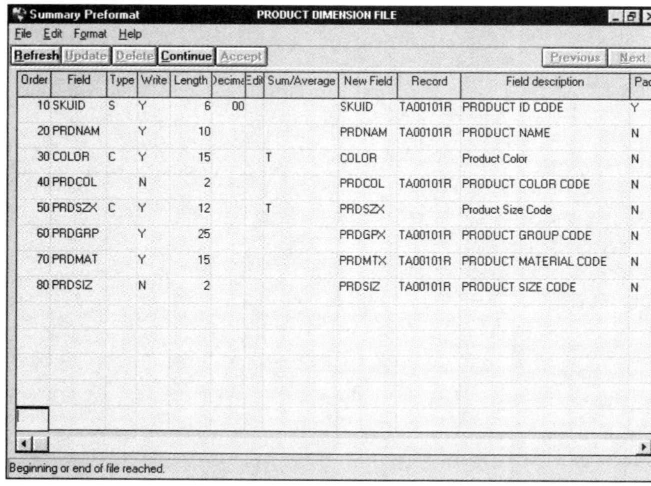

Order	Field	Type	Write	Length	Decima	Edit	Sum/Average	New Field	Record	Field description	Pac
10	SKUID	S	Y	6	00			SKUID	TA00101R	PRODUCT ID CODE	Y
20	PRDNAM		Y	10				PRDNAM	TA00101R	PRODUCT NAME	N
30	COLOR	C	Y	15		T		COLOR		Product Color	N
40	PRDCOL		N	2				PRDCOL	TA00101R	PRODUCT COLOR CODE	N
50	PRDSZX	C	Y	12		T		PRDSZX		Product Size Code	N
60	PRDGRP		Y	25				PRDGPX	TA00101R	PRODUCT GROUP CODE	N
70	PRDMAT		Y	15				PRDMTX	TA00101R	PRODUCT MATERIAL CODE	N
80	PRDSIZ		N	2				PRDSIZ	TA00101R	PRODUCT SIZE CODE	N

FIGURE 15.20

Selecting Fields for an Update Procedure

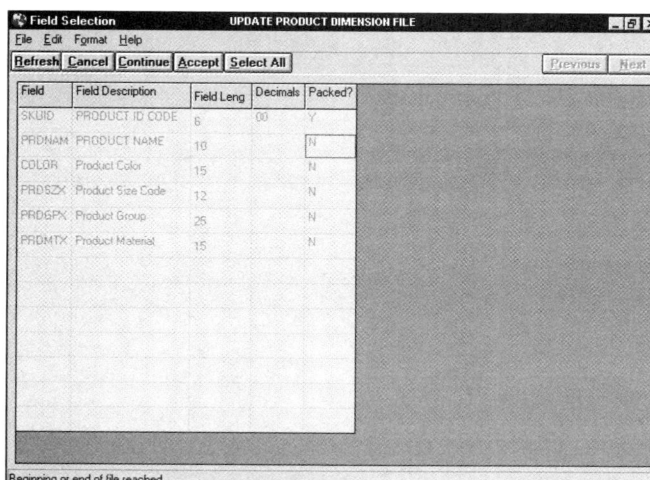

Field	Field Description	Field Leng	Decimals	Packed?
SKUID	PRODUCT ID CODE	6	00	Y
PRDNAM	PRODUCT NAME	10		N
COLOR	Product Color	15		N
PRDSZX	Product Size Code	12		N
PRDGPX	Product Group	25		N
PRDMTX	Product Material	15		N

FIGURE 15.21

Specifying a Key Field for an Update Procedure

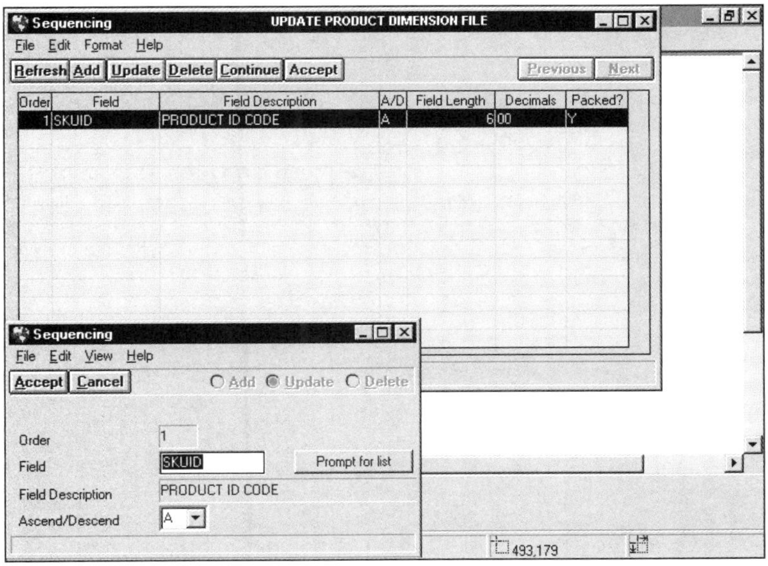

FIGURE 15.22

Formatting an Update Procedure

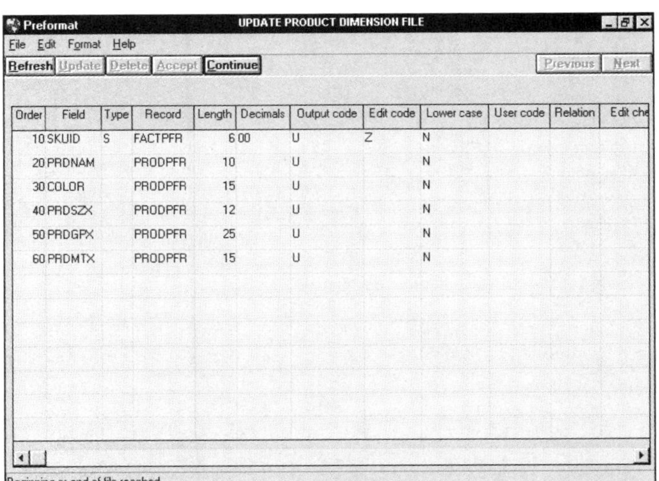

FIGURE 15.23
Customizing Processing Options for an Update

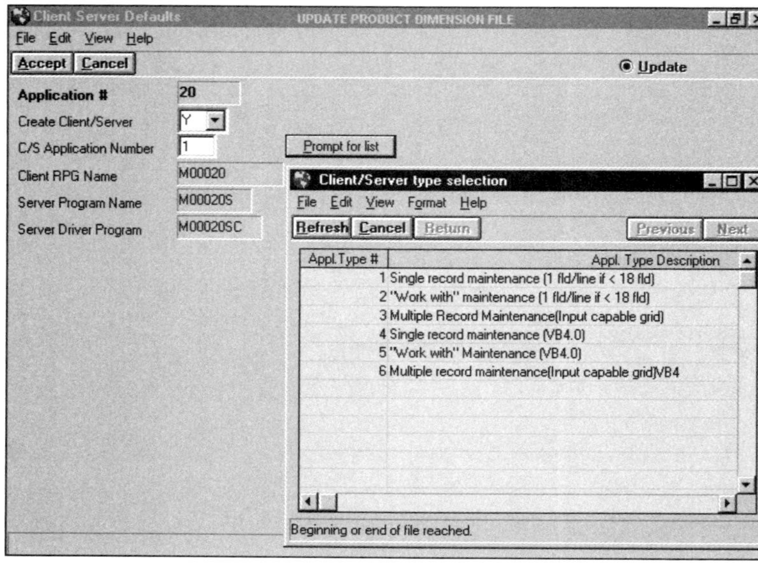

FIGURE 15.24
Updating a Product Record

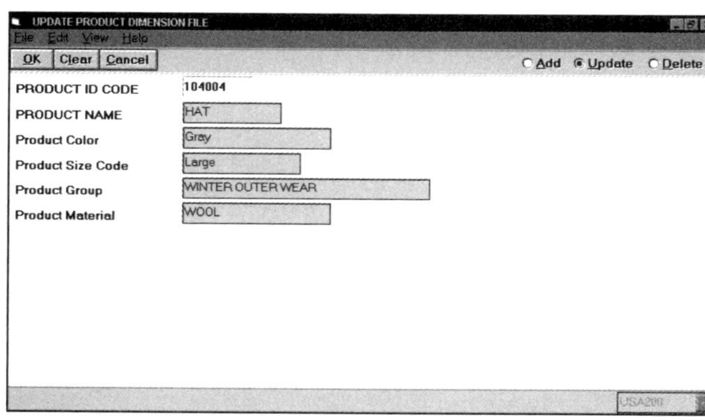

Once a data warehouse has been initialized, we can use amis Quester to display its contents. For example, Figure 15.25 depicts a tabular view of sales data that has been retrieved from our sample data warehouse via a query.

To perform analyses with amis V8, end users use amis Desktop to view and manipulate data. Figure 15.26 depicts an amis Desktop query result screen

FIGURE 15.25

Revenue Figures by SKU

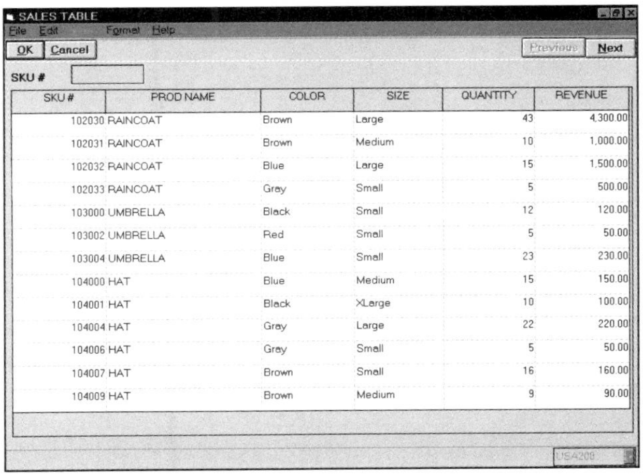

SKU #	PROD NAME	COLOR	SIZE	QUANTITY	REVENUE
102030	RAINCOAT	Brown	Large	43	4,300.00
102031	RAINCOAT	Brown	Medium	10	1,000.00
102032	RAINCOAT	Blue	Large	15	1,500.00
102033	RAINCOAT	Gray	Small	5	500.00
103000	UMBRELLA	Black	Small	12	120.00
103002	UMBRELLA	Red	Small	5	50.00
103004	UMBRELLA	Blue	Small	23	230.00
104000	HAT	Blue	Medium	15	150.00
104001	HAT	Black	XLarge	10	100.00
104004	HAT	Gray	Large	22	220.00
104006	HAT	Gray	Small	5	50.00
104007	HAT	Brown	Small	16	160.00
104009	HAT	Brown	Medium	9	90.00

FIGURE 15.26

Revenues and Unit Prices by Size for Raincoats

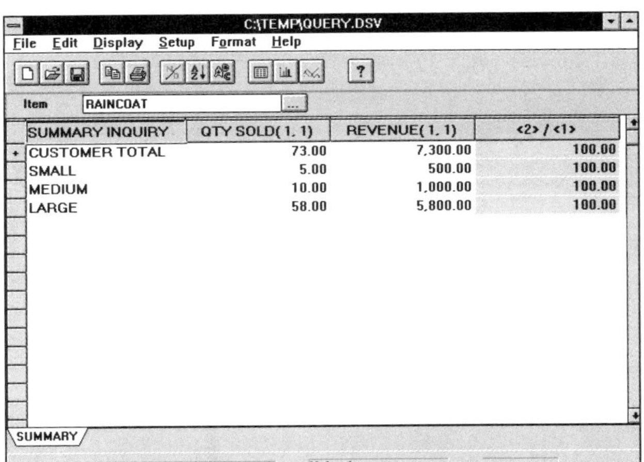

SUMMARY INQUIRY	QTY SOLD(1, 1)	REVENUE(1, 1)	<2> / <1>
CUSTOMER TOTAL	73.00	7,300.00	100.00
SMALL	5.00	500.00	100.00
MEDIUM	10.00	1,000.00	100.00
LARGE	58.00	5,800.00	100.00

that lists sales volumes, revenues, and average selling prices for small, medium, and large raincoats. In this instance, the average selling price is a calculated field. By clicking on the select button to the right of the displayed item (which in this case is raincoat), end users can invoke amis Desktop's Item Selector dialog box.

Figure 15.27 shows various SKU numbers as they appear in this dialog box. End users also can view SKU descriptions from the metadata repository by selecting the Description option at the bottom of the Item Selector dialog box.

Figure 15.28 depicts how results appear if an end user selected SKU 102030. Using our sample data warehouse, amis Desktop also lets end users view summary results by product category. For example, Figure 15.29 depicts sales volumes and sales revenues for each product category. The third column is a calculated field that lists the percent of revenue that each product category contributed to total sales revenue. This summary listing has been sorted alphabetically by product category.

Also, you may notice that a plus (+) sign appears to the left of each product category. This symbol indicates that more detailed information is available about each product category. For example, if you click on the plus sign next to the word BOOTS, the underlying sales figures are displayed alongside each boot SKU number.

amis Desktop also lets end users quickly create graphical depictions of data. For example, to graph the revenue amounts in Figure 15.29, they would drag the cursor over the revenue figures and then click on the bar chart icon underneath the Help menu at the top of the screen. Figure 15.30 (page 284) contains the resulting bar chart for this action. They can then easily examine the same figures via other graphs and charts. For instance, by clicking on the appropriate icon, they would create a pie chart such as the one in Figure 15.31 (page 284).

FIGURE 15.27

Selecting a New Item for an Existing Query

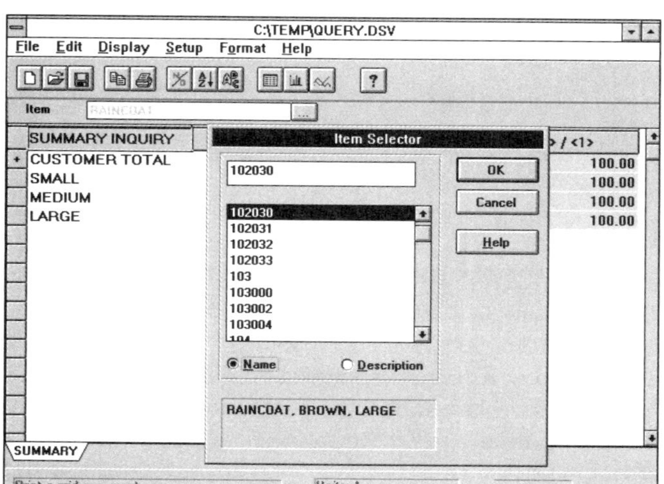

FIGURE 15.28

Revenues and Unit Prices by Size for the Newly Selected Item

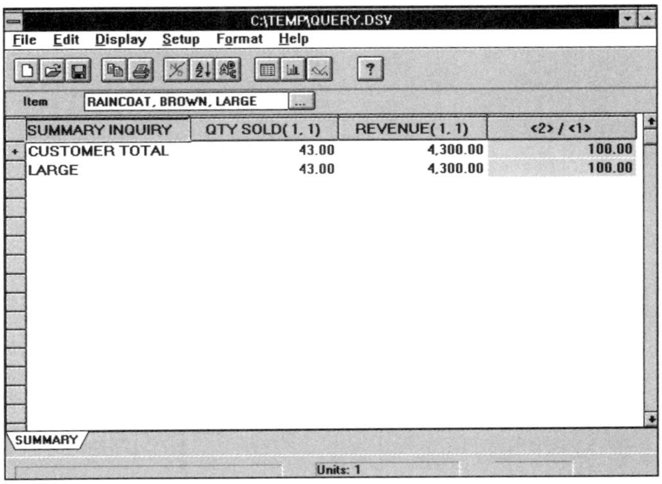

FIGURE 15.29

Revenue Figures by Product Category — Tabular View

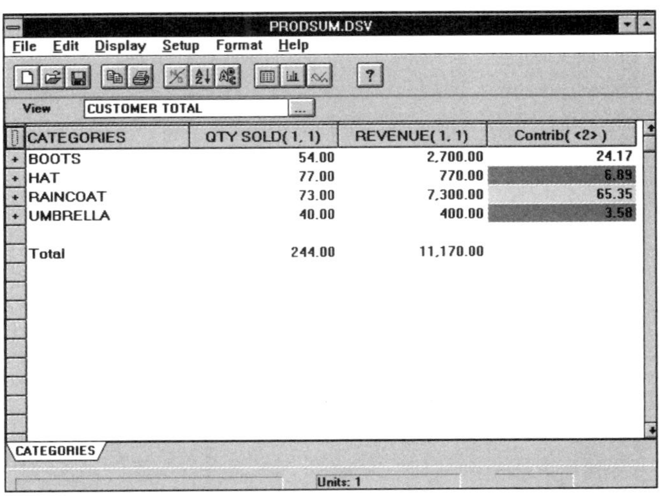

amis Desktop is also adept at displaying data in cross-tabular formats. Figure 15.32 (page 285) shows sales volumes by product category and size. amis Desktop's Setup menu manages such cross-tabular views. This pull-down menu lets end users swap axes and control column and row totals. They also can graph cross-tabular data by clicking on appropriate icons. For example,

FIGURE 15.30
Revenue Figures by Product Category — Bar Chart View

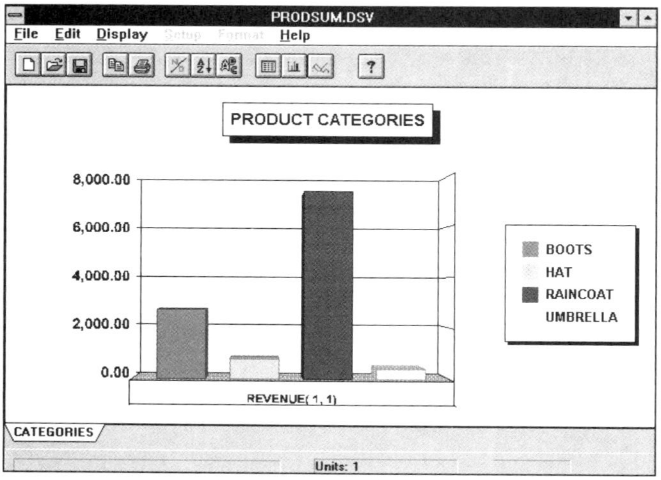

FIGURE 15.31
Revenue Figures by Product Category — Pie Chart View

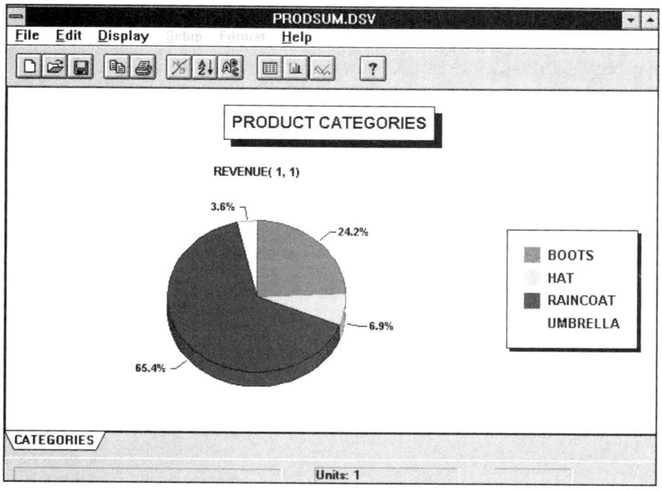

Figure 15.33 depicts a bar chart for sales volumes by product category grouped according to size. If end users switch axes, the bar graph dynamically adjusts to reflect the new orientation of the axes. The bar graph represented in Figure 15.34 (page 286), for example, shows sales volumes by size grouped according to product category.

FIGURE 15.32

Revenue Figures by Product Category — Cross-Tabular View

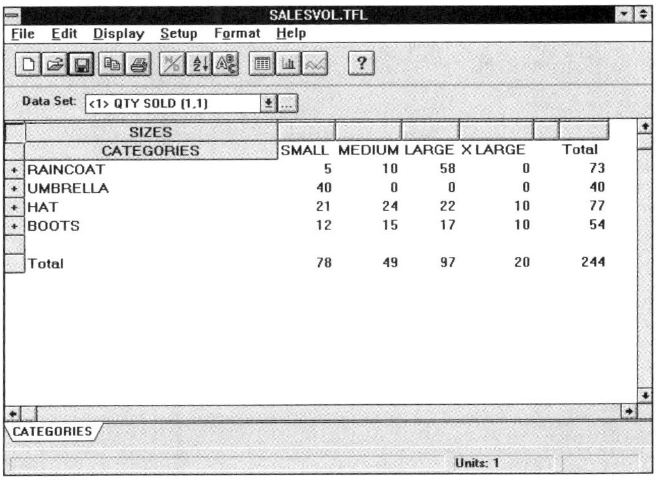

FIGURE 15.33

Revenue Figures by Size and Product Category — Bar Chart View

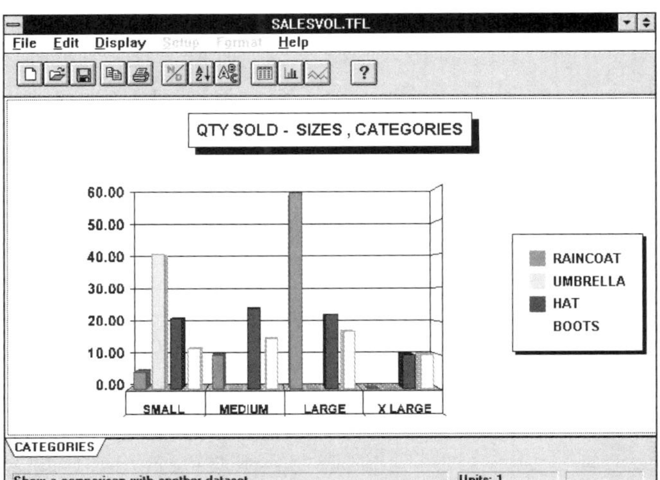

By tightly integrating the functionality of amis Desktop with underlying data models, amis V8 lets end users perform sophisticated, multidimensional analyses while shielding them from the underlying complexity of data-mart schema.

FIGURE 15.34
Revenue Figures by Product Category and Size — Bar Chart View

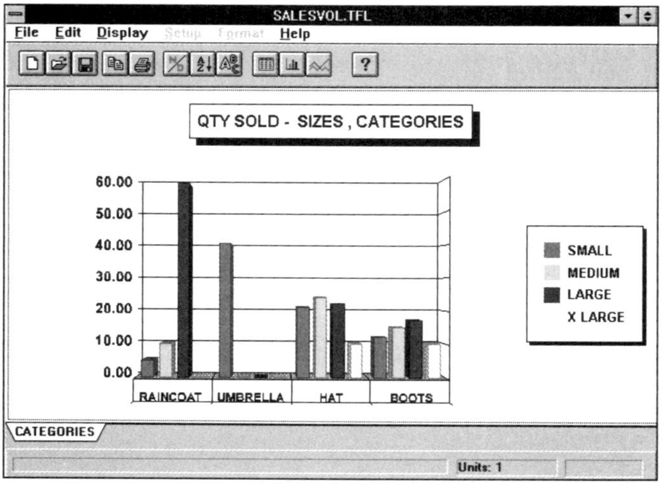

PRODUCT SUMMARY AND POSITIONING

amis V8 is a comprehensive data-warehousing solution. On the back end, the package supports the creation and maintenance of primary warehouse repositories and one or more relational OLAP data marts. Because the product automatically creates data repositories that adhere to the star schema (based on your input, of course), you do not have to manually design and build data-warehouse repositories.

On the front end, amis V8 facilitates sophisticated multidimensional analyses as well as the advanced presentation of data via graphs, charts, cross-tabs, reports, and EIS-style images such as grids and maps. For spreadsheet users, the product also supports direct links to the major spreadsheet packages. For end users, amis V8 features a consistent, integrated GUI. amis Desktop Developer is necessary for customers seeking to integrate amis V8 with third-party products.

Olympic amis Limited has traditionally served the banking and insurance industries, and the company has designed data-store models specifically for these fields. For organizations such as banks and insurers, these predefined data models hold extra appeal. In a bid to grow beyond its traditional customer base, Olympic amis is actively developing data models for JD Edwards' OneWorld distribution software. Starting at $25,000, amis V8 is targeted for medium- to high-end AS/400 data-warehouse implementations.

Chapter 16

ShowCase Corporation and ShowCase STRATEGY

Company Background

Founded in 1989, ShowCase Corporation offers an integrated suite of data-warehousing software marketed collectively as ShowCase STRATEGY. Headquartered in Rochester, Minnesota, privately held ShowCase has approximately 200 employees serving more than 2,600 client sites worldwide. The company maintains regional sales and support offices in Rochester, Chicago, Brussels, and Kuala Lumpur, and markets its products in the Pacific Rim and continental Europe through a variety of distribution channels. In addition, ShowCase has developmental partnerships with leading software vendors such as AppSource, Arbor Software, and IBM. The company has also established synergistic partnerships with more than 30 application developers including JD Edwards and Software 2000. ShowCase Corporation positions STRATEGY as an end-to-end, integrated, enterprise-wide data-warehousing solution.

Product Overview

Introduced in 1996, STRATEGY has roots in several ShowCase products developed earlier in the decade. ShowCase introduced VISTA, the world's first Windows-based AS/400 query package, in 1991. VISTA EIS, an advanced presentation package designed for VISTA, followed the next year. After developing an ODBC driver with Microsoft in 1993, ShowCase introduced a report writer called VISTA Pro in 1994. The company focused on developing service and support programs in 1995 and unveiled STRATEGY in 1996.

STRATEGY consists of six integrated components: Server, Query, Report Writer, Distributor, Essbase/400, and Analyzer. Two optional components in this suite are ported from other platforms: Essbase/400 and Analyzer. Essbase/400, a proprietary multidimensional database, is modeled after Arbor Software Corporation's Essbase. Arbor first introduced Essbase, a leading MD-OLAP product in the Unix and Windows NT Server markets, in 1991. ShowCase, in conjunction with Arbor and IBM, ported Essbase to the AS/400 in 1996; ShowCase has exclusive distribution rights to the product for five years. ShowCase also has ported Wired for OLAP, an advanced presentation and analysis tool developed by AppSource Incorporated, to the AS/400. Dubbed STRATEGY Analyzer, you can use this component to develop advanced EIS applications for your data warehouse.

The remainder of this chapter details each module and explores the suite's applicability in the AS/400 data-warehousing arena.

Server

Server, the foundation of STRATEGY, provides you with administrative functionality to manage end-user access to the data warehouse. Server consists of five components, which I discuss in the following sections.

Corporate Views Manager

Server's Corporate Views Manager performs metadata management. This module lets you assign more meaningful names to files (up to 128 characters) and fields (up to 30 characters), as shown in Figure 16.1. Query and Report Writer access these names, or aliases, to provide more intuitive end-user access to STRATEGY warehouse repositories. The assignment of aliases does not require the recompilation of underlying files. We also can use Corporate Views Manager to define which columns are eligible for join operations during Query and Report Writer access.

FIGURE 16.1
Assigning Descriptive Text to Fields

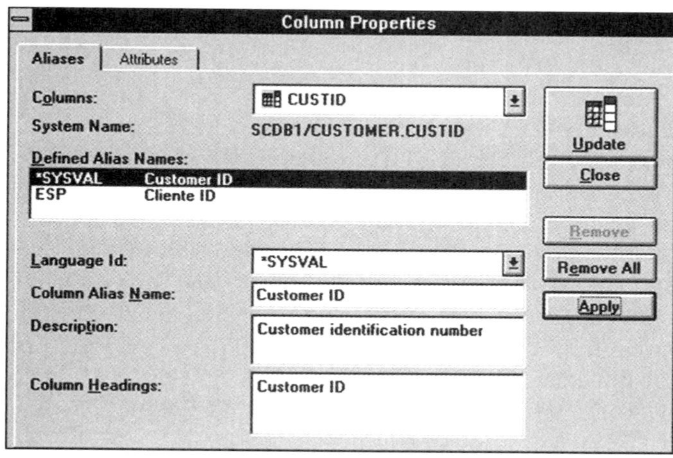

Security Manager

Security Manager lets you bolster AS/400 security without having to make changes to existing applications. For example, we can control access to data-warehouse tables via Query and Report Writer at the library, collection, table, row, and column levels for both individual and group profiles. You also can maintain user profiles via Security Manager's graphical interfaces. Figure 16.2 depicts the removal of finance users' rights to a salary column (i.e., field).

FIGURE 16.2
Maintaining Field-Level Security

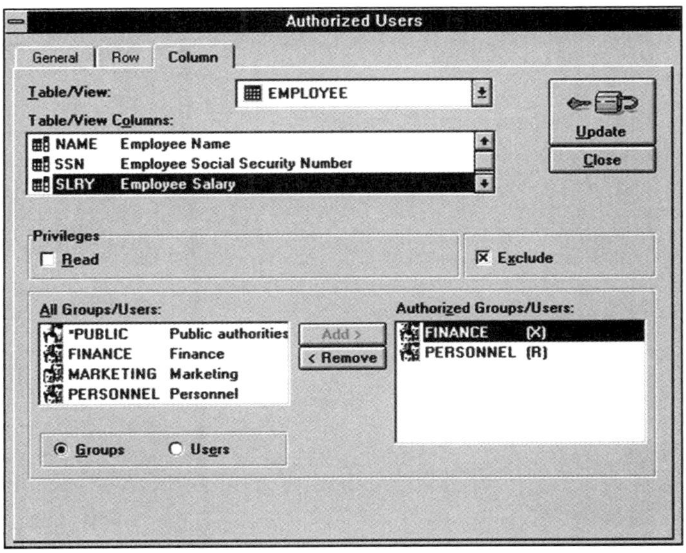

Resource Manager

To better manage system performance, you can use Server's Resource Manager to specify those users whose jobs can run interactively and/or in batch. It also lets you limit query priorities and specify user and group profiles that have authority to build new queries. In addition, you can assign query priorities and limits on a user and group-profile basis. Resource Manager also provides a means to control the manipulation of warehouse data at the client level (e.g., printing locally, saving data to diskettes, linking to PC applications). Figure 16.3 (page 290) shows Resource Manager's Query and Report Writer Settings screen.

FIGURE 16.3
Query and Report Writer Settings Screen

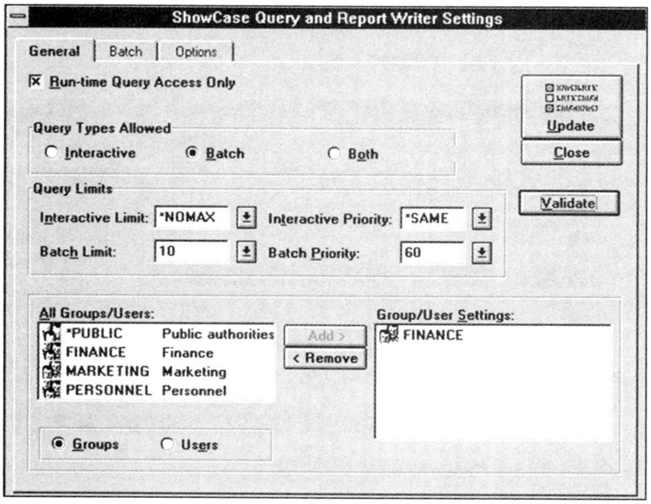

License Manager

Server's License Manager lets you administer passwords and grant end-user access to various STRATEGY features. For example, you can permit specific users or groups of users to access the data warehouse via Query, but not via Report Writer. Figure 16.4 illustrates the assignment of Query rights to QSECOFR and to all user profiles with *PUBLIC rights.

FIGURE 16.4
Maintaining Security by Function

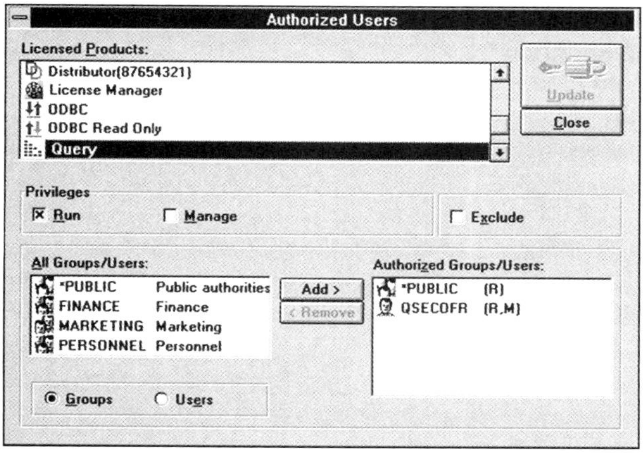

Warehouse Manager

Warehouse Manager provides an interface between STRATEGY and many OS/400 features. It is through Warehouse Manager, for example, that you can assign more descriptive text to AS/400 files and fields. This Server component also enables batch subsystem control, date conversion, query optimization, stored-procedure-call support, and many other functions.

Query

An enhanced version of ShowCase's first query product (VISTA), Query lets experienced end users access, retrieve, and manipulate information stored in DB2/400-based warehouse repositories. Alternatively, you can design queries for inexperienced users to execute. This module ships along with STRATEGY's Server component. These components, together with consulting services, constitute a core product offering.

Through Query, users can design queries with multilevel control breaks, aggregate functions (sum, average, minimum, maximum, count), and interactive runtime prompts. Prompts also can dynamically request input parameters (e.g., customer numbers, date ranges) from users. Query includes a Query Guide that walks users through the process of designing a query. Figure 16.5, familiar to users of ShowCase VISTA, depicts Query's Columns specification screen.

FIGURE 16.5
Query's Columns Specification Screen

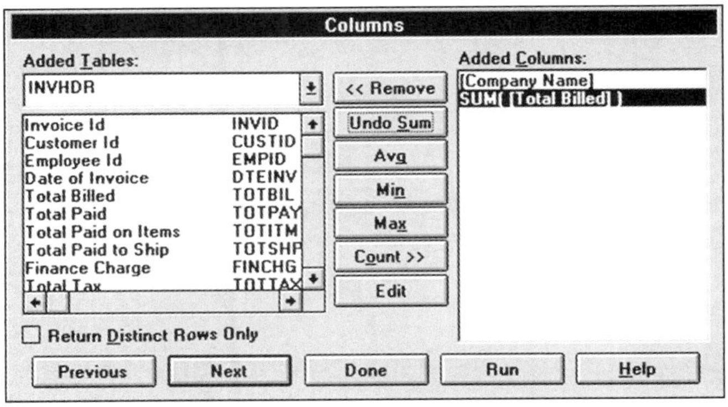

Users also can access Query's functionality directly through STRATEGY's add-on functions for Lotus 1-2-3 and Microsoft Excel. Through these spreadsheet products, users can execute queries and save results in spreadsheet files. They can then analyze and/or graph the results using available spreadsheet functionality. For example, a sales manager can use Lotus 1-2-3 or Excel to execute a query that retrieves revenue figures for top customers from a DB2/400-based data warehouse. Once the figures have been transferred to a spreadsheet, the manager can use the spreadsheet to create a pie chart that details the relative percentages of customers' contributions to total revenue. This functionality lets users leverage their experience with spreadsheets. Figure 16.6 shows the use of Query's Microsoft Excel plug-in.

FIGURE 16.6
Query's Excel Plug-In

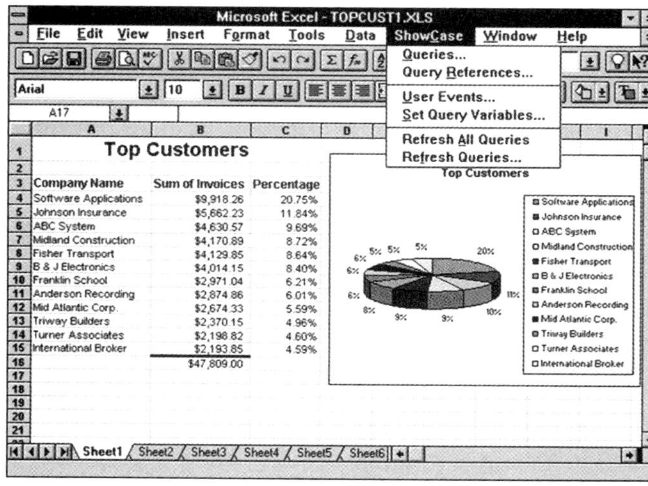

In instances when users prefer to view results in STRATEGY, Query also provides a desktop viewer that lets them interactively format resultant data; for example, they can change font sizes, colors, styles, and column widths.

To safeguard system performance, you also can use Query to limit the number of rows queries return. This feature prevents poorly designed queries from degrading system performance in instances when an inordinant number of rows would otherwise be retrieved from the data warehouse. To further safe-guard system performance, Query users can schedule queries to run during off-peak hours.

Report Writer

An enhanced version of ShowCase's first report writer, VISTA Pro, STRATEGY Report Writer is tightly integrated with Query. Using Report Writer, IT personnel and experienced end users can create presentation-quality reports from four standard templates, including columnar, cross-tab, form, and label. Figure 16.7 features Report Writer's template-selection screen. Report Writer supports subtotals, grand totals, multilevel sorts, runtime variable prompts, colors, borders, shading, and multiple fonts. Report Writer also lets users design reports that feature both text and images (typically including charts, tables, graphs, logos, and other bitmap-compatible files).

FIGURE 16.7
Report Writer's Template Selection Screen

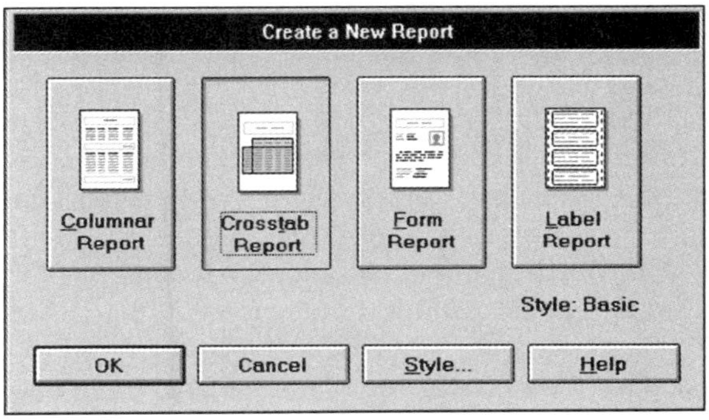

STRATEGY's Distributor

The Distributor module gives you basic capabilities to extract, transform, and propagate DB2/400-based OLTP data to DB2/400-based warehouse repositories or to STRATEGY's own Essbase/400 MD-OLAP database. Through a GUI interface similar to that of Query and Report Writer, you can access single and multiple tables and filter data by rows and columns. Once this data is isolated, you can transform it into meaningful information before it is propagated to STRATEGY warehouse repositories. When you load data into Essbase/400, Distributor can dynamically build dimensions and recalculate derived figures — but be aware that if your multidimensional database has many dimensions and a significant amount of data, then this process can require a considerable period of time. You also can use Distributor to derive new fields, summarize data, and perform date operations. The product lets you track the history and current status of transferred distribution sets. You also can use it to schedule transfers periodically (daily, weekly, monthly, etc.) or by event. However, Distributor's scheduling function is very basic, so many ShowCase sites rely on third-party scheduling products such as Robot/400.

Essbase/400

Essbase/400 is an AS/400-resident version of Essbase, Arbor Software Corporation's multidimensional (MD-OLAP) database offering. (Arbor, a public company headquartered in Sunnyvale, California, pioneered the use of MD-OLAP technology in 1991. Previously available for OS/2, Unix, and Windows NT, Essbase was already licensed to more than 900 companies worldwide when ShowCase Corporation ported it to the AS/400.)

On the AS/400, Essbase databases (or cubes) are not stored in DB2/400. Instead, they are loaded from DB2/400 and stored in stream files that reside in the Integrated File System. To accommodate what may be 10+ GB of data, these stream files are often very large. Essbase/400 cubes can be updated incrementally, but you may choose to simply perform full refreshes for these structures at regularly scheduled intervals. Incremental rebuilds require OLTP systems that carefully track when records are added, deleted, and updated. Many OLTP systems do not provide comprehensive support for this, so full refreshes of data marts (e.g., such as those created in Essbase/400) are the oft-chosen workaround. In the case of companies that maintain 5+ GB Essbase/400 cubes, full refreshes will probably have to be performed on the weekend when requisite processing resources are available.

ShowCase offers three optional modules for Essbase/400. A Currency Conversion module is designed to support the manual maintenance of currency exchange rates. Upon input, specified calculations are rerun to update the Essbase/400 database. You can use an SQL Interface module to access DB2/400 data in cases where Essbase/400 does not contain enough detailed information to satisfy a query. Finally, a set of Essbase/400 APIs can integrate Essbase/400 data with custom applications written in Visual Basic, PowerBuilder, C, or C++. You can access Essbase/400 data through STRATEGY's Analyzer component, as well as through add-ons for Lotus 1-2-3 and Excel. Note that Essbase/400 is available for RISC-based AS/400s only.

As is the case with any MD-OLAP product, loading and maintaining data in Essbase/400 can require a significant period of time. For this reason, I highly recommend performance trials, if possible, with your own data in your own environment.

Analyzer

An enhanced version of AppSource Corporation's Wired for OLAP software offering, Analyzer provides end users with the means to analyze information stored in both Essbase/400 MD-OLAP data stores and DB2/400 relational databases. Analyzer is positioned as STRATEGY's front-end OLAP tool. You also can use this product to design EIS-style GUIs complete with geographical maps and hotspots. For example, you can associate a particular sales query that summarizes revenue by region with various regions on a map of the United States.

To analyze relational data residing in DB2/400, users first employ Analyzer's Data Modeler to construct relational databases that Analyzer can link to. We can think of these derived relational data stores as personal data marts. Data Modeler lets IT personnel and advanced end users apply selection criteria in the data-extraction process. Knowledge of database design techniques is useful in this process. To smooth the learning curve, a Query Guide wizard leads users through the process. Data Modeler's interface is similar to that of STRATEGY's Query module.

To further enable multidimensional analyses, Analyzer provides a Cube Navigator that lets users manipulate dimensions of information via intuitive drag-and-drop motions. After re-arranging data into a meaningful format, users can examine the data through a spreadsheet package or via graphs and charts. They also can use Analyzer's Cube Navigator to quickly design ad hoc multi-dimensional reports. Figure 16.8 depicts Analyzer's Cube Navigator definition screen. As an OLAP tool, Analyzer is well suited for "what if" analyses, time-series analyses, budgeting, forecasting, and other advanced analytic modeling.

FIGURE 16.8
Opening Screen for Analyzer's Cube Navigator

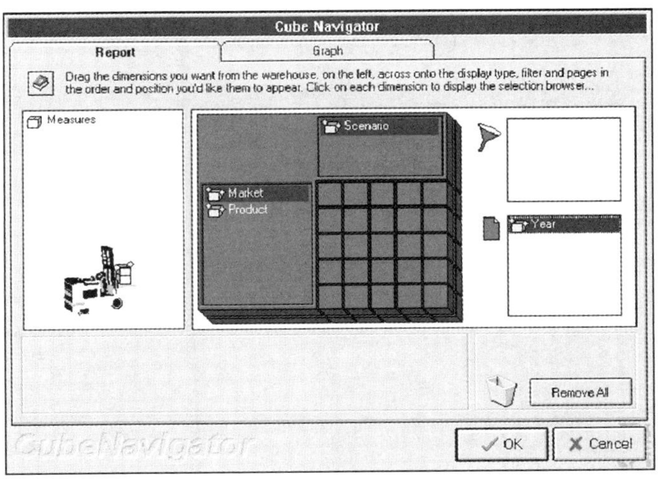

Analyzer for the Web

In late 1997, ShowCase released a Java 1.1-based version of Analyzer, dubbed Analyzer for the Web, that lets remote users interactively examine warehouse data on an ad hoc basis through standard Web browsers. Notably, the product does not require hard-coded HTML or CGI scripts. Essentially a Java applet, Analyzer for the Web requires Netscape 3.0 (or later) or Microsoft Explorer 3.2[1] (or later) Web browsers.

[1]Figure 4.8 in Chapter 4 illustrates Analyzer for the Web as it would be used with Microsoft Explorer.

IMPLEMENTATION EXAMPLE

To further convey the functionality of STRATEGY, this section features numerous screens of distribution sets, transformation processes, queries, and resultant tables, graphs, and reports for our implementation example. For simplicity, let's assume that the data warehouse resides on the same AS/400 as the OLTP database. For heterogeneous database support or robust propagation needs, you can integrate STRATEGY with third-party replication products.

In the first step of our implementation example, we access, summarize, and transfer invoice information from our sample invoice header and detail files, IN001PF and IN002PF. Figure 16.9 depicts STRATEGY's Source Definition function as we can use it to display a list of tables in an SQL collection called AS/400DW. Note that we already have assigned aliases to the table names to facilitate intuitive access to the data warehouse.

FIGURE 16.9
STRATEGY's Source Definition Screen

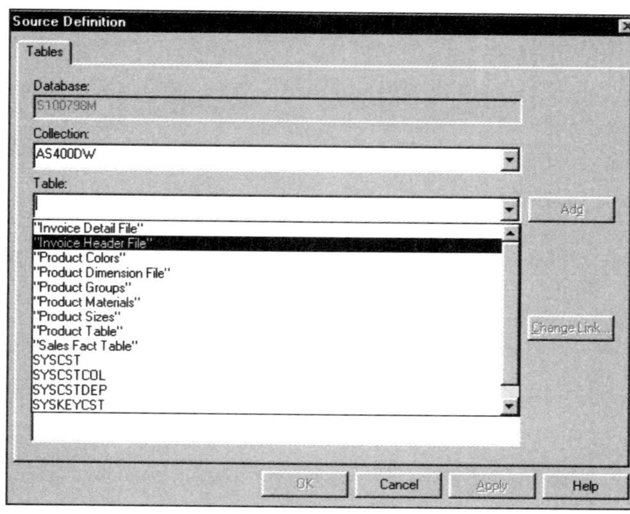

Figure 16.10 shows the selection of our invoice header and detail files for use in a STRATEGY distribution set, while Figure 16.11 depicts the selection of columns required for the summarization of invoice figures.

To further highlight Distributor's functionality, Figure 16.12 (page 298) shows the creation of a distribution set that will move product information to the data warehouse. Figure 16.13 (page 298) details the selection of product columns that the distribution set will actually transfer to the data warehouse. At this point, the color codes in our implementation example have not yet been remapped, as the sample data in Figure 16.14 (page 299) demonstrates.

FIGURE 16.10
Selecting Two Source Tables for the Warehouse

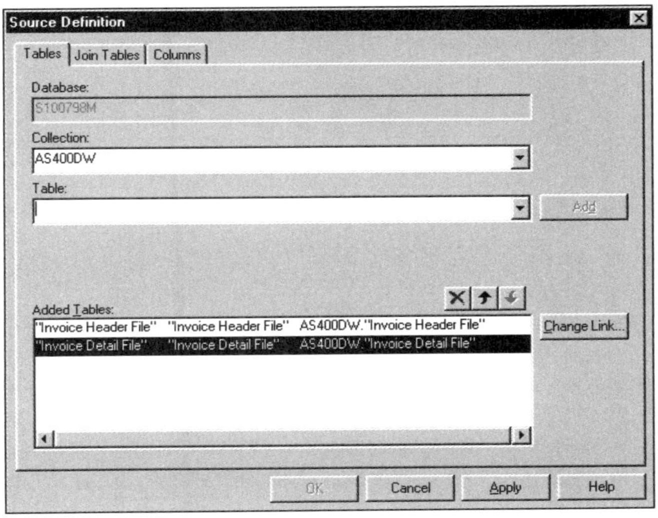

FIGURE 16.11
Selecting and Deriving Invoice Columns for the Warehouse

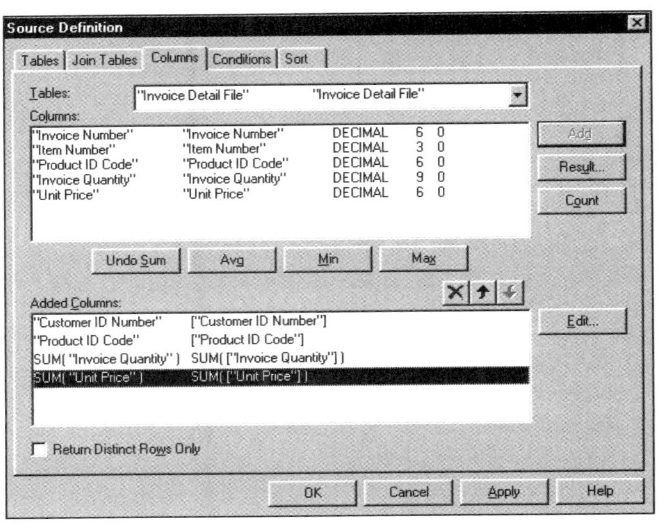

FIGURE 16.12
Selecting the Product Table as a Source for the Warehouse

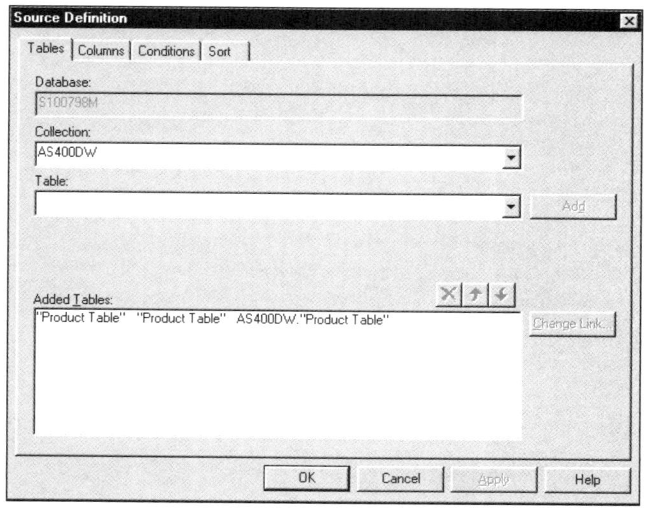

FIGURE 16.13
Selecting Product Columns for the Warehouse

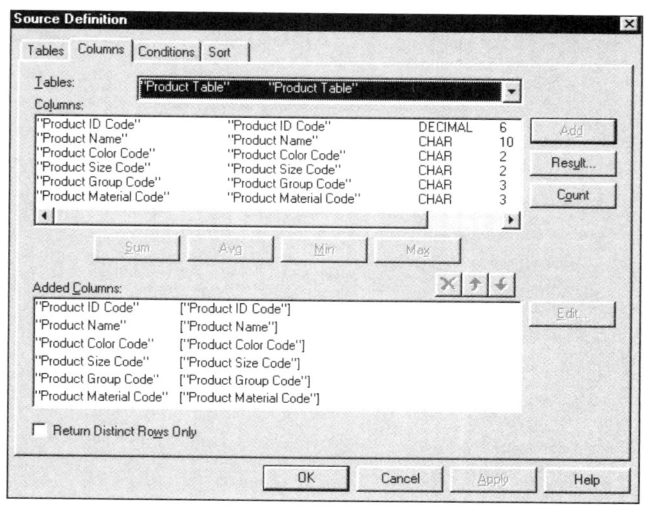

Before we remap color codes in the data warehouse, we must create a product dimension table. Figure 16.15 depicts the creation of our sample product dimension table, while Figure 16.16 (page 300) illustrates the definition

FIGURE 16.14
Sample Data Generated by Distributor

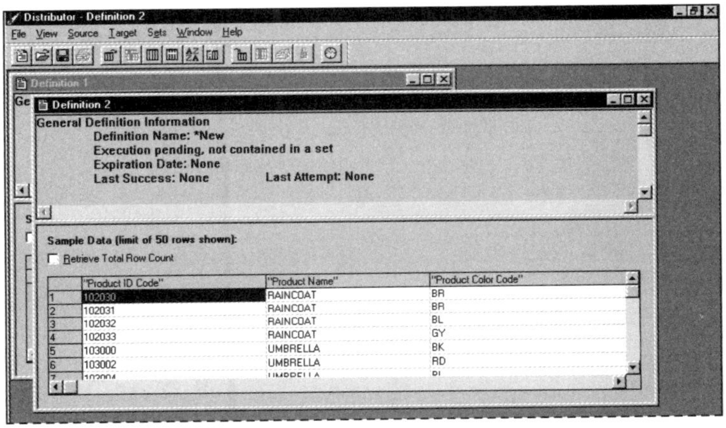

of columns and associated attributes. Figure 16.17 (page 300) highlights Distributor's Post-Transfer SQL feature as we use it to create SQL statements that transform color codes into meaningful textual descriptions. Distributor's Post-Transfer SQL feature lets us transform data either through SQL statements or through calls to transformation programs written in other languages such as RPG or COBOL.

FIGURE 16.15
Defining the Product Dimension Table

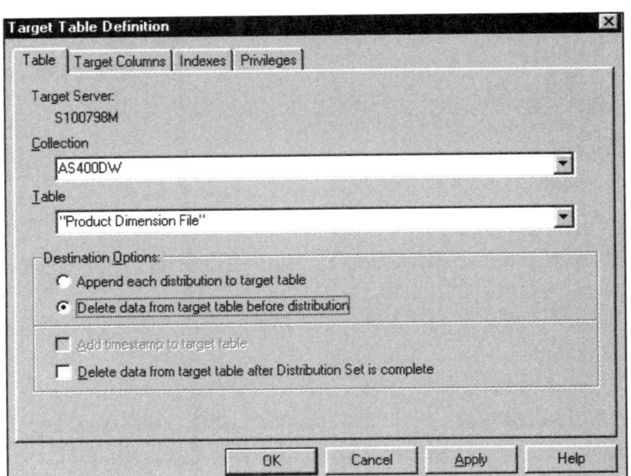

FIGURE 16.16
Maintaining Column Attributes

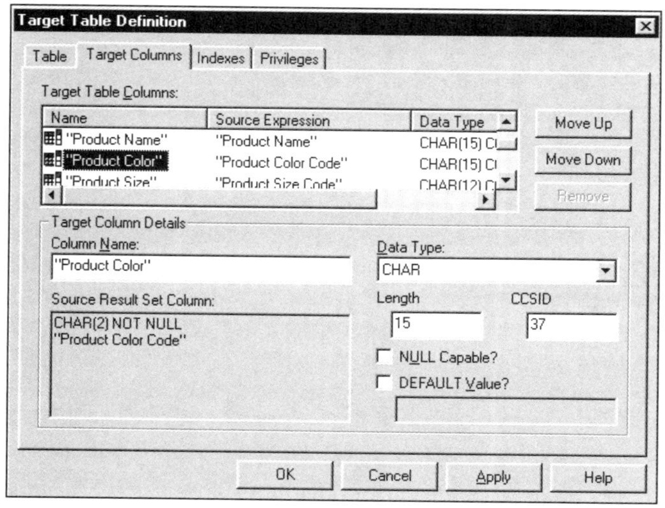

FIGURE 16.17
Using Post-Transfer SQL Functionality to Map Color Codes to Descriptions

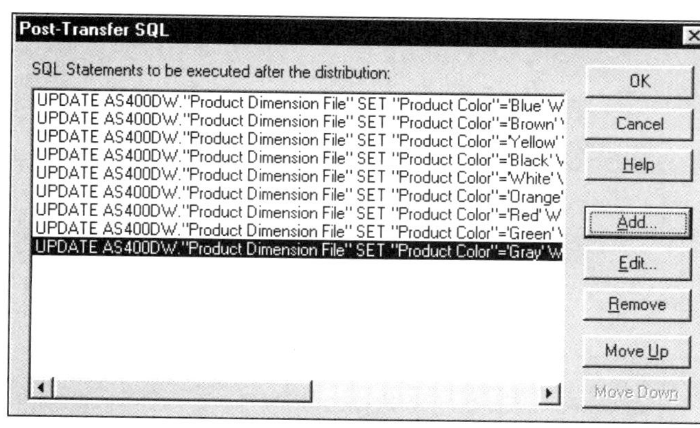

We can use the Post-Transfer SQL feature of distributor on a target AS/400 after we have transferred the data. STRATEGY also supports the dynamic execution of SQL statements that we can use to update distributed product data. Figure 16.18 highlights this feature, showing the color code BL remapped to BLUE.

Once data has been distributed and transformed, all query results reflect the remapped color values. In Figure 16.19, we no longer see cryptic color or size codes (size codes were remapped in the same way that color codes were transformed into meaningful text).

A query designed with STRATEGY's Query component generated the results in Figure 16.19. To highlight the creation of a more complex query, Figure 16.20 (page 302) features the STRATEGY Query Guide as we can use it to define a product sales summary. The resultant data set, which appears in

FIGURE 16.18

Using Dynamic SQL Call to Map Color Codes to Descriptions

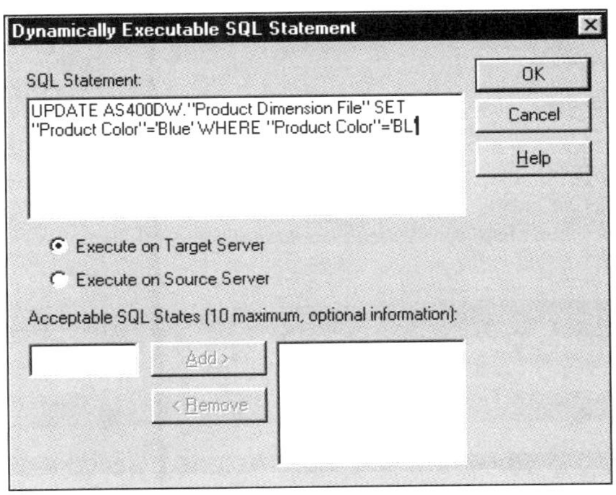

FIGURE 16.19

Query Results After Mapping Codes to Descriptions

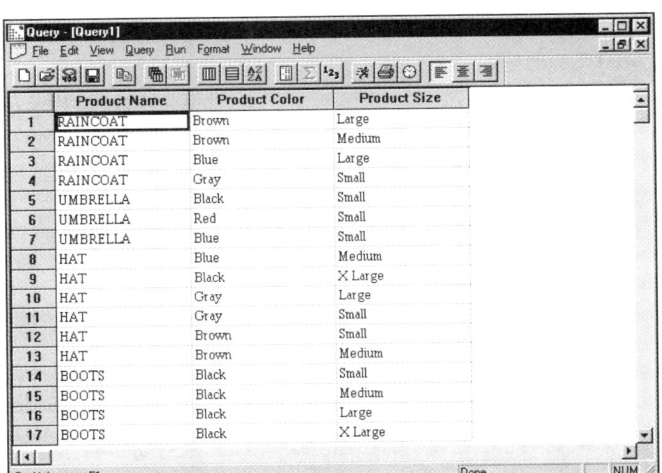

	Product Name	Product Color	Product Size
1	RAINCOAT	Brown	Large
2	RAINCOAT	Brown	Medium
3	RAINCOAT	Blue	Large
4	RAINCOAT	Gray	Small
5	UMBRELLA	Black	Small
6	UMBRELLA	Red	Small
7	UMBRELLA	Blue	Small
8	HAT	Blue	Medium
9	HAT	Black	X Large
10	HAT	Gray	Large
11	HAT	Gray	Small
12	HAT	Brown	Small
13	HAT	Brown	Medium
14	BOOTS	Black	Small
15	BOOTS	Black	Medium
16	BOOTS	Black	Large
17	BOOTS	Black	X Large

Figure 16.21, includes SKU number, product name, color, size, sales volumes, and revenues.

FIGURE 16.20
Using Query Guide to Define a Sales Summary Query

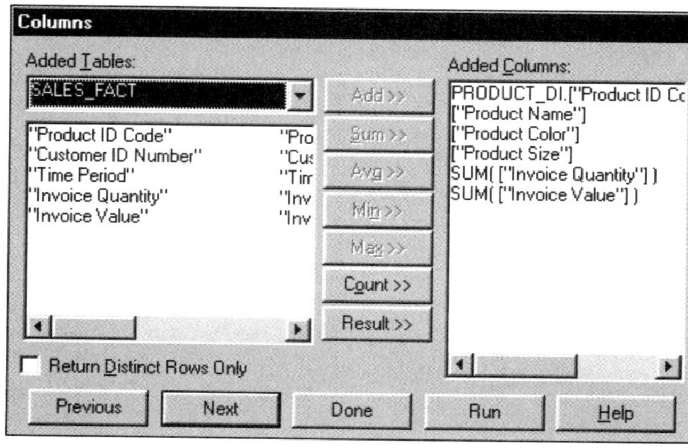

FIGURE 16.21
Sample Report Detailing Sales Values by SKU Number

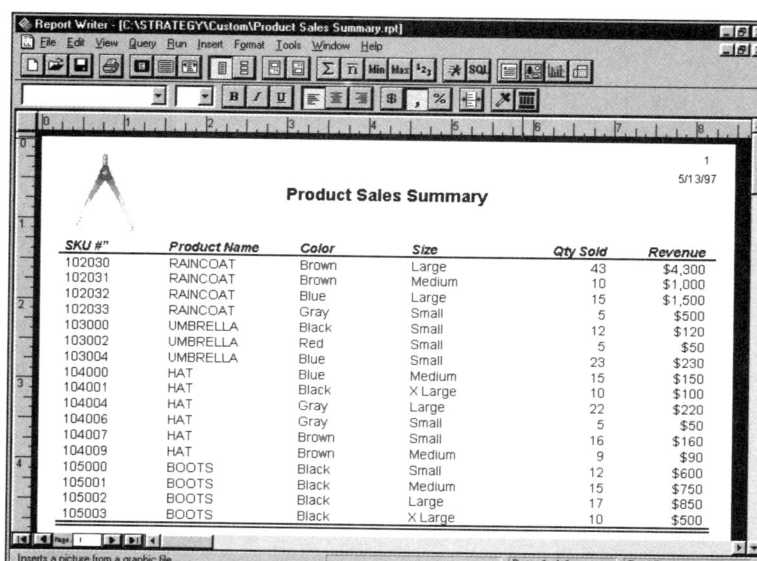

SKU #"	Product Name	Color	Size	Qty Sold	Revenue
102030	RAINCOAT	Brown	Large	43	$4,300
102031	RAINCOAT	Brown	Medium	10	$1,000
102032	RAINCOAT	Blue	Large	15	$1,500
102033	RAINCOAT	Gray	Small	5	$500
103000	UMBRELLA	Black	Small	12	$120
103002	UMBRELLA	Red	Small	5	$50
103004	UMBRELLA	Blue	Small	23	$230
104000	HAT	Blue	Medium	15	$150
104001	HAT	Black	X Large	10	$100
104004	HAT	Gray	Large	22	$220
104006	HAT	Gray	Small	5	$50
104007	HAT	Brown	Small	16	$160
104009	HAT	Brown	Medium	9	$90
105000	BOOTS	Black	Small	12	$600
105001	BOOTS	Black	Medium	15	$750
105002	BOOTS	Black	Large	17	$850
105003	BOOTS	Black	X Large	10	$500

STRATEGY also supports the analysis of information via drilling up, drilling down, and slicing and dicing operations. In Figure 16.22 (page 304), we see a product category summary enabled via Essbase/400. Note that a third figure, Percent of Revenue, has been calculated for each product category. Furthermore, bar graphs depict sales volume and revenue figures. Using Essbase/400, end users do not write SQL-like queries to access information in the MD-OLAP structure. Rather, they manipulate figures via intuitive point, click, and drag operations.

To further highlight STRATEGY's analytic functionality, Figure 16.23 (page 304) shows the product category summary, without graphs, as we view it through STRATEGY's Analyzer component. In this instance, we have color-coded a results grid to let end users quickly determine which product categories are performing poorly based on percent of revenue. Analyzer, which we can use to access data in Essbase/400 or DB2/400 tables, can also present data via other advanced EIS-style images such as graphs and maps.

End users who are comfortable with spreadsheet software may opt to analyze and graph data with Lotus 1-2-3 or Microsoft Excel. Figure 16.24 (page 305) depicts STRATEGY's Excel plug-in as end users would view sales volume and revenue by product category. As you can see, we have used Excel's graphing capabilities to create two bar charts representing sales volume and sales revenue, respectively.

Alternatively, end users also can analyze information using STRATEGY's comprehensive Report Writer. In Figure 16.25 (page 305), Report Writer has created a cross-tabular view of sales volumes by product category and size. If we wanted, we could easily integrate this cross-tab with additional text and graphic images such as corporate logos. Report Writer supports both AS/400 and PC printers.

Cross-tabular views of data are not limited to STRATEGY's Report Writer module. In Figure 16.26 (page 306), we see the same figures as they appear in a color-coded grid designed with Analyzer. In this instance, notice that a legend appears to the left of the grid.

FIGURE 16.22
Product Category Sales Summary Enabled via Essbase/400

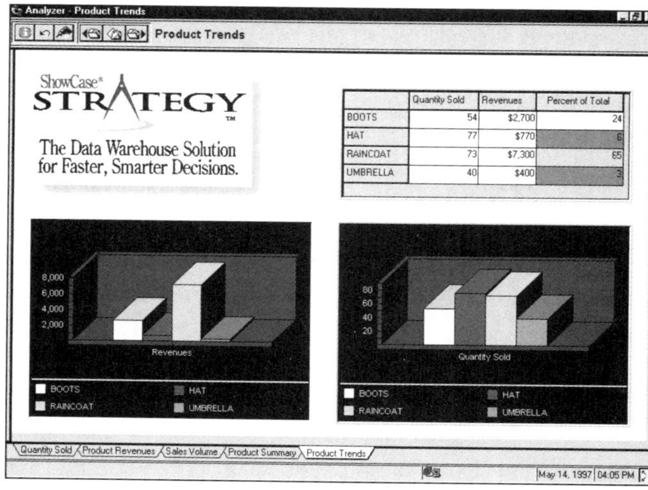

FIGURE 16.23
Product Category Sales Summary Enabled via Analyzer

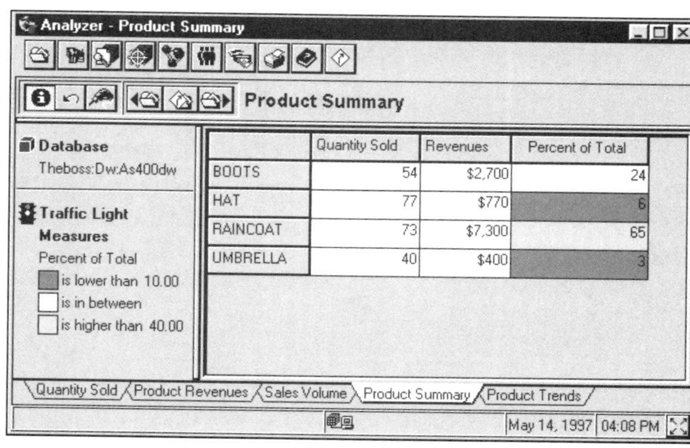

FIGURE 16.24

Product Category Sales Summary Enabled via Excel Plug-In

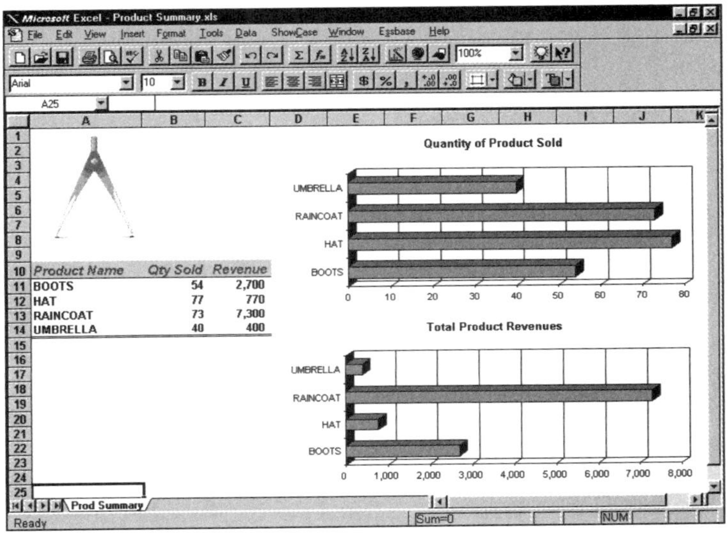

FIGURE 16.25

Product Category Sales Summary Enabled via Report Writer

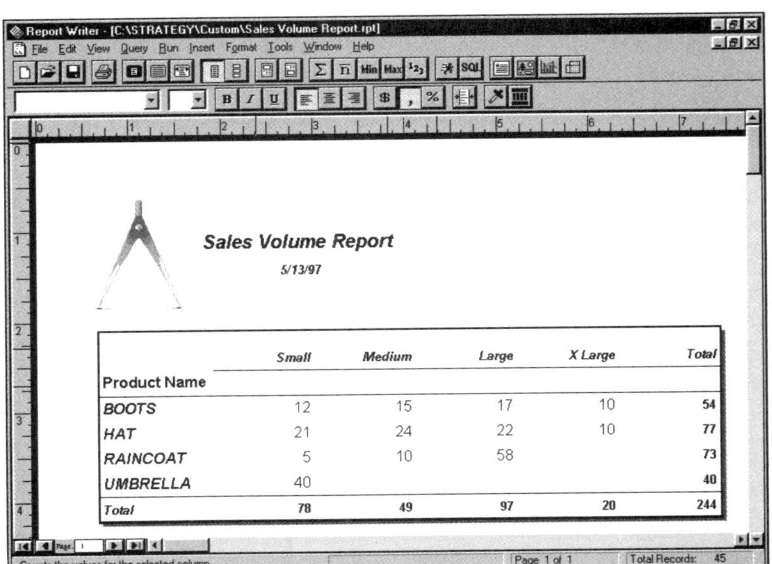

FIGURE 16.26
Product Category Sales Summary Enabled via Analyzer (with Traffic Light Feature)

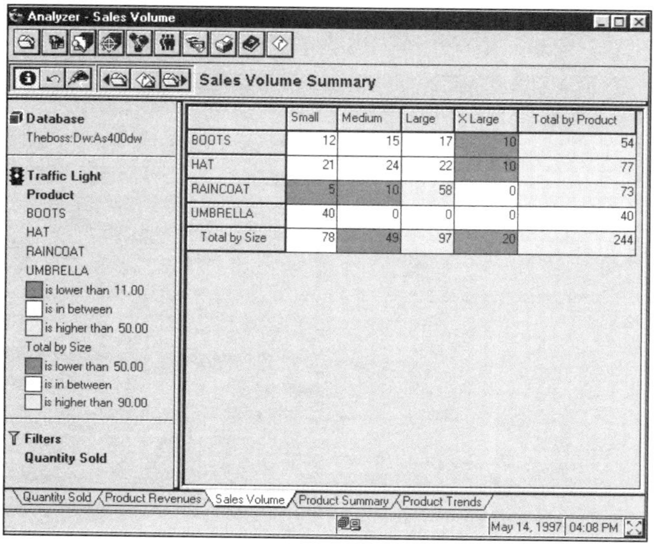

PRODUCT SUMMARY AND POSITIONING

STRATEGY is an integrated data-warehousing solution with exceptional strengths in its front-end capabilities. The product facilitates intuitive end-user access to data through feature-rich OLAP, query, report-writing, graphing, and EIS capabilities. Its functions are accessible through a consistent, well-designed GUI.

On the back end, STRATEGY provides solid support for the creation and maintenance of MD-OLAP data marts. Be aware that this process can require considerable time in a multidimensional database that has many dimensions and a significant amount of data. However, once loaded, STRATEGY's Essbase/400 enables the type of advanced analyses you would expect from an MD-OLAP product: forecasting, budgeting, what if analyses, and the like. You would be well-advised to temper user expectations when rolling out Essbase/400 cubes. As soon as users begin working with these models, they tend to inundate IT with requests for cubes with more and more dimensions.

STRATEGY also supports the creation of DB2/400-based warehouse repositories. However, support for these repositories is less robust, and you remain largely responsible for designing appropriate database schema (i.e., star or snowflake).

ShowCase considers its consulting and support a critical first step in every STRATEGY implementation. Because of STRATEGY's broad range of functionality, its implementations do require careful planning and a firm commitment on the part of both IT and the user community. Do not expect to roll out an end-to-end solution in a month!

At $20,000 for a 10-user relational implementation and $80,000 for a full relational/MD-OLAP implementation, STRATEGY is squarely aimed at the medium to high end of the AS/400 data-warehousing market. Annual maintenance fees are 20 percent of the product's cost.

Chapter 17

Silvon Software and DataTracker

Company Background

Founded in 1987, Silvon Software develops a variety of applications and tools for the IBM AS/400 and Microsoft Windows NT Server markets. Silvon's flagship business-intelligence offering, DataTracker, supports the development of application-specific IBM DB2/400 and Microsoft SQL Server-based data-warehousing solutions. The company also offers HELPLINE, a Help desk and customer-service-management package; INSITE, an asset-management package; INTO 2000, a date-conversion tool; and its Software Development Management (SDM) product suite, an integrated collection of change-management, release-management, quality-assurance and application-development tools.

Headquartered in Westmont, Illinois, privately held Silvon has approximately 175 employees and more than 3,500 customers worldwide. DataTracker, its data-warehousing product suite, is licensed by more than 800 customers and is deployed at approximately 1,000 sites. The company manages North American sales and support through its head office in Illinois and maintains additional offices in Europe, Latin America, Asia, and the Pacific Rim. Distributors located throughout the world market Silvon's products in 25 countries. The company maintains partnerships with IBM, Microsoft, MAPICS, Orcom, Oracle, JDA, Marcam, and Sybase. This chapter focuses on DataTracker for the AS/400 and its derivative vertical data-warehousing applications including SalesTracker, MarginTracker, RetailTracker, and MFGTracker.

Product Overview

DataTracker is a comprehensive, AS/400-based data-warehousing solution that is well-suited for large-scale information-warehousing applications. The product features a highly scalable relational OLAP database engine, data-transformation tools, a metadata repository, and custom-designed analysis and presentation tools.

Working in the DataTracker environment, IT personnel can extract operational DB2/400-based data, transform that data, and load the transformed data into what Silvon refers to as Application-Specific Data Marts, or ADMs. The company's philosophy is to provide business intelligence for specific functional areas of your business. In keeping with this philosophy, its products are not designed to function as monolithic primary repositories.

Using dimension specifications such as product, customer, and region, DataTracker generates relational OLAP data marts based on the star schema. DataTracker databases accommodate up to 70 dimensions and can be optimized through DataTracker's built-in performance tools. In addition to DataTracker,

Silvon also offers APIs and prebuilt extraction procedures for third-party manufacturing applications that SSA (BPCS), Marcam (PRISM and MAPICS), Computer Associates (PRMS), and JD Edwards (World) have developed. Coded in RPG, these extraction routines propagate data to Silvon ADMs on a full-refresh or incremental net-change basis. You can also use DataTracker to export DB2/400 data to Microsoft SQL Server databases. The product currently does not support Oracle or Informix, nor does it support a proprietary MD-OLAP database. However, Silvon plans to eventually support all popular RDBMs used on Windows NT and Unix platforms.

For end users, DataTracker features a GUI-based analysis tool for Windows 3.1, Windows 95, and Windows NT clients. Designed in PowerSoft, the product lets users interactively query, analyze, and graph DB2/400-based data-mart information. DataTracker also supports basic character-based report-writing functionality.

DataTracker is a modular software suite consisting of eight integrated components: Data Sourcing Kit (DSK), to support data transformation; DBGenerate, to create ROLAP data repositories; DBLoad, to initialize and maintain ROLAP data repositories; DBAdmin, to manage end-user access to data; DBRemote, to create standalone, PC-based data marts from larger ADMs; DBConnect, to integrate DataTracker with any ODBC-capable desktop application; DBView, to enable end-user access and analysis via local PCs; and DBNet, to enable end-user access via Web browsers. A description of each of these components follows.

Data Sourcing Kit (DSK)

Designed for IT personnel, DSK is a library of programs, procedures, and templates that facilitate direct connections to operational DB2/400 databases. These databases can be part of a home-grown application or a third-party software package. For the latter, DSK includes information about leading applications' database schema and transaction histories. After connections to databases have been established, you can extract and prepare data for Silvon's ADMs. DSK supports the initial selection of data by field and by record. You can use DSK to derive new fields, update field content, change field names, reformat field sizes, translate field values, and modify field types. It also supports the use of numerous mathematical and string functions. Transformed data is stored in a series of transient DB2/400 files that DataTracker's DBLoad module later accesses.

DBGenerate

After you have used DSK to transform raw operational data into denormalized OLAP structures, you use DBGenerate to automatically create a star-schema database with requisite aggregation tables and metadata. A native AS/400 application, DBGenerate examines configuration parameters entered in DataTracker's DBAdmin module and then creates a series of DB2/400 fact and dimension tables. The module also generates associated join-logical files. To improve query performance, DBGenerate dynamically creates aggregation tables based on usage. DBGenerate also creates and maintains a metadata repository that includes file names, field specifications, and associated aliases.

DBAdmin

DBAdmin provides you with the means to specify the initial dimensions and levels of aggregation in application data-mart schema. You also can use the module to modify field attributes and reconfigure dimensions once a data mart is operational. DBAdmin also lets you define security by user profile, by table, and by field. DBAdmin includes a performance workbench environment for creating tuned query paths that are automatically recognized by the DBOLAP engine.

DBLoad

DBLoad is the mechanism through which information stored in DSK's preparation files is moved to Silvon ADMs. The module first accesses DataTracker's metadata repository to obtain details about the target ADM schema. Afterward, it aggregates the data contained in the preparation files to match predefined drill-down specifications. After it has performed the aggregation processes, DBLoad executes insert and update operations to physically propagate data to the target ADM.

DBView

Custom-designed using PowerSoft and available in 16- and 32-bit versions, DBView provides end users with the means to interactively query and analyze Silvon databases. In addition to its GUI-based query capabilities, this module features spreadsheet, graphing, and OLAP functionality. You can use DBView to interactively filter and sort query results. The product also lets users drill up and down through various levels of aggregated information. You can save DBView's query and presentation specifications as reusable templates. For example, you can direct queries to automatically move results to a spreadsheet. DBView also supports the ad hoc creation of new fields that you can use to enable what-if scenarios. DBView does not directly support EIS-style presentation graphics (e.g., maps and other images). However, you can integrate third-party packages with DataTracker via DBConnect and ODBC drivers.

DBRemote

An optional DataTracker module, DBRemote's function is to create standalone data marts that reside on PC-based servers, desktop PCs, or laptop computers. End users first use DBRemote's graphical interface to extract subsets of data from an AS/400-based ADM. These data sets are then downloaded via ODBC and converted to Sybase SQL Anywhere data files. End users can then slice, dice, filter, graph, and manipulate the downloaded data with DataTracker's front-end analysis tools. No host attachment is required to analyze downloaded information. DBRemote provides facilities to maintain synchronization between downloaded PC files and AS/400-resident application data marts. Unlike Silvon's ADMs, remote data marts are not based upon the star schema. Rather, they consist of SQL Anywhere files that are basically unrelated flat files.

DBConnect

Also optional, DataTracker's DBConnect module features a Windows-based interface that you can use to integrate Silvon ADMs with software packages that support ODBC. AS/400-resident information can then be exchanged with a variety of third-party applications such as report writers (e.g., Crystal Reports) and EIS packages (e.g., Forest & Trees and Brio Query).

DBNet

Another optional DataTracker module, DBNet is a Web server-based application that lets end users access Silvon ADMs over the Internet or via private intranets. Users can then execute DataTracker views, perform basic analyses, and export data in comma-separated (CSV) or delimited formats. DBNet does not support graphing, charting, or all the features found in DBView, nor does it support direct links to PC applications. You can use DBNet in conjunction with any browser that supports HTML 2.0. The product is positioned as an economical way to view DataTracker information over the Internet and is not intended to function as an industrial-strength analysis tool.

Derivative Solutions

In addition to DataTracker, Silvon offers several derivative data-mart solutions that have been created with DataTracker. Offered as SalesTracker, MFGTracker, RetailTracker, and MarginTracker, these applications possess DataTracker's functionality and are designed for specific industries and organizations.

Introduced in 1988, SalesTracker is designed to meet the business intelligence needs of sales and marketing departments and organizations. Its ROLAP database and accompanying analytic software have been designed to process actual, budgeted, and forecast sales information. SalesTracker includes support for common sales dimensions as well, including territories, products, customers, and sales reps. The product also supports multiple currencies and exchange rates that end users might input or that have been extracted from operational systems.

MarginTracker, introduced in 1997 and marketed jointly with IBM, is designed to meet the analytic needs of wholesale distributors. In addition to many features found in SalesTracker, the product supports cost assignment for activity-based accounting and activity-based management. MarginTracker targets the food and beverage industries.

Also introduced in 1997, MFGTracker targets discrete and process manufacturers and is designed to provide Enterprise Resource Planning (ERP) capabilities. MFGTracker attaches directly to ERP applications that JD Edwards, SSA, Marcam, and other major software developers offer. Through its customized RPG-access programs, MFGTracker can extract both current and historical data from these packages.

Finally, RetailTracker targets major retailers whose business model is defined by a considerable number of products and locations.

Implementation Example

To help convey DataTracker's functionality, this section includes sample screens and explanations for our implementation example. For simplicity, let's assume that the data warehouse resides on the same AS/400 as the OLTP database. For heterogeneous database support or robust propagation needs, we can integrate DataTracker with third-party replication products.

The first step in implementing a DataTracker ADM is to determine which dimensions end users require. In our relatively simple implementation example, this information has already been specified, so we'll get right to this task. Figure 17.1 shows how we would use DataTracker's Database Maintenance Utility to connect to the source data. This step, in which we can create new databases or maintain existing ones, builds AS/400 libraries that are used to extract source data. Next, we invoke the Maintain Dimensions program shown in Figure 17.2 (page 314) to define dimensions.

FIGURE 17.1

Connecting to the Source Database

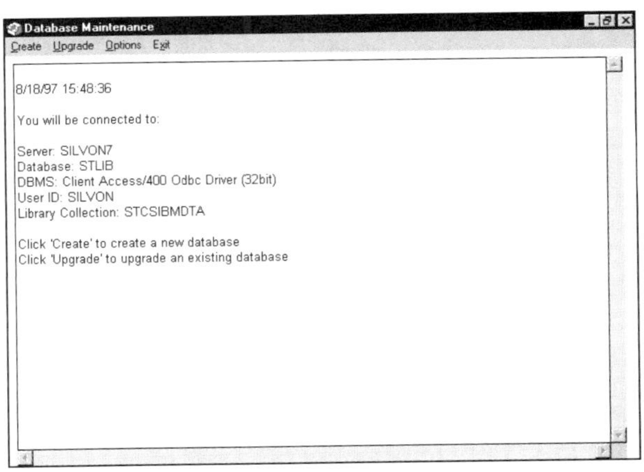

FIGURE 17.2
Defining Dimensions for the Application Data Mart

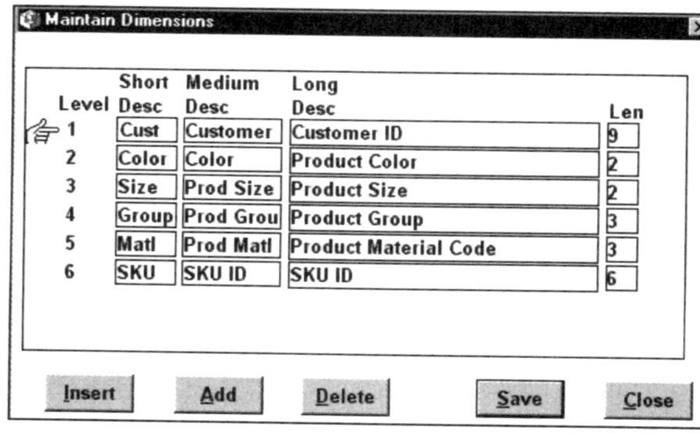

Tracking data over time is an important feature in any data warehouse, and Silvon offers comprehensive support for this function. Figures 17.3 demonstrates how DataTracker's Table Structure utility enables the definition of time-period buckets for data values. As shown in the lower left window, Structure Codes are used to classify data values and specify applicable time periods.

FIGURE 17.3
Specifying Time Periods for the Application Data Mart

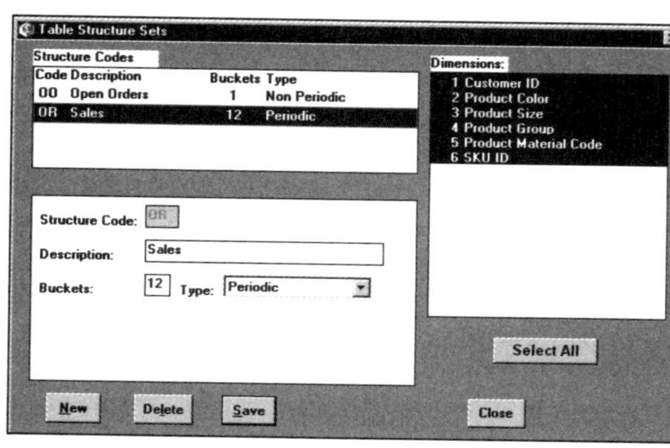

In Figure 17.4, Data Tracker's Create Tables utility uses dimensions and time-period definitions as the basis for the product's relational star-schema database. It is here that tables are actually created on the AS/400.

Once tables have been created, we use a series of OS/400-based commands to extract data from the OLTP data source. Figure 17.5 shows Data-Tracker's EXTMST command, which we use to load the master files that serve

FIGURE 17.4
Creating Tables for the Application Data Mart

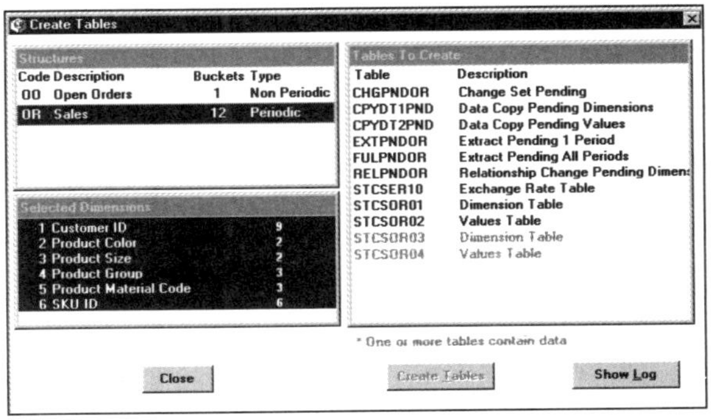

FIGURE 17.5
Specifying Data Extraction on a Net-Change Basis

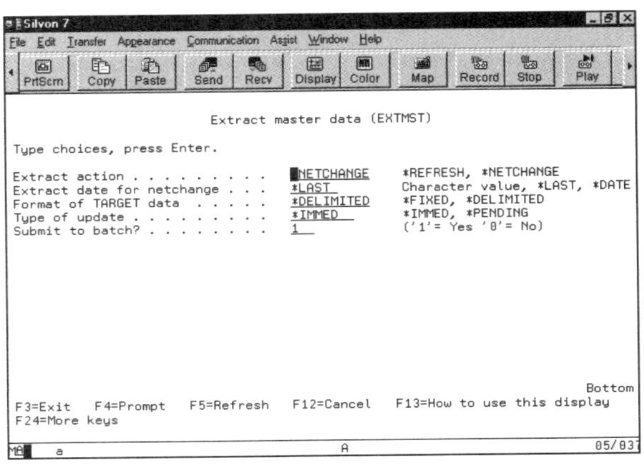

as descriptions of fact tables. We can then use the product's IMPDTL command, as shown in Figure 17.6 (page 316), to initiate an extraction procedure. This process creates a staging file that is used to actually populate the DataTracker database.

To move data from the staging file to the DataTracker database, we invoke the MOVSINDTA command, as shown in Figure 17.7 (page 316).

We use DataTracker Administration programs to physically map metadata to the data mart. Figure 17.8 (page 317) shows how the product's Dimension Maintenance and Field Definition functions are used to map descriptive text, or aliases, to the database. In Figure 17.9 (page 317), we see how the product's Value Administration function describes and sequences the data that is used to populate the data mart.

FIGURE 17.6
Initiating the Data Extraction Process

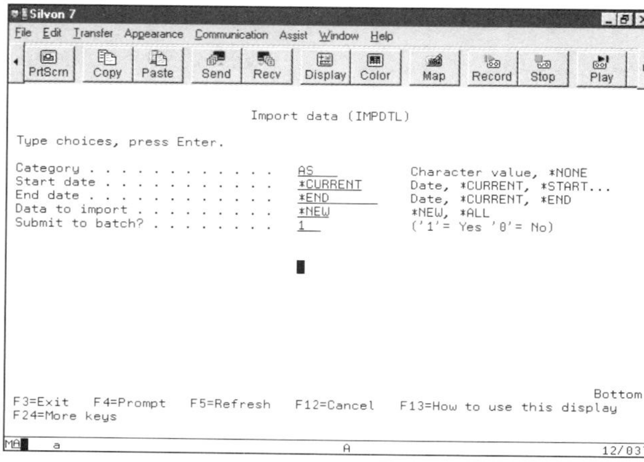

FIGURE 17.7
Moving Data from Staging Tables to the Application Data Mart

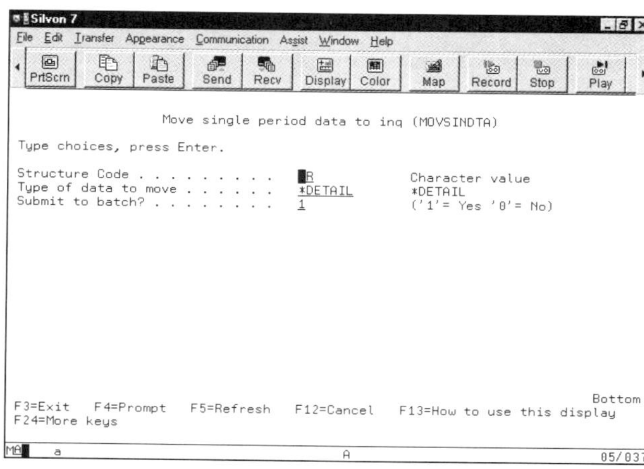

Using Category Maintenance, as shown in Figure 17.10 (page 318), related fields are grouped together by dimensions for use. Here, we've assigned invoice quantity and revenue to a category called actual sales. These categories let users access multiple data elements in a more timely and meaningful way.

Next, we use DataTracker's Viewset function, as depicted in Figure 17.11 (page 318), to assign values to each time period. Here, we've simply defined month buckets for a calendar year. This function offers a great deal of flexibility

FIGURE 17.8
Maintaining Dimensions

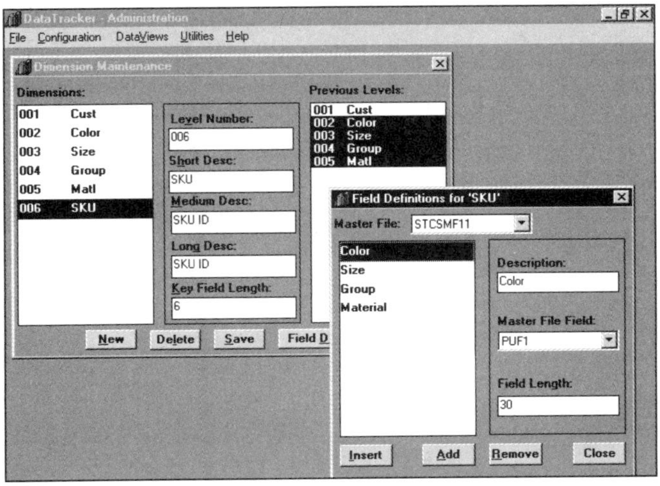

FIGURE 17.9
Maintaining Fields

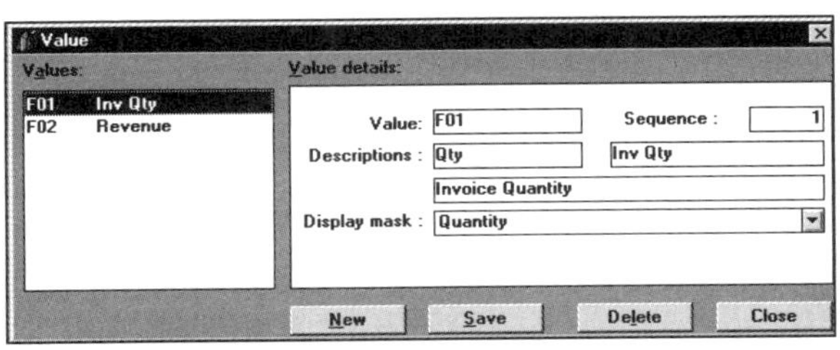

to users who track information based on nonstandard periods such as company-specific fiscal calendars or manufacturing schedules.

Using Silvon's ViewBuckets function, as shown in Figure 17.12 (page 319), we associate time periods to "sales group."

Of course, once a database has been initialized, access to it must be carefully controlled. Figure 17.13 (page 319) demonstrates how dimensional access rights are assigned to a user profile called Silvon. We also can assign rights to group profiles on this screen. Figure 17.14 (page 320) demonstrates how rights to specific category values are also assigned to user profile Silvon.

Now that we have had a brief look at DataTracker's back-end data-mart initialization capabilities, let's see how we can use the product's PC-based interface to examine our implementation example's sample data.

FIGURE 17.10
Maintaining Categories

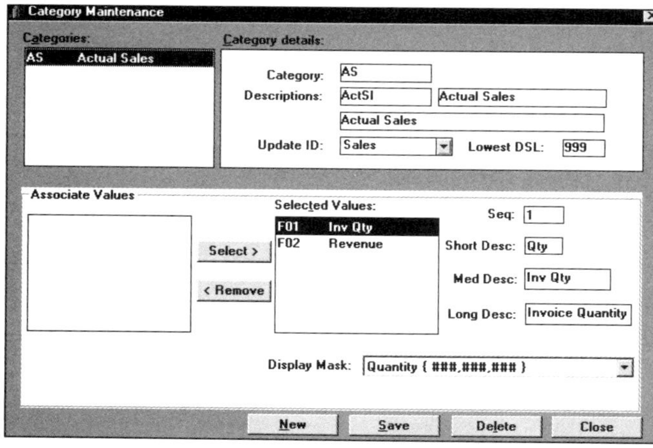

FIGURE 17.11
Defining Time Periods

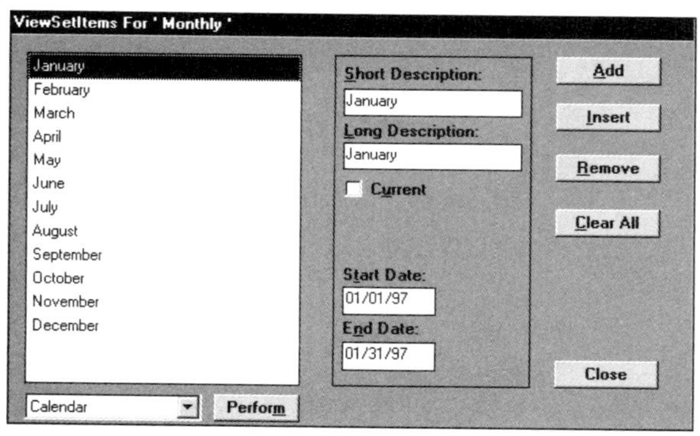

Figure 17.15 on page 320 shows a concise cross-tabulation of our products by both size and invoice date. By selecting the SKU dimension in the Modify Dimensions window, we can in turn view a cross-tabulation of our database by SKU number, as depicted in Figure 17.16 (page 321). We also have the option to use DataTracker's Quick Filter window to limit the contents of the cross-tabulation view, the result of which appears in Figure 17.17 (page 321). In addition, we can save our views and associate them with various icons, as depicted in Figure 17.18 (page 322).

As we saw in Chapter 5, metadata is a critical component of every data warehouse. Referring to Figure 17.17, we see how metadata (i.e., date/time

FIGURE 17.12

Associating Time Periods to Category SalesGroup

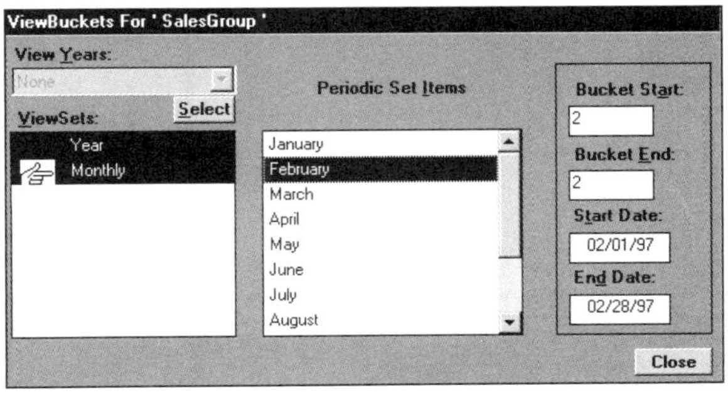

FIGURE 17.13

Assigning Security Rights per Dimension

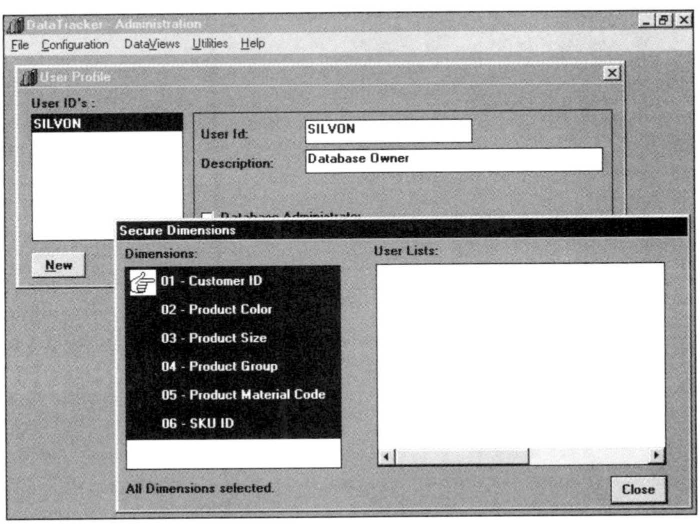

stamps) can be viewed along with tabular results. And in Chapter 4, you learned that graphs are an indispensable component of data warehouses. Figures 17.19 (page 322) and 17.20 (page 323) depict the creation of a pie chart based on a section of a cross-tabular summary, while Figure 17.21 (page 323) uses a bar graph to depict revenue by SKU number. Finally, Figure 17.22 (page 324) uses a cross-tabulation summary to depict sales by SKU, along with SKU attributes.

FIGURE 17.14
Assigning Security Rights per Category Value

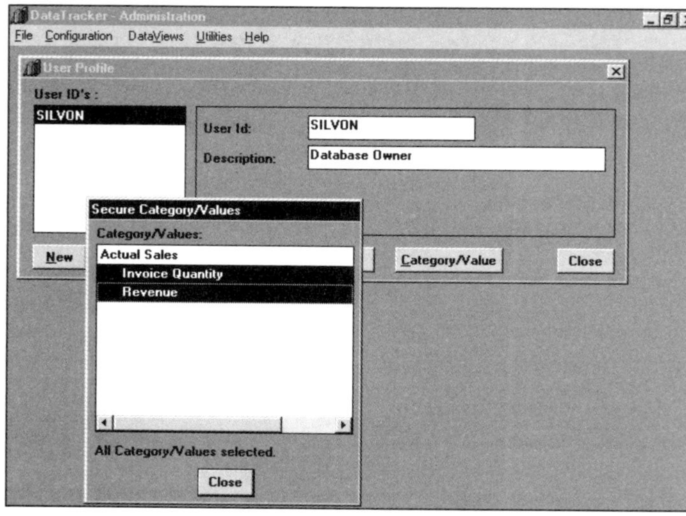

FIGURE 17.15
Cross-Tabular Sales Summary by Product Size and Invoice Dates

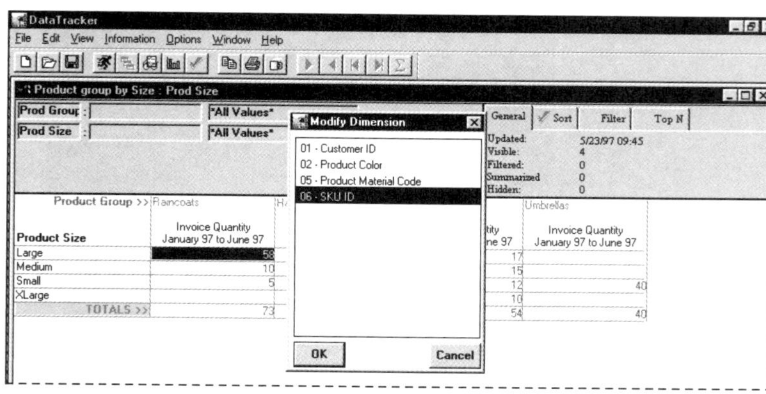

FIGURE 17.16
Cross-Tabular Sales Summary After Modifying Dimensions

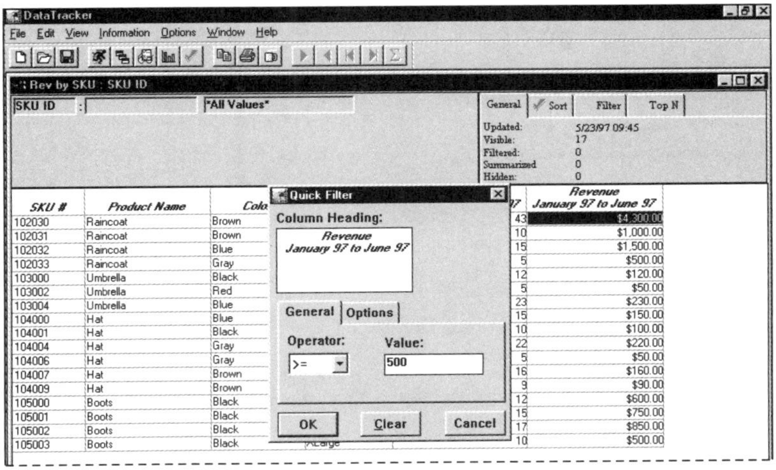

FIGURE 17.17
Cross-Tabular Sales Summary After Applying Quick Filter

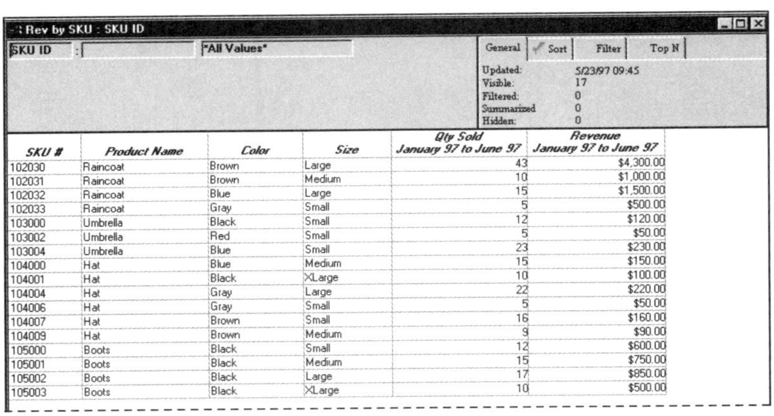

FIGURE 17.18
Assigning Views to Icons

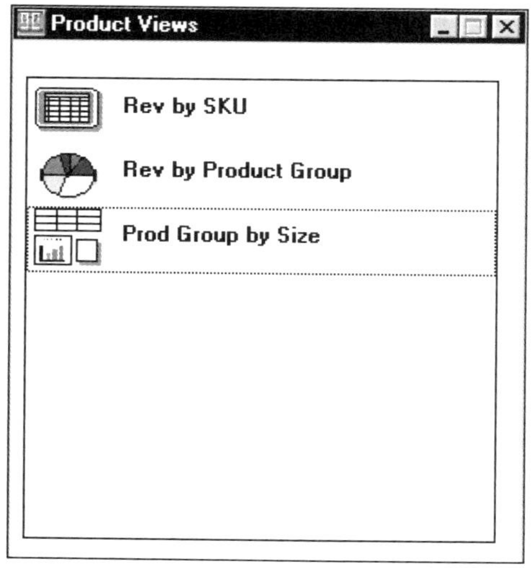

FIGURE 17.19
Selecting Section of Cross-Tabular Summary for a Pie Chart

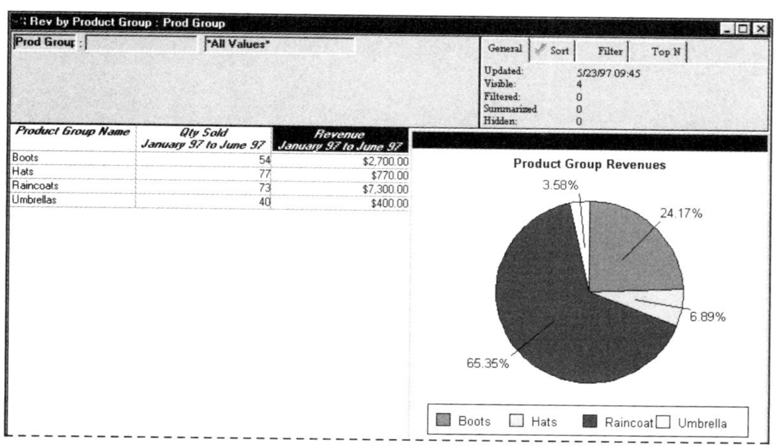

PRODUCT SUMMARY AND POSITIONING

DataTracker is a very powerful data-warehousing solution with considerable strength in its back-end capabilities. Using clear, concise screens that prompt you for information about dimensions, the product builds highly scalable data

FIGURE 17.20
Viewing Pie Chart of Revenue by Product Group

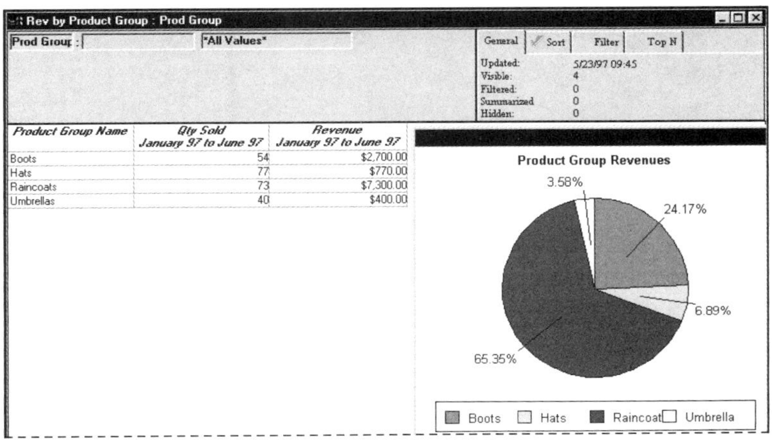

FIGURE 17.21
Viewing Bar Chart of Revenue by SKU

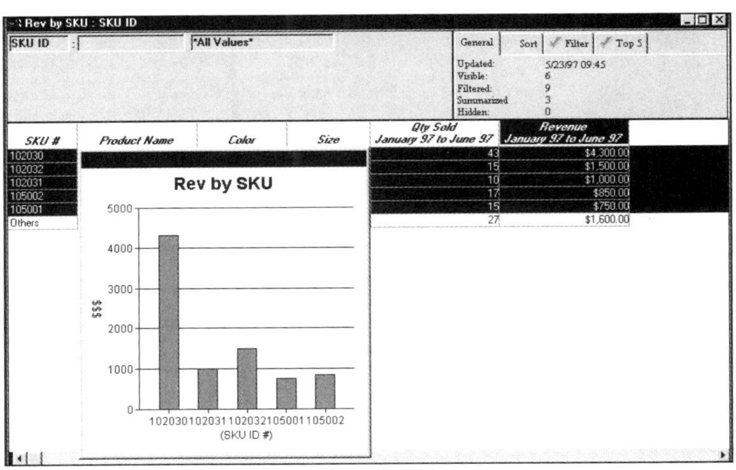

marts that adhere to the star schema. Designed for medium to very large data-warehouse implementations, DataTracker (as well as its derivative products) can capably scale to 100+ GB in size. To maintain databases of this magnitude, DataTracker supports high-volume data-load processing. Figure 17.23 (page 325) features impressive CPW benchmark statistics that bear this out.

FIGURE 17.22
Viewing Cross Tabular Summary of Revenue by SKU

Rev by SKU : SKU ID

SKU ID : *All Values*

General | Sort | Filter | Top N

Updated: 5/23/97 09:45
Visible: 8
Filtered: 9
Summarized 0
Hidden: 0

SKU #	Product Name	Color	Size	Qty Sold January 97 to June 97	Revenue January 97 to June 97
102030	Raincoat	Brown	Large	43	$4,300.00
102031	Raincoat	Brown	Medium	10	$1,000.00
102032	Raincoat	Blue	Large	15	$1,500.00
102033	Raincoat	Gray	Small	5	$500.00
105000	Boots	Black	Small	12	$600.00
105001	Boots	Black	Medium	15	$750.00
105002	Boots	Black	Large	17	$850.00
105003	Boots	Black	XLarge	10	$500.00

As I mentioned earlier in the chapter, DataTracker is available with predefined extraction processes for a number of popular third-party applications. Organizations that use these applications and are in need of focused business intelligence will find this aspect of DataTracker quite appealing. Recall that Silvon's data-warehousing philosophy is to provide business intelligence for specific functional areas of your business. Its products are not designed to function as monolithic primary repositories.

On the front-end, DataTracker features a mix of 5250 green screens and GUI interfaces for IT personnel tasked with initializing and maintaining the system. For end users, the product facilitates intuitive data access through GUI-based query, graphing, OLAP, and character-based report-writing tools. The product is not designed to support advanced EIS-style presentation capabilities.

In terms of its user interface and query/report writing functionality, DataTracker is not as integrated or as advanced as other solutions such as ShowCase Corporation's STRATEGY. However, depending on your environment, more advanced query/EIS/report-writing capabilities may not be required. Furthermore, if need be, they can be enabled by integrating DataTracker's database with third-party products such as Seagate Software's Crystal Reports and Platinum Technology's Forest & Trees.

Your affinity for DataTracker will depend upon several factors. These include your current choice of OLTP applications; the degree to which you need a high-volume, highly-scalable data-warehousing solution; the degree to which you require advanced presentation of data; and finally, your budget.

Pricing for 10 concurrent seats of DataTracker starts at $47,000. Annual maintenance fees for the project are 15 percent of the purchase price. When supplied by Silvon, implementation services range from $15,000 to $35,000 and extend over a two- to four-month period.

FIGURE 17.23

Silvon's Performance Benchmarks for DataTracker

System Type/ Performance	Business Transaction File Size (records)	Transformed Flat File Size (records)[2]	Total Data Mart Records Including Aggregation Tables[3]	Insert/Update Time of Low Level Records & Aggregation Tables[4]	Data Mart Loading Rate (records per hour)[5]
AS/400 M40S #2111, 256MB CPW=59.8	30,000	300,000 10 Facts 14 Dims.	602,850	49 min. (.817 hrs)	738,000
AS/400 M50S #2120, 750MB CPW=77.7	633,000[1]	1,900,000 3 facts 21 Dims.	2,713,000	2 hr 48 min (2.8 hrs)	970,000
AS/400 M50S #2120, 750MB CPW=77.7	500,000[1]	680,000 3 facts 21 Dims.	914,000	54 min (.90 hrs)	1,016,000
AS/400 M53 #2154, 750MB CPW=162.7	500,000[1]	680,000 3 facts 21 Dims.	914,000	26 min (.433 hrs)	2,111,000

[1]Dimensions: 4 × Products, 5 × Organization, 5 × Geographic, 5 × Customer, 1 × Returns, 1 × Promotions. Fact Table: Price, Units, Cost. Lowest level detail: Product by Ship-to.

[2]File created externally by transforming business transactions into a Transformed (denormalized) input file for the DataTracker DBLoad process.

[3]Total size of the DBLoad work file expanded to include the aggregation tables that were inserted/updated (net-changed) into the DataTracker Application Data Mart.

[4]Total time to create, update, and insert nightly net-change records and indexes.

[5]Critical Application Data Mart load rate for all processes after the denormalized file preparation was completed.

Note: All tests were run using V2.1 DataTracker Server code and V3R7.

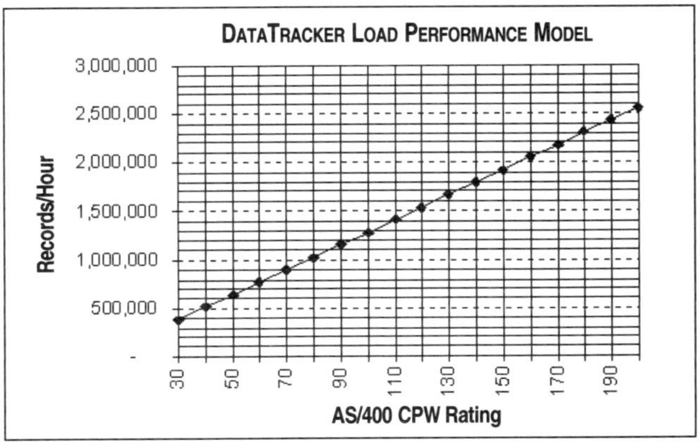

Load Performance Model: CPW × 12,800 = Records per hour

Assumptions/Requirements:

1. Minimum memory size should be 256 MB. Larger memory is required with large input files.
2. Performance is only applicable to AS/400 Uni-processors. N-Way AS/400 processors may increase the performance.

Bibliography

Books

Soltis, Frank G. *Inside the AS/400, Second Edition.* Loveland, Colorado: Duke Press, 1997.

IBM Publications

Data Mining — An IBM Overview. IBM Corporation. 1996.

DB2 for OS/400 SQL Programming, Version 3. IBM Corporation. November 1996 (IBM Publication No. SC41-4611-0).

IBM Intelligent Miner for AS/400, API and Utility Reference, Second Edition. IBM Corporation. October 1996 (IBM Publication No. SH12-6214-01).

IBM Intelligent Miner for AS/400, User's Guide, Second Edition. IBM Corporation. October 1996 (IBM Publication No. SH12-6213-01).

White Papers

Arbor Software Corporation. *Relational OLAP: Expectations and Reality.* Arbor Software Corporation. 1995.

Atre, Shaku. *Data Warehouse and AS/400.* Atre Associates, Inc. 1995.

Finkelstein, Richard. *Understanding the Need for On-Line Analytical Servers.* Performance Computing, Inc. Out of print. Available for viewing at Arbor Software Corporation's Web site: http://www.arborsoft.com/essbase/demos.html.

Gordon, K. I. *The Why of Data Standards: Do You Really Know Your Data?* K. I. Gordon. 1996.

Kenan Systems Corporation. *An Introduction to Multidimensional Database Technology.* Kenan Systems Corporation. 1995.

The Metadata Council. *The Metadata Interchange Initiative.* The Metadata Council. 1995–1997.

Pilot Software, Inc. *An Introduction to OLAP, An Explanation of Multidimensional Terminology and Technology.* Pilot Software, Inc. 1996.

Raden, Neil. *Star Schema 101.* Archer Decision Sciences, Inc. 1996.

Saylor, Michael J., Manish G. Archarya, and Robert Trenkamp. *The Case for Relational OLAP.* MicroStrategy, Inc. 1995.

Steinacher, Scott. *Data Warehousing Strategies for Windows NT Server and the AS/400.* Duke Communications International. August 1996.

Trajecta, Inc. *dbProphet: Predictive Modeling with Neural Networks.* Trajecta, Inc. 1997.

ARTICLES

Codd, Edgar F., Sharon B. Codd, and Clynch T. Salley. "Beyond Decision Support." *Computerworld*, July 16, 1993.

Edelstein, Herb. "Mining Data Warehouses." *InformationWeek*, January 8, 1996.

Foley, John, and Barbara DePompa. "Data Marts: Low Cost, High Appeal." *InformationWeek*, March 18, 1996.

Fulton, John. "Warehouse District." *AS/400 Magazine*, September 1997.

Nadile, Lisa. "Databases in Step." *InformationWeek*, December 9, 1996.

Rock, Doug. "More Power to You." *AS/400 Magazine*, September 1997.

Small, Robert D. "Debunking Data-Mining Myths." *InformationWeek*, January 20, 1997.

Steinacher, Scott. "Tired of Cryptic Queries?" *NEWS/400*, December 1991.

Steinacher, Scott. "Users Harvest AS/400 Report Data with Monarch." *NEWS/400 Product Quarterly*, Summer 1996.

Steinacher, Scott, and Robert Lamendola. "The EIS That MIS Built." *Information Management*, August 1991.

Stokes, Nigel. "The Power of Data Replication." *NEWS/400*, September 1995.

Weir, Jason. "Data Replication with DataMirror/400." *NEWS/400*, January 1997.

Wulf, Mark. "A Practical Guide to Data Mining." *NEWS/400*, January 1997.

Appendix A

How to Use the CD-ROM

The CD-ROM is set up to run automatically under Windows 95 and Windows NT 4.0. If Autorun is enabled on your machine, you should be able to insert the disk into your CD-ROM drive, and it will start automatically. If Autorun is disabled on your machine, or if you are using Windows 3.1, you can choose Run from the Start menu and type **z:\warehous.exe**, where "z" is the letter of your CD-ROM drive. In addition, we have provided Microsoft Internet Explorer 3.02 on the CD-ROM for you to install if you don't have a Web browser.

Requirements

The Macromedia Director© movie that comprises the shell for this CD-ROM is designed to run under Windows 95, Windows NT 4.0, or Windows 3.1 with an Intel processor, as is most of the software included on the CD. At minimum, you need a 486 66MHz processor, 8 MB free RAM, a double-speed CD-ROM drive, a 256-color monitor, and a sound card. For ease of use, we recommend using a Pentium 100MHz or better processor, 12 MB free RAM, and an 8x or better CD-ROM, as well as a 256-color monitor and a sound card.

CD-ROM Contents

The disk is organized as a Macromedia Director© movie and is self-running as described above.

Software

The CD-ROM includes the following software:

1. Advanced Systems Concepts, Inc.'s SEQUEL and SEQUEL Viewpoint. See page 123 for a product overview.
2. DataMirror Corporation's Transformation Server for AS/400. See page 163 for a product overview.
3. Datawatch Corporation's Monarch. See page 189 for a product overview.
4. FIS Banking Demo: Ferguson Information Systems markets InfoManager OY's InfoManager. See page 203 for a product overview.
5. FIS HealthObjects Demo: Ferguson Information Systems markets InfoManager OY's InfoManager. See page 203 for a product overview.
6. amis V8 Banking Works Demo: Olympic amis Limited's amis V8. See page 265 for a product overview.

7. amis V8 Insurance Works Demo: Olympic amis Limited's amis V8. See page 265 for a product overview.
8. amis V8 Banking Manufacturing Demo: Olympic amis Limited's amis V8. See page 265 for a product overview.
9. Silvon Software, Inc.'s DataTracker. See page 309 for a product overview.

Web Vendor Links

The CD contains the following links to vendor Web sites:

1. Advanced Systems Concepts, Inc.: http://www.asc-as400.com
2. DataMirror Corporation: http://www.datamirror.com
3. Datawatch Corporation: http://www.datawatch.com
4. Ferguson Information Systems, Inc.: http://www.infomanager.fi
5. Olympic amis Limited: http://www.amis.co.uk
6. Silvon Software, Inc.: http://www.silvon.com
7. Duke Press: http://www.dukepress.com

Disclaimer

All software on the CD is provided on an "as is" basis. Duke Press makes no claims for it nor accepts any responsibility for any damage it may do to an individual user's computer. Support for the CD by Duke Press is limited to the workings of the shell structure only. For support of the software provided on the CD, please contact the individual software vendors.

Index

K

L

M

N

O

Internet Security with Windows NT

By Mark Joseph Edwards

Security expert and *Windows NT Magazine* news editor Mark Edwards provides the quintessential guide to Internet and intranet security from the Windows NT platform. Security is the number one concern of NT users, and this comprehensive book covers network security basics as well as IIS and MPS, and includes specific advice about selecting NT tools and security devices. The accompanying CD-ROM includes security-related utilities, tools, and software packages — firewalls, port scanners, network-monitoring software, and virus detection and prevention utilities. These tools, combined with the tips and techniques in the book, are powerful weapons in your security efforts. 520 pages.

The Microsoft Outlook E-Mail and Fax Guide

By Sue Mosher

Here's a book for Microsoft Outlook 97 end users and the administrators who support them. This easy to read volume will expand your knowledge of Outlook's e-mail functions and explain the real world tasks that you are likely to encounter. Sue Mosher explains the setup of individual e-mail services and components, e-mail options and when you might want to use them, and many time-saving techniques that take you beyond the basics. Users at all levels will learn from this comprehensive introduction to Microsoft's next generation of messaging software. The book includes coverage of the Internet Mail Enhancement Patch, Rules Wizard, and special features for Microsoft Exchange Server users. 500 pages

Also Published by Duke Press

Database Design and Programming for DB2/400

By Paul Conte

This textbook is the most complete guide to DB2/400 design and programming available anywhere. The author shows you everything you need to know about physical and logical file DDS, SQL/400, and RPG IV and COBOL/400 database programming. Clear explanations illustrated by a wealth of examples demonstrate efficient database programming and error handling with both DDS and SQL/400. In addition, the author provides an extensive section on practical database design for DB2/400. 772 pages.

ILE: A First Look

By George Farr and Shailan Topiwala

This book begins by showing the differences between ILE and its predecessors, then goes on to explain the essentials of an ILE program — using concepts such as modules, binding, service programs, and binding directories. You'll discover how ILE program activation works and how ILE works with its predecessor environments. The book covers the new APIs and new debugging facilities and explains the benefits of ILE's new exception-handling model. You also get answers to the most commonly asked questions about ILE. 183 pages.

An Introduction to AS/400 System Operations

By Patrice Gapen and Heidi Rothenbuehler

Here's the textbook that covers what you need to know to become a successful AS/400 system operator. It covers a broad range of topics, including system architecture; DB2/400 and Query; user interface and Operational Assistant; managing jobs and printed reports; backup and restore; system configuration and networks; performance; security; and Client Access (PC Support). 233 pages.

Mastering the AS/400

A Practical, Hands-On Guide

By Jerry Fottral

This introductory textbook to AS/400 concepts and facilities has a utilitarian approach that stresses student participation. A natural prerequisite to programming and database management courses, it emphasizes mastery of system/user interface, member-object-library relationship, utilization of CL commands, and basic database and program development utilities. 484 pages.

The Microsoft Exchange Server Internet Mail Connector

By Spyros Sakellariadis

Achieve Internet connectivity using Exchange Server 4.0 and 5.0. This book presents four Internet connectivity models, shows how to set up the Internet Mail Connector with an Internet Service Provider, and illustrates how to monitor Internet traffic. It also includes troubleshooting and reference guides. 234 pages.

The Microsoft Exchange User's Handbook

By Sue Mosher

Microsoft Exchange is all about making connections — connections to a Microsoft Mail server, to Exchange Server, to a fax machine, or to online services. Here's the must-have, complete guide for users who need to know how to set up and use all the features of the Microsoft Exchange client product. Includes chapters about Microsoft Exchange Server 5.0 and Microsoft Outlook. 692 pages. CD included.

Migrating to Windows NT 4.0

By Sean Daily

This book is a comprehensive yet concise guide to the significant changes users will encounter as they make the move to Windows NT 4.0. The author, a Microsoft Certified Systems Engineer (MCSE), eases the transition with his enthusiastic presentation of a wealth of tips and techniques that give readers the sense they're receiving "insider information." 475 pages.

Powering Your Web site with Windows NT Server

By Nik Simpson

Powering Your Web Site with Windows NT Server explores the tools necessary to establish a presence on the Internet or on an internal corporate intranet using Web technology and Windows NT Server. The author helps readers navigate the process of creating a new information infrastructure, from the basics of justifying the decision to management through the complete implementation cycle. 640 pages. CD included.

Programming in RPG IV, Revised Edition

By Judy Yaeger, Ph.D., a NEWS/400 *technical editor*

This textbook provides a strong foundation in the essentials of business programming, featuring the newest version of the RPG language: RPG IV. Focusing on real-world problems and down-to-earth solutions using the latest techniques and features of RPG, this book provides everything you need to know to write a well-designed RPG IV program. 435 pages.

Starter Kit for the AS/400, Second Edition

An indispensable guide for novice to intermediate AS/400 programmers and system operators

By Wayne Madden, NEWS/400 *publisher and editor in chief,*
with contributions by Bryan Meyers, Andrew Smith, and Peter Rowley

This second edition contains updates of the material in the first edition and incorporates new material to enhance its value as a resource to help you learn important basic concepts and nuances of the AS/400 system. New material focuses on installing a new release, working with PTFs, AS/400 message handling, working with and securing printed output, using operational assistant to manage disk space, job scheduling, save and restore basics, and more basic CL programming concepts. Optional diskette available. 429 pages.

TECHNICAL REFERENCE SERIES: DESKTOP GUIDES

Edited by Bryan Meyers, a NEWS/400 *technical editor*

Written by experts, these unique desktop guides put the latest AS/400 applications and techniques at your fingertips. These "just-do-it" books are priced so you can keep your personal set handy. Optional online Windows help diskette available for each book.

Desktop Guide to CL Programming

By Bryan Meyers, a NEWS/400 *technical editor*

This first book of the NEWS/400 *Technical Reference Series* is packed with easy-to-find notes, short explanations, practical tips, answers to most of your everyday questions about CL, and CL code segments you can use in your own CL programming. Complete "short reference" lists every command and explains the most-often-used ones, along with names of the files they use and the MONMSG messages to use with them. 230 pages.

We Want Your Response

Mail it 

Fax it 

Web it 

omplete this form to join ur network of computer rofessionals

/e'll gladly send you a free copy of

- ❑ *Windows NT Magazine*
- ❑ *Selling NT Solutions* magazine
- ❑ *NEWS/400* magazine
- ❑ *Controller Magazine*

Publisher of practical, hands-on technical books for Windows NT and AS/400 computer professionals. Providing help not hype.

Name ____________________

Title ____________________ Phone ____________________

Company ____________________

Address ____________________

City/State/Zip ____________________

E-mail ____________________

Where did you purchase this book?

❑ Trade show ❑ Computer store ❑ Internet ❑ Card deck ❑ Bookstore
❑ Magazine ❑ Direct mail catalog or brochure

What new applications do you expect to use during the next year?

____

____

How many times this month will you visit one of Duke Communication's Web sites (Duke Press, *NEWS/400, Windows NT Magazine, Selling NT Solutions, Controller Magazine*)**?** ____________________

Please share your reaction to *Data Warehousing and the AS/400*

____

____

____

❑ YES! You have my permission to quote my comments in your publications.
(initials) __________

[98SCXBOOK]

COPY THIS PAGE AND MAIL TO:
DUKE PRESS • 221 EAST 29TH STREET • LOVELAND, CO 80538
OR FAX TO (970) 667-2321
OR RESPOND VIA OUR WEB SITE AT www.dukepress.com